INTELLIGEN

Behavioral and Social Scientific Foundations

Baruch Fischhoff and Cherie Chauvin, *Editors*

Committee on Behavioral and Social Science Research to Improve
Intelligence Analysis for National Security

Board on Behavioral, Cognitive, and Sensory Sciences

Division of Behavioral and Social Sciences and Education

NATIONAL RESEARCH COUNCIL
OF THE NATIONAL ACADEMIES

THE NATIONAL ACADEMIES PRESS
Washington, D.C.
www.nap.edu

THE NATIONAL ACADEMIES PRESS   500 Fifth Street, N.W.   Washington, DC 20001

NOTICE: The project that is the subject of this report was approved by the Governing Board of the National Research Council, whose members are drawn from the councils of the National Academy of Sciences, the National Academy of Engineering, and the Institute of Medicine. The members of the committee responsible for the report were chosen for their special competences and with regard for appropriate balance.

This study was supported by Grant No. 2008*1199327*000 between the National Academy of Sciences and the Office of the Director of National Intelligence. Any opinions, findings, conclusions, or recommendations expressed in this publication are those of the author(s) and do not necessarily reflect the views of the organizations or agencies that provided support for the project.

International Standard Book Number-13: 978-0-309-17698-9
International Standard Book Number-10: 0-309-17698-0

Additional copies of this report are available from the National Academies Press, 500 Fifth Street, N.W., Lockbox 285, Washington, DC 20055; (800) 624-6242 or (202) 334-3313 (in the Washington metropolitan area); Internet, http://www.nap.edu

Suggested citation: National Research Council. (2011). *Intelligence Analysis: Behavioral and Social Scientific Foundations*. B. Fischhoff and C. Chauvin, eds. Committee on Behavioral and Social Science Research to Improve Intelligence Analysis for National Security. Board on Behavioral, Cognitive, and Sensory Sciences, Division of Behavioral and Social Sciences and Education. Washington, DC: The National Academies Press.

Pennsylvania. She is interested in how people make judgments and decisions, with a special focus on deviations between normative theories and actual behavior. Her current research examines ways in which anticipated emotions and moods influence choice. She is also interested in the effects of the context and the question format on preference measurement. She holds a B.A. in psychology from the University of California at Berkeley and an M.A. and a Ph.D. in psychology from the University of Illinois at Urbana–Champaign.

Kiron K. Skinner is the W. Glenn Campbell research fellow at Stanford University's Hoover Institution and an associate professor of international relations and political science at Carnegie Mellon University. One of her books uses insights and applications from rational choice theory and the framework of comparative presidential studies to investigate how Ronald Reagan and Boris Yeltsin, statesmen once considered to be on the political fringe, came to commandeer the electoral centers of their respective countries. Her government service includes serving as a member of the U.S. Defense Department's Defense Policy Board, Chief of Naval Operations Executive Panel, and National Security Education Board. She is a member of the board of the Atlantic Council of the United States and a member of the Council on Foreign Relations. She holds an A.B. in political science from Spelman College and an A.M. and a Ph.D. in political science and international relations from Harvard University. She also received an honorary doctorate of laws from Molloy College on Long Island.

Barbara A. Spellman is professor of psychology and professor of law at the University of Virginia. Her research concerns higher order cognition (i.e., thinking, reasoning, decision making), spanning issues in cognitive, social, developmental, and legal psychology. She has also studied decision making in the face of potentially unreliable and deceptive information. She is an elected fellow of the American Association for the Advancement of Science and of the Association for Psychological Science (APS) and has been on the governing boards of APS and the Psychonomic Society. She has also served on many editorial boards and is currently editor-in-chief of *Perspectives on Psychological Science*. She received a B.A. in philosophy from Wesleyan University, a J.D. from New York University School of Law, and a Ph.D. in psychology from the University of California at Los Angeles.

Philip E. Tetlock is the Annenberg University Professor in the Department of Psychology and the Wharton School of Business at the University of Pennsylvania. His research covers three general areas: learning from experience, including how experts think about possible pasts (historical counterfactuals) and probable futures (conditional forecasts); designing accountability systems, including when such systems promote mindless conformity, defensive bolstering of prior positions, or thoughtful self-critical analysis; and the challenges of de-biasing judgment and choice, including how organizations structure norms and incentives to check common cognitive biases and avoid triggering mirror-image biases. He has served on numerous editorial boards, including the *Annual Review of Psychology* and the *Journal of Personality and Social Psychology*, and he has received awards from the American Psychological Association, the American Political Science Association, and the American Association for the Advancement of Science. He has a Ph.D in psychology from Yale University.

Catherine H. Tinsley is an associate professor at the McDonough School of Business at Georgetown University, a Zaeslin fellow at the College of Law and Economics at the University of Basel, and a research fellow at the National Aeronautics and Space Administration. She studies how factors such as culture, reputations, and negotiator mobility influence how people negotiate and how they manage conflict. She also looks at how near-miss events bias perceptions of risk and how these biases instantiate themselves in individual and organizational decisions regarding low-probability, high-consequence events such as: natural disasters, man-made disasters (terrorist attacks), and organizational disasters (oil spills and space flight mishaps). She has served on the editorial boards of numerous publications. She holds an M.A. and a Ph.D. in organizational behavior from the J.L. Kellogg Graduate School of Management at Northwestern University.

Amy Zegart is associate professor at the School of Public Affairs of the University of California at Los Angeles and a research fellow at the Hoover Institution at Stanford University. Previously, she served on the Clinton Administration's National Security Council staff, as a foreign policy advisor to the Bush–Cheney 2000 presidential campaign, and as a consultant on strategy and organizational effectiveness for McKinsey & Company. Her research examines the organizational deficiencies of American national security agencies. Her most recent book, *Spying Blind: The CIA, the FBI, and the Origins of 9/11*, won the Louis Brownlow Book Award of the National Academy of Public Administration. She is a lifetime member of the Council on Foreign Relations and a member of the Pacific Council on International Policy. She holds an A.B. in East Asian studies from Harvard University and a Ph.D. in political science from Stanford University.

THE NATIONAL ACADEMIES
Advisers to the Nation on Science, Engineering, and Medicine

The **National Academy of Sciences** is a private, nonprofit, self-perpetuating society of distinguished scholars engaged in scientific and engineering research, dedicated to the furtherance of science and technology and to their use for the general welfare. Upon the authority of the charter granted to it by the Congress in 1863, the Academy has a mandate that requires it to advise the federal government on scientific and technical matters. Dr. Ralph J. Cicerone is president of the National Academy of Sciences.

The **National Academy of Engineering** was established in 1964, under the charter of the National Academy of Sciences, as a parallel organization of outstanding engineers. It is autonomous in its administration and in the selection of its members, sharing with the National Academy of Sciences the responsibility for advising the federal government. The National Academy of Engineering also sponsors engineering programs aimed at meeting national needs, encourages education and research, and recognizes the superior achievements of engineers. Dr. Charles M. Vest is president of the National Academy of Engineering.

The **Institute of Medicine** was established in 1970 by the National Academy of Sciences to secure the services of eminent members of appropriate professions in the examination of policy matters pertaining to the health of the public. The Institute acts under the responsibility given to the National Academy of Sciences by its congressional charter to be an adviser to the federal government and, upon its own initiative, to identify issues of medical care, research, and education. Dr. Harvey V. Fineberg is president of the Institute of Medicine.

The **National Research Council** was organized by the National Academy of Sciences in 1916 to associate the broad community of science and technology with the Academy's purposes of furthering knowledge and advising the federal government. Functioning in accordance with general policies determined by the Academy, the Council has become the principal operating agency of both the National Academy of Sciences and the National Academy of Engineering in providing services to the government, the public, and the scientific and engineering communities. The Council is administered jointly by both Academies and the Institute of Medicine. Dr. Ralph J. Cicerone and Dr. Charles M. Vest are chair and vice chair, respectively, of the National Research Council.

www.national-academies.org

Preface

The U.S. intelligence community (IC) is a complex human enterprise whose success depends on how well the people in it perform their work. Although often aided by sophisticated technologies, these people ultimately rely on their own intellect to identify, synthesize, and communicate the information on which the nation's security depends. Their individual and collective "brainpower" is the human capital of the IC. Their role is the pivotal middle point between gathering information and policy making. The IC's success depends on having trained, motivated, and thoughtful people working within organizations able to understand, value, and coordinate their capabilities.

For a century or more, the behavioral and social sciences have studied how individuals and groups perform these fundamental intellectual processes. That research has found that people perform some of these tasks much better than others. In some cases, the research has demonstrated ways to overcome weaknesses (e.g., through training or structuring analytical processes); in other cases, the research has identified problems that reflect limits to analysis that are important for decision makers to understand as aspects of the uncertainties that they face.

Recognizing the potential value of this research, the Office of Analytic Integrity and Standards of the Office of the Director of National Intelligence (ODNI) requested the National Research Council (NRC), through its Board on Behavioral, Cognitive, and Sensory Sciences, to form a committee to synthesize and assess the behavioral and social science research evidence relevant to (1) critical problems of individual and group judgment and of communication by intelligence analysts and (2) the kinds of analytic processes that are employed or have potential in addressing these problems.

To this end, the Committee on Behavioral and Social Science Research to Improve Intelligence Analysis for National Security has produced a consensus report, *Intelligence Analysis for Tomorrow: Advances from the Behavioral and Social Sciences*, summarizing its analysis and presenting its conclusions and recommendations, and this collection of individually authored papers, which presents the more detailed evidentiary base for the committee's conclusions and recommendations.

The papers in this collection represent the individual work of committee members, with two (Chapters 7 and 11) involving collaborations with colleagues having related expertise. The papers summarize research relevant to recruiting, cultivating, deploying, and retaining human capital. The specific topics in this volume were selected by the committee as central to the IC's mission.

The first chapter sets the context for the volume by describing the analytic process, in terms of its behavioral and social demands. The remaining chapters provide critical assessments of the science relevant to meeting those demands, organized into the three essential elements of successful analysis, analytic methods (Chapter 2–5), analysts (Chapter 6–9), and organizations (Chapter 10–13).

The committee envisions this volume as a resource for the IC's leadership and workforce, to help the IC to develop its own programs and be a critical consumer of services secured externally. The committee also envisions this volume being used by the broader audience of those who teach, study, and perform analysis. Even more broadly, the papers in this volume may benefit researchers and educators in other domains who face similarly complex, uncertain analytical problems, such as technological risk management, entrepreneurship, and international development.

In addition to specific acknowledgements made by the authors in their individual chapters, the NRC wishes to thank several individuals who assisted in preparing this collection of papers. Among the NRC staff, special thanks are due to Barbara Wanchisen and Mary Ellen O'Connell who provided oversight and support of the study. Two senior program assistants, Matthew McDonough and Gary Fischer, provided administrative and logistic support over the course of the study. We also thank an NRC consultant, Laura Penny, for her work in the final editing of the collection. Finally we thank the executive office reports staff of the Division of Behavioral and Social Sciences and Education, especially Eugenia Grohman, who provided valuable help with the editing and production of the report, and Kirsten Sampson Snyder, who managed the report review process.

Each paper has been reviewed in draft form by individuals chosen for their diverse perspectives and technical expertise, in accordance with procedures approved by the NRC's Report Review Committee. The purpose of this independent review is to provide candid and critical comments that will assist the institution in making its published report as sound as possible and to ensure that the report meets institutional standards for objectivity, evidence, and responsiveness to the study charge. The review comments and draft manuscript remain confidential to protect the integrity of the deliberative process. We wish to thank the following individuals for their review of this report: Nancy J. Cooke, Applied Psychology Program, Arizona State University; Susan T. Fiske, Department of Psychology, Princeton University; John Gannon, Global Analysis, BAE Systems, McLean, VA; Robert L. Jervis, School of International and Public Affairs, Columbia University; Tania Lambrozo, Department of Psychology, University of California, Berkeley; John McLaughlin, Paul H. Nitze School of Advanced International Studies, Johns Hopkins University; Jonathan Moreno, Department of History and Sociology of Science, Center for Bioethics, University of Pennsylvania; Scott E. Page, Santa Fe Institute, University of Michigan, Ann Arbor; Charles Perrow, Department of Sociology (emeritus), Yale University; Paul R. Pillar, Security Studies Program, Georgetown University; Stephen M. Robinson, Department of Industrial and Systems Engineering (emeritus), University of Wisconsin, Madison; R. Scott Rodgers, Behavioral Influences Analysis Flight (GTRB), National Air and Space Intelligence Center; Frank Yates, Ross School of Business, University of Michigan.

Although the reviewers listed above provided many constructive comments and suggestions, they were not asked to endorse the content of the papers, nor did they see the final draft before its release. The review of this collection of papers was overseen by Richard J. Bonnie, Institute of Law, Psychiatry and Public Policy, University of Virginia. Appointed by the NRC, he was responsible for making certain that an independent examination of the papers was carried out in accordance with institutional procedures and that all review comments were carefully considered. Responsibility for the final content of this publication rests entirely with the authors and the institution.

Baruch Fischhoff, *Chair*
Cherie Chauvin, *Study Director*
Committee on Behavioral and Social Science Research
to Improve Intelligence Analysis for National Security

Contents

xi

Part I

Introduction

In Chapter 1, Thomas Fingar provides an overview of the structure, missions, and characteristics of the intelligence community (IC), and describes the role of analysis in reducing uncertainty, providing warning, and identifying opportunities for national security decision makers. Fingar argues that analysts' primary mission is to provide timely information and insights that help decision makers understand developments with potentially consequential implications for American interests.

Fingar's detailed description of what analysts do, in supporting both the general national security enterprise and specific missions, agencies, and decision makers, shows how intelligence analysts play critical roles that share properties with analysts in other organizations. He describes the intelligence analyst's job as enhancing decision makers' understanding of complex situations, often with scant and problematic information. Timely input is often more important than precise estimates, as long as analysts communicate clearly what they do and do not know, what assumptions they have made in closing information gaps, how confident they are in their sources and judgments, and which alternatives they have set aside as less likely.

Fingar also describes challenges in the current operating environment. Those challenges include a shift from threats against the nation to threats against individual Americans anywhere, any time; expansion of national security to include such threats as infectious disease and transnational crime; dramatic increases in demand for precision and "actionable" intelligence;

compression of timelines for collecting, evaluating, and interpreting intelligence on increasingly complex issues; and exponential increases in the amount of information of potential value.

Fingar's introductory chapter demonstrates why IC analysts need the insights and tools of the behavioral and social sciences, as discussed in Parts II–IV of this volume.

1

Analysis in the U.S. Intelligence Community: Missions, Masters, and Methods

Thomas Fingar

The intelligence establishment of the United States is a vast enterprise with more than a dozen agencies, roughly 100,000 employees (Sanders, 2008), and a budget larger than the gross domestic product of many nations.[1] Approximately 20 percent of the employees are analysts,[2] a category that subsumes photo interpreters, those who interpret intercepted signals, specialists on foreign military systems, and a number of other specialists in addition to those who analyze political, economic, societal, and other security-related developments. All are members of the intelligence community (IC), but their missions, customers, professional identities, and organizational cultures are to a substantial extent determined by the agency (or agency component) to which they are assigned.[3] They work on different kinds of problems for diverse sets of institutional and individual customers. The diversity of missions and masters has resulted in a pluralistic structure with sensible—if not always optimal—divisions of labor and professional specialization.

---

[1]The National Intelligence Program budget for fiscal year 2008 was $47.5 billion (Office of the Director of National Intelligence, 2009).

[2]The approximate percentage of analysts is based on the number of analysts listed in the *Analytic Resources Catalog* and the total number of military and civilian U.S. government personnel working in the IC (Sanders, 2008).

[3]For descriptions of IC organizations and their primary missions, see *Members of the Intelligence Community* at http://www.dni.gov/members_IC.htm [accessed December 2009], *2009 National Intelligence: A Consumer's Guide* at http://www.dni.gov/IC_Consumers_Guide_2009 .pdf [accessed December 2009], and *An Overview of the United States Intelligence Community for the 111th Congress* at http://www.dni.gov/overview.pdf [accessed December 2009].

This essay is intended to set the stage for the discipline- and field-specific essays of the other contributors. It seeks to identify key characteristics of the IC and to explicate, albeit in abbreviated fashion, why the IC is organized as it is and how mission, expectations, and structure empower and constrain the work of individuals, agencies, and the IC as a whole.

ANALYTIC MISSION OF THE INTELLIGENCE ENTERPRISE

The mission of intelligence analysis is to evaluate, integrate, and interpret information in order to provide warning, reduce uncertainty, and identify opportunities. Providing insight on trends, the political calculus of particular foreign leaders, or the way problems are perceived by people outside the United States is often more helpful to decision makers than is the presentation of additional "facts" or speculation about "worst case" possibilities.[4] Discovering that a country is cheating on a treaty commitment may be less important than providing insight into why it is doing so.[5] Ferreting out all details of an adversary's new weapon system may be less useful than finding a vulnerability that can be exploited. Prompting decision makers to rethink their own assumptions and preliminary judgments may be more beneficial to the national security enterprise than providing definitive answers to specific questions.[6]

Intelligence, especially analytic support, is useful to decision makers in direct proportion to the degree to which it is timely, targeted, and trusted by those who receive it. Thorough examination of all relevant factors and how they interact is seldom possible within the real-world decision timelines of U.S. officials, and getting it completely right is often less important than providing useful information and insights to the right people at the right time. Even data-rich and methodologically brilliant analytic products may contribute little to the national security enterprise they are supposed

---

[4]Examples of trends affecting the agendas and capabilities of governments include the rapid "graying" of populations in Europe and Japan and youth bulges in African and Central Asian countries already struggling to meet demands for education and jobs (National Intelligence Council, 2008a). Political leaders widely considered "close" to the United States who found it expedient to distance themselves from Washington when running for reelection include Iraqi Prime Minister Nouri al-Maliki (Steele, 2008) and Afghan President Hamid Karzai (Voice of America, 2009). For an example of how other countries view U.S. policies, see Tiron (2007).

[5]For example, "Russia" failed to honor its obligations under the Chemical Weapons Convention because the retired general assigned to oversee dismantlement of now-prohibited activities failed to do what he was supposed to do. When this was discovered, the general was fired by President Yeltsin (Boudreaux, 1994).

[6]For example, the way in which U.S. policy makers approached the problem of illicit Chinese sales of chemical weapon precursors changed when they understood that part of the problem stemmed from the limited ability of the Chinese government to enforce its own export regulations (Nuclear Threat Initiative, 2007).

to support if they are prepared without understanding the knowledge, timelines, and objectives of officials working on the issue.[7]

In addition to being factually accurate, intelligence analysis must be—and be seen to be—both objective and germane to the needs of those for whom it is intended. The importance of tailored support is one of the reasons the U.S. intelligence enterprise has so many different and somewhat specialized components. Oversimplifying greatly, the 16 constituent agencies—with 19 analytic components counting the National Intelligence Council, National Counterintelligence Executive, and National Counterterrorism Center—exist because each serves different, and somewhat unique, customers and missions. Each has developed expertise and analytic tools to meet the needs of its primary customers. Their customers have confidence in the work performed by "their" intelligence unit because they know the people and routinely find the work they produce to be more useful than that provided by analysts elsewhere who perforce are less well attuned to the specific intelligence requirements of the parent department.[8]

FORM FOLLOWS FUNCTION

Legacy arrangements whereby individual and institutional customers rely primarily on analysts and agencies that look at issues and intelligence through lenses keyed to their own mission requirements are logical and often sufficient to meet core requirements. Indeed, the approach adopted by the Office of the Director of National Intelligence (ODNI) in 2005 and implemented thereafter has sought to preserve and build on the best features of a de facto federated system of intelligence support. That approach made it easier to take advantage of complementary skills, achieve more rational divisions of labor, and improve the overall performance of the analytic community by improving the performance of all analysts and each of the analytic components.[9]

This approach deliberately eschewed institutional consolidation and the formation of country- and/or issue-specific centers intended to "rationalize"

---

[7]For example, after U.S. policy makers became convinced that they needed to work with the Chinese government to halt the sale of missiles to countries in the Middle East, they wanted information and insight from the IC that would help them to determine how to do that, not additional reports confirming that sales had occurred in the past (Gordon, 1990).

[8]The Central Intelligence Agency does not have a "parent department" in the sense that this term is used here, but it is the primary source of analytic support for the National Security Council staff and a primary or secondary source for customers across the U.S. government.

[9]The ODNI was established by the *Intelligence Reform and Terrorism Prevention Act of 2004*. The position of Director of National Intelligence was created to enhance integration of the IC and was given a specific mandate to improve the quality of analytic products. See Fingar (2006) for discussion of many elements of the approach adopted by the ODNI.

organization charts and lower institutional barriers to information exchange and collaboration because the ODNI judged that potential gains from co-locating analysts working on similar problems would be less than the probable loss of insight and trust resulting from proximity to particular customers.[10] Rather than consolidating analysts, the ODNI approach sought to preserve and enhance the advantages of analytic boutiques (e.g., the Marine Corps Intelligence Activity and the State Department's Bureau of Intelligence and Research) that were able to provide tailored support while making it easier for them to contribute to, and benefit from, the work of colleagues elsewhere in the IC. Furthermore, the approach aimed to reduce the autarky and isolation of analysts by facilitating knowledge of, access to, and collaboration with colleagues and counterparts in other components of the intelligence enterprise. The notional "model" for the analytic enterprise was more like Radio Shack's networking of widely dispersed affiliates located near their customers than Walmart's distribution of standardized goods through megastores located far from people previously served by neighborhood shops.

PARAMETERS AND PRESSURES AFFECTING ANALYTIC PERFORMANCE

Implementation of the blueprint summarized above has begun, and the initial results suggest it is both workable and worthwhile. The results also demonstrate, however, that several more challenges must be understood and addressed to minimize unnecessary duplication while providing more accurate, insightful, and useful analytic support to the IC's large, diverse, and demanding customer base.[11] The magnitude of the task is complicated and compounded by the explosive growth of requirements and

---

[10]The call for formation of subject-specific centers was made, i.a., in *The 9/11 Commission Report* (National Commission on Terrorist Attacks, 2004, pp. 411–413). Preservation of multiple analytic components that had evolved independently in a context that made it difficult to rely on work done by colleagues in other components— because of impediments to knowing precisely who did what, the expertise of analysts elsewhere, or how responsive they would be to requests for assistance—also preserved unnecessary as well as appropriate duplications of effort. It also perpetuated cultural differences, bureaucratic rivalries, and other organizational pathologies (in this volume, see Zegart, Chapter 13; Tinsley, Chapter 9; and Spellman, Chapter 6). Knowing more about the capabilities, staffing, and missions of each component was a requisite for identifying which capabilities were redundant and which could be eliminated without risking a single point of failure or jeopardizing the ability of the IC to obtain multiple independent analyses of critical issues. Reducing and realigning independent capabilities was postponed until more was known about individual and aggregate strengths and weaknesses.

[11]These are the personal observations of a participant observer. I made many of the decisions incorporated into the approach summarized here and closely monitored their implementation, but the judgments about their efficacy are largely subjective and impressionistic.

escalating expectations of customers, overseers, and the attentive public. Simply stated, in addition to their many other challenges, IC analysts must contend with more requirements from more customers, and must answer more difficult questions more quickly and with greater precision than ever. Moreover, they must do so while coping with exponentially increasing volumes of information (for further discussion, see Fingar, 2011b). Each of these interconnected challenges warrants both explication and illustrative examples of their implications for the analytic enterprise.

In the years since the demise of the Soviet Union, and especially since the attacks of 9/11, "national security" has been redefined, often implicitly, in ways that require radically different approaches to analysis, the way analysts engage with one another, and the missions they support. Once limited almost exclusively to concerns about military, diplomatic, and political/ideological threats to "American national interests," national security now subsumes concerns about the geopolitics of energy, global financial flows, spread of infectious disease, and the safety of individual American citizens anywhere on the globe.[12] Expansion of the concept and concerns of "national security" has also expanded the scope (i.e., number and variety) of institutions and individuals who desire or demand analytic support from the IC.[13] Because intelligence support has long been treated as a "free good," there are few constraints on what customers can request or what members of Congress expect to be provided.[14]

The proliferation of customers and topics on which the IC was expected to acquire information, develop expertise, and deliver analytic insights raised questions about how to do so. The default setting was for new customers to go to the Central Intelligence Agency (CIA) because its

---

[12]The broader scope of questions addressed to the IC is illustrated by the titles of unclassified reports published by the National Intelligence Council during the past decade. They include: *The Impact of Climate Change to 2030: Commissioned Research and Conference Reports* (National Intelligence Council, 2009), *Strategic Implications of Global Health* (National Intelligence Council, 2008b), *SARS: Down But Still a Threat* (National Intelligence Council, 2003), and *Global Humanitarian Emergencies: Trends and Projections 2001–2002* (National Intelligence Council, 2001).

[13]Perhaps the clearest example of this expansion is the creation of the Homeland Security Council by the George W. Bush Administration and the subsequent incorporation of "domestic" agencies into the restructured National Security Council undertaken by the Obama Administration. It is also reflected in the redefinition of "national intelligence" in the *Intelligence Reform and Terrorism Prevention Act of 2004* (Section 1012).

[14]Members of the Intelligence Oversight Committees in both the Senate and the House of Representatives have raised questions about the appropriateness of devoting intelligence resources to nontraditional issues and customers, but members who sit on committees with responsibility for the nontraditional issues and agencies generally take the opposite view. For examples of debate over the proper scope of topics to be addressed by the IC, see the blog, Kent's Imperative (n.d.), http://kentsimperative.blogspot.com/ [accessed May 2010]. For an example of disagreement among members of Congress, see *Congressional Record–House* (2007).

mandate was to support all national security customers, and the CIA initially accepted the new requirements. Rather quickly, however, customers and intelligence analysts rediscovered the value of proximity and tasking authority that had spawned the creation of so many different analytic components. Simply stated, the U.S. government faced, at least implicitly, the question of whether to replicate the old approach of creating new specialized units co-located with customers, or to develop better ways to frame requirements and tap expertise without creating new units. In other words, the IC had to find a way to provide boutique-like service and attention to customers without creating new bureaucratic units or substantially increasing the number of analysts.

In addition to coping with a wider range of requirements from a larger and more diverse set of customers, intelligence analysts had to address many questions that were inherently more complex than most of those that had become routine during the Cold War. One dimension involved the shift of focus from the national level (e.g., what does Moscow or Cairo want?) to subnational and nongovernmental organizations and groups (e.g., is the basis for the insurgency political, tribal, economic, religious, or something else?). Addressing such questions requires both greater and different kinds of expertise and analytic techniques than were sufficient in the past. These challenges are further compounded by shorter deadlines—to be useful now, analytic insights often must be provided in days or hours rather than weeks or months—and the demand for more "actionable intelligence" (i.e., information that can be used to disrupt a terrorist plot, prevent the delivery of chemical precursors, or freeze bank accounts being used for illicit purposes).[15]

More numerous and more complex issues require use of more and different types of information. Much of the required information is readily available to anyone at no or little cost; other types of information can only be acquired, if at all, through clandestine methods. Knowing what to look for, where to seek it, and how to provide guidance to collectors have become much more demanding aspects of an analyst's job than in days when much

---

[15]The kinds of difficulties and dilemmas inherent in meeting demands for actionable intelligence can be illustrated with a simple, but typical, example. Foreign governments being asked to search a shipment or block a flight suspected of carrying illicit material want detailed information about the content and source of the intelligence that triggered the request because they want to make an independent judgment about whether it is sufficiently reliable to jeopardize their own interests by taking the requested action. Sometimes, such requests for information about the intelligence are also intended to learn more about U.S. intelligence capabilities; foreign governments want to know how much—and how—the United States knows about what happens in their countries. It is not always easy to provide information that is sufficiently detailed to be persuasive and to minimize the likelihood of error without jeopardizing sources and methods (for further discussion, see Fingar, 2011b).

of the job often entailed evaluating and explaining secrets and other bits of information collected and disseminated "because it was obtainable" rather than because it addressed high-priority analytic questions. Moreover, the dramatic increase in publicly available information that has characterized the past two decades, and the extraordinary capabilities of new methods of technical collection and data storage, have greatly increased the height of the information haystack. It probably does contain more "needles" than before, but they are often much harder to find.

WHAT ANALYSTS DO: INDIVIDUAL AND COLLECTIVE RESPONSIBILITIES

Every analyst's job is multifaceted and somewhat unique, but all entail core responsibilities and employ—or should employ—the same high standards of analytic tradecraft. The challenge, and it is a significant one, is for every individual and the analytic community as a whole to strike the right balance when allocating time and effort to each component of the job. This cannot be achieved by assigning arbitrary priorities or percentages of time. The generic tasks summarized below are—or should be—complementary, but they are more often characterized as zero-sum with a bias for addressing what is current at the expense of what might be more important. This is a long-standing lament, but most proposals to alleviate competing demands do not go beyond calling for more long-term strategic analysis and less attention to current issues (e.g., Russell, 2007; Commission on the Intelligence Capabilities of the United States Regarding Weapons of Mass Destruction, 2005).

Answer Questions

A portion of every analyst's job involves answering questions. Sometimes the questions are posed in the course of a meeting and may require both an immediate answer and a longer and more considered response. One's ability to provide confident answers with adequate levels of detail is a function of one's expertise and ability to anticipate what the customer or meeting is likely to require; the adequacy of the response is, in part, a function of the degree to which those present have confidence in the analyst.[16] Sometimes the most important "answers" are the ones provided by

---

[16]For purposes of this paper, "expertise" is a function of formal academic study; time spent working on particular places, people, or problems; and understanding of U.S. interests and objectives germane to one's areas of specialization.

an analyst to questions that customers should have asked, but did not.[17] To be useful, the analyst needs to find out what his or her customers "know," what they are trying to accomplish, and what approach is being used to formulate and evaluate policy options. Questions that are more difficult to address include those that come to an analyst indirectly, with little or no information on why the question was asked.[18] The objective in all cases is to provide more than "just the facts." Good analytic tradecraft requires providing information on context, patterns, the quantity and character of intelligence germane to the subject, and other insights likely to help customers to understand the issues that prompted the query (Commission on the Intelligence Capabilities of the United States Regarding Weapons of Mass Destruction, 2005).[19] Three keys to providing timely and useful answers are (1) command of one's portfolio, (2) knowledge of where to go for data and help to interpret what it means, and (3) practice of good tradecraft even on routine or quick turnaround matters.

---

[17]The following examples of questions that should have been asked, but were not addressed until an intelligence analyst injected them into the conversations, are real, not hypothetical. The first occurred in the context of a long discussion of how Moscow would respond to a variety of U.S. and/or European moves intended to affect developments in the Caucasus and how various scenarios were likely to play out. A question that should have been asked early in the discussion was, "How do the Russians view the situation and what do they want to happen?" The second occurred in the context of a discussion of the efficacy of a new program to protect Iraqi oil pipelines from attack by insurgents by paying local militias to act as a pipeline protection force. The indicator used to gauge the efficacy of the program was the number of attacks after the stand-up of the new protection force, and several people noted with pleasure that no attacks had been made on a particular section of the pipeline for more than 6 weeks. What should have been asked—and addressed sooner than it was—was whether the pipeline was operative before or during the period under discussion. It wasn't. Until noted by the intelligence analyst, no one had considered that the reason there had been no attacks on the pipeline was probably because it had already been put out of commission.

[18]When I was Chairman of the National Intelligence Council, I received a message from the staff of a senior director at the National Security Council requesting an update on political reconciliation, economic reconstruction, and public safety in Iraq. The request was misleadingly clear in that it seemed to require updated information of the kind that was regularly incorporated into spreadsheets and graphics used to depict progress and problems. The IC contributed to, but usually did not prepare, those graphics, which were the responsibility of officials in the State and Defense Departments. When I sought clarification, I learned from the senior director that he was looking for an analytical assessment of the relationships among reconciliation, reconstruction, and the security of different ethnic and religious groups. The operative assumption up to that time had been that progress toward political reconciliation—elections—would facilitate progress on the other dimensions of interest. He was asking if the evidence supported that hypothesis. It did not.

[19]The need to identify assumptions, characterize sources of information, and specify levels of confidence in both judgments and underlying information is codified in IC directives (see Director of National Intelligence, 2007a, 2007c).

Provide Warning

Every analyst has a responsibility to monitor developments and trends in his or her portfolio in order to determine where they seem to be headed and whether they might "threaten" American interests or the viability of approaches being considered or implemented by those they support. Analysts should also be alerted to potential opportunities for policy intervention to mitigate or capitalize on what is taking place. For most analysts, most of the time, the focus should be on providing strategic warning—informing customers what could happen far enough in advance to allow deliberation and the formulation of policies to encourage what appears desirable and to thwart or mitigate unfavorable or dangerous developments. But no policy maker likes to be surprised. Too often their expectations and demands for "warning" are conveyed or interpreted as demands to be informed or alerted about any development that might be made known to colleagues and counterparts, or about which they might be asked questions by Congress or the media. This desire for "no surprises" often skews the work of analysts too far in the direction of "current intelligence," amounting to little more than duplicative and ill-informed commentary on developments that, in the grand scheme of things, are not all that important (e.g., Russell, 2007).

Monitor and Assess Current Developments and New Information

The ability to provide warning of what lies over the horizon, around the bend, or behind a tree requires continuous and close monitoring of developments that might affect places, problems, people, or policy maker requirements in every analyst's portfolio. This dimension of the analyst's job involves more than just evaluating, assessing, interpreting, and transmitting the latest fruits of collection efforts.[20] Many analysts feel overwhelmed because they attempt to—and cannot—"read everything" that collectors push at them and they know is available in unclassified materials ("open source" in the argot of the IC). The days when an analyst could, or could be expected to, read everything are long gone. It would be counterproductive and fruitless to try to solve the problem by narrowing the scope of

---

[20]"Evaluation" of intelligence involves determination of its use (e.g., whether it contains new information, whether it corroborates or contradicts previously acquired information, and whether it requires reconsideration of previously reached judgments). "Assessment" deals with other dimensions of a report's possible use such as its reliability, credibility, and importance to understanding the particular issues under study. "Interpretation" of intelligence addresses "what does it mean" questions germane to understanding capabilities, intentions, trends, and drivers. "Transmission" of intelligence requires communication of information about its provenance, reliability, significance, and implications to other analysts and to customers outside of the IC.

portfolios and adding more analysts.[21] What is required is better understanding of complex problems, not a large contingent of analysts who know
more and more about less and less.

To perform this part of the job, analysts must begin with a clear (or as
clear as their relationship with customers allows) understanding of what
customers are working on, worry about, and want to know.[22] Armed with
this knowledge, and the analyst's own subject matter expertise and understanding of the issues and dynamics involved, the analyst can narrow the
scope of his or her search and analysis efforts to what are thought to be
key drivers, key indicators, and key developments germane to the concerns
of customers and, as importantly, to their own ability to understand what
is happening, why, and where events appear to be headed. There are obvious advantages to divisions of labor with fellow analysts and increasing
opportunities to work together via collaborative tools such as A-Space and
other capabilities to access and assemble data and to garner insights from
colleagues. However, at the end of the day, each analyst is responsible for
identifying and interpreting information germane to the interests of his or
her customers that might affect their understanding of the situation and
ability to achieve their objectives.[23]

---

[21]In the past, when many existing systems and procedures were developed, a substantial part
of the intelligence enterprise was devoted to ferreting out secrets and attempting to learn "anything we could" about dangerous and denied areas on the assumption that knowing a little
about some dimension of a place or problem was better than knowing very little about most
dimensions. The job of the analyst was to explain and interpret whatever "facts" happened
to be collected on a subject in his or her portfolio. Now such an approach is impractical, unnecessary, and often unhelpful. Much—even most—of the time, analysts begin with a question
that, if answered, will provide key insights into the subjects they study and seek information
that promises to help answer that question.

[22]This can happen in many ways. One is the "EAP Informal," a weekly meeting chaired by
the Assistant Secretary of State for East Asia and the Pacific that I found to be an exceptionally effective forum and format for ensuring that policy maker and intelligence counterparts
understand what each is working on, attempting to accomplish, and worried about. The six
or seven senior participants from the Department of State, Department of Defense, the Joint
Chiefs, the National Security Council, the National Intelligence Council, and the Department
of State's Bureau of Intelligence and Research (INR) come together as peers who check their
bureaucratic roles at the door so they can speak freely about issues, options, and objectives
without worrying about turf or other bureaucratic issues. I participated in these meetings as
Director of INR's Office of Analysis for East Asia and the Pacific and found them extremely
useful for providing guidance to collectors and focusing the work of IC analysts.

[23]A-Space is a pathbreaking collaborative workspace that enables analysts from across the
IC to access and share highly classified information, pose questions, and post observations
without having to know precisely who might have answers or find the observations of interest,
mentor and obtain help at a distance, and collaborate to produce and update reports and data
repositories. *Time* named A-Space (which the media calls Facebook for Spies) one of the 50
best inventions of 2008 (*Time*, 2008).

Building Expertise and Strategic Analysis

Observations—and criticism—that analysts devote too much time to "current intelligence" often lament that too little time is spent on "strategic analysis." Many prescribe corrective measures that include setting up separate staff to conduct long-range studies or assigning all "current intelligence work" to a small staff so that most analysts can engage in strategic analysis (e.g., Treverton and Gabbard, 2008). From my perspective, both the diagnosis and the prescriptions are somewhat off the mark. The IC certainly can do a lot better in terms of the way it monitors and reports breaking developments (what Secretary Powell correctly referred to as "the news"). Yet that does not obviate the need for the vast majority of analysts to address issues already or soon to be on the agendas of those they support because if they do not and cannot do that, the IC will not meet the requirements and expectations of those it supports.

Second, although many proclaim the need for more strategic analysis, I have found the "market" for such work to be both small and episodic. So-called "tyranny of the inbox" is a bigger problem for policy makers than for analysts, and the needs of customers drive the process. Perhaps policy makers should think more about the long-term future, but few do so on more than an intermittent basis, and all tend to have less interest in long-term issues as they spend more time on the job. One can lament or decry the situation, but it is difficult for officials to think about how events might play out after their term of office while piranhas are working on their legs.[24] Intelligence is fundamentally a support function; it exists to provide information and insight that will help customers to perform their assigned missions in the national security enterprise (for further discussion, see George and Rishikof, 2011). Analysts can, should, and do regard reminding customers of long-term trends and strategic implications of current decisions as an important part of their job, but they must do so within the parameters of trust, temporal pressures, and the agendas of those they support. The alternative is to be regarded as unhelpful or irrelevant (e.g., Treverton, 2008).

Rather than focusing on structural solutions such as creating strategic analysis units, or on changing the behavior and expectations of decision makers, the most useful proposals to improve analytic support begin from the premise that providing useful insights and context when addressing "current" issues requires both deep expertise and understanding of strategic

---

[24]One senior official with whom I worked earlier in my career described the problem somewhat more colorfully when he said, "I'd love to spend more time thinking about the future but right now I'm up to my ass in alligators."

trends and long-term dynamics. The implication of this is that "every" analyst not only should—but also must—continuously examine "strategic" questions to enhance his or her ability to provide better daily support to the national security enterprise. One can imagine multiple ways to combine current and strategic work, but the key is continuous integration of insights from the strategic dimension into what the analyst carries in his or her head and contributes to the policy-making process through oral and written assessments and projections. A State Department colleague once likened the process to continuously updating the "elevator briefing" that an analyst should be prepared to deliver in the time to accompany a key customer from his or her office to the basement of the building. Such a briefing would summarize what was new, what it seemed to mean, and how it affected trends and strategic concerns.

Analysis of Topics Assigned in Accordance with Agency Production Plans

The job elements described above assume and require regular interchange between analysts and customers. They involve a high degree of contingency because analysts must adapt and respond to changing requirements, the serendipity of events, and the fruits of collection efforts. The degree to which analysts focus on or are consumed by these job elements is a function of where they work, what accounts they follow, whom they support, and a number of other situational factors.[25] For some analysts, these tasks are all consuming, but a subset must also devote time

---

[25]IC components generally employ one of two broad approaches to assigning responsibilities and developing their analytic workforces. Which approach is adopted depends primarily on the size of the agency, the number of analysts, and the scope of the issues it is expected to cover. One approach is to assign broad and diverse portfolios to all analysts, including new arrivals. This has long been the pattern in smaller components and has the advantage of forcing analysts to learn quickly and giving them the opportunity to work on high-profile issues that sustain their interest and deepen relationships with their key customers. This fosters breadth of expertise, sometimes at the expense of greater depth, but job satisfaction is generally high. The second approach is more akin to apprenticeship in a guild. New analysts are assigned initial portfolios that are quite narrow and acquire depth at the expense of breadth and context. More typical of large agencies than smaller ones, this approach to professional development assumes and requires a relatively long sequence of jobs before earning the chance to become a recognized expert on a country or transnational phenomenon. Over the long term, analysts who progress through this career trajectory can become very good, but in the near term, the approach discourages many ambitious analysts and reduces flexibility in deploying analytic talent against assigned tasks. In both cases, however, overall job satisfaction is high. Indeed, in 2009 the IC was named one of the best places to work in the federal government (Partnership for Public Service, 2009).

and attention to topics assigned in accordance with agency or IC production plans. Other analysts, probably the majority, are able and expected to devote most of their time to production intended to close intelligence gaps, illuminate new issues, or satisfy internally or externally mandated requirements to update information on leadership biographies, military orders of battle, developments in foreign science and technology, foreign direct investment in particular countries or industries, and other such issues. Some of this work is crucial and contributes directly to the work of other analysts; some of it requires more effort than may be warranted to produce information and insights of interest to only a small number of people who may or may not have any reason or ability to act on that information.[26]

Contribute to Community and Collaborative Products

Contributing to the *President's Daily Brief* and participating in the production of *National Intelligence Estimates* and other formally "coordinated" assessments impose heavy demands on analysts, but for all but a tiny number, the duration is short and the frequency is very occasional. Meeting the standards and procedural requirements of the IC's flagship products takes a great deal of work, but only a small percentage of all analysts write or make significant contributions more than a few times per year, if that. When they do, it is all consuming for a short period; how easy or difficult it is depends on how efficiently and effectively they perform other tasks in their job jars. Nevertheless, the high standards, obvious importance, and requirement to look closely at sources, assumptions, alternative hypotheses, and other facets of good tradecraft make this job element more important than suggested by the infrequency of individual participation. Expectations and enforcement of high standards in this arena exert an

---

[26]How specialized analysis can contribute to the work of all-source analysts responsible for broader portfolios and issues with more direct relevance to policy deliberations is easily demonstrated by the example of experience-based judgments by imagery analysts about how much time will be required to finalize preparations for a missile launch after certain intermediate stages have been completed. This and similar specialized input helps all-source analysts to assess intent and tell policy makers how long they have to work on the problem if they wish to prevent the launch, reassure allies, or influence international opinion. An example of information and insight of less utility is knowledge of the personal peccadilloes of mid-level foreign officials or businesspersons acquired in the course of monitoring other matters.

upward pull on the quality of work done by analysts in other venues and by the IC as a whole.[27]

Efforts to integrate the IC and to forge a "community of analysts" who collaborate without regard to parent agency have added new dimensions to the analyst's job.[28] One new element is the increased requirement for consultation and coordination in the production of items for the *President's Daily Brief* and briefing materials prepared by the National Intelligence Council for the National Security Council and other high-level meetings (for additional detail, see Fingar, 2011a). Though intended to require minimal time commitment on the part of those asked to comment on or coordinate most products, the importance of the products causes most analysts to take this task seriously and to invest as much time as they believe is necessary to "get it right." As a result, many will identify this dimension of their job as more time consuming than it probably is.

Bottom-up, analyst-initiated collaboration is an even more significant new element in the job jar. This takes many forms, including informal collaboration with colleagues within and beyond an analyst's home agency to produce better products, to the use of Wiki, blog, and other collaborative tools in Intellipedia (the IC's classified version of Wikipedia) and A-Space (for additional information on Intellipedia, see Calabresi, 2009; for

---

[27]The *President's Daily Brief* is both a product (a daily compilation of intelligence-based assessments keyed to the President's agenda and responsibilities) and a process that begins with the identification of intelligence germane to pending or previously made decisions, and sometimes culminates with oral briefings in the oval office presented by the analysts who have prepared the assessment. *National Intelligence Estimates* are considered to be the most authoritative judgments of the IC. They are produced by the National Intelligence Council (NIC) with input from all component agencies with information and expertise germane to the topic. They are frequently described as consensus documents, but their goal is clarity, not consensus. If analysts from different agencies or within a single agency reach different judgments than do others working with the same information, and those judgments meet the requirements of good analytic tradecraft, both/all alternatives are explicated in the text and incorporated into the executive summary (called Key Judgments). This was not always the case before the NIC was transferred from the Director of Central Intelligence to the DNI. "Coordinated" intelligence products have been shared with all components known or thought to have relevant expertise in order to compare independently developed assessments, to ensure that all relevant intelligence has been considered, and to discover any analytic differences. The coordination process for *National Intelligence Estimates* is highly structured, but many other products are "coordinated" in effective but less formal ways. See also Fingar (2011b).

[28]ODNI efforts to forge a "community of analysts" remain a work in progress. The goal is to have analysts think of themselves as members of a single intelligence enterprise rather than as employees of a specific component agency. This is one of many interdependent measures to address cultural impediments to integration and collaboration without sacrificing the advantages of having specialized components keyed to the missions and requirements of different bureaucratic customers.

A-Space, see Shaughnessy, 2008). Analysts in and influenced by the "digital generation" find these tools to be helpful, but using them to share information, enhance understanding, build "living documents," and perform other analytic tasks has taken the IC in new directions that have no roadmaps, few standards, and only limited understanding on the part of most managers.[29] No matter how great a boon or burden, actual or perceived, these increasingly used forms of collaboration are still a matter of dispute. It is not uncommon to hear complaints from both analysts and managers that analysts "must" spend too much time collaborating with colleagues or using new analytic tools.[30]

Provide Guidance to Collectors

The existence and utility of the National Intelligence Priorities Framework (NIPF) notwithstanding, analysts play the primary role in translating

---

[29]The term "living documents" is intended to capture a process that produces authoritative and regularly updated analytic products, but is more formal than a blog or Wiki. The IC is still learning how to do this, but the basic idea is that an assessment—such as a biographic profile or analysis of economic conditions in a particular country—prepared by one or more analysts using Intellipedia or A-Space will be reviewed by senior analysts or supervisors using criteria identical to those used in the review of materials prepared for publication by the agency conducting the review and given a metaphorical stamp of approval signifying that, as of a particular date and time, the content of the document has been endorsed by the reviewing agency. This will signal to customers and analysts that the product has been subjected to formal review and that at least one component of the IC is prepared to stand by its judgments. Analysts in other agencies could disseminate and use the product in the same way that they would use other types of products released by the endorsing agency. As new information was obtained or analysts developed new insights, they could be added to the original document until someone determined that it was necessary to conduct another formal review, perhaps by a different agency, so the product could be used with a different set of customers or in response to a request for an update. The simple idea behind this approach is that it is more efficient to produce and update a single document accessible to all than to reinvent and reproduce the same assessment in multiple publications, and that if all agencies are applying the same standards (see Director of National Intelligence, 2007a, 2007c), analysts and customers can have the same confidence in the quality of the product as they do in products produced by the component of the IC with which they work most often.

[30]Analytic tools had a deservedly bad reputation among IC analysts because of a long sequence of oversold, but underproducing, "solutions" to real and imagined problems. When Intellipedia and A-Space were introduced, they were greeted with considerable skepticism, but the speed with which they were voluntarily adopted by analysts was phenomenal. For example, it took less than a year for 90 percent of analysts eligible to participate in A-Space (approximately 12,000) to open accounts. The rate of active participation, that is, the percentage of users who edit or post materials as opposed to merely reading what is already posted, is much higher for A-Space than it is for Wikipedia or similar sites.

customer needs into guidance for collectors.[31] The IC collection system is both vast and nimble. It can be tweaked to go after specific topics and targets, and collectors do their best—which is a substantial effort—to meet the ever-changing panoply of needs given to them by analysts. Analysts do not—or should not—simply relay questions from customers. They translate such requests by asking themselves—and their colleagues—what the question is intended to illuminate, what kind of information would produce the greatest understanding of the underlying problem, and where collectors should look to find that information. The formal process for translating information needs into guidance to collectors is still a work in progress and is still more cumbersome than it should be, but analysts are and will remain the key to its success.[32]

The schematic summary above somewhat obscures the extent to which all of these job elements are interrelated and occupy a continuum rather than compartmented activities. It also omits activities such as updating databases that occupy significant portions of some analysts' time. That said, many analysts and commentators speak as if the different elements are in zero-sum competition and lament that certain ones constrain what can be done to address others. As one might imagine, there is a natural tendency to decry and exaggerate the amount of time that must be allocated to tasks an

---

[31]The NIPF is the formal mechanism for translating policy-maker priorities into collection and analytic requirements. A matrix is formed by arraying 32 intelligence topics (subdivided into 3 prioritized bands) against roughly 220 countries and non-state actors. Each cell in the matrix receives a "score" ranging from zero to five, with zero meaning the cell is empty and that the topic will receive essentially no attention from the IC. One is the highest priority, and topics in that group will receive a great deal of attention. Category five topics are essentially "global coverage" accounts maintained to support diplomatic and other ongoing responsibilities, or "fire extinguisher" accounts maintained at a low level of effort because of their potential to flare up with significant implications for U.S. interests (for additional information on the NIPF, see Director of National Intelligence, 2007b).

[32]In addition to the formal NIPF process through which senior policy makers update their priorities every 6 months, analysts provide regular guidance to collectors through a variety of less formal, but more nimble, procedures. One is a biweekly update compiled by the Analytic Mission Management team in the Office of the Deputy Director of National Intelligence for Analysis by soliciting input from the 12 National Intelligence Officers (NIOs; 6 regional and 6 dealing with transnational issues). These updates reflect input and insight obtained through close interaction between the NIOs and their counterparts on the National Security Council and other executive branch agencies as well as similar input from senior analysts in individual IC components. A second mechanism, also managed by the Analytic Mission Management team, involves the convening, usually by a National Intelligence Officer, of senior analysts working on a particular place or problem. The purpose of these meetings is to clarify what policy makers want and need to understand and determine collectively what kinds of information might provide greatest insight into the problem. This is refined into specific guidance to collectors to "look in these places for this kind of information on these topics." The guidance is also keyed to decision timelines to ensure that input from the IC is delivered in time to make a difference.

individual finds more difficult or less rewarding than those on which he or she would rather spend time. All are important and interconnected efforts to make analysis more accurate, more useful, and more efficient. They will have the greatest impact if they address all of the elements in the job jar as parts of an integrated whole rather than as specialties that can be compartmentalized and assigned to discrete groups of analysts.

MAKING NECESSITY A VIRTUE LEADS TO A BETTER WAY OF DOING BUSINESS

In the past—and here the past is as recent as the immediate post-9/11 period during which there was tremendous growth in the IC budget and the number of analysts—the standard response to increased demands was to add people and/or create new analytic components.[33] To improve information sharing, reduce "cultural" barriers to collaboration, and consolidate work on important issues, the 9/11 Commission recommended and the *Intelligence Reform and Terrorism Prevention Act of 2004* (IRTPA) endorsed the creation of specialized "centers." The IRTPA also gave statutory authority to the National Counterterrorism Center (NCTC) that had been created four months earlier by Executive Order (National Commission on Terrorist Attacks upon the United States, 2004; Section 1021 of the 2004 IRTPA).

The newly established ODNI made a conscious decision not to adopt that approach. By mid-2005, calls to integrate and rationalize the IC and competing demands for "more analysts" made it impractical and imprudent to create and staff new analytic units to support new missions and new customers. New units would have had to be either too small to achieve critical mass on any issue or so large that duplication of effort would have been inevitable. Moreover, the start-up problems of the NCTC and the fact that no agency abolished or significantly downsized its own counterterrorism unit when NCTC was established underscored previously learned lessons about distancing analysts from their primary customers and providing what looks like one-size-fits-nobody analytic support (see DeYoung, 2006; Whitelaw, 2006; for additional analysis, see Fingar, 2011a).[34] The ODNI

---

[33]The IC budget was classified until 2008, but authoritative figures were released occasionally. In 1998, Director of Central Intelligence George Tenet cited the figure of $26.7 billion (Central Intelligence Agency, 1998). The figure for 2009 was $49.8 billion (Office of the Director of National Intelligence, 2009).

[34]The NCTC's start-up problems resulted from the concatenation of many factors, including ambiguities in law and policy, resistance from certain agencies, and the sheer magnitude of the task. In addition, agencies were understandably reluctant to downsize their existing capabilities before the NCTC had proven that it could meet their specific counterterrorism requirements.

was determined to find a better way to organize and integrate IC analytic capabilities.

To address the need to bring new types of expertise to bear on new problems for new customers without creating new units or adding significantly to the analytic workforce, the ODNI set out to discover whether such expertise existed anywhere in the IC, where this expertise was considered critical to the performance of core missions, and where it was vestigial or serendipitous.[35] This effort also revealed how strong or weak the analytic community was in each area, now and when factoring in projected retirements and other forms of attrition. Using loose and subjective criteria, the ODNI set out to determine where the IC had sufficient expertise (if it could be harnessed effectively), where gaps existed in specific agencies and in the IC as a whole, and where there was potential to "grow" expertise by mentoring across agency boundaries.

Developing the "better way" is still a work in progress, but the principal building blocks of the approach are relatively clear and experience to date provides an empirical basis for adjustments and improvement. The first building block was to identify with a fair degree of precision what each of the component analytic elements did (i.e., the missions and customers they supported, the areas of expertise they had developed, and the kinds of assessments they produced). This inventory revealed less redundancy than many assumed, especially when one examined specific areas of focus subsumed under broad rubrics such as "China" or "missiles." Yet it also indicated that many agencies had developed small elements to address subjects tangential to their core missions because they did not know where relevant expertise could be found elsewhere in the IC, could not "task" analysts elsewhere to provide necessary input, or could not have confidence in the quality of the work done by people they did not know and could not evaluate on their own.[36] This mapping exercise also revealed that most components judged that they lacked a "critical mass" of expertise on all but

---

[35]Vestigial capabilities exist for many reasons, ranging from the magnitude of the IC effort against the former Soviet Union and its Warsaw Pact allies to expertise on Libya's weapons of mass destruction programs that became less relevant when Muammar Gaddhafi decided to dismantle those programs and surrender key components to the United States. Serendipitous capabilities also have many variations, including the linguistic abilities and cultural knowledge of first- and second-generation Americans, the skills and knowledge individuals acquired in previous assignments, and the ability to use friendships and professional ties to secure assistance on certain types of issues.

[36]In the parlance of the IC, the ability to "task" an assignment entails the ability to ensure that it is carried out and to hold individuals and organizations accountable for their performance. "Tasking" carries a lot more weight than merely "asking" that something be done. The former is mandatory; the latter can be trumped by assignments that have been specifically "tasked" to an analyst or agency.

a small number of topics. When combined, these agency-by-agency mapping exercises provided a reasonably complete picture of the customers and activities supported by the IC and a first-cut approximation of duplication and deficiencies.

The second building block was to inventory the skills and experience of the analysts themselves by reinvigorating and making enrollment mandatory in the Analytic Resources Catalog (ARC).[37] A primary objective of the ARC was to map what analysts know, individually and collectively. An assumption confirmed by the ARC data was that expertise on many subjects is deeper than organizational and staffing charts would suggest because analysts retain knowledge from previous assignments even as they assume new responsibilities. The mapping exercise, in conjunction with demographic data using years of experience as a proxy for age and similar ways to avoid running afoul of privacy laws, also revealed areas where expertise was concentrated in particular age cohorts (e.g., a disproportionate percentage of those working a given subject had 20 or more years of experience, suggesting an upcoming problem of simultaneous retirements with no suc-

---

Prior to the creation of the ODNI and the adoption of uniform tradecraft standards for all agencies, there were both real and exaggerated differences in the quality of work done by different components of the IC. Cultural differences and their consequences magnified negative perceptions and stereotyping of the people in and work done by counterparts in other agencies. This was a serious impediment to collaboration and meaningful divisions of labor. In addition to the adoption of uniform tradecraft standards, the ODNI launched a course in basic analytic tradecraft attended by new analysts from across the IC. More than 3,000 analysts have graduated from "Analysis 101." They have trained together and know that their counterparts elsewhere are as talented and well prepared as they are because they have learned the same skills at the same time in the same classrooms (see Kelly, 2007).

[37]The ARC was the brainchild of John Gannon, the first Assistant Director of Central Intelligence for Analysis and Production (ADCI/AP) and one of my predecessors as Chairman of the National Intelligence Council. Gannon's objective was to facilitate more efficient use of analytic skills and the ability to make better informed decisions about what skills to pursue when filling vacant positions. His efforts were thwarted by officials who used counterintelligence concerns and other arguments to stifle this early effort to integrate the analytic community. A few years later, Mark Lowenthal, who succeeded Gannon as ADCI/AP, revived the ARC with somewhat more success, but he gave it a rationale that caused both individual analysts and managers to avoid entering pertinent information out of concern that the ARC would provide the basis for recruiting analysts for task forces, undesirable assignments, or other activities they might not wish to do. When I inherited their positions and the ARC, I made clear that it was to be a database of expertise, not a free agent list or roster of candidates for reassignment. The ARC has now become the model and foundation for similar and integrated databases of collectors, scientists, and other IC professionals.

cessors in the pipeline).[38] One objective of this inventory of expertise was to make it easier for analysts to find potential collaborators and for analytic managers to find persons with the skills and experience needed to address subjects beyond the competence of their own agency. Stated another way, the goal was to be able to harness the totality of expertise in the analytic community, not just that of persons currently occupying particular billets (e.g., "Southeast Asia terrorism" or "Andean economics").

The exercise described above made clear that the IC had more expertise than suggested by staffing patterns *if* it could find a way to tap what people already knew, even if that knowledge was from previous assignments, and *if* the IC found a way to enable analysts to collaborate at a distance. The goal was to facilitate voluntary formation of "virtual" teams with the advantages of proximity to key customers and synergistic benefits from collaboration.[39] Realizing the potential benefits inherent in this vision required overcoming a number of technical, policy, and cultural obstacles.[40] Some have been surmounted; others have yet to be tackled. It also made clear, however, that the IC did not have and was unlikely ever to have enough people with

---

[38]The specific case referenced in the text was drawn from a pilot project to map with precision the capabilities and experience profiles of analysts working on Africa. When the initial results were shown to me, my first reaction was that the numbers were dangerously small, but the demographic profile of IC Africa analysts did not look that bad. When I looked more closely at the high end of the experience curve, however, I realized that we had a more serious problem than indicated by the data. Specifically, the profile showed that roughly 10 percent of the analysts had more than 20 years of experience (that was the way the question had been asked). But I knew several of the analysts in that category, and also knew they had all served for more than 30 years and were already eligible to retire. This discovery lent new urgency to efforts to recruit at higher levels of experience and to use the experienced veterans to mentor more junior analysts without regard to home agency affiliation.

[39]The impetus for formation of virtual teams was the desire to create "critical masses" of expertise sufficient to address the complex analytic problems assigned to the IC without sacrificing the advantages of proximity to key customers that would result from the creation of "centers" (as called for by the 9/11 Commission) or similar arrangements intended to overcome cultural differences and impediments to information sharing through proximity. It was also the result of my experience in the Bureau of Intelligence and Research, where I had a number of teams composed of analysts scattered across three floors of the State Department. They interacted primarily through e-mail, a method that could easily be used to link analysts in different buildings, different agencies, and different cities. This experience was reinforced by the findings of the study of teams prepared for the Intelligence Science Board (Hackman and O'Connor, 2004).

[40]Technical impediments included incompatibilities among legacy systems that made it difficult to "wire" together certain components of the IC and use of different meta-data standards that impeded use of materials resident in different databases. Policy obstacles ranged from measures to address counterintelligence concerns spawned under conditions very different from those of today to "rules" that precluded e-mailing certain categories of documents to anyone in certain agencies. Fixing the technical obstacles was easier than reducing policy impediments. Cultural obstacles often boiled down to some version of "why would I want to work with anyone in that organization?"

sufficient expertise to cover all of its missions in the small time frames that had become the norm. It was imperative to find ways to develop continuing relationships with scholars, journalists, think tank researchers, diplomats, and others with deep knowledge of subjects of interest to policy makers and essential to the analytic mission of the IC.[41] This had to involve more than just compiling a list of "experts on everything." Indeed, one objective was to make the incorporation of information and insights from outside experts a regular part of each analyst's job in order to raise the level of individual and corporate expertise in the IC. A second was to be able to use the outside expert as a sounding board for ideas and as a source of guidance on where to look for answers to specific questions. A third objective was to nurture these relationships so they could be activated immediately in the event of a crisis or extremely short fuse requirements. The advantages are obvious, but not enough to overcome concerns, many of them legitimate, about interchange with people outside the IC.[42] The proposed arrangements also raise important questions about deference to authority figures, protection of sources and methods, and other methodological concerns.

DEMOGRAPHICS

Perhaps the most important characteristic of the analytic workforce is its youth. Any plans to improve the quality of analytic products must give proper attention to the fact that more than 50 percent have joined the IC since 2001. A second is that the age distribution of the other 50 percent is skewed toward the retirement end of the scale, largely because the hiring freezes, downsizing, rightsizing, and organizational turmoil of the 1990s limited intake and caused many younger analysts to seek employment elsewhere, often in firms that do contract work for the IC. These demographics create a number of challenges (e.g., the need to use and capitalize on the expertise of senior analysts now serving in managerial positions, and to pull junior analysts up the learning curve faster than would normally have been the case in the IC).[43] This also means that more formal training is required

---

[41]Arguments for more and continuous interchange between IC analysts and specialists from outside the IC are developed at greater length in Fingar (2007). See also *Intelligence Community Directive (ICD) 205: Analytic Outreach* (Director of National Intelligence, 2008).

[42]Concerns about interchange between IC analysts and experts from outside of the IC include the potential for unintentional disclosure of sensitive intelligence or information about sources and methods, increased vulnerability to the intelligence collection efforts of other nations, and the desire of some "collectors" to monopolize contacts with outside experts.

[43]The IC has a long tradition of developing talent and shaping careers through approaches that would be familiar to guilds in the Middle Ages. Analysts gradually are exposed to more dimensions of the intelligence business and expected to more or less replicate the career paths and behaviors of those who have gone before. Such approaches are no longer adequate for the challenges of today or acceptable to the talented and ambitious new analysts who have joined

to compensate for the brevity of on-the-job learning through observation of how more senior analysts practice their craft.

Those are the downsides of demography, but there are a great many upsides as well. For example, the cohort that has joined in the past 7 to 8 years is extremely talented and exceptionally well trained in the disciplines they pursued in graduate school (and most of the new analysts do have graduate training, many from leading universities). They are also of the "digital generation" and completely at home in environments requiring collaboration at a distance, sharing and providing information to trusted interlocutors, experimenting with analytic tools, searching the Internet and classified databases, and performing other tasks (Palfrey and Gasser, 2008). They routinely communicate with friends across institutional boundaries and expect to do the same in their professional lives. Persuading them to adopt new techniques and to work differently than the generations they are succeeding is easy. What is less easy—but essential—is developing modern-day means to vet information, exercise quality control on products developed using Wikis and blogs, and maintain the requisite security safeguards when dealing with persons outside of the IC.[44] In doing so, IC leaders must diligently adapt policies and procedures developed for a different time, different types of problems, and different generations to suit the capabilities and expectations of the youthful workforce.

WILL AND ABILITY TO ADAPT

The IC as a whole and the analytic community in particular are neither broken nor bad, but they can and want to be better. They want to be better for the right reasons: to ensure the security of our country, the safety of our fellow citizens, and the success of policies to protect American interests and promote American ideals. The majority of analysts are new to the IC, but they are not new to analysis. As a group, they represent and reflect the best training available in America's best universities. Their seniors, in both age and position, are among the most knowledgeable subject matter experts in their fields. Most of them feel a strong sense of professional responsibility to move successors up the learning curve as rapidly as possible. Top analytic managers "get it" and are (mostly) eager to do what is necessary to transform the way analysis is done in the IC in order to satisfy burgeoning

---

the IC in the past decade and will leave if they feel inhibited by hoary traditions that no longer make sense to them or their expectations of the intelligence profession.

[44]Vetting information entails discovering and conveying to others details about its provenance that could affect judgments about reliability, accuracy, and intent (e.g., Was it published in a government- or party-controlled newspaper? Did the source have first-hand or only indirect access to the information? Or is it simply the repackaging of information published previously in another media outlet?).

requirements, support new missions, realize the full potential of the analytic workforce, and retain the talented people who have joined the IC in the past decade. Getting it right will not be easy or quick, but conditions for sustained improvement have never been better.

REFERENCES

Boudreaux, R. 1994. Yeltsin fires chemical warfare chief. *Los Angeles Times.* April 8. Available: http://articles.latimes.com/1994-04-08/news/mn-43642_1_chemical-weapons [accessed May 2010].

Calabresi, M. 2009. Wikipedia for spies: The CIA discovers Web 2.0. *Time.* Wednesday, April 8. Available: http://www.time.com/time/nation/article/0,8599,1890084,00.html [accessed October 2010].

Central Intelligence Agency. 1998. *Statement by the Director of Central Intelligence regarding the disclosure of the aggregate intelligence budget for fiscal year 1998.* Press release, March 20. Available: https://www.cia.gov/news-information/press-releases-statements/press-release-archive-1998/ps032098.html [accessed May 2010].

Commission on the Intelligence Capabilities of the United States Regarding Weapons of Mass Destruction. 2005. *Report to the President of the United States.* March 31. BookSurge, LLC. Available: http://www.gpoaccess.gov/wmd/pdf/full_wmd_report.pdf [accessed April 2010].

Congressional Record–House. 2007. Proceedings and debates of the 110th Congress, first session, 153: 77—Part II, May 10, pp. H4895–H4896. Available: http://www.gpo.gov/fdsys/pkg/CREC-2007-05-10/pdf/CREC-2007-05-10-pt2-PgH4881-3.pdf [accessed October 2010].

DeYoung, K. 2006. A fight against terrorism and disorganization. *Washington Post,* August 9. Available: http://www.washingtonpost.com/wp-dyn/content/article/2006/08/08/AR2006080800964_pf.html [accessed May 2010].

Director of National Intelligence. 2007a. *Intelligence community directive (ICD) 203: Analytic standards.* June 21. Available: http://www.dni.gov/electronic_reading_room/ICD_203.pdf [accessed May 2010].

Director of National Intelligence. 2007b. *Intelligence community directive (ICD) 204: Roles and responsibilities for the National Intelligence Priorities Framework.* September 13. Available: http://www.dni.gov/electronic_reading_room/ICD_204.pdf [accessed May 2010].

Director of National Intelligence. 2007c. *Intelligence community directive (ICD) 206: Sourcing requirements for disseminated analytic products.* October 17. Available: http://www.dni.gov/electronic_reading_room/ICD_206.pdf [accessed May 2010].

Director of National Intelligence. 2008. *Intelligence community directive (ICD) 205: Analytic outreach.* July 16. Available: http://www.dni.gov/electronic_reading_room/ICD_205.pdf [accessed May 2010].

Fingar, T. 2006. DDNI/A [Deputy Director of National Intelligence for Analysis] addresses the DNI's information sharing conference and technology exposition. *Intelink and Beyond: Dare to Share.* Denver, CO, August 21. Available: http://www.dni.gov/speeches/20060821_2_speech.pdf [accessed May 2010].

Fingar, T. 2007. *Remarks and Q&A by the Deputy Director of National Intelligence for Analysis & Chairman.* National Intelligence Council at the ODNI Open Source Conference. Washington, DC, July 17. Available: http://www.dni.gov/speeches/20070717_speech_3.pdf [accessed May 2010].

Fingar, T. 2011a. Office of the Director of National Intelligence: Promising start despite ambiguity, ambivalence, and animosity. In R. Z. George and H. Rishikof, eds., *The national security enterprise: Navigating the labyrinth*. Washington, DC: Georgetown University Press.

Fingar, T. 2011b. *Reducing uncertainty: Intelligence analysis and national security*. Stanford, CA: Stanford University Press.

George, R. Z., and H. Rishikof (Eds.). 2011. *The national security enterprise: Navigating the labyrinth*. Washington, DC: Georgetown University Press.

Gordon, M. R. 1990. Beijing avoids new missile sales assurances. *The New York Times*. March 30. Available: http://www.nytimes.com/1990/03/30/world/beijing-avoids-new-missile-sales-assurances.html [accessed May 2010].

Hackman, J. R., and M. O'Connor. 2004. *What makes for a great analytic team? Individual versus team approaches to intelligence analysis*. February. Available: http://www.fas.org/irp/dni/isb/analytic.pdf [accessed May 2010].

Kelly, M. L. 2007. *Intelligence community unites for "Analysis 101."* National Public Radio, May 7. Available: http://www.npr.org/templates/story/story.php?storyId=10040625 [accessed May 2010].

National Commission on Terrorist Attacks Upon the United States. 2004. *The 9/11 Commission report*. New York: W.W. Norton. Available: http://www.9-11commission.gov/report/911Report.pdf [accessed April 2010].

National Intelligence Council. 2001. *Global humanitarian emergencies: Trends and projections 2001–2002*. Available: http://www.dni.gov/nic/special_globalhuman2001.html [accessed May 2010].

National Intelligence Council. 2003. *SARS: Down but still a threat*. Available: http://www.dni.gov/nic/special_sarsthreat.html [accessed May 2010].

National Intelligence Council. 2008a. *Global trends 2025: A transformed world*. Available: http://www.dni.gov/nic/PDF_2025/2025_Global_Trends_Final_Report.pdf [accessed May 2010].

National Intelligence Council. 2008b. *Strategic implications of global health*. Available: http://www.dni.gov/nic/PDF_GIF_otherprod/ICA_Global_Health_2008.pdf [accessed May 2010].

National Intelligence Council. 2009. *The impact of climate change to 2030: Commissioned research and conference reports*. Available: http://www.dni.gov/nic/special_climate2030.html [accessed May 2010].

Nuclear Threat Initiative. 2007. *China's chemical and biological weapon-related exports to Iran*. Available: http://www.nti.org/db/China/cbwiran.htm [accessed May 2010].

Office of the Director of National Intelligence. 2009. *DNI releases budget figure for 2009 National Intelligence Program*. October 30. Available: http://www.dni.gov/press_releases/20091030_release.pdf [accessed January 2010].

Palfrey, J., and U. Gasser. 2008. *Born digital: Understanding the first generation of digital natives*. New York: Basic Books.

Partnership for Public Service. 2009. *The best places to work in the federal government 2009*. Available: http://data.bestplacestowork.org/bptw/index [accessed May 2010].

Russell, R. L. 2007. *Sharpening strategic intelligence*. New York: Cambridge University Press.

Sanders, R. 2008. *Conference call with Dr. Ronald Sanders, associate director of national intelligence for human capital*. August 27. Available: http://www.asisonline.org/secman/20080827_interview.pdf [accessed April 2010].

Shaughnessy, L. 2008. *CIA, FBI push "Facebook for Spies."* CNN.com/technology. September 5. Available: http://edition.cnn.com/2008/TECH/ptech/09/05/facebook.spies/ [accessed May 2010].

Steele, J. 2008. *Maliki drops the mask: With his tough stance on U.S. withdrawal, Sunni militias and the Kurds Iraq's leader risks doom.* September 5. Available: http://www.guardian.co.uk/commentisfree/2008/sep/05/iraq.middleeast [accessed December 2009].

Time. 2008. *Time's* best inventions of 2008. October 29. Available: http://www.time.com/time/specials/packages/completelist/0,29569,1852747,00.html [accessed May 2010].

Tiron, R. 2007. Afghanistan officials question drug-eradication, nomination. *The Hill.* Available: http://thehill.com/business-a-lobbying/2261-afghanistan-officials-question-drug-eradication-nomination [accessed May 2010].

Treverton, G. F. 2008. Intelligence analysis: Between "politicization" and irrelevance. In R. Z. George and J. B. Bruce, eds., *Analyzing intelligence: Origins, obstacles, and innovations* (pp. 91–106). Washington, DC: Georgetown University Press.

Treverton, G. F., and C. B. Gabbard. 2008. *Assessing the tradecraft of intelligence analysts.* The RAND Corporation, National Security Research Division. Available: http://www.rand.org/pubs/technical_reports/2008/RAND_TR293.pdf [accessed May 2010].

Voice of America. 2009. *Afghan election poses policy dilemmas for U.S.* August 3. Available: http://www.voanews.com/english/2009-08-03-voa34.cfm [accessed May 2010].

Whitelaw, K. 2006. The eye of the storm. *U.S. News and World Report* 141(7):48–52.

Part II

Analytic Methods

In Part II, four papers present the contributions of four social science approaches to intelligence analysis: operations research, game theory, signal detection theory, and qualitative analysis. These four approaches were selected for their immediate applicability to the needs of intelligence analysts and because their benefits and limitations are well understood as the result of extensive scientific research and testing.

In Chapter 2, Edward H. Kaplan introduces readers to the field of operations research (OR). After reviewing the field's origins in the applications of applied mathematics to military decision-making problems, Kaplan describes current methods in OR, showing how they could be adopted for intelligence analysis. He stresses OR's value in organizing diverse pieces of information for understanding the operational capabilities and challenges of all actors in a situation. He focuses on optimization, probability modeling, and decision analysis as OR tools that are particularly well suited for intelligence analysis. He shows how OR from its inception has recognized the value of timely but imperfect analysis—as is often needed with intelligence analysis.

In Chapter 3, Bruce Bueno de Mesquita describes the fundamental assumptions of game theory and its applications to intelligence analysis. He notes its ability to help analysts pay attention to events that do not happen; explain discontinuities; understand the constraints of uncertainty, risks, costs and benefits; and coordinate multiple actors. As an example, he shows how game theory clarifies the potentially misleading role of selection effects in interpreting historical patterns. Bueno de Mesquita also shows the value of game theory reasoning itself, which is enhanced when it can be combined with empirical and quantitative analysis.

In Chapter 4, Gary H. McClelland presents the contributions of signal detection theory to improving the performance and evaluation of analytic judgments and tradecraft. Signal detection theory provides an orderly way of treating how well analysts understand uncertain situations and what decision rules guide their judgments about them. McClelland illustrates the approach with applications to technology, medicine, and science policy, which parallel the challenges faced by intelligence analysts who must understand uncertain situations and convey their conclusions to policy makers. In particular, the paper shows how signal detection theory can be used to clarify the lessons of 9/11 and the "failures" of intelligence about Iraq weapons of mass destruction—distinguishing decision rules (e.g., systematic bias toward false alarms) from failures to understand distortion.

In Chapter 5, Kiron K. Skinner describes the essential roles of formal qualitative analysis in intelligence analysis. She shows how political science provides disciplined methods for increasing the usefulness and accuracy of qualitative analysis. Skinner's paper illustrates these methods with lessons from two historical intelligence failures, drawing on the "strategic perspective," a theory of decision making that integrates observations of state behavior, political leadership, and the connections between domestic politics and international relations.

2

Operations Research and Intelligence Analysis

Edward H. Kaplan[1]

This chapter presents an overview of the field of operations research (OR), with a glimpse toward its applicability to problems in intelligence analysis. I first define the field of operations research, and suggest the types of intelligence problems that it can and cannot best address. A brief review of the World War II origins of OR and subsequent developments follows. I then offer a selective tour of current OR applications to illustrate the range of activities in which operations research is used, and provide some evidence indicating the value gained from using OR in practice. I next suggest how operations researchers approach new problems, provide a brief survey of different OR modeling methods that have been developed over the years, and note that the use of these techniques is now facilitated by computerized spreadsheet programs. I then provide a few "back of the envelope" models more to illustrate the flavor of operations research reasoning than to highlight any particular discoveries. I close by suggesting some possible applications of these ideas to intelligence analysis, including the use of OR to study the intelligence production process.

WHAT IS OPERATIONS RESEARCH AND HOW IS IT USEFUL?

Massachusetts Institute of Technology (MIT) physicist, Philip Morse, defined operations research as the scientific study of operations (Morse, 1956). Operations are the physical means by which organizations "get

[1]The author acknowledges the Daniel Rose Fund supporting the Technion–Yale Initiative in Homeland Security and Counterterror Operations Research.

31

things done." They are the organized, often repetitive activities and/or tasks carried out by firms, agencies, the military, or virtually any other organization in support of its mission. Examples include the steps involved in the production of manufactured goods, the servicing of customers in call centers (or restaurants or hospitals or online), the determination of routes and schedules for delivering parcels (e.g., FedEx) and/or people (e.g., the airlines), or the planning of terrorist attacks (and countermeasures to prevent such attacks).

As will be elaborated below, the scientific study of operations reflects the methods of physical science, which is not surprising because the founders of OR were physical scientists. Early studies focused on establishing the physical principles underlying the mainly military operations in question via the analysis of operational data, the formulation of (often simple) mathematical models from first principles, and the design and analysis of experiments to test the results of such models. Over time, however, the formulation and analysis of mathematical models became the hallmark of operations research studies, while the mathematics underlying such models developed to the point where today, the term "operations research" is as likely to refer to the mathematical methods involved as to field studies of actual operations.

The rationale for studying operations is not only to understand them (which is the usual goal of scientific investigation), but also to use such understanding to make better operational decisions. "Better" refers to improving matters in terms of the organization's fundamental objectives: What decisions lead to higher (if not maximal) profits, lower (if not minimal) costs, increased numbers of infections averted, or reduced numbers of successful terror attacks? Thus, perhaps a more complete definition of OR is the scientific study of operations to make better decisions.

For intelligence analysts, operations research offers powerful tools for understanding and analyzing certain classes of problems. However, OR is by no means a "one-size-fits-all" approach to solving intelligence problem sets. Questions that address the operations, capabilities, or procedures underlying adversaries' (or sometimes allies') "systems of interest" can be studied using mainstream OR ideas, while operations research can assist in the study of questions that focus more on an adversary's intentions by complementing other methods such as game theory (see Fingar, Chapter 1, and Bueno de Mesquita, Chapter 3, both in this volume).[2] As an example,

---

[2] As will be discussed later, the interdisciplinary field of decision analysis focuses on individual and group decision making; this field includes some operations research ideas, but also relies heavily on research in psychology, economics, and statistics. Intelligence questions addressing intentions can, in principle, be approached via decision analysis and related game-theoretic models, but most OR methods are better suited for studying operations per se.

although OR ideas are less helpful in answering whether Iran's opposition leaders want to develop nuclear weapons, such ideas could be employed to estimate how long Iran would take to develop them. Although OR cannot tell us if Hezbollah intends to launch an attack on American soil, the methods of operations research could be used to estimate the number of operatives required to execute different types of terror attacks, or perhaps even estimate the number of Hezbollah operatives or sympathizers in the country. In applying OR to intelligence problems, the expectation is not that this approach will provide magic answers to otherwise unanswerable questions, but rather that the methods of OR can serve as powerful organizing devices for connecting different pieces of information, and suggest what unknown parameters for the system of interest are most important to ascertain.

THE ORIGINS OF OPERATIONS RESEARCH

Prior to the outbreak of World War II, Britain's preparation for the anticipated conflict included experimental investigations into the deployment of newly developed radar technology to provide early warning and real-time tracking of German bomber attacks. By mid-1938, air-defense drills revealed that although it was technically feasible for the radar system to detect aircraft, " . . . its operational achievements fell far short of requirements" (Larnder, 1984, p. 471). The superintendent of the Bawdsey Research Station,[3] A. P. Rowe, is credited with proposing that " . . . research into the operational—as opposed to the technical—aspects of the system should begin immediately" (Larnder, 1984, p. 471), and the term "operational research" was created to describe this new area of endeavor. Initial investigations included methods for managing fighters to counterattack bombers in both formation and individual combat. As the war progressed, staff of the then-formalized (in 1941) Royal Air Force Operational Research Section employed statistical analysis, deductive methods from the physical sciences, and common sense to analyze both offensive and defensive operations with an eye toward reducing their own casualties while inflicting maximal damage on the enemy (Dyson, 2006).

The leading British scientist associated with wartime OR is the Nobel Prize-winning physicist Patrick Blackett, who in 1940 was appointed as the Director of Naval Operational Research (*Nobel Lectures, Physics 1942–1962*, 1964; McCloskey, 1987). He was involved in the early radar studies and is credited with leading the team that discovered the relationship between the size of merchant marine convoys and the number of merchant ships sunk in U-boat pack attacks. As detailed in Falconer (1976) and Morse

---

[3]This was where Britain's Army and Air Force conducted its prewar radar experiments.

and Kimball (1951), the key finding was that the number of merchant vessels sunk per attack, while proportional to the number of attacking U-boats and inversely proportional to the number of naval escorts, was essentially independent of the number of merchant ships in a convoy. This led to the recommendation that merchant ships travel in larger convoys, which in turn greatly reduced shipping losses to the allied forces in the North Atlantic (see Kirby, 2003, for further details of the British origins of operational research).

Philip Morse (not incidentally Blackett's friend and colleague), is regarded widely as the father of operations research in the United States. In 1942, Morse agreed to join the war effort by organizing a group of scientists to help the U.S. Navy study its antisubmarine operations (Morse, 1986). The different problems addressed and methods developed by Morse and his associates, originally contained in classified reports and memorandums, have been documented in Morse and Kimball's *Methods of Operations Research* (1951), the first published text in the field. In addition to the merchant marine convoy problem discussed earlier, reported applications include finding the best search patterns to locate enemy ships and submarines, evaluating the trade-offs in the following situations:

- Using planes as merchant marine escorts and having these same planes bomb U-boat docks;
- Attacking enemy ships versus attacking the factories that produce ships;
- Determining the required forces of different types to undertake various military operations;
- Evaluating rapid maneuvering versus antiaircraft fire to defend warships against Kamikaze suicide plane attacks;
- Developing countermeasures to enemy radar; and
- Evaluating weapons effectiveness and determining the best methods for using them.

Basic physical reasoning (as captured in simple flow or differential equations), probability modeling, statistical analysis of both experimental and operational (i.e., field) data, and a good deal of (sophisticated!) common sense were used throughout the decision making. In later writing, Morse noted that for operations researchers, "Any field of mathematics, any technique of measurement that will bring results is used," and that OR " . . . uses any and all of these techniques to study *operations* so that they may be understood, and thus understandingly controlled" (Morse, 1956, p. 6). Additional reflections on early OR methods and applications in the United States can be found in two Morse publications (Morse, 1948, 1952).

One additional development with military roots has had a profound impact on the field of OR. In 1946, mathematician George Dantzig was on leave from his doctoral program at the University of California–Berkeley and working for the U.S. Air Force Office of Statistical Control. One challenge he faced was to help the Air Force mechanize the process by which it scheduled and deployed forces, equipment, training, and other functions. This challenge led Dantzig to the formulation of the linear programming problem, a technique with wide applicability to decision-making problems, and the simplex algorithm for solving linear programs (Gass, 2005; Dantzig, 1963). Linear programming and associated optimization techniques have since blossomed into one of the largest subfields of OR.

OR did not develop in isolation in the decades following World War II. At the intersection of the engineering, mathematical, social, and physical sciences, it shared methods, application areas, and personalities with other growing disciplines, especially economics, statistics, and computer science. For example, the OR technique of linear programming was crucial to the development of practical solution methods in game theory (McKinsey, 1952); game theory in turn has provided fundamental tools in economics and political science. A concise and entertaining account of such developments in operations research can be found in Gass and Assad (2005).

OR thus evolved as small groups of scientists worked to understand and improve military operations using whatever tools were available, or by developing new models if the situation so demanded. Only after World War II did operations researchers seek to organize professionally and in academia. In 1948, the Operational Research Club (later the Operational Research Society) was established in London, and the Operations Research Society of America (now the Institute for Operations Research and the Management Sciences) was founded in 1952. Morse initiated the Operations Research Center at MIT in 1953 and awarded its first Ph.D. to John D.C. Little in 1955 (Larson, 2007). Today, OR programs exist within engineering and/or management schools[4] in major research universities around the world. The International Federation of Operational Research Societies boasts 48 active national member societies, and current applications beyond those found in the military abound in both the public and private sectors, as discussed next.

SELECTED CURRENT OPERATIONS RESEARCH APPLICATIONS

Manufacturing and Supply Chain Management

Returning to the definition of OR as the scientific study of operations for the purpose of making better decisions, manufacturing operations

---

[4]Some operations research programs can also be found within or in conjunction with mathematics or statistics departments.

provide a natural setting for study and application. Engineering the design of a product is one thing, but managing its production is another. How should the required production steps be scheduled to most efficiently use the available capacity of labor and machines? What is the "right" (i.e., profit maximizing) level of production over time? Given the need to assemble a myriad of parts and store partially finished and finished product (with attendant inventory holding costs) in the face of uncertain end-product demand, how much inventory (and what types) should be held over time, and when should orders for additional supply be placed? What are the best ways to measure quality levels and ensure the attainment of appropriate quality in production? How can one coordinate the activities of several different actors (or players)—such as suppliers, manufacturers, and retailers, each with their own incentives—to better coordinate entire supply chains? These questions and more fall within the subfield of manufacturing and supply chain management. OR methods for investigating such questions are a standard part of the curriculums found in schools of business/management and in industrial engineering programs (see Cachon and Terwiesch, 2008, and Hopp and Spearman, 2007, for introductory texts), while major manufacturing companies rely on such ideas in their daily activities.

Distribution and Logistics

Closely related to manufacturing and supply chain management is the area of distribution and logistics, which involves " . . . the efficient transfer of goods from the source of supply through the place of manufacture to the point of consumption in a cost-effective way whilst providing an acceptable service to the customer" (Rushton et al., 2006, p. 6). To appreciate the problems and opportunities that arise in distribution management, one need only consider the success of companies such as United Parcel Service and FedEx, which have built entire businesses around efficient distribution systems (indeed, FedEx was identified by the Defense Science Board as a case study for learning how OR has been institutionalized successfully in the private sector; see Defense Science Board, 2009). The design and operation of such systems reflect some of the most famous problems in the study of network flows, including the transportation problem (what is the cheapest way to ship products from a set of supply nodes [or sources] to a set of demand nodes [or sinks]?), the shortest path problem (how can one find the shortest distance between any starting location and any set of destinations on a given transportation network?), the longest path problem (which in project management applications reveals the bottleneck activities capable of delaying completion time of the project in question), and the traveling salesperson problem (someone starting out from an origin point must visit a given set of locations before returning to the origin; what sequence of visits minimizes the total travel distance?) (Ahuja et al., 1993). Distribution problems are not restricted to the shipment of discrete units; consider the flow (and pricing) of electricity, oil, natural gas, or electronic funds.

Private and Public Services

The key distinction between services and physical products is that services are usually produced and consumed at the same time. Customer satisfaction, often determined by the experience of waiting (Larson, 1987) along with the price of service, is a key objective in managing service operations (Wright and Race, 2004). Determining the appropriate service capacity (e.g., number of servers) is a problem common for services ranging from call centers (Aksin et al., 2007) to hospitals (Green, 2004); operations researchers typically apply queueing (or waiting line) theory to this type of problem (Gross et al., 2008). In the public sector, operations researchers have devoted considerable attention to the study and improvement of emergency services, including police (Larson, 1972), fire (Walker et al., 1979), and emergency medical services (Willemain and Larson, 1977). Additional public-sector applications include the criminal justice system, public transportation, energy, and the environment (Pollock et al., 1994). In the private sector, the real-time pricing of services, known as yield or revenue management, is another aspect of services management where OR has had a major impact. Revenue management methods are employed routinely in the airline, hotel, and car rental industries, among others (Talluri and van Ryzin, 2005).

Medicine and Public Health

Along with scholars and practitioners from many other academic disciplines, operations researchers have focused attention on different aspects of health care in recent years. Applications include clinical concerns such as optimizing radiation treatment for cancer, matching the supply and demand of transplantable organs, preparing for influenza or other pandemics, allocating resources for HIV prevention programs, and evaluating specific prevention and/or treatment interventions from the standpoint of program operations (see Brandeau et al., 2004, for numerous examples). The focus on the operations involved in delivering healthcare services is what distinguishes OR from other studies. Needle exchange programs provide an example of this perspective. These controversial programs enable drug injectors to exchange used needles and syringes for clean ones to prevent HIV transmission via needle sharing (National Research Council and Institute of Medicine, 1995). Although many studies focused on surveys of program clients to determine whether rates of needle sharing declined as a result of such programs, an operations research study was what established the following principles: increased needle exchange rates reduce needle circulation times; the less time a needle spends circulating among drug injectors, the less likely it is to carry HIV (needles are shared by fewer people); and the lower the level of HIV among needles, the less likely drug injectors are to become infected with HIV. By systematically coding, tracking, and testing the needles in an exchange program for HIV infection over time, this study demonstrated that the predictions of this "circulation theory" were supported by the data, with the result that HIV transmission in this community was reduced substantially (Kaplan, 1995).

Homeland Security and Counterterrorism

Since the terrorist attacks of September 11, 2001, many operations researchers have turned their attention to problems related to terrorism. Examples include the defense of critical infrastructure such as electricity grids, pipelines, and transportation hubs, including airports and subway stations, chemical plants, nuclear reactors, and major ports. Models for these scenarios have been developed, and in many cases the recommended courses of action have been adopted (Brown et al., 2006). Other examples include the operational (as opposed to scientific) effectiveness of detectors of suicide bombers (Kaplan and Kress, 2005), evaluation and proposed improvements to US-VISIT (the Department of Homeland Security biometric identification program for immigration and border management at U.S. points of entry) (Wein and Baveja, 2005), and preparedness for potential bioterror attacks (Wein et al., 2003; Wein and Liu, 2005).

THE OPERATIONS RESEARCH VALUE PROPOSITION

In manufacturing and services applications, the monetary benefits that OR projects have generated, whether by increasing revenues or decreasing costs, have been documented in specific instances. Pringle (2000) reports several examples, including the following:

- Working for Sears, Roebuck and Company, operations researchers designed a scheduling system that " . . . generated a one-time cost reduction of $9 million as well as ongoing savings of $42 million per year" (p. 30);
- Weyerhaeuser operations researchers solved the problem of " . . . where to cut the stem into logs of what length and to what use should the resulting logs be allocated (export, lumber, plywood, paper) . . . resulting in savings well in excess of $100 million" (p. 30); and

- Operations researchers at National Car Rental developed and implemented a revenue management system that improved revenue by $56 million in its first year of operation.

Horner (2000) relates the success of Sabre, the spin-off formed by American Airlines' OR group that is widely credited with the creation of revenue management (by merging of real-time pricing with reservations and scheduling). Interviewing Thomas Cook, the former head of American's operations research group, Horner reports that by 1998, " . . . the revenue management system at American Airlines was generating nearly $1 billion in annual incremental revenue. To put that figure into perspective, consider that the airline's total operating profit didn't approach $1 billion until 1997" (p. 47).

Further examples of monetary benefits generated by industry OR groups appear in Bell et al. (2003), while Alden (2009) estimates conservatively that from 1972 through 2008, the total benefits generated by finalists for the Franz Edelman Award for achievement in operations research and the management sciences, the top award for applied operations research with about six finalists each year, exceed $160 billion. Clearly much can be gained by applying OR ideas in industry.

THE OPERATIONS RESEARCH APPROACH
TO PROBLEM SOLVING

How do operations researchers get started with a new project? Leaving to the side purely mathematical studies meant to improve the quantitative methods of OR, the goal of an applied study is to improve decision making. Historically, this has placed OR groups in an advisory role in which responsible decision makers (e.g., military commanders, business executives, agency heads) request assistance to help improve matters in some regard. This does not imply that problems always arrive as well-posed questions; indeed, Morse and Kimball (1951, p. 5) wrote, "It often occurs that the major contribution of the operations research worker is to decide what is the real problem." This latter statement applies equally well to independent operations researchers conducting research to achieve better outcomes in their area of interest.

Understanding the problem often requires understanding the environment and/or system in which the issue is embedded. For example, issues that might be addressed are the basic processes that characterize the flow of material in production processes; the transmission of infections in contagious outbreaks; the routing of Internet traffic; the movement of offenders through the criminal justice system; the generation and distribution of electricity; or the interdiction of terrorists en route to attack. What part of these processes represents cause for concern (e.g., excessive delays at airports or hospitals) or alternatively presents an opportunity (e.g., differences in individuals' willingness to pay for airline seats, hotel rooms, or cell phone minutes)? Basic understanding of the problem terrain enables decision makers and OR analysts to communicate more effectively about problems and/or opportunities in the environment.

Understanding the environment and/or system in question requires substantive expertise. Such expertise is often best gained via direct observation, which is why operations researchers have been known to ride around in police patrol cars, spend time on factory floors or in warehouses, or observe the formation and dissipation of lines at banks, on highways, in call centers, or at Disney World. Certainly the formative years of military OR saw analysts "living in the system," able to witness new versions of "the problem" surface repeatedly over the course of World War II.

Another important part of getting started is figuring out just what the decision maker is trying to achieve. What are the objectives? If faced with two ways to implement the operation(s) in question, could the decision maker state which one is preferred and why? Getting decision makers to explicitly state their *objectives* in terms of *performance measures* represents a major step toward understanding the problem (see Fischhoff, this volume, Chapter 10). Possible objective/performance measure pairings include *maximize profit, minimize cost, maximize lives saved,* and *minimize response time.* With a common understanding of objectives and performance measures, problem identification becomes much easier.

The hallmark of an OR study is the creation of a mathematical model that represents the operations of the system under study, and the choices and alternatives available to the decision maker, and that situates both within the appropriate environment. Crafting a model is a creative act that is as much art as science. The relationship between observation and data collection on the one hand and model development on the other is bidirectional, in that the model can suggest new data to collect as easily as field observation can cause revision (or abandonment) of the model in question. Most OR students are familiar with mathematical problem sets meant to drill and further teach the nuances of the modeling methods under study. Modeling real applications is more like taking an operational situation into the real world, and decomposing it to the point where one can create problem set-like questions that address the system's most important features and properties. For an empirical study of how operations modelers approach problems and formulate new models, see Willemain (1995).

THE SCOPE OF OPERATIONS RESEARCH METHODS

Although operations researchers employ many mathematical tools in their studies, and other quantitative disciplines apply many of these same mathematical techniques, three sets of modeling approaches have become identified with OR: optimization, probability modeling (or stochastic processes), and decision analysis. All of these methods have and continue to be used in applications such as those outlined earlier. Although the interested reader can learn the basics of these methods from any good introductory textbook in operations research (e.g., Hillier and Lieberman, 2010), one should be aware that the methods themselves are active subjects of research among mathematical operations researchers, and new extensions and results for these techniques continue to be discovered.

Optimization problems involve the maximization or minimization of some *objective function* (e.g., maximize profit, minimize cost) of variables under the decision maker's control (the *decision variables*), subject to resource or other constraints on the allowable values of these variables. The techniques used to solve optimization problems depend on the underlying mathematical specifics (e.g., whether the objective function is linear or nonlinear, whether the decision variables are continuous or integer valued), and include linear programming, nonlinear programming, integer programming, and dynamic programming, among others (Bradley et al., 1977). The solution to an optimization problem identifies the values of the decision variables that lead to the best outcome for the decision maker within the assumptions of the model, along with the value of that outcome (e.g., maximized profit or minimized cost), and also provides tools for examining the sensitivity of these results (values of the decision variables and the objective function) to changes in the assumptions made in constructing the model.

Probability modeling represents those operational situations where randomness and uncertainty dominate; these are known as *stochastic processes*. For example, *queueing theory* addresses problems where customers arrive at a service system according to some random process and the duration of service is uncertain. It provides answers to questions such as how long customers must wait for service, how many customers are in the system, and how busy service providers are; such models are fundamental to applications in service systems (Gross et al., 2008). *Inventory theory* provides additional models for understanding the flow and storage of intermediate and finished goods in production processes, blood/plasma supplies, and supply chains (Porteus, 2002). *Reliability theory* (also known as *survival analysis*) examines the probability of (and time to) failure of complicated systems such as nuclear power plants, space transport systems, or individuals suffering from disease by analyzing the interrelationships among components or subsystems that can give rise to total system failure or death in the case of the patient (Bazovský, 2004). For extremely complicated problems where a mathematical solution proves too difficult, *simulation models* are used to represent the operation of the system and generate data of interest on a computer; the resulting data can then be analyzed statistically to infer relationships between system operations and performance measures of interest (Rubinstein and Kroese, 2007).

Decision analysis is a hybrid family of optimization and probability methods that has been developed to help decision makers evaluate alternative courses of action in the face of uncertain outcomes that evolve over time (Clemen and Reilly, 2001; Howard and Matheson, 1983; Raiffa, 1968). Helpful graphical tools such as *decision trees* and *influence diagrams* have been developed to represent the problem environment and further structure such problems. Decision analysis is where OR intersects most with psychology, where scholars of judgment and decision making have invested tremendous effort to study how individuals actually make decisions (with attendant biases) (see Fischhoff, Chapter 10; Arkes and Kajdasz, Chapter 7; and Spellman, Chapter 6, all in this volume). Another point of intersection is with rational choice and game theory models in economics and political science, which proceeds under the assumption that individuals behave *as if* they are experts at solving decision analysis problems and regularly do so in their strategic decision making (see Bueno de Mesquita, this volume, Chapter 3). The OR perspective is *advisory*; given a decision maker's preferences, understanding of the alternative actions available, and valuation of the possible consequences associated with these alternatives, what is the best course of action? Decision analysis also provides methods for estimating the value of additional information that could be learned about the problem, in order to examine the sensitivity of recommended courses of action to the specific assumptions made when modeling the problem (as with optimization models) (see Fischhoff, this volume, Chapter 10).

OPERATIONS RESEARCH FOR THE MASSES

The theory underlying the mathematical methods described above is quite deep. For this reason, OR modeling work was limited to those with advanced mathematical training (and founders of the field, such as Blackett and Morse, certainly were gifted mathematicians). However, as with common statistical methods such as hypothesis testing and regression analysis, using OR properly in applied studies is possible without mastering all of the underlying mathematical theory. Indeed, over the past decade, OR methods have been computerized in easy-to-use spreadsheet packages such as Microsoft Excel, making it much easier to formulate and solve a variety of models (Winston and Albright, 2009). Also, often the analysis of seemingly complex models gives rise to insights that are shockingly elegant in their simplicity, as the examples of the next section are meant to demonstrate.

OPERATIONS RESEARCH ON THE BACK OF AN ENVELOPE

Go/No Go (Decision Analysis)

Many decisions can be represented as a choice between the "business as usual" status quo mode of operations (or *no go*), and changing to a risky alternative that might or might not succeed (*go*). Suppose that the risky alternative, if it succeeds, would deliver an incremental benefit of b units (e.g., additional profit, additional lives saved) relative to the status quo, while this same alternative, if it fails, would impose an incremental cost of c units relative to the status quo. Also, suppose the probability of the risky alternative succeeding is equal to p. This situation is depicted graphically in the decision tree in Figure 2-1; the square represents the decision between the status quo and the risky alternative that must be made, the circle represents the uncertain performance of the risky alternative (with the probabilities of success and failure indicated on the corresponding "branches" of the tree), and the incremental values associated with the various possible outcomes appear at the end of each branch.

The decision maker seeks to maximize the value expected from the consequences of this decision. Compared to the status quo (which has an expected incremental value of zero when compared to itself), the risky alternative is worth $p \times b - (1 - p) \times c$, which exceeds zero providing that $p > c / (b + c)$. This model thus suggests a very simple rule. Note that knowing the precise value of the success probability p is unnecessary; one only needs to recognize whether this probability is above or below the threshold of $c / (b + c)$. If the incremental penalty c greatly exceeds the incremental benefit b, one should only pursue the risky alternative if one is extremely certain it will succeed. On the other hand, if the incremental benefit is much larger than the incremental cost, unless one is quite certain that the risky alternative will fail, it appears advantageous to "go for it."

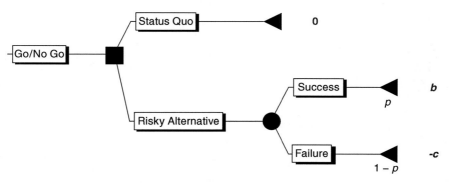

FIGURE 2-1 Go/no go decision tree.

Of course, decision analysis offers more complex methods than the simple example above. Perhaps of special relevance to intelligence analysts, decision analysis has developed tools that apply to decision makers who are risk averse (or conversely, risk prone). For example, given a coin toss that pays $0 if the coin lands tails, but $10 if the coin lands heads, a risk-averse decision maker would be willing to sell the rights to this lottery for, say, $4 even though the expected value of the gamble equals $5. Conversely, a risk-prone decision maker might not be willing to part with this gamble unless offered at least, say, $6. Decision analysis offers both methods for assessing whether a decision maker is risk averse or risk prone (or risk neutral for that matter), along with a methodology detailing how such decision makers should choose among their options (Clemen and Reilly, 2001; Howard and Matheson, 1983; Raiffa, 1968).

Little's Theorem (Queueing)

Little's Theorem is named after John D.C. Little, MIT's first Ph.D. student in operations research. It states that the average number of customers in a queueing system (L) is equal to the product of the customer arrival rate (λ) and the mean time spent in the system (W), or simply $L = \lambda W$ (Little, 1961). The power of this simple formula stems from the nearly endless number of situations that can be construed as customers waiting for service. For example, if λ is the rate at which a new product enters a certain production stage, and W is the mean time spent per unit in that production stage, then $L = \lambda W$ is the mean work-in-process inventory for that production stage. If λ is the annual number of guns that illicitly enter circulation, and W is the mean time that an illicit gun remains in use, then $L = \lambda W$ is the average number of illicit guns in circulation available for use. If λ is the average number of airplanes that take off each day, and W is the mean time spent airborne per flight, then $L = \lambda W$ is the average number of airplanes in the sky. If λ is the average number of terror plots instigated each year, and W is the mean time spent from the time a new plot is hatched until it is either carried out successfully or abandoned/interdicted, then $L = \lambda W$ is the average number of terror plots currently in the "terror queue" (Kaplan, 2010). If λ is the average number of new intelligence reports initiated each year, and W is the mean time required to research and produce a report, then $L = \lambda W$ represents the expected number of reports currently being produced (or the intelligence work-in-process inventory). If λ is the annual rate of new HIV infections, and W is the mean time following infection during which a newly infected individual would present a result of "recently infected" on a test such as the BED[5] assay that specifically tests for evidence

---

[5]BED is a trademark of Calypte Biomedical Corporation. For more information see http://www.calypte.com/technologies-incidence-testing.asp [accessed October 2010].

of recent infection, then $L = \lambda W$ is the average number of persons who can be considered newly infected. Recent research estimating the annual rate of new HIV infections in the United States has turned this logic around by estimating L from samples of HIV-infected persons, and then estimating the HIV infection rate λ by inverting Little's Theorem (Hall et al., 2008).

Waiting for the Bus (Probability)

Sometimes sampled information can look very different across observers simply because of differences in the physical processes by which data are collected. Imagine observing successive buses on an urban bus line as they arrive at and depart from the same bus stop. Suppose that 8 of 9 waits between successive buses are 1 minute (short gaps), but that 1 in 9 such intervals equals 10 minutes (long gaps). Now imagine a would-be passenger arriving at the bus stop exactly as a bus departs; our poor passenger literally has just missed the bus. What is the probability that this passenger faces a long wait of 10 minutes for the next bus? Clearly the answer equals 1/9, as by construction 1 in 9 of all intervals between buses equal 10 minutes. Now suppose that a second would-be passenger arrives at the same bus stop, but at a time that is random with respect to bus arrivals. What is the chance that this passenger faces a 10-minute gap? The answer is no longer equal to 1/9; the randomly arriving passenger has a 5 in 9 chance of landing in a long gap! The reason is that the chance of arriving in a gap of a given length is proportional both to the frequency with which such gaps occur and the gap duration. Thus, the chance of arriving in a long gap is proportional to $(1/9) \times 10$, while the chance of arriving in a short gap is proportional to $(8/9) \times 1$, yielding the probability of arriving during a long gap equal to $(10/9)/(10/9 + 8/9) = 5/9$ as claimed. The situation is even odder than this: The first passenger who just missed the bus must wait an average of $1 \times 8/9 + 10 \times 1/9 = 2$ minutes for the next bus, while the second passenger on average waits $(10/2) \times 5/9 + (1/2) \times 4/9 = 3$ minutes; on average, a person who just misses the bus in this example faces a shorter wait for the next one than a person who arrives at a random time.

This is an example of what operations researchers call *random incidence* (or *length-biased sampling* in statistical parlance). It can explain how different people observing presumably the same phenomenon can see quite different things. For example, if one is interested in studying the progression of persons infected with a disease, one will obtain a different picture by following newly infected persons over time versus sampling ill patients with the same disease in the hospital and following them over time. Similarly, studies of the duration of unemployment spells will reveal quite different results for samples of newly unemployed persons as compared to random samples from persons currently receiving unemployment insurance.

Knapsack Problem (Optimization)

A common optimization problem is to allocate a budget across different activities. For example, given a fixed budget to spend on different healthcare programs, how much money should the government allocate to different care and prevention activities (Stinnett and Paltiel, 1996; Institute of Medicine, 2001)? One model for such problems that yields a practical allocation rule is the *knapsack model*. In this model, a number of possible activities (or programs) can receive funding. Let b_i and c_i respectively denote the unit benefits and costs of the ith activity (e.g., each unit could correspond to an incremental employee or facility), and suppose there is an upper limit to the number of units of activity i allowed (e.g., due to program capacity, or perhaps for political reasons that restrict the amount of funds any single program can receive). The goal is to maximize total benefits within a given budget, and the solution is particularly simple. First, rank the activities from the largest to smallest value of their "bang for the buck" ratios b_i/c_i. Then, allocate the largest amount of money possible to that activity with the highest such ratio (i.e., the smaller of the total budget and the maximum allowable amount). This activity produces the most benefit per dollar among all activities and is thus the most cost-effective means of generating benefits. Next, consider the budget that remains after subtracting the amount awarded to the most efficient program and move to the activity with the second highest bang for the buck ratio. Again, allocate the largest amount of money possible, update the budget, and move to the next most efficient activity. Continue in this manner until either all activities have been fully funded, or the remaining budget is exhausted while funding whatever activity currently ranks as the most efficient (in which case this activity will receive only partial funding). At the end of such an exercise, there will be a set of fully funded activities (those with the largest bang for the buck ratios), a set of activities that receive no funding, and potentially one activity that receives partial funding. Of course, it is possible that partial funding is not possible—constructing half a tank or two-thirds of a bridge, for example, probably has little value. In this case, more sophisticated optimization techniques are available to ensure that all funded activities are fully funded (e.g., integer or dynamic programming [Bradley et al., 1977]).

The most important aspect of this problem is the intuition behind the solution: Allocate resources in order of most to least efficient activities, that is, from the largest to smallest bang for the buck. In the HIV prevention example, this rule says that prevention programs should be funded in order of most to least infections prevented per dollar (Institute of Medicine, 2001). Although resource allocation problems typically are more complicated than the simple knapsack formulation, the principle of securing funding for more efficient activities and programs before considering less efficient alternatives often provides a good heuristic.

Project Scheduling and the Critical Path (Optimization)

A common problem faced by project managers is to schedule the various activities that must be completed to finish a project. The term "project" can be interpreted quite broadly, with examples ranging from construction projects to fundraising campaigns to weapons development programs to terror attacks. One of the most important questions one can ask is, how long will completing the entire project take?

An easy approach for answering this question that can be implemented by hand for small problems (or with the aid of specialized computer programs such as Microsoft Project for larger ones) is as follows (for a spreadsheet implementation, see Winston and Albright, 2009): First, produce a list of all project tasks that must be completed along with estimates for the duration of each task. Second, for each task, note the "immediate predecessor" activities that must be completed immediately before the task in question can begin. Third, starting with those tasks for which there are *no* prerequisite activities (and hence can begin at "time zero" when the project starts), determine the earliest time that these activities can be completed. These are "first round" activities, and because their completion does not rely on other activities, their "early finish" times are simply the task durations. Fourth, for each remaining downstream task, the earliest time each task can begin is computed from the formula

Early Start Time = *maximum* {Early Finish Times}

where the maximum is taken over all the Early Finish Times of the immediate predecessors of the task in question. These Early Finish Times are computed as

Early Finish Time = Early Start Time + Task Duration

Note that the first round activities with no prerequisite activities all have Early Start Times of zero, while the second round of tasks that do have immediate predecessors will have Early Start Times determined from the first of the two formulas above. Applying these steps recursively until all tasks have been addressed yields the duration of the entire project.

This "critical path method" also identifies those activities that, if delayed, slow the completion of the entire project. For project managers, such critical activities are those that must be expedited. Alternatively, in an adversarial situation where one wishes to impede the progress of an enemy project, delaying a critical activity in, for example, the planning of a terror attack can delay the entire project.

I have presented a highly simplified view of project scheduling that can be made more realistic. For example, task durations are unlikely to be known with certainty; more advanced models treat such durations as random variables, enabling one to compute the *probability* that a project is completed by a given date. Or, one could focus on cost/completion trade-offs to examine how quickly one might complete a project given an expedition budget. In the next section, I discuss some applications of project management to intelligence problems.

OPERATIONS RESEARCH FOR INTELLIGENCE ANALYSIS

Operations research shares at least two common features with intelligence analysis. First, as stated in the *Intelligence Community Directive* (ICD 203) Analytic Standards, intelligence analysts are expected to ". . . perform their analytic and informational functions from an unbiased perspective" and "independent of political considerations" (Director of National Intelligence, 2007, p. 2). The intelligence analyst does not make decisions, but provides information in support of government (or military) executive decision makers. Operations researchers similarly play the advisory role of unbiased analysts in relation to executive decision makers. Writing about the separation of OR support and executive decision making, Morse and Kimball (1951, p. 2) state, "The requirement that the executive reach a decision concerning an operation is to some extent antagonistic to the requirement that he look at it scientifically and impersonally, *as would be required in operations research*" (emphasis added). The second shared concern is timeliness; the Analytic Standards directive states "Analytic products that arrive too late to support the work of the consumers weaken utility and impact. Analysts will strive to deliver their products in time for them to be actionable by customers" (Director of National Intelligence, 2007, p. 2). Writing more than half a century earlier, Morse and Kimball (1951, p. 10a) state, "An important difference between OR and other scientific work is the sense of *urgency* involved. In this field a preliminary analysis based on incomplete data may often be much more valuable than a more thorough study using adequate data, simply because the crucial decisions cannot wait on the slower study but must be based on the preliminary analysis. The big improvements often come from the first quick survey of a new field; later detailed study may only gain small additional factors."

Given the military origins of OR and both the military and systems aspects of intelligence analysis, it should not prove surprising that operations research has been applied to intelligence analysis on occasion. For example, Caldwell et al. (1961) report on "A model for evaluating the output of intelligence systems" where the object was to learn the relative contributions of different pieces of intelligence to the overall value of an intelligence assessment. Steele (1989) uses operations research models to illustrate the advantages and disadvantages posed by different communication protocols when the goal is to keep a secret. However, evidence for regular application of OR in intelligence analysis is hard to find. Heuer (1978, 1999), Schum (1987), Schum and Morris (2007), and Zlotnick (1967, 1972) all discuss the use of basic probability models, including Bayes' Rule, with an eye toward assessing the likelihoods of various events or "states of affairs," but there is no focus on operations in this otherwise engaging work. Operations ideas are almost entirely absent from intelligence analysis primers distributed by national intelligence agencies (Defense Intelligence Agency, 2008; U.S. Government, 2009). Indeed, in contrast to excellent military resources such as the operations research group at the Naval Postgraduate School[6] and the Military Operations Research Society,[7] with the exception of focused technical expertise in operations research such as that found at the National Security Agency,[8] apparently few operations researchers work within the intelligence community (Defense Science Board, 2009).

Without suggesting that intelligence analysts should master OR, there are opportunities for improving intelligence analysis through appropriate application of operations research. Such opportunities present themselves when intelligence analysts focus on making inferences about adversarial supply chains, weapons development programs, the planning of terror attacks, the distribution of personnel or materiel, or any other operations of interest. Furthermore, as in the application of Little's Theorem, issues that might not initially pose as operations can sometimes be construed as such. The following examples are meant to illustrate such opportunities for applying OR to intelligence problems.

Example: Producing Nuclear Weapons

The development of nuclear weapons provides an intriguing case study for applying operations research to intelligence questions. In asking whether or not a "proliferator" is pursuing a nuclear weapons program, it is important to understand the possible forms a project designed to produce such

---

[6]http://www.nps.edu/Academics/Schools/GSOIS/Departments/OR/index.html [accessed October 2010].

[7]http://www.mors.org [accessed October 2010].

[8]The National Security Agency runs a summer program for operations research graduate students to work as apprentices to operations research and simulation modeling analysts; see http://www.nsa.gov/careers/opportunities_4_u/students/graduate/sport.shtml [accessed October 2010].

weapons could take. An OR approach to this problem focuses on identifying the infrastructure tasks necessary for weapons production in addition to the weapons production process itself, and paying careful attention to the necessary sequencing and timing of such tasks. Such project management and scheduling problems can be approached using more sophisticated versions of the critical path method described earlier. Harney et al. (2006) report precisely such a study. The basic scientific information required to design such weapons has been known and publicly available for quite some time (see Office of Technology Assessment, 1993, especially Chapter 4: Technical Aspects of Nuclear Proliferation). Working with this and other sources, Harney and colleagues were able to estimate that, depending on assumptions regarding resource availability (e.g., available budget, whether highly enriched uranium is produced or available immediately [i.e., stolen or purchased]), the time required to complete a first batch of six weapons would be 4 to 6.5 years. In a companion paper (Brown et al., 2009), the same researchers ask which tasks in the project network, if delayed, would maximally set back the weapons development project. Under many different scenarios, the authors identify two bottleneck tasks ("cascade loading" and "acquisition of pumps and piping") that if interdicted can increase the duration of time to produce weapons by 37 percent if the proliferator is unaware of the interdiction effort (perfect covert action). Even if the proliferator is aware of the interdiction effort and modifies the production process accordingly (as modeled using game theory), interdicting these activities can still delay the overall project by 34 percent. Again, the idea is not that this model tells intelligence analysts the precise state of a proliferator's nuclear weapons program, but it does suggest which production activities are crucial in the overall development project, and consequently what parameters might deserve a more focused intelligence effort.

Example: Detecting Terror Plots and Tracking Terror Operations

Estimating the size of hidden populations is a common problem across many fields of endeavor. Public health officials would like to know the number of persons newly infected with HIV (Hall et al., 2008), wildlife managers wish to know the size of various animal (Blower et al., 1981) or plant (Alexander et al., 1997) populations, and policy makers and professionals in law enforcement, drug treatment, and public health seek estimates of the number of drug injectors (Kaplan and Soloshatz, 1993; Rossi, 1999; Friedman et al., 2004). Similarly, the unknown number of undetected terrorists (or terror plots) is of great interest to counterterrorism, law enforcement, and homeland security decision makers. Although human intelligence from undercover agents or confidential informants has been vital in interrupting specific plots (and the lack of such intelligence is an oft-mentioned failure leading up to 9/11), operations research offers an opportunity to estimate the number of undetected terror plots from undercover activity and utilization data. The relationships between the instigation and planning of terror attacks and the use of undercover intelligence agents can be characterized using queueing theory. Viewing terror plots as the "customers" and undercover agents as the "servers," queueing theory allows one to estimate the number of waiting customers based on the servers' utilization in a manner analogous to how one might estimate the number of waiting customers in a call center from the utilization of servers there (Kaplan, 2010). An important feature of the terrorist-detection process is that unlike the customers in most service systems, terrorists do not wish to be "served" and will leak false information to throw counter-terrorism investigators off track, while undercover agents and informants make "false positive" mistakes that lead to time wasted in pursuit of false leads (for more on assessing the credibility of human intelligence sources, see Schum and Morris, 2007). The hope is that the use of a model of the form proposed could provide an approach to making inferences about the overall level of terrorist activity from a body of intelligence reports that are otherwise studied only for information about specific individuals of interest. Additional applications that follow from this idea include determining the appropriate amount of resources to invest in undercover intelligence gathering, or evaluating the trade-off between investments in human sources versus improved detection technologies.

A different approach to tracking terror threats that developed recently builds on ideas from probability theory and project management. As reported by Godfrey and Mifflin (2009) and Godfrey et al. (2007), the various activities required to execute a terror attack can be organized in the form of a project network, with careful attention paid to the precedence relationships among tasks and the estimated probability distributions of the durations of each task. Given intelligence assessments regarding the status of different tasks, this TerrAlert model produces assessments of the time remaining until an attack takes place. It also suggests which project tasks to disrupt for maximum delay. To cite the authors, "For example, bombing a factory where we suspect a manufacturing task is being performed is most effective when that task is ongoing, less effective when the task is not yet started (raw materials can be rerouted to a different facility), and ineffective when the task is finished (final product has already been produced and distributed)" (Godrey et al., 2007, p. 354). TerrAlert has been installed at the Defense Threat Reduction Agency and the Office of Naval Intelligence's Advanced Maritime Analysis Cell, though its current usage status is unknown.

Example: Connecting the Dots

Perhaps the most fundamental problem in intelligence analysis is that of "connecting the dots," meaning " . . . selecting and assembling disparate pieces of information to produce a general understanding of a threat . . . " (Hollywood et al., 2004, p. xv). Direct application of statistical tools such as data mining to large databases documenting travel or financial transactions invariably suffer from the false positive problem that follows from searching databases in which the base rate of individuals involved in terrorism is extremely low (Hollywood et al., 2009). Even systems oriented specifically for the tracking of terrorists suffer from this low base rate problem. For example, between July 2004 and November 2007, the Federal Bureau of Investigation's (FBI's) terrorist threat and suspicious incident tracking system (known as Guardian) received roughly 108,000 reports of potential terror threats and suspicious incidents, yet the FBI determined that the overwhelming majority of these were in no way connected to terrorism (U.S. Department of Justice, 2008). An operations research approach to this problem would begin by constructing deliberately oversimplified models of the current relationship between intelligence data collection and reporting on the one hand, and how seasoned intelligence analysts process such data to generate and test new hypotheses on the other, and evaluate (within the model) the success of this current approach. Only after understanding the current relationship could an attempt be made to employ OR methods to improve the results (to connect more dots within the same resource constraints currently faced). Hollywood et al. (2004) report a research proposal to resolve this issue.

Example: Modeling Intelligence Operations

The production of intelligence analysis can itself be viewed as a process characterized by oft-repeated operations of different types. For example, at the macro level, one can ask whether the "intelligence cycle"—requirements planning, data collection, data processing and exploitation, intelligence analysis and the production of intelligence reports, and product dissemination to government or military decision makers (the "consumers")—is balanced in the sense that the overall intelligence budget has been divided appropriately among these different activities to maximize the value of intelligence produced by the entire system. For example, the Defense Science Board (2009, p. 31) considered the following potential operations research application with regard to expensive new biometric data collection capability to accompany Unmanned Aerial Systems (UAS): "OR techniques could be used to analyze the capability of the entire ISR[9] system to effectively use the contemplated new collection capability and/or understand what additional costs would have

---

[9]Intelligence, surveillance, and reconnaissance.

to be incurred. An obvious case in point would be whether or not appropriate investment has been made in the analytical resources (specific skills, recruitment, and training) and dissemination capability needed to handle the volume of new product that would be produced by a UAS investment."

As another example, consider the allocation of intelligence analysts to different geographic regions of interest, or to different intelligence problem sets. The allocation of workers to tasks forms the basis for a classic OR model known as the assignment problem (Ahuja et al., 1993; Hillier and Lieberman, 2010). Rather than simply assigning a task to the best available analyst on an as-available basis, allocations based on the assignment model should result in better overall matches between intelligence coverage/ expertise and analytical tasks. Both this and the prior example show that viewing the very creation of intelligence as a production process could itself prove to be a beneficial yet challenging application of operations research.

REFERENCES

Ahuja, R. K., T. L. Magnanti, and J. B. Orlin. 1993. *Network flows: Theory, algorithms, and applications.* Englewood Cliffs, NJ: Prentice-Hall.

Aksin, O. Z., M. Armony, and V. Mehrota. 2007. The modern call center: A multi-disciplinary perspective on operations management research. *Production and Operations Management* 16(6):665–688.

Alden, J. M. 2009. Operations research, the multi-billion dollar profit center. *Edelman Awards Gala* (pp. 14–16). Hanover, MD: Institute for Operations Research and the Management Sciences. Available: http://www.scienceofbetter.org/Edelman/09edelmanbook.pdf [accessed May 2010].

Alexander, H. M., N. A. Slade, and W. D. Kettle. 1997. Application of mark-recapture models to estimation of the population size of plants. *Ecology* 78(4):1230–1237.

Bazovský, I. 2004. *Reliability theory and practice.* New York: Courier Dover.

Bell, P. C., C. K. Anderson, and S. P. Kaiser. 2003. Strategic operations research and the Edelman Prize finalist applications 1989–1998. *Operations Research* 51(1):17–31.

Blower, J. G., L. M. Cook, and J. A. Bishop. 1981. *Estimating the size of animal populations.* London, UK: George Allen and Unwin.

Bradley, S. P., A. C. Hax, and T. L. Magnanti. 1977. *Applied mathematical programming.* Reading, MA: Addison-Wesley.

Brandeau, M. L., F. Sainfort, and W. P. Pierskalla, eds. 2004. *Operations research and health care: A handbook of methods and applications.* Boston, MA: Kluwer Academic.

Brown, G., M. Carlyle, J. Salmerón, and K. Wood. 2006. Defending critical infrastructure. *Interfaces* 36(6):530–544.

Brown, G. G., W. M. Carlyle, R. C. Harney, E. M. Skroch, and R. K. Wood. 2009. Interdicting a nuclear-weapons project. *Operations Research* 57(4):866–877.

Cachon, G., and C. Terwiesch. 2008. *Matching supply with demand: An introduction to operations management.* New York: McGraw-Hill/Irwin.

Caldwell, W. V., C. H. Coombs, R. M. Thrall, M. S. Schoeffler, and M. Hill. 1961. A model for evaluating the output of intelligence systems. *Naval Research Logistics Quarterly* 8(1):25–40.

Clemen, R. T., and T. Reilly. 2001. *Making hard decisions.* Pacific Grove, CA: Duxbury/ Thomson Learning.

Dantzig, G. B. 1963. *Linear programming and extensions*. Princeton, NJ: Princeton University Press.

Defense Intelligence Agency. 2008. *A tradecraft primer: Basic structured analytic techniques*. Washington, DC: Directorate for Analysis, Defense Intelligence Agency.

Defense Science Board. 2009. *Operations research applications for intelligence, surveillance and reconnaissance (ISR)*. Defense Science Board Advisory Group on Defense Intelligence. Washington, DC: Office of the Under Secretary of Defense for Acquisition, Technology, and Logistics.

Director of National Intelligence. 2007. *Intelligence Community Directive (ICD) 203: Analytic Standards*. June 21. Available: http://www.dni.gov/electronic_reading_room/ICD_203.pdf [accessed May 2010].

Dyson, F. 2006. A failure of intelligence. *Technology Review* 109(5):62–71.

Falconer, N. 1976. On the size of convoys: An example of the methodology of leading wartime OR scientists. *Operational Research Quarterly* 27(2):315–327.

Fisk, C. E. 1972. The Sino-Soviet border dispute: A comparison of the conventional and Bayesian methods for intelligence warning. *Studies in Intelligence* 16(2):53–62.

Friedman, S. R., B. Tempalski, H. Cooper, T. Perlis, M. Keem, R. Friedman, and P. L. Flom. 2004. Estimating numbers of injecting drug users in metropolitan areas for structural analyses of community vulnerability and for assessing relative degrees of service provision for injecting drug users. *Journal of Urban Health* 81(3):377–400.

Gass, S. I. 2005. The life and times of the father of linear programming. *Operations Research/Management Science Today* 32(4):40–48.

Gass, S. I., and A. A. Assad. 2005. *An annotated timeline of operations research: An informal history*. New York: Kluwer Academic.

Godfrey, G. J., and T. Mifflin. 2009. *Likelihood-based optimization of threat operation timeline estimation*. 12th International Conference on Information Fusion, Seattle, WA, July 6–9.

Godfrey, G. A., J. Cunningham, and T. Tran. 2007. A Bayesian, nonlinear particle filtering approach for tracking the state of terrorist operations. *Intelligence and Security Informatics*, IEEE, May 23–24, pp. 350–355.

Golany, B., E. H. Kaplan, A. Marmur, and U. G. Rothblum. 2009. Nature plays with dice—terrorists do not: Allocating resources to counter strategic versus probabilistic risks. *European Journal of Operational Research* 192(1):198–208.

Green, L. V. 2004. Capacity planning and management in hospitals. In M. L. Brandeau, F. Sainfort, and W. P. Pierskalla, eds., *Operations research and health care: A handbook of methods and applications* (pp. 15–43). Boston, MA: Kluwer Academic.

Gross, D., J. F. Shortle, J. M. Thompson, and C. M. Harris. 2008. *Fundamentals of queueing theory*. Hoboken, NJ: John Wiley and Sons.

Hall, H. I., R. G. Song, P. Rhodes, J. Prejean, Q. An, L. M. Lee, J. Karon, R. Brookmeyer, E. H. Kaplan, M. T. McKenna, and R. S. Janssen. 2008. Estimation of HIV incidence in the United States. *Journal of the American Medical Association* 300(5):520–529.

Harney, R., G. Brown, M. Carlyle, E. Skroch, and K. Wood. 2006. Anatomy of a project to produce a first nuclear weapon. *Science and Global Security* 14(2–3):163–182.

Heuer, R. J., Jr., ed. 1978. *Quantitative approaches to political intelligence: The CIA experience*. Boulder, CO: Westview Press.

Heuer, R. J., Jr. 1999. *Psychology of intelligence analysis*. Washington, DC: Center for the Study of Intelligence, Central Intelligence Agency.

Hillier, F. S., and G. J. Lieberman. 2010. *Introduction to operations research*, 9th ed. New York: McGraw-Hill.

Hollywood, J., D. Snyder, K. McKay, and J. Boon. 2004. *Out of the ordinary: Finding hidden threats by analyzing unusual behavior*. Santa Monica, CA: RAND Corporation.

Hollywood, J., K. Strom, and M. Pope. 2009. Can data mining turn up terrorists? *Operations Research/Management Science Today* 36(1):20–27.

Hopp, W. J., and M. L. Spearman. 2007. *Factory physics*. New York: McGraw-Hill/Irwin.

Horner, P. 2000. The Sabre story. *Operations Research/Management Science Today* 27(3):46–47.

Howard, R. A., and J. Matheson, eds. 1983. *The principles and applications of decision analysis* (2 vols). Palo Alto, CA: Strategic Decisions Group.

Institute of Medicine. 2001. *No time to lose: Getting more from HIV prevention*. Committee on HIV Prevention Strategies in the United States. M. S. Ruiz, A. R. Gable, E. H. Kaplan, M. A. Stoto, H. V. Fineberg, and J. Trussell, eds. Division of Health Promotion and Disease Prevention. Washington, DC: National Academy Press.

Kaplan, E. H. 1995. Probability models of needle exchange. *Operations Research* 43(4):558–569.

Kaplan, E. H. 2010. Terror queues. *Operations Research* 58(4):773–784.

Kaplan, E. H., and M. Kress. 2005. Operational effectiveness of suicide-bomber–detector schemes: A best-case analysis. *Proceedings of the National Academy of Sciences of the United States of America* 102(29):10,399–10,404.

Kaplan, E. H., and D. Soloshatz. 1993. How many drug injectors are there in New Haven?: Answers from AIDS data. *Mathematical and Computer Modelling* 17(2):109–115.

Kirby, M. W. 2003. *Operational research in war and peace: The British experience from the 1930s to 1970*. London, UK: Imperial College Press.

Larnder, H. 1984. The origin of operational research. *Operations Research* 32(2):465–475.

Larson, I. Y., ed. 2007. *The Operations Research Center at MIT*. Hanover, MD: Institute for Operations Research and the Management Sciences.

Larson, R. C. 1972. *Urban police patrol analysis*. Cambridge, MA: MIT Press.

Larson, R. C. 1987. Perspectives on queues: Social justice and the psychology of queueing. *Operations Research* 35(6):895–905.

Little, J. D. C. 1961. A proof for the queueing formula $L = \lambda W$. *Operations Research* 9(3):383–387.

McCloskey, J. F. 1987. The beginnings of operations research: 1934–1941. *Operations Research* 35(1):143–152.

McKinsey, J. C. C. 1952. *Introduction to the theory of games*. New York: McGraw Hill.

Morse, P. M. 1948. Mathematical problems in operations research. *Bulletin of the American Mathematical Society* 54(12):602–621.

Morse, P. M. 1952. Operations research, what is it? *Journal of Applied Physics* 23(2):165–172.

Morse, P. M. 1956. Statistics and operations research. *Operations Research* 4(1):2–18.

Morse, P. M. 1986. The beginnings of operations research in the United States. *Operations Research* 34(1):10–17.

Morse, P. M., and G. E. Kimball. 1951. *Methods of operations research*. Cambridge, MA: MIT Press.

Nobel Lectures, Physics 1942–1962. 1964. Amsterdam, The Netherlands: Elsevier. Available: http://nobelprize.org/nobel_prizes/physics/laureates/1948/blackett-bio.html [accessed March 2010].

National Research Council and Institute of Medicine. 1995. *Preventing HIV transmission: The role of sterile needles and bleach*. J. Normand, D. Vlahov, and L. E. Moses, eds. Panel on Needle Exchange and Bleach Distribution Programs. Commission on Behavioral and Social Sciences and Education. Washington, DC: National Academy Press.

Office of Technology Assessment. 1993. *Technologies underlying weapons of mass destruction*. U.S. Congress, Office of Technology Assessment Report OTA-BP-ISC-115. Washington, DC: U.S. Government Printing Office.

Pollock, S. M., M. H. Rothkopf, and A. Barnett, Eds. 1994. *Operations research and the public sector*. Amsterdam, The Netherlands: North-Holland.

Porteus, E. L. 2002. *Foundations of stochastic inventory theory*. Stanford, CA: Stanford University Press.

Pringle, L. 2000. Operations research: The productivity engine. *Operations Research/Management Science Today* 27(3):28–31.

Raiffa, H. 1968. *Decision analysis: Introductory lectures on choices under uncertainty*. Reading, MA: Addison-Wesley.

Rossi, C. 1999. Estimating the prevalence of injecting drug users on the basis of Markov models of the HIV/AIDS epidemic: Applications to Italian data. *Health Care Management Science* 2(3):173–179.

Rubinstein, R. Y., and D. P. Kroese. 2007. *Simulation and the Monte Carlo Method*. New York: John Wiley and Sons.

Rushton, A., P. Croucher, and P. Baker. 2006. *The handbook of logistics and distribution management*. London, UK: Kogan Page.

Schum, D. A. 1987. *Evidence and inference for the intelligence analyst*. New York: University Press of America.

Schum, D. A., and J. R. Morris. 2007. Assessing the competence and credibility of human sources of intelligence evidence: Contributions from law and probability. *Law, Probability and Risk* 6(1–4):247–274.

Steele, J. M. 1989. Models for managing secrets. *Management Science* 35(2):240–248.

Stinnett, A., and A. D. Paltiel. 1996. Mathematical programming for the efficient allocation of health care resources. *Journal of Health Economics* 15(5):641–653.

Talluri, K. Y., and G. van Ryzin. 2005. *The theory and practice of revenue management*. New York: Springer Science+Business Media.

U.S. Department of Justice. 2008. *The Federal Bureau of Investigation's terrorist threat and suspicious incident tracking system*. Audit Report 09-02. Washington, DC: U.S. Department of Justice, Office of the Inspector General.

U.S. Government. 2009. *A tradecraft primer: Structured analytic techniques for improving intelligence analysis*. Available: https://www.cia.gov/library/center-for-the-study-of-intelligence/csi-publications/books-and-monographs/Tradecraft%20Primer-apr09.pdf [accessed March 2010].

Walker, W. E., J. M. Chaiken, and E. J. Ignall. 1979. *Fire department deployment analysis*. New York: Elsevier North Holland.

Wein, L. M., and M. Baveja. 2005. Using fingerprint image quality to improve the identification performance of the U.S. Visitor and Immigrant Status Indicator Technology Program. *Proceedings of the National Academy of Sciences of the United States of America* 102(21):7,772–7,775.

Wein, L. M., and Y. Liu. 2005. Analyzing a bioterror attack on the food supply: The case of botulinum toxin in milk. *Proceedings of the National Academy of Sciences of the United States of America* 102(28):9,984–9,989.

Wein, L. M., D. L. Craft, and E. H. Kaplan. 2003. Emergency response to an anthrax attack. *Proceedings of the National Academy of Sciences of the United States of America* 100(7):4,346–4,351.

Willemain, T. R. 1995. Model formulation: What experts think about and when. *Operations Research* 43(6):916–932.

Willemain, T. R., and R. C. Larson, eds. 1977. *Emergency medical systems analysis*. Lexington, MA: DC Heath and Company.

Winston, W. L., and S. C. Albright. 2009. *Practical management science*. Florence, KY: South-Western Cengage Learning.

Wright, J. N., and R. Race. 2004. *The management of service operations*. London, UK: Thomson Learning.

Zlotnick, J. 1967. A theorem for prediction. *Studies in Intelligence* 11(4):1–12.

Zlotnick, J. 1972. Bayes' theorem for intelligence analysis. *Studies in Intelligence* 16(2):43–52.

3

Applications of Game Theory in Support of Intelligence Analysis

Bruce Bueno de Mesquita

Intelligence analysts are often asked to identify the likely—and unlikely—consequences of alternative courses of action for specific, real-time foreign policy problems. With limited time and potentially critical consequences, analysts must sort through the uncertainties surrounding the specific problem, providing a best estimate of what is likely to happen, estimating the probability of outcomes different from the best estimate, and assessing contingencies that might lead to alternative outcomes. In each instance, there is an interest to work through the logic of a situation to ascertain what might be done to alter or to facilitate particular outcomes. Keeping the intelligence assessment open to the prospects of a discontinuous change is especially important because the past is not a reliable predictor of the future (Feder, 2002; Fingar, this volume, Chapter 1).

The analyst's task is daunting. Every case is fraught with unique features, the time for examining each case is limited, and the potential always exists for deleterious consequences if the analysis proves incorrect. Expert knowledge is the sensible starting place for understanding any specific case, but area or problem expertise should not be the only means of analyzing important, complex problems (Tetlock, 2005). Such expertise can be complemented by reliance on well-tested, rigorous methods of analysis. Such methods can provide an independent perspective that informs and stimulates debate.

I examine how game theory reasoning, combined with empirical, mostly quantitative, analysis, can help inform foreign policy analysis by (1) fostering reliable predictions about the likelihood of alternative outcomes and by assessing how alternative tactics and strategies might improve the expected results; (2) identifying conceptual categories that can be combined to reflect the essence of most foreign policy problems, providing an organizational tool for recognizing commonalities across seemingly disparate events; and (3) highlighting some important ways in which inferences about specific events can go awry because of unstated assumptions or logical leaps from past observations to the current, specific situation.

This chapter proceeds as follows: First it explains briefly what game theory is and how it differs from some methods that seem to be closely related. The chapter then builds toward the ultimate goal: reliable means to predict and engineer policy outcomes. To do so, the chapter discusses the generic classes of constraints commonly designed into different game theory models, especially conceptual constraints that can help inform and organize approaches to foreign policy problems. It then turns to some of the common empirical or research-design challenges that can result in mistaken inferences and, therefore, unreliable assessments of specific situations. The chapter then reviews the record of game theory models as a means to facilitate the prediction and engineering of outcomes, especially in the intelligence/national security setting. Following that discussion, some of the important limitations of game theory are reviewed, touching on alternative methods that may be better suited for certain types of problems. I close with a concluding section.

WHAT IS GAME THEORY?

Game theory is a body of reasoning, grounded in mathematics but readily understood intuitively as a reflection of how people may behave, particularly in situations that involve high stakes for them. It is part of a family of theories that assume people are rational, meaning that they do what they believe (perhaps mistakenly) is in their best interest. Models of decision making such as prospect theory (Kahneman and Tversky, 1984; Kahneman and Miller, 1986) and operations research (Kaplan, this volume, Chapter 2), for instance, examine rational choices in situations in which people confront constraints such as limited time, limited budget, incomplete or uncertain information, or other structural impediments. Game theory models examine choices under these constraints while also specifically attending to strategic interaction in which decision makers select their actions, taking into account expectations about how others will respond to them.

Although all games have shared characteristics, including points at which choices need to be made—terminal points reflecting the possible outcomes of a game and player pay-offs or expected pay-offs—they also vary in other features. In some models, players move sequentially; in others, simultaneously. The two ways of ordering moves often are blended together by recognizing that uncertainty can be captured partially by treating moves as simultaneous. Thus, games may be played under conditions of uncertainty. Although they must have at least two players, they can have any number above that. Games may be single-shot, repeated (meaning the same players interact over the same set of pay-offs more than once), or iterated (meaning that the same players interact more than once with the pay-offs varying across iterations). The various ways in which the features of a game combine can provide a framework for interpreting specific foreign policy matters in a broad setting whose logic has been carefully explored. I will try to illustrate that with examples in the next section.

Games are solved by looking ahead, anticipating (rational) responses by others to each action a player can take, and working backward to formulate a plan of action—a strategy—for the best way to reply to each of the actions others could choose. This is, of course, exactly what players of games like chess or checkers do. They try to anticipate how others will respond to different moves and they pick the move they believe is best for them given their expectations about how their rivals will play the game. In that sense, all game theory models compel us to think about counterfactual circumstances and not just about what actually happens (Tetlock and Belkin, 1996; Fearon, 1991).

Just observing what "really" happened, while ignoring counterfactual actions (actions off-the-equilibrium-path in game theory jargon), can result in misleading inferences about both the process leading to an outcome and the content of the outcome itself (Fingar, this volume, Chapter 1). Game theory diminishes this risk. The solution to any game ensures insight both into what really happened (the actions taken and therefore on the equilibrium path) and why alternative actions were not taken.[1] Why, for instance, did President Kennedy choose a naval blockade as a key response to the introduction of long-range ballistic missiles into Cuba by the former Soviet Union? He certainly understood that the blockade could not remove the missiles already in Cuba. He also understood that other military means might have had a better chance of either destroying the missiles or compelling the Soviets to withdraw them. But the expected cost–benefit assessment from alternative approaches such as a tactical airstrike against the missile installations or an invasion of Cuba to overthrow the Castro regime (all moves considered and not made) were inferior to the expected net gains

---

[1]Games are solved by finding Nash equilibrium strategies. A strategy is a complete plan of action covering every contingency that can arise within the game. A Nash equilibrium is defined as a set of strategies such that no player has a unilateral incentive to switch to some other plan of action. Equilibria describe the path of play leading to an outcome and also the actions not taken; that is, placed off the equilibrium path, because they are not best replies for some player.

from the chosen approach. That is, these other approaches were placed off the equilibrium path because they were deemed inferior in expected results.

Games can have multiple equilibria. A change from one equilibrium outcome to another can appear as a discontinuity. Because different equilibria typically result from having crossed a threshold value on one or more predictor variables, seemingly discontinuous outcomes—a switch from one plan of action to another when the values on the explanatory variables no longer support a previous strategy—can follow after a long period of smooth, continuous changes in the values of those variables. The collapse of the former Soviet Union illustrates this point.

Some look at the demise of the Former Soviet Union as an unpredictable, discontinuous event (Gaddis, 1992). Others, as reported in the Soviet newspaper, *Izvestiya*,[2] examining strategic decision making under economic and political constraints, predicted that the Soviet Union was steadily approaching a cut-point between alternative outcomes. On one side—the cold war years—the Soviet economy was running down, but it was not yet bad enough to jeopardize the leadership's hold on power. On the other side of the cut-point, a small further decline in the economy led to insufficient resources to sustain the system and so called for radical internal change. Thus, from a game theory perspective, the discontinuous outcome was the predictable consequence of a continuous, long-term process of economic erosion and shifting political incentives.

Of course, game theory is not the only method for evaluating change. Statistical methods, for instance, are at least as well suited for trend analysis. Likewise, game theory is not the only mode of reasoning appropriate for studying problems related to questions such as regime stability, the efficacy of carrots and sticks in extracting policy concessions, or the propensity for some issues to be resolved through negotiation and for others to escalate to violence. Political psychology is rich with individual-level assessments of decisions affecting fundamental national security matters (McDermott, 2007). Organizational theory and social forces (see this volume's Spellman, Chapter 6; Tinsley, Chapter 9; and Zegart, Chapter 13) help us to understand how decisions are shaped by and shape group dynamics (see Hastie, this volume, Chapter 8). But equally hard to escape is the fact that strategic interaction—the intentional maneuvering between contending parties—is central to international affairs and is at the heart of many problems confronted by intelligence analysts.

Indeed, game theory provides ways to integrate much of the important knowledge derived from structural, organizational, behavioral, and psychological theories. Structure is a central element in games of sequential decision making in which choices are constrained by the situation in which

---

[2]April 3, 1995, based on the Central Intelligence Agency's Foreign Broadcast Information Service's translation.

decision makers find themselves (Acemoglu and Robinson, 2005; Bueno de Mesquita et al., 2003; North et al., 2009; Shepsle, 1979; Hastie, this volume, Chapter 8). Those situations, or organizational structures, in turn, can be traced back to the strategic interplay among an organization's founders, leaders, and members (Morrow, 1994; Downs et al., 1996). Beyond structural constraints, games also address individual decision-maker characteristics such as their preferences, orientation toward risk taking, and beliefs. Although preferences and risk orientations are taken as psychological features of the individual, beliefs may be a combination of personal predilections and experience. They are assumed to be sustained as long as there is no substantial evidence to contradict them, but they are modified in accordance with Bayes' rule (Kaplan, this volume, Chapter 2) when new information proves to be inconsistent with prior beliefs. Of course, game theory recognizes that many decisions must be made with uncertainty about virtually any and every aspect of a situation.

No single game or model fits all international affairs. Rather, classes of games reflect particular combinations of constraints that act as potential impediments to any player getting what it wants. Therefore, the intelligence analyst, whether formally trained in game theory or not, can benefit from working out the strategic implications of different mixes of individual and structural constraints that are crucial to any given situation. By doing so, the analyst can gain an upper hand in thinking about the strategic lay of the land and, if the right tools are available for more formal, rigorous analysis, can also employ those tools to help work through the complex array of plausible (and implausible) developments and potential ways to alter them. I now turn to these crucial classes of constraints.

CATEGORIZING CONSTRAINTS ON FOREIGN POLICY ACTIONS

In thinking about national security problems, five constraints draw our attention to features of different games that can help illuminate the analysis of national security issues. These constraints are: (1) **Uncertainty**; (2) **Risks**; (3) **Distribution of costs and benefits**; (4) **Coordination**; and, in the case of recurring situations, (5) **Patience**. Let's consider each constraint, identifying the essential elements and providing illustrative examples.

Uncertainty

Uncertainty is a nearly ever-present concern. Information is hard to come by about the intentions of rivals, their capability to implement their intentions, their resolve to do so at different levels of costs borne by them (whether inflicted by others or self-imposed), and their beliefs about U.S. intentions, capabilities, and resolve. Uncertainty creates the opportunity for rivals to bluff about their true qualities, sometimes with the objective of making analysts or decision makers believe they are more hawkish—or more dovish—than they actually are. As in poker and many other games, a successful bluff can produce bigger rewards than could be attained if all information were open for everyone to see and evaluate. But, of course, bluffs are risky. They can also lead to undesired outcomes.

Game theory looks at uncertainty two ways. One source of uncertainty arises because of random shocks to a situation. These random developments can change player expectations and, therefore, the actions they choose.[3] Key figures might die unexpectedly (Jones and Olken, 2009) or some event, such as a natural disaster (Bommer, 1985; Brancati, 2007), might alter the focus of decision makers or the ease with which rivals can organize. Models that allow inputs to be randomly altered (i.e., to experience stochastic shocks) provide a way to think about unanticipated, random events that might alter developments and probe the robustness of alternative outcomes (Bueno de Mesquita, 1998).

Uncertainty also arises in the form of not knowing some critical piece of information about a player, such as his or her preferences, capabilities, or expectations. These situations are sometimes described as circumstances in which players do not know what game they are playing. This form of uncertainty—about player types in game theory jargon—is dealt with by attaching probabilities to player types and having nature—a nonstrategic actor—draw the player types in accordance with the explicitly assumed probability distribution.[4] Let me illustrate this approach to uncertainty while also illustrating the principle that uncertainty reduction, contrary to intuition, does not necessarily increase the odds of finding a cooperative solution to a conflict-prone problem.

Indeed, reducing uncertainty often increases the chances of resolving a dispute cooperatively by making clear to both sides how events are likely to unfold. Less uncertainty can help the side that sees it will pay a heavy cost find a negotiated agreement that leaves it better off than it expected to be by resisting. The improvement in welfare arises because concessions now

---

[3]Modelers often refer to developments or circumstances that are not determined within the logic of the situation, but nevertheless are relevant to shaping choices as exogenous. Weather conditions, for example, are exogenous. However, a decision to initiate a military action or to hold back is not exogenous; it is, in game theory jargon, endogenous because there is a choice to be made about when to attack given expectations about weather, the exogenous factor. I return to this important distinction later.

[4]Uncertainty is addressed by converting incomplete information (not knowing player payoffs or expectations at the end-points of the game) into imperfect information (not knowing the prior history of play) by creating player types and a subjective probability distribution over the types (Harsanyi, 1967–1968). In this way, players do not know where in the game they are when prior choices are consistent with the interests of different types, but subsequent actions will follow different strategic paths depending on the types.

are partially compensated by the transaction costs avoided later (Fearon, 1995). But sometimes reducing uncertainty increases the risk of conflict escalation instead of defusing it. Consider this highly simplified example of potential interactions between a government and terrorists.[5]

Some governments—the U.S., British, and Israeli governments are notable examples—have declaratory policies that they will not negotiate with terrorists. Imagine a disgruntled, relatively weak group that feels ill treated and would like the government to be more responsive to its perceived grievances. Its members are uncertain whether the government will take them seriously if they come forward to try to negotiate a resolution of their grievances. Some group members propose that the government will pay more attention if the group launches an act of terrorism to raise awareness of their cause. These members note that this worked for the Palestinian Liberation Organization, the Irish Republican Army, and others. Although the group is divided on this question, the hardliners prevail. Following the terrorist action, the group debates whether to now come forward and seek concessions from the government in exchange for laying down their arms and eschewing future violence.

Imagine that on average the group values a negotiated agreement with the government more than engaging in another attention-getting act of terrorism, but the members agree that such an act would be better than coming forward, seeking to make a deal only to find their group ignored or even suppressed. For arguments sake, let's say that they value a prospective negotiated deal at 100, being ignored or suppressed at 0, and another act of attention-getting terrorism at 40.

If the government has no declaratory policy about negotiating with terrorists, then the group is likely to be uncertain about how the government will respond if they now come forward-seeking concessions. They do not know the government's type: suppressor or compromiser. If the group thinks the chance that the government is the compromiser type is 0.5 and the chance that it is the suppressor type is also 0.5 (so that they have maximum uncertainty about the likely response by the government), then their expected value from coming forward, trying to negotiate, is $0.5(100) + 0.5(0) = 50$. Because this is better than the value (40) they attach to a second act of terrorism, they take their chances and try to negotiate. Perhaps they are lucky and the government turns out to be the compromiser type that grants some concessions in exchange for the group disarming and perhaps they are unlucky, with the government being the suppressor type.

Although uncertainty about the government's type might result in the

---

[5]For more nuanced game-theoretic treatments of terrorism, see Bueno de Mesquita (2005, 2008); Bueno de Mesquita and Dickson (2007); Kydd and Walter (2002); Lapan and Sandler (1988, 1993); and Rosendorff and Sandler (2004).

opportunity for negotiation, consider what happens if the government reduces uncertainty about its true type. Suppose the government has a declaratory policy that it will never negotiate with terrorists. Because reneging on a public declaration of this sort can be costly for democratic leaders, jeopardizing their chances of reelection and encouraging future adversaries to see them as weak or lacking commitment to their stated intentions (Fearon, 1994; Smith, 1998; Schultz, 1998), the declaratory policy increases confidence in the belief that the government is the type that will not negotiate with terrorists. That is, the declaratory policy has reduced—if not completely eliminated—uncertainty about how the government will respond to a request for negotiations by the alienated group. Suppose the group now places the odds that the government is the suppressor type at 0.7 instead of 0.5. With reduced uncertainty about the government's type, the group's expected value from seeking negotiations now is 0.3(100) + 0.7(0) = 30. A second act of terrorism is valued at 40 so, with uncertainty reduced, the prospect of more terrorism increases.[6]

Uncertainty generally increases the number of possible equilibrium outcomes in strategic settings. Even though players do their best to digest whatever information comes their way, what they believe and what is actually true can deviate, resulting, as in the terrorist example, in an outcome that is not optimal from anyone's point of view. This reminds us that rational, strategic actors can, nevertheless, end up with bad outcomes.

Risks

Whereas uncertainty is about not knowing an important piece of information—say whether a government will pursue negotiations with terrorists—risk is concerned with the probability of alternative results, given different choices of action. In making a bet that I will roll a 6-sided die and come up with a 6, there is no uncertainty about the probability of a 6 being the outcome, although the bet is certainly risky. If the die is fair, then there is a 1/6 chance of rolling a 6 and winning the bet. Plus, there is a 5/6 chance of losing: Risky choices can, of course, lead to bad outcomes.

Different people respond to known risks differently. Some are reluctant to take risks, while others attach so much value to a successful outcome relative to the low value they attach to failure that they favor gambling for the big win over even a fairly valued sure outcome. Estimating the willingness

---

[6]This is a stylized example to make clear how uncertainty reduction can exacerbate rather than diminish tensions. Of course, a fuller analysis would need to take into account the reputational effects of alternative courses of action, the elasticity of demand to be a terrorist conditional on changes in the expectation that the government will inflict costs on such groups, the credibility of the government's commitment to provide policy concessions, and the credibility of the terrorist group's promise to disarm, as well as many other considerations.

to gamble—a player's risk aversion or risk acceptance—in a foreign policy context is a difficult, iffy business, but it also is an important undertaking if we are to design and solve strategic problems that can be of practical use to intelligence analysts (Bueno de Mesquita, 1985; Morrow, 1987; O'Neill, 2001; see also Fischhoff, this volume, Chapter 10).

Risk-proneness draws attention to how risks, weighted by the value or utility attached to alternative outcomes, shape expected pay-offs. Risk by itself is central to all rational choice models of decision making (Kahneman and Tversky, 1984; Kahneman and Miller, 1986; Riker, 1996; McDermott, 1998; see also Kaplan, this volume, Chapter 2). The fall of Iran's Shah provides insight into how attentiveness to actuarial risks and their strategic implications might have informed analysis about regime change.

Nondemocratic leaders who survive in office past approximately 1 or 2 years experience a significant year-to-year decline in the risk of being ousted (Bueno de Mesquita et al., 2003; Egorov and Sonin, 2005), all else being equal. That does not tend to be true for democrats. So, looked at from this angle, it is easy to see why analysts and decision makers would have been taken by surprise when the Shah was deposed in 1979, 38 years into his rise to power and 22 years after his coronation. However, all things are not equal. Mortality, for instance, cuts against the general trend of long-term political survival. The longer a leader is in power, the older the leader gets, and, therefore, the greater the risk of contracting a serious or even terminal illness.

Analyses of political survival indicate that nondemocratic leaders known to be suffering from a terminal illness—as the Shah was—are particularly vulnerable to being deposed by a coup or revolution, apparently because their supporters, especially in the military, can no longer count on them to deliver a flow of largesse, so they factionalize as they look for a new patron to take care of them (Bueno de Mesquita et al., 2003; Goemans, 2008). The risk of revolution when a dictator is dying is likely also to be increased by the propensity of such leaders to surround themselves with relatively incompetent advisors—that is, advisors who are not likely to be good candidates to become rivals of the incumbent (Sonin and Egorov, 2005). Of course, autocrats understand what drives the risk of deposition, so they commonly try to keep their illnesses secret. But when the best medical care can be had only outside their country, as was true for the Shah (and Mobutu Sese Seko in then-Zaire and many others), then there is little they can do to avoid the risk that the illness becomes common knowledge. The Shah's illness was known for some time before he was overthrown. The risk to the stability of his regime was, therefore, something that could have been anticipated and calculated. Of course, terminal illness does not guarantee a revolution, but it certainly raises the odds.

Distribution of Costs and Benefits

Distributional conflicts arise over the relative costs and benefits associated with different outcomes of a game. For example, wars are sometimes fought to gain wealth or territory (Huth, 1996; Vasquez, 2009), or, in the case of certain regime types, to impose policies on recalcitrant adversaries (Bueno de Mesquita et al., 2003; Bercovitch and Lutmar, 2010) or to spread values (O'Donnell et al., 1986; Karl, 1990). Each of these factors involves distributional issues between rivals, so they can be assessed in a game-theoretic framework.

The combination of uncertainty and distributional issues creates complex situations in which rivals have incentives to bluff in an effort to steer action toward their desired outcome. Thus, a player might claim to be more resolved to get its way than it truly is. It might try to signal this resolve by making verbal threats or by taking visibly costly actions, such as mobilizing its military, in the hope that its words or actions will convince others to sacrifice what they want in order to avoid threatened costs. Thus, uncertainty about costs and benefits not only can provoke bluffs, but also can provide a means to reduce the odds of being taken in by a bluff.

Consider the difference between bluffs that are costly to make and bluffs that cost nothing. Threats intended to deter an adversary can be purely verbal cheap talk (private communication, for instance, that "there will be dire consequences if . . . ") or they can be accompanied by a costly signal, such as the visible mobilization of armed forces (or a public declaration that "there will be dire consequences if . . . ", especially if made by a politician up for reelection [Fearon, 1994; Smith, 1998]).[7] A private declaration of resolve, for instance, to deter Iran from building a nuclear weapon, would not be the same as public statements or costly actions demonstrating such resoluteness by, for example, conducting military flights over Iran's nuclear sites or massing troops on Iran's border.

Talk is cheap unless the declaration is accompanied by self-imposed high costs. Costly actions increase the threatening party's own costs without guaranteeing that the threatening party will receive offsetting gains. Therefore, the higher the self-imposed costs, the more likely it is that the threatened action is serious and not a mere bluff (Banks and Sobel, 1987). It is noteworthy that the United States makes only vague statements about

---

[7]Cheap talk refers to signals (communication, statements) between players that do not influence the costs and benefits; that is, the pay-offs, to the players in the game. In the unusual foreign policy case of pure coordination, cheap-talk signals are taken as meaningful because players have no incentive to bluff or deceive each other (Crawford and Sobel, 1982; Spence, 1973; Sartori, 2005). In situations not only involving coordination, such as when there are disagreements about the allocation of scarce resources, cheap-talk statements are equivalent to babbling. They convey no information.

not tolerating an Iranian nuclear bomb, but undertakes actions—such as economic sanctions—that inflict small costs on American voters and, therefore, on American politicians.

The focus on sanctions is more often on the costs to the target than the costs borne by the threatening party. This raises a closely associated distributional question in strategic environments that lead to sanctions. A perennial question is whether sanctions successfully alter the likely outcome of a game and, therefore, the distribution of costs and benefits across players. Often they do not (Hufbauer et al., 2007; Martin, 1993; Smith, 1996a). When the self-inflicted costs are small—as is true for the costs borne by the United States in sanctioning Iran—then the adversary is relatively unlikely to believe that the sanctioner is serious about altering the outcome of the situation. Furthermore, if the costs to some sanctioning parties get to be significant, then it is likely that they will try to renegotiate the terms of their agreement to sanction to avoid continued costs (Abreu et al., 1993). In addition, despite widespread advocacy for imposing sanctions to redistribute costs and benefits in many difficult foreign policy situations, both logic and evidence show that sanctions are more likely to be effective at the threat stage than at the implementation stage. This is because they are only likely to need to be implemented if their target has already concluded that the prospective costs of the sanctions are smaller than the prospective costs of granting the concessions that would avoid sanctions (Smith, 1996a; Drezner, 1999). Therefore, the threat of sanctions can be a powerful tool for altering the outcome of some disputes, but their implementation rarely is.

Finally, distribution issues often reveal commitment problems. Sometimes disputants make promises (e.g., cease-fire agreements), but the mere existence of a cheap-talk promise reveals nothing about what action should be expected. The Taliban, for instance, promised not to disrupt the 2009 Afghan election, yet reneged on that promise. Why? Because low turnout could help advance the Taliban's interests. Likewise, repeated efforts to forge land-for-peace or peace-for-land deals between Israel and the Palestinian Authority suffer from commitment problems associated with the overriding difference in distributional interests of the two sides. Promising peace for land runs into the problem that once land concessions are granted, they are costly to withdraw. So, once land concessions are implemented, the other side has incentives to say the concession is not sufficient to warrant peace (Powell, 1999). Peace for land has exactly the same problem. Once militants disarm in expectation of getting land concessions, the Israelis have little incentive to carry out their part of the bargain because the militants have given up their threat power. Distributional issues often prompt these sorts of commitment issues in foreign affairs. Analysis that treats promises as meaningful, even when carrying them out is contrary to their maker's interests, is bound to lead to overly optimistic conclusions.

Coordination

An interest in coordinated action arises among players when they want to work toward a common resolution of an issue. For example, whether allies can be counted on to help out in time of war is a question of incentives to coordinate (Altfeld and Bueno de Mesquita, 1979; Siverson and King, 1980; Smith, 1996b; Leeds, 2003).

Although some coordination problems are not complicated by other factors, most are. The rare pure coordination issue, like whether allied tanks should drive on the left or right side of the road in a combat zone, responds well to cheap-talk signals because the parties involved have no incentive to bluff or misrepresent themselves (Calvert, 2006; Crawford and Sobel, 1982; Spence, 1973). Resolution based only on exchanging information does not work if the coordination problem is complicated by differences in distributional preferences.

Interests in coordination—though rarely pure coordination—are widespread in international crises. When disputes involve multiple parties, for instance, adversaries have an interest in building a coalition capable enough to deter or defeat the other side. Coalition formation inherently involves coordination, combined with finding distributive concessions—shares in the spoils of victory or subsidized costs, for instance—that make coordinated action worthwhile. Lalman and Newman (1990) and Morrow (1991a) have examined the question of alliance formation, for example, when the interests of the parties are not to attain mutual security gains. Morrow (1991a) in particular shows theoretically and empirically that states can coordinate by joining a mutual alliance in which one gains improved security against threats from enemies at the expense of some loss in foreign policy autonomy and the other sacrifices some degree of its own security, by risking entanglement in its partners' problems, in exchange for improvement in its ability to act independently on foreign policy matters.

Not all coordination solutions need to involve costs, but generally those that impinge as well on distribution questions do when the issue is a one-shot circumstance. Even with distributional differences at play, however, it is sometimes possible to find ways to coordinate as long as the situation involves indefinitely repeating interaction. In these circumstances, cheap talk can help identify a coordination mechanism whereby players alternate on distributional gains or find some other distributional scheme that leaves them all better off in the long run (Taylor, 1976; Axelrod, 1984). Because many foreign policy problems are inherently of unknown duration—such as negotiations over nuclear policy with North Korea or Iran—it is possible (though difficult) to find coordinated solutions to differences in distributional interests.

Patience

Patience calibrates the value a given cost or benefit has tomorrow compared to the same cost or benefit today. The more patient a person is, the closer the future value is to the current value. Greater impatience, therefore, means more greatly discounting future costs or benefits compared to the same values today.

Repeated strategic situations have important qualities that separate them from single-shot games. When games are repeated an indefinite or unknown number of times, then there can be a great many equilibria. Even for situations that in single play have only one equilibrium strategy, as is true for the prisoner's dilemma, with indefinite repetition a vast number of equilibria are possible. One is when players always cooperate with each other. In the single-shot game they cannot rationally do so. The key to cooperation in these circumstances is that with enough time and patience, the cumulative benefits of cooperation can outweigh the short-term incentive to cheat or behave aggressively (Axelrod, 1984).[8] Repeated interaction, however, is not always beneficial. Just as reducing uncertainty sometimes exacerbates a situation, so too can repeated interaction. To anticipate whether repetition promotes conflict or cooperation, it is important to understand how patient or impatient players are and what the sequence of gains and losses looks like. For instance, repeated play can lead to cooperation in the prisoner's dilemma if the participants in the game are patient, that is, if they value continuous modest benefits more than they value larger immediate gains followed by ongoing greatly reduced benefits. The more impatient a player is, the more difficult it is to inspire cooperation because the anticipated cumulative benefits are heavily discounted.

In an arms race, in contrast, patience can make cooperation less likely (Powell, 1999; Slantchev, 2003). Arms races are characterized by absorbing costs now to prevent defeat later. Governments recognize that what they spend on arms comes at the expense of consumption, savings, and other beneficial aspects of a national economy. They also recognize that if they fail to spend while a rival builds up its military might, then they make themselves vulnerable by giving their adversary a first-strike advantage. The more highly valued the future flow of benefits is that can be derived by using a first-strike advantage by conquering a rival, the more willing a regime's leaders are to bear the high cost of spending more money on arms today to ensure victory and a steady stream of benefits in the future. In this case, costs are borne upfront and a stream of gains results from undertaking

---

[8]Repetition provides an avenue for creating benefits, as well, from building a reputation for being someone others can work with and trust (Kydd, 2005; Sartori, 2005).

those costs now. Therefore, the more valuable the future, time-discounted cumulative worth of those gains, the more a state is inclined to spend on arms in pursuit of the long-term gains from a first-strike advantage. In this case impatience makes leaders more reluctant to sacrifice today for tomorrow's gains. Patience has the opposite effect.

Game theory models of patience remind us to be careful not to leap to general conclusions from specific insights. Patience neither leads inevitably to cooperation nor does it lead inevitably to conflict. Which arises depends on the structure of the circumstance. Thus, the intelligence analyst can capitalize on the conditional predictions of models of strategic interaction to provide insight into what might look like unique circumstances in any specific case.

EMPIRICAL CONSIDERATIONS RELATED TO STRATEGIC INTERACTION

Hypotheses derived from game theory models can be difficult to test. This is so because actions are, as we have discussed, part of an equilibrium strategy intended to produce the best outcome each player can get. This means some outcomes are placed off the equilibrium path because of strategic consideration. Some common problems in moving from hypotheses to empirical evaluations result from a failure to attend to these strategic considerations. Here I discuss two of these empirical challenges.

Because potential outcomes are placed off the equilibrium path when there is a strategy that is expected to produce a better result for a player, what we get to observe has been selected based on the anticipated inferior results of what we do not get to observe: the results off the equilibrium path. This means that outcomes—and the cases we can observe—are the product of *selection effects*, or the elimination of certain possible actions because of their expected negative consequences. Another strategic concern that shapes the cases we can examine is closely associated with selection effects. Many—perhaps most—foreign policy decisions reflect endogenous choices, or choices that create the value attached to explanatory variables—such as the demands made by contending sides in a dispute—to improve each player's expected results. For example, security-conscious calculations about what to seek as the resolution of a dispute take into account not only what the player wants, but also what the player anticipates will minimize its risks of a particularly bad outcome (Morrow, 1991b; Smith, 1998). In this way, endogenous, strategic decision making can lead to selection effects in that the anticipation of alternative outcomes shapes current choices so that, in a sense, causality is reversed, with the future "causing" current decisions. Let's examine each of these factors more closely. Then we will be ready to turn to prediction.

Selection Effects: Confounding Inferences

Nearly all historical research on topics such as the causes of big wars, or on nuclear proliferation, both topics of likely concern for intelligence analysts, suffers from selection effects. Scholars concerned with big wars, for instance, almost never examine events that threatened to become big wars but did not escalate beyond low levels of dispute. Scientific analyses, with a strong concern for control groups, and especially game theoretic analyses with their emphasis on counterfactual actions, help reduce errors of inference that may prevail in other forms of investigation. A mind experiment regarding war can help clarify this claim.

All else being equal, consider which events in history were probably *expected* to yield bigger costs if they became wars: those that actually became wars or those that were resolved peacefully through negotiations. One important reason for finding a negotiated resolution to an international dispute is that the costs of fighting are expected to be too high. When the costs of war are expected to be relatively low, however, then fighting becomes more acceptable.[9] It follows that we cannot understand the causes of big wars without examining many crises that had the potential to become big wars, but were averted by reaching a negotiated settlement beforehand. The Cuban Missile Crisis is a nearly perfect example of such an event and has been widely studied (Allison and Zelikow, 1999). But one can see similar patterns in a mostly forgotten dispute between Bavaria and Prussia over Hesse in 1850. In that case, there is little historical research perhaps because, in the end, almost nothing happened. Yet contemporaneous newspaper accounts of the 1850 dispute were dominated by fears that the conflict would erupt into a general war in Europe. Fear of just such a war prompted Prussia to grant concessions that otherwise might not have been granted to a rival as weak as Bavaria, or even to Bavaria's Austrian allies (Bueno de Mesquita and Lalman, 1992).

We see these effects even more dramatically in cases in which nothing at all happened, so we do not even get to observe a low-level conflict. Selection effects that result in "the dog that didn't bark" often lead to selection bias in empirical research. Let me illustrate how strategic selection effects and the case selection bias they lead to can result in unwarranted inferences by discussing the reputed unreliability of military alliances.

Here is a useful fact with which to begin: Often—perhaps as often as 70 percent of the time, depending on how the estimate is done—when a nation with allies is attacked, the allies, despite their treaty obligations, fail

---

[9]Here we should be careful to distinguish between expected costs and benefits and a war's previous sunk costs. At any moment, the rationality behind continuing to fight is related to expected future costs—not past costs—and expected benefits (Wittman, 1979, 2009).

to come to their ally's defense (Sabrosky, 1980; Leeds et al., 2000, 2002).[10] Some infer from the high percentage of alliance partners who do not fight for their partner that treaty obligations are not a meaningful signal of a shared commitment to coordinate under costly conditions. Notice, however, that this inference is drawn by looking at the response of the alliance partner "if the ally is attacked." That, as we will see, is a problematic qualifier if we want to evaluate alliance reliability.

Consider the following mind experiment. Suppose the leader of nation A has a rival, an enemy state called B. That rival has an ally, C. Countries like C frequently do not assist B following an attack by A. We know that information from data analyses whose dependent variable asks whether allied states got help from their partners when attacked. But such analyses do not ask whether an attack took place; attack is taken as given. Yet the underlying question of interest is the reliability of alliance commitments. By ignoring cases in which nothing happened—no attack took place—an empirically incorrect inference is drawn because of improper case selection.

The reported pattern of behavior is insufficient to infer that alliances are unreliable. In fact, the observation is exactly what we should expect if alliance commitments are credible. Consider the following two cases in which A is equally motivated to extract something of value from B and concludes that the valued good can only be gotten by attacking B. In case 1, A attacks B, and in case 2, A does not attack B. To keep matters simple, I assume A believes it can defeat B and gain a benefit that exceeds the anticipated costs of a fight just with B. Suppose, however, that A does not believe the benefits warrant the expected costs of a fight against both B and C. Then, if A believes C's alliance commitment to B is reliable, A does not attack B and we do not include the ongoing peaceful interaction between A and B in our data analysis. If A believes the alliance is unreliable, A attacks B and the case is included in the data analysis. Naturally, some of the time A's beliefs will be mistaken because of uncertainty about a state's true degree of commitment (Gartzke, 1999; Coletta and Gartzke, 2003). However, in general we expect that A's beliefs will be consistent with the subsequent behavior of C because the cost to A of getting this wrong is likely to be high (Huth, 1988; Huth and Russett, 1984; Wu, 1990).

By examining only cases of attack, we fail to test alliance reliability properly. A focus on strategic interaction instructs us to anticipate that we should expect that the applicable alliances will generally prove to be unreliable *if* an attack has taken place. A, after all, has already taken into account

---

[10]Nearly five times as many alliance partners become war participants following an attack as do nonallied states (Siverson and King, 1980), so clearly alignment helps predict choices if an attack happens, but, as we will see, that is not particularly informative about the general reliability of alliance commitments.

the anticipated reliability of C's commitment as part of A's strategic decision making about whether to attack B. If A believes C will assist B, then A
chooses not to attack, making C's reliability an unobserved state of affairs
because A places "attack" off the equilibrium path. The empirical expectation, then, is that the most reliable alliances do not get tested because they
succeed in deterring attacks, while the relatively less reliable alliances are
more likely to be tested and, as expected, prove wanting. The evidence supports the selection argument regarding alliance reliability (Smith, 1996b).

Dominant arguments among international relations scholars and practitioners about the effects of bipolarity, multipolarity, and the balance of
power on stability suffer from just such theoretical selection effects and
empirical selection bias, as does much writing on the rise or decline of
great powers. A careful examination of the arguments for why bipolar or
multipolar systems or balanced or imbalanced power systems are likely to
promote stability shows, for instance, that the logic behind these arguments
depends on assumptions that lead to hypotheses not supported by studies
without selection bias (Bueno de Mesquita, 2009; Kim and Morrow, 1992;
Niou et al., 1989; Powell, 1999; Vasquez, 1997).

Endogenous Choice

Selection bias in sampling often results from a failure to think through
how the strategic setting creates values on key explanatory variables that,
in turn, lead to strategic selection of actions. Statistical analysis runs into
this failure because it generally assumes that the values taken by independent variables are exogenous; that is, are determined outside the strategic
setting rather than shaped by it.[11] In strategic settings—and most foreign
policy problems involve a substantial element of strategic interplay between
contending sides—the assumption that the values of the explanatory variables do not depend on expectations about how they will shape outcomes
is problematic. When choices are made strategically, they are forward looking. One course of action is chosen over others because it is expected to
have better consequences down the road. In this sense, attending to reverse
causality is of fundamental importance—looking ahead to work out what
the best action is now. One simple example is to consider whether Christmas tree sales cause Christmas or the anticipation of Christmas causes
tree sales. Behind this example lies an important consideration for policy

---

[11]The exception to this statement involves the application of Bayesian statistical estimation
techniques. These are rarely found in studies of foreign affairs. For two excellent examples
of the use of such methods, each motivated by game theory's strategic reasoning, see Smith
(1999) and Ward et al. (2007).

analysis. Let me illustrate that consideration with a discussion of arms races and their relation to war.

Many contend that arms races cause war (Richardson, 1960; Wallace, 1982; Diehl and Crescenzi, 1998; Gibler et al., 2005). This belief contributes to efforts to pursue arms control agreements in the expectation of improving the prospects of peace. The standard account of how arms races cause war builds on stimulus-response, nonstrategic explanations of arms racing. The claim is that when a country builds up its arms, it makes its adversaries fear that their security is at risk. In response, they build up their own arms to defend themselves. The other side looks at that build-up—seeing their own as purely defensive—and responds by developing even more and better weapons to protect themselves, fearing that the other side intends to take advantage or even attack them. Eventually, so the argument goes, the arms race (inexplicably) spirals out of control and war starts.

In support of this contention, evidence is adduced that wars are preceded by arms races. The arms build-up is taken as exogenous, as independent of the threat or expectation of war. Here we have correlation masquerading as causation, with little regard to the underlying strategic environment. After all, the most basic economics teaches us that when the cost of anything goes up, holding quality constant, we buy less, not more of it. Arms build-ups increase destructive power and, therefore, the expected cost of war. By raising the expected cost of war while leaving the value of war's benefits unaltered, arms racing should reduce, not increase, the incidence of war although, if a war occurs, it will be costlier because of the arms build-up.

Just about every war has been preceded by a build-up in weapons, but then many wars are also avoided by the deterrent impact of an arms build-up (Powell, 1990, 1999; Bueno de Mesquita and Riker, 1982). Much of the empirical literature on arms races results in poor sampling of cases because of a failure to understand that arms acquisition is endogenous to the expectation of war. That is, the fear of vulnerability to an adversary causes arms races, rather than the decision to acquire arms being the cause of war (Altfeld, 1983; Powell, 1990, 1999). Thus, the idea of forward-looking, endogenous choice confounds assessments that treat the value on explanatory variables as being independent of expectations about future events.

PREDICTION OF FUTURE EVENTS

The discussion of strategic constraints and the empirical challenges they create should encourage testing hypotheses by observing past patterns (whether through case studies or statistically in large-N studies) and then projecting the expectations they imply on out-of-sample cases. That is the problem faced by intelligence analysts. They know what happened in the past and they must figure out which past patterns are germane to the problem they confront at the moment, a problem whose resolution is still unknown. The intelligence analyst's problem is perhaps the most challenging for any theory. Prediction (forecasting) is demanding exactly because the researcher cannot fit arguments to unknown results. This is a fundamental difference between real-time prediction and so-called post-diction. Not surprisingly, few theories of international relations are routinely exposed to the demands of real-time prediction.

Among quantitative efforts to predict national security problems, a few stand out for their success and the ease with which they can be applied in real-time. Artificial neural network models, for instance, are a statistical means to "train" their algorithm to new cases by discerning patterns among variables based on prior observations, then updating the weights of variables as new observations are added, using the "training" to anticipate the next out-of-sample case. Beck et al. (2000) and King and Zeng (2001) have used such methods to predict patterns of conflict initiation and of state failure with considerable success.

Other quantitative, but not statistical, approaches to foreign policy problems have also proven effective in predicting the dynamics and the outcomes of out-of-sample events. Some applied game theory models, for instance, have been used to evaluate national security problems and have even found use among some intelligence analysts. Statistical assessments, including regression, maximum likelihood, artificial neural network models, and others, are especially valuable when the past is a good predictor of the future. Applied game theory models provide a useful alternative to more conventional statistical analyses in that applied games have greater case-specific qualities. They also are equally helpful in looking at ongoing situations and cases involving the prospect of discontinuity. Furthermore, they highlight sources of selection effects, compel attentiveness to endogenous choices, and keep the derivation of hypotheses—done through formal logic—independent of the data used to evaluate them. Game theory also provides explicit means of modeling how uncertainty alters the strategic interplay among decision makers and provides a means—through Bayes' rule—for taking learning into account. Other methods address many of these items as well, but to my knowledge game theory modeling is the only approach structured to draw explicit analytic attention to all of them.

A final reason for focusing attention on game theoretic approaches to international relations is their track record when applied to national security matters. Indeed, Stanley Feder (2002), a former Central Intelligence Agency (CIA) analyst and national intelligence officer, emphasizes the virtues that strategic models bring to the job of intelligence analysts precisely because such models help anticipate divergence from past patterns. Feder reports that at least one such model that he tested more than 1,200 times during his tenure at the CIA produced accurate results 90 percent of the time and provided a means to extrapolate to significant implications about matters such as regime stability, leadership change, and responsiveness to alternative approaches to a given problem (Feder, 1995, 2002). Others report similar reliability when reviewing academic publications concerning the same applied game theory models (Ray and Russett, 1996).

Feder contends that the intelligence community would benefit from greater use of such models (for ways to evaluate this expectation, see Tetlock and Mellers, this volume, Chapter 11). He argues that these models do not get greater use because analysts tend to think of quantitative or mathematical approaches as the domain of methodologists rather than as part of their domain of country-specific or problem-specific analysis. Fortunately, analysts do not need to be methodologists or game theorists to capitalize on the insights that can be gained from thinking about problems in a strategic vein. They can combine their deep understanding of history, culture, and idiosyncratic factors impinging on any case with the case-oriented insights of applied game theory models, rendering their analysis more complete and transparent.

LIMITATIONS

Of course, a cultural divide between humanistic and social science approaches to intelligence analysis—as highlighted by Feder (2002)—is not the only factor that restricts the adoption of statistical or game theoretic methods by the intelligence community. Humanistic modes—examinations of history, culture, and local conditions—provide important insights into intelligence problems. When coupled with social science methods, the two together have demonstrated much more insight than either alone (Feder, 1995, 2002). We should not lose sight of the fact that humanistic modes of analysis face limitations of their own. They lack analytic transparency; different subject or area experts often draw different inferences when confronted with the same facts; and tools for evaluating accuracy are inaccurate either with regard to outcomes or the process leading to them. Likewise, we must also be explicit about the limitations of more social-science–oriented methods.

Game theory forecasting methodology used to evaluate political decisions, as reviewed by Feder (1995, 2002), Ray and Russett (1996), and others (e.g., Thomson et al., 2006; Schneider et al., 2010), can combine the benefits of detailed case assessment while exploiting the advantages of broad hypothesis testing through the application of the same model to numerous individual cases. But game theory applications make strong assumptions about information and people.

Games require that at least some critical element of information must be common knowledge; that is, at least some information must be known to each player, who must know that each other player knows that information, and each player must know that each other player knows that each player knows the information and so forth. Although there is considerable ongoing research to escape the common knowledge conundrum—especially when it comes to assumptions about the probability that players hold this or that belief about others—standard game theory models still have not overcome the common knowledge constraint. Some argue that this requirement cannot be overcome in a foreign policy context (Fey and Ramsay, 2007).

Additionally, the path to outcomes in game theory models is well defined and (perhaps overly) precise. The path to outcomes in the real world tends to be fairly noisy, involving more randomness and often taking longer, with many more steps, than in formal game theory models. This has stimulated several complementary technologies. One approach focuses attention on the costs and benefits of searching for the best action to take. These models, known as "satisficing" models—in which players choose the first adequate approach to a problem that they identify—and other models in which players have bounded, that is, limited rationality, are two modifications to standard game theory models designed to cope with potentially overly defined outcome paths (Simon, 1957; Sargent, 1994; Byron, 2004). But in doing so, these perspectives introduce their own problems. They increase the number of equilibria and suggest paths to outcomes that may be no closer—and might even be less close—to the choices of actual decision makers than is true in standard game theory modeling. Indeed, evolutionary models—that incorporate various forms of short-sighted behavior—stabilize at a Nash equilibrium outcome of a more standard game designed to capture the strategic setting.[12] Yet evolutionary models can arrive at the evolutionarily stable equilibrium from a nearly infinite number of paths, implying that the process of decision making leading to outcomes is unpredictable. If that is true, then outcome predictions may still be reliable, but predictions about process are unlikely to be. The evidence from intelligence applications of game theory models, however, challenges this inference. Standard games

---

[12]Evolutionary game theory builds on the insights of evolution in biology. Essentially, evolutionary models assume that players continue a strategy or course of action as long as it produces good results for them, switching to a different strategy when their behavior proves excessively costly. Nash equilibrium is the fundamental concept for solving games. In game theory, players have strategies, defined as a complete plan of action for every contingency that could arise in the game. A Nash equilibrium is a set of player strategies in which no player has a unilateral incentive to deviate from his or her strategy.

seem to provide insight into the choice process as well as into the outcome of events (Feder, 1995, 2002).[13]

Although no rational choice models assume that decision makers have perfect foresight or that decision makers explore all possible avenues of action, they do make strong assumptions about how problems are solved. Because the actors in these models are trying to do what is best for them, they are assumed to play skillfully and without emotion. The game theoretic decision maker is cold, calculating, and self-interested. Of course not everyone behaves that way all of the time so, as with any method, it is prudent to view the results of a game as information to be taken as one of several inputs. In forming a well-rounded assessment of a problem, it is also important to examine the insights from many authors in this volume, as follows: from psychology (see this volume's Spellman, Chapter 6, and Tinsley, Chapter 9), organizational theory (see this volume's Kozlowski, Chapter 12, and Zegart, Chapter 13), group dynamics (Hastie, this volume, Chapter 8), and history and culture (Skinner, Chapter 5). But at the same time, we should not overstate the limitations that arise from discounting factors such as emotion. After all, Feder (1995, 2002), Ray and Russett (1996), and numerous other independent auditors of game theoretic results about national security matters all conclude that some applied models prove highly reliable, hitting, as Feder puts it, "the bull's eye" twice as often as the intelligence analysts whose data were used to estimate variables in the applied models.

CONCLUSION

International relations and foreign policy problems are readily clustered according to the broad categories of constraints examined by game theory approaches. Recall that these constraints include (1) uncertainty; (2) risk; (3) distributional concerns; (4) coordination; and (5) patience. Attention to these constraints, coupled with a focus on strategic interaction, highlights the ways in which selection effects and endogenous choice shape events and, therefore, how ignoring these factors can result in mistaken inferences.

By monitoring which strategic constraints are operative in a situation and how they relate to what is or is not observed, the analyst will have a clearer evaluation of the array of plausible and implausible outcomes. Even done intuitively, the factors highlighted by game theory should help

---

[13]Charles Buffalano, then deputy director of research at the Defense Advanced Research Projects Agency, in private correspondence dated June 12, 1984, reported that "one of the last (and most successful) projects in the political methodologies program was the expected utility theory. . . . The theory is both explanatory and predictive and has been rigorously evaluated through post-diction and in real time. . . . [I]t has the power to predict *specific* policies, their nuances, and ways in which they might be changed."

diminish the analytic pitfalls that make the intelligence analyst's job so daunting.

The knowledge derived from quantitative and formal methods has been successful in informing intelligence analysis. Many of these methods are relatively easy to learn and apply. In all likelihood when the intelligence community is organized to use these social science methods and when its culture changes to welcome these approaches, then, as suggested by the chapters in this volume, quantitative and formal modeling perspectives applied together, with more qualitative and more humanistic methods, will improve analysis and enhance national security.

REFERENCES

Abreu, D., D. Pearce, and E. Stacchetti. 1993. Renegotiation and symmetry in repeated games. *Journal of Economic Theory* 60(2):217–240.

Acemoglu, D., and J. A. Robinson. 2005. *Economic origins of dictatorship and democracy.* New York: Cambridge University Press.

Allison, G. T., and P. Zelikow. 1999. *Essence of decision: Explaining the Cuban missile crisis,* 2nd ed. White Plains, NY: Longman.

Altfeld, M. 1983. Arms races? And escalation? *International Studies Quarterly* 27:225–232.

Altfeld, M. F., and B. Bueno de Mesquita. 1979. Choosing sides in wars. *International Studies Quarterly* 23(March):87–112.

Axelrod, R. 1984. *The evolution of cooperation.* Boston, MA: Basic Books.

Banks, J. S., and J. Sobel. 1987. Equilibrium selection in signaling games. *Econometrica* 55:647–661.

Beck, N., G. King, and L. Zeng. 2000. Improving quantitative studies of international conflict. *American Political Science Review* 94(1):21–36.

Bercovitch, J., and C. Lutmar. 2010. Beyond negotiation deadlocks: the importance of mediation and leadership change. In A. Narlikar, ed., *Deadlocks in multilateral settings: Causes and solutions* (pp. 232-253). New York: Cambridge University Press

Bommer, J. 1985. The politics of disaster—Nicaragua. *Disasters* 9(4):270–278.

Brancati, D. 2007. Political aftershocks: The impact of earthquakes on intrastate conflict. *Journal of Conflict Resolution* 51(5):715–743.

Bueno de Mesquita, B. 1985. The war trap revisited. *American Political Science Review* 79:156–173.

Bueno de Mesquita, B. 1998. The end of the Cold War: Predicting an emergent property. *Journal of Conflict Resolution* 42(2):131–155.

Bueno de Mesquita, B. 2009. *Principles of international politics,* 4th ed. Washington, DC: CQ Press.

Bueno de Mesquita, B., and D. Lalman. 1992. *War and reason.* New Haven, CT: Yale University Press.

Bueno de Mesquita, B., and W. H. Riker. 1982. Assessing the merits of selective nuclear proliferation. *Journal of Conflict Resolution* 26(2):283–306.

Bueno de Mesquita, E. 2005. Conciliation, counterterrorism, and patterns of terrorist violence. *International Organization* 59(1):145–176.

Bueno de Mesquita, E. 2008. Terrorist factions. *Quarterly Journal of Political Science* 3(4):399–418.

Bueno de Mesquita, E., and E. Dickson. 2007. The propaganda of the deed: Terrorism, coun-terterrorism, and mobilization. *American Journal of Political Science* 51(2):364–381.

Bueno de Mesquita, B., A. Smith, R. M. Siverson, and J. D. Morrow. 2003. *The logic of politi-cal survival.* Cambridge, MA: MIT Press.

Byron, M., ed. 2004. *Satisficing and maximizing: Moral theorists on practical reason.* New York: Cambridge University Press.

Calvert, R. L. 2006. Deliberation as coordination through cheap-talk. Presented at Midwest Political Science Association annual meeting, April 20–23, Chicago, IL. Available: http://www.nyu.edu/gsas/dept/politics/seminars/Calvert_Paper.pdf [accessed October 2010].

Coletta, D., and E. Gartzke. 2003. Testing war in the error term. *International Organization* 57(Spring):445–448.

Crawford, V., and J. Sobel. 1982. Strategic information transmission. *Econometrica* 50:1431–1451.

Diehl, P. F., and M. J. C. Crescenzi. 1998. Reconfiguring the arms race war debate. *Journal of Peace Research* 35(1):111–118.

Downs, G. W., D. M. Rocke, and P. N. Barsoom. 1996. Is the good news about compliance good news about cooperation? *International Organization* 50:379–407.

Drezner, D. W. 1999. *The sanctions paradox.* New York: Cambridge University Press.

Egorov, G., and K. Sonin. 2005. The killing game: Reputation and knowledge in politics of succession. *Game Theory and Information.* Available: http://ideas.repec.org/p/wpa/wuwpga/0505003.html [accessed May 2010].

Fearon, J. D. 1991. Counterfactuals and hypothesis testing in political science. *World Politics* 43(January):169–195.

Fearon, J. D. 1994. Domestic political audiences and the escalation of international disputes. *American Political Science Review* 88:577–592.

Fearon, J. D. 1995. Rationalist explanations for war. *International Organization* 49:379–414.

Feder, S. 1995. Factions and policon: New ways to analyze politics. In H. Westerfield, ed., *Inside CIA's private world: Declassified articles from the agency's internal journal, 1955–1992* (pp. 274–293). New Haven, CT: Yale University Press.

Feder, S. A. 2002. Forecasting for policy making in the post-cold war period. *Annual Review of Political Science* 3:149–166.

Fey, M., and K. Ramsay. 2007. Mutual optimism and war. *American Journal of Political Sci-ence* 51(4):738–754.

Gaddis, J. 1992. International relations theory and the end of the cold war. *International Security* 17(3):323–345.

Gartzke, E. 1999. War is in the error term. *International Organization* 53:567–587.

Gibler, D. M., T. J. Rider, and M. L. Hutchison. 2005. Taking arms against a sea of trou-bles: Conventional arms races during periods of rivalry. *Journal of Peace Research* 42(2):131–147.

Goemans, H. E. 2008. Which way out: The manner and consequences of losing office. *Journal of Conflict Resolution* 52(6):771–794.

Harsanyi, J. C. 1967–1968. Games with incomplete information played by "Bayesian" play-ers. *Management Science* 14:157–182, 320–324, 486–502.

Hufbauer, G. C., J. J. Schott, K. A. Elliott, and B. Oegg. 2007. *Economic sanctions reconsid-ered,* 3rd ed. Washington, DC: Peterson Institute for International Economics.

Huth, P. K. 1988. *Extended deterrence and the prevention of war.* New Haven, CT: Yale University Press.

Huth, P. K. 1996. *Standing your ground: Territorial disputes and international conflict.* Ann Arbor: University of Michigan Press.

Huth, P. K., and B. M. Russett. 1984. What makes deterrence work? Cases from 1900 to 1980. *World Politics* 36:496–526.

Jones, B. F., and B. A. Olken. 2009. Hit or miss? The effect of assassinations on institutions and war. *American Economic Journal: Macroeconomics* 1(2):55–87.

Kahneman, D., and A. Tversky. 1984. Choices, values and frames. *American Psychologist* 39(4):341–350.

Kahneman, D. and D. T. Miller. 1986. Norm theory: Comparing reality to its alternatives. *Psychological Review* 93:136–153.

Karl, T. 1990. Dilemmas of democratization in Latin America. *Comparative Politics* 23:1–23.

Kim, W., and J. D. Morrow. 1992. When do power shifts lead to war? *American Journal of Political Science* 36:896–922.

King, G., and L. Zeng. 2001. Improving forecasts of state failure. *World Politics* 53(4):623–658.

Kydd, A. 2005. *Trust and mistrust in international relations*. Princeton, NJ: Princeton University Press.

Kydd, A., and B. F. Walter. 2002. Sabotaging the peace: The politics of extremist violence. *International Organization* 56(2):263–296.

Lalman, D., and D. Newman. 1990. Alliance formation and national security. *International Interactions* 16:239–254.

Lapan, H. E., and T. Sandler. 1988. To bargain or not to bargain: That is the question. *American Economic Review* 78(2):16–21.

Lapan, H. E., and T. Sandler. 1993. Terrorism and signaling. *European Journal of Political Economy* 9(3):383–397.

Leeds, B. A. 2003. Alliance reliability in times of war: Explaining decisions to violate treaties. *International Organization* 57(Fall):801–827.

Leeds, B. A., A. G. Long, and S. McLaughlin Mitchell. 2000. Re-evaluating alliance reliability: Specific threats, specific promises. *Journal of Conflict Resolution* 44:686–699.

Leeds, B. A., J. Ritter, S. McLaughlin Mitchell, and A. G. Long. 2002. Alliance treaty obligations and provisions, 1815–1944. *International Interactions* 28:261–284.

Martin, L. L. 1993. *Coercive cooperation*. Princeton, NJ: Princeton University Press.

McDermott, R. 1998. *Risk-taking in international politics*. Ann Arbor: University of Michigan Press.

McDermott, R. 2007. *Presidential leadership, illness and decision making*. New York: Cambridge University Press.

Morrow, J. D. 1987. On the theoretical basis of a measure of national risk attitudes. *International Studies Quarterly* 31:423–443.

Morrow, J. D. 1991a. Alliances and asymmetry: An alternative to the capability aggregation model of alliances. *American Journal of Political Science* 35:904–933.

Morrow, J. D. 1991b. Electoral and congressional incentives and arms control. *Journal of Conflict Resolution* 35:243–263.

Morrow, J. D. 1994. Modeling the forms of cooperation: Distribution versus information. *International Organization* 48:387–423.

Niou, E., P. Ordeshook, and G. Rose. 1989. *The balance of power*. Cambridge, UK: Cambridge University Press.

North, D., J. J. Wallis, and B. Weingast. 2009. *Violence and social orders: A conceptual framework for interpreting recorded human history*. New York: Cambridge University Press.

O'Donnell, G., P. Schmitter, and L. Whitehead, eds. 1986. *Transitions from authoritarian rule*. Baltimore, MD: Johns Hopkins University Press.

O'Neill, B. 2001. Risk aversion in international relations theory. *International Studies Quarterly* 45:616–640.

Powell, R. 1990. *Nuclear deterrence theory*. Cambridge UK: Cambridge University Press.

Powell, R. 1999. *In the shadow of power*. Princeton, NJ: Princeton University Press.

Ray, J. L., and B. M. Russett. 1996. The future as arbiter of theoretical controversies: Predictions, explanations and the end of the cold war. *British Journal of Political Science* 26(4):441–470.

Richardson, L. F. 1960. *Arms and insecurity*. Chicago, IL: Quadrangle.

Riker, W. H. 1996. *The strategy of rhetoric*. New Haven, CT: Yale University Press.

Rosendorff, P., and T. Sandler. 2004. Too much of a good thing? The proactive response dilemma. *Journal of Conflict Resolution* 48(4):657–671.

Sabrosky, A. 1980. Interstate alliances: Their reliability and the expansion of war. In J. D. Singer, eds. *The correlates of War II: Testing some realpolitik models*. New York: Free Press.

Sargent, T. 1994. *Bounded rationality in macroeconomics*. New York: Oxford University Press.

Sartori, A. 2005. *Deterrence by diplomacy*. Princeton, NJ: Princeton University Press.

Schneider, G., D. Finke, and S. Bailer. 2010. Bargaining power in the European Union: An evaluation of competing game–theoretic model. *Political Studies* 58(1):85–103.

Schultz, K. 1998. Domestic opposition and signaling in international crises. *American Political Science Review* 92:829–844.

Shepsle, K. A. 1979. Institutional arrangements and equilibrium in multidimensional voting models. *American Journal of Political Science* 23:27–59.

Simon, H. A. 1957. *Models of man: Social and rational*. New York: John Wiley and Sons.

Siverson, R. M., and J. King. 1980. Attributes of national alliance membership and war participation, 1816–1965. *American Journal of Political Science* 24(1):1–15.

Slantchev, B. 2003. The power to hurt: Costly conflict with completely informed states. *American Political Science Review* 97(1):123–133.

Smith, A. 1996a. The success and use of sanctions. *International Interactions* 21(3):229–245.

Smith, A. 1996b. To intervene or not to intervene: A biased decision. *Journal of Conflict Resolution* 40(1):16–40.

Smith, A. 1998. International crises and domestic politics. *American Political Science Review* 92(3):623–638.

Smith, A. 1999. Testing theories of strategic choice: The example of crisis escalation. *American Journal of Political Science* 93(4):1,254–1,283.

Sonin, K., and G. Egorov. 2005. *Dictators and their viziers: Agency problems in dictatorships*. Available: http://www.nyu.edu/gsas/dept/politics/seminars/sonin_s05.pdf [accessed October 2010].

Spence, M. 1973. Job market signaling. *Quarterly Journal of Economics* 86:355–374.

Taylor, M. 1976. *Anarchy and cooperation*. London, UK: John Wiley and Sons.

Tetlock, P. 2005. *Expert political judgment*. Princeton, NJ: Princeton University Press.

Tetlock, P., and A. Belkin. 1996. *Counterfactual thought experiments in world politics*. Princeton, NJ: Princeton University Press.

Thomson, R., F. N. Stokman, C. H. Achen, and T. König., eds. 2006. *The European Union decides*. Cambridge UK: Cambridge University Press.

Vasquez, J. A. 1997. The realist paradigm and degenerative versus progressive research programs: An appraisal of neotraditional research on Waltz's Balancing Proposition. *American Political Science Review* 91(4):899–912.

Vasquez, J. A. 2009. *Territory, war, and peace*. New York: Routledge.

Wallace, M. 1982. Armaments and escalation: Two competing hypotheses. *International Studies Quarterly* 26:37–56.

Ward, M. D., R. M. Siverson, and X. Cao. 2007. Disputes, democracies, and dependencies: A re-examination of the Kantian peace. *American Journal of Political Science* 51(3):583.

Wittman, D. 1979. How a war ends: A rational model approach. *Journal of Conflict Resolution* 23(4):743–763.

Wittman, D. 2009. Bargaining in the shadow of war: When is a peaceful resolution most likely? *American Journal of Political Science* 53:588–602.

Wu, S. 1990. To attack or not to attack: A theory and empirical assessment of extended immediate deterrence. *Journal of Conflict Resolution* 34:531–552.

4

Use of Signal Detection Theory as a Tool for Enhancing Performance and Evaluating Tradecraft in Intelligence Analysis

Gary H. McClelland

Many individuals and organizations make predictions of future events or detection and identification of current states. Examples include stock analysts, weather forecasters, physicians, and, of course, intelligence analysts. Consumers of these predictions need to know the expected accuracy of the forecasts and the confidence with which the predictions and putative detections are made. Those making the predictions need to know how well they are doing and if they are improving. Being able to assess prediction accuracy is especially important when evaluating new methods believed to improve forecast performance. However, in a problem that is not unique to the intelligence community (IC), forecasters are notoriously reluctant to keep scorecards of their performance, or at least to make those scorecards publicly available. As discussed extensively in Tetlock and Mellers (this volume, Chapter 11), *Intelligence Community Directive Number 203* (Director of National Intelligence, 2007) emphasizes process accountability in evaluating IC performance rather than accuracy. This chapter suggests methods for improving the assessment of accuracy.

The chapter relies extensively on recent advances in assessing medical forecasts and detections, where signal detection theory specifically and evidence-based medicine more generally have led to many advances. Although medical judgment tasks are not perfectly analogous to IC analyses, there are enough strong similarities to make the examples useful. Just as physicians often have to make quick assessments based on limited and sometimes conflicting information sources with no two cases ever being quite the same, so too intelligence analysts evaluate and characterize evolving situations using partial information from sources varying in credibility.

In both medicine and intelligence analysis the stakes are often very high. That, combined with time pressure, can generate considerable stress for the person making the forecasts and detections. As the medical examples illustrate, rigorous evaluation of physician judgments and practices using the methods proposed in this chapter have improved medical outcomes substantially. It is reasonable to expect similar benefits if these methods are applied in intelligence analysis.

Without scorecards and assessment of accuracy of the many forecasts an individual or organization makes, judgments of forecaster performance are likely to be based on a few spectacular, newsworthy, atypical events. These events are more likely to be failed rather than successful predictions. For example, public assessments of the IC in this century are largely based on missing the 9/11 terrorist attacks and falsely claiming that Iraq had weapons of mass destruction (WMD). The dangers of forecasters being evaluated on the basis of a few events are obvious. The many day-to-day predictions that were correct are ignored, especially true negatives (e.g., no credit is given for *not* having invaded other countries that did not have these weapons). Also, post-hoc analyses of a few events are plagued by the problems of hindsight bias. Finally and perhaps most importantly, a few isolated events do not provide adequate data for assessing whether new methods (e.g., Intellipedia, A-Space, red cell analysis, having an overarching Office of the Director of National Intelligence) improve performance. Keeping score in the IC is likely to reveal much better day-to-day performance than they are given credit for by policy makers and the public.

Forecasters are not only reluctant to keep score, but also they often avoid making predictions with sufficient precision to allow scorekeeping. An important exception is contemporary weather forecasting that involves, for example, explicit probabilities of precipitation and confidence bands around predicted hurricane tracks. By contrast, many forecasts in other disciplines are too vague to support scorekeeping. In this context, an examination of unclassified National Intelligence Estimates (NIEs) from the past several years provides an interesting case study. Heuer (1999, pp. 152–153) explicitly warns: "Verbal expressions of uncertainty—such as 'possible,' 'probable,' 'unlikely,' 'may,' and 'could'—are a form of subjective probability judgment, but they have long been recognized as sources of ambiguity and misunderstanding. . . . To express themselves clearly, analysts must learn to routinely communicate uncertainty using the language of numerical probability or odds ratios." Sherman Kent (1964) had similar concerns and concludes:

> Words and expressions like these are far too much a part of us and our habits of communication to be banned by fiat. . . . If use them we must in NIEs, let us try to use them sparingly and in places where they are least

likely to obscure the thrust of our key estimative passages. . . . Let us meet these key estimates head on. Let us isolate and seize upon exactly the thing that needs estimating. Let us endeavor to make clear to the reader that the passage in question is of critical importance—the gut estimate, as we call it among ourselves. *Let us talk of it in terms of odds and chances*, and when we have made our best judgment let us assign it a word or phrase that is chosen from one of the five rough categories of likelihood on the chart. [emphasis added]

However, in recent years, all NIEs contain a boilerplate page explaining that instead of using quantitative probability estimates that might imply overprecision, a set of probability words ("remote," "unlikely," "even chance," "probably, likely," and "almost certainly") will be used instead. A graphic locates those words along an unnumbered probability scale. The actual use of such words in the predictions made in NIEs would allow some scorekeeping. However, a search of unclassified[1] NIEs from the past several years reveal scant use of those words and much more frequent use of nebulous words like "could" that do not allow an assessment of accuracy. The boilerplate page includes this sentence: "In addition to using words within a judgment to convey degrees of likelihood, we also ascribe 'high,' 'moderate,' or 'low' confidence levels based on the scope and quality of information supporting our judgments." Again, although associating such confidence words with predictions would facilitate scorekeeping, the issue is moot because the word "confidence" did not appear in a search of a number of recent NIEs.

This chapter suggests signal detection theory as a useful method for keeping score, develops some examples in the context of intelligence analysis, and describes some benefits of keeping score that have been achieved in other disciplines, such as weather forecasting and medicine.

SIGNAL DETECTION THEORY

Proposing signal detection theory as a method for keeping score—to evaluate prediction quality—in intelligence analysis, specifically, or detection and diagnosis, more generally, is neither novel nor surprising. The theory developed from the operations analysis (Kaplan, this volume, Chapter 2) of the military problem of using radar to detect aircraft. The seminal paper by Tanner and Swets (1954) was based on research funded by the U.S. Army Signal Corps. Lusted (1971) provides an early use of signal detection in

---

[1]Of course it is possible that the probability words were used in classified NIEs, possibly even the nonredacted versions of the NIEs that were included in these counts. The probability word counts reported here are based only on unclassified NIEs.

radiology, demonstrating its value for assessing radiologists, more informally trained assistants, and putative improvements in radiological examination systems. Numerous studies in radiology and medical diagnosis have relied on signal detection concepts. Several recent National Research Council reports on using polygraphs for lie detection (National Research Council, 2003) and evaluating emerging trends in cognitive neuroscience for identifying psychological states and intentions (National Research Council, 2008) both use signal detection concepts.

Basic Concepts of Signal Detection Theory

I briefly review the basic concepts underlying signal detection theory and illustrate them in the context of intelligence analysis. This is not meant to be a primer for signal detection concepts (see McNichol, 2004; Swets et al., 2000; Wickens, 2001), but instead an introduction and discussion of how signal detection measures could be used for scorekeeping within the IC. Whether or not one adopts signal detection for scorekeeping, knowledge of the concepts can usefully change how problems of detection and prediction are framed and discussed (see Oliver et al., 2008, for an example of the rhetorical power of signal detection in neurology). Sorkin and one set of colleagues (2001) and Sorkin and another set of colleagues (2004) provide excellent applications of signal detection of group or team decision making that may be especially relevant for IC applications (see Hastie, this volume, Chapter 8).

In essence, signal detection theory quantifies the ability of a detection system (whether it be an individual, a team of individuals, a test, a procedure, or a device) to distinguish between *signal* (i.e., an event of interest) and *noise* (i.e., background events of no interest). The most important aspect of this quantification is to separate the true accuracy of the detection system from the system's (or individual's) response bias—the propensity to be cautious and overwarn (false alarms) versus avoiding crying wolf, thereby underwarning (misses). These concepts and the important trade-offs between them are discussed in detail below.

2 × 2 World View

Table 4-1 depicts signal detection theory's rather simplistic 2 × 2 view of the world. The truth is whether there is a signal to be detected (e.g., dictator X will be overthrown next month, country Y has materials to make WMD, the image on the satellite photo is a mobile missile launcher) or there is noise (e.g., dictator X will continue, country Y does not have materials to make WMD, the image on the satellite photo is benign). Colloquially, a

TABLE 4-1 Signal Detection Theory's 2 × 2 World View

		Truth:	
		Signal	Noise
Analyst Says:	Alert	Hit	False alarm
	Quiet	Miss	Correctly quiet

signal means "something is going on" that the intelligence analyst needs to alert someone about and noise means "nothing is going on." The analyst can be correct by issuing an alert when there truly is a signal (a "hit") or by correctly remaining quiet when there truly is no signal.

Note that the examples above appear to be of two different kinds: detection—the detection and identification of existing states of the world (e.g., country Y does have materials to make WMD)—and forecasting future states of the world (e.g., dictator X will be overthrown next month). Weather service tasks relevant to tornadoes illustrate both. A weather forecaster estimates the probability there will be tornadoes in a given time period, and weather observers try to detect tornadoes that have actually formed. So long as the validity of a forecast is eventually known, the distinction between detection and forecasting is not important for signal detection analysis, which unfortunately bears a name reflecting more its World War II origins in detection of airplanes than its wider current use.

Two types of errors The simplistic 2 × 2 world view of signal detection emphasizes that there are inherently two kinds of errors—misses and false alarms. Or there are errors of omission versus errors of commission. Absent a perfect detection system, the analyst must decide whether to err in the direction of a miss or a false alarm.

Graded response Although the analyst's or decision maker's response is dichotomous—alert or not—the strength of the evidence is likely to be a graded response on a more-or-less continuous scale. The inherent problem for the analyst is to decide when the graded evidence is strong enough to issue an alert.

Hit and false alarm rates Commonly used basic measures of detection performance are the hit rate—probability of correctly alerting when a signal is present—and the false alarm rate—incorrectly alerting when a signal is not present. Medical studies of signal detection often report the sensitivity (equivalent to the hit rate, and referred to as the recall rate in some other fields) and specificity (equivalent to one false alarm rate). The more traditional hit rate and false alarm rate are used here, but it is important to recognize that similar measures with different names are sometimes used in different fields. They are all transformations of one another, so the choice is one of convenience.

Assessing detection performance The key issue in this context is how to use the hit and false alarm rates to assess the performance of the detection system, whether that system is an electronic device (e.g., the Preliminary Credibility Assessment Screening System, or PCASS), a human intelligence analyst, or the IC as a whole. If the system were simply guessing, we would expect the hit and false alarm rates to be equal, with the exact rate depending on the system's propensity to "alert." The performance equivalent to guessing is represented by the diagonal line in Figure 4-1, which depicts the relationship between the hit and false alarm rate. The system does better than guessing the extent to which the hit rate exceeds the false alarm rate.

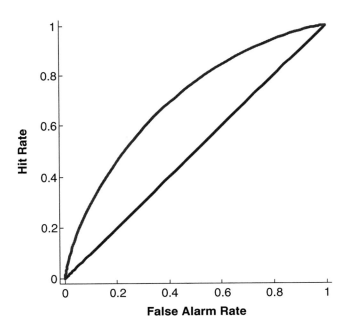

FIGURE 4-1 Inherent trade-off between hit rate and false alarm rate. SOURCE: Generalized from Green and Swets (1966).

The performance of a moderately good detector is depicted in Figure 4-1 by the curved line above the diagonal.

The relationship between the hit and false alarm rates is constrained by curves similar to the one depicted in Figure 4-1, often referred to as ROC (for "receiver operating characteristic") curves. The actual hit and false alarm rates, a point along the curve, is determined when the detector or analyst sets the threshold that the graded response must exceed before an alert is sounded. A conservative threshold—one requiring strong evidence—would produce relatively few false alarms, but consequently, also relatively few hits; this is represented by the open circle at the left lower end of the ROC curve in Figure 4-2. Such a conservative threshold would be appropriate when false alarms were feared much more than misses. If misses were to be avoided at all costs, a liberal threshold would be appropriate, such as the black circle at the upper right end of the ROC curve in Figure 4-2. Note, however, the high hit rate (equivalent to avoiding misses) comes at the expense of a high false alarm rate. The gray circle mid-way

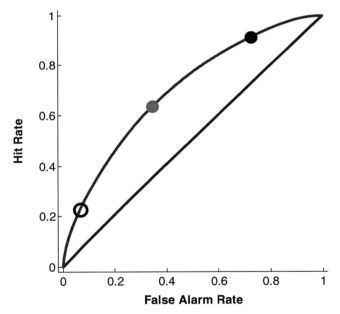

FIGURE 4-2 Differential weighting of misses and false alarms.
NOTE: Lower open circle represents fear of false alarms; upper black circle represents fear of misses; middle gray circle represents balance between the two fears.
SOURCE: Generalized from Green and Swets (1966).

along the ROC curve represents a balancing of the fears or costs of misses and false alarms. None of the marked points on the curve represent better or worse prediction, but simply reflect differential concern for the costs of misses and false alarms. Thus, it is not the actual hit and false alarm rates that characterize performance of the detection system. Instead, either the standardized difference between the hit and false alarm rates $d' = z_{HR} - z_{FAR}$ or the area under the ROC curve (AUC) represent detection accuracy. Figure 4-3 depicts ROC curves representing increasing discriminability as they are further from the diagonal line. An important feature of signal detection theory is that it separates the inherent capability of the detection system (represented by d' or AUC) from the threshold motivated by relative costs of misses and false alarms. Hence, d' or AUC should be used to assess the performance of detection systems, whether they be electronic devices or intelligence analysts.

Changing response bias The actual hit and false alarm rates are determined by the threshold used to change the graded response into an action.

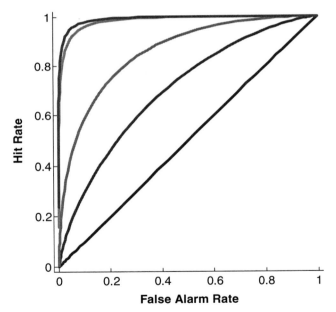

FIGURE 4-3 ROC curves representing increasing detection performance with increasing distance from the diagonal.
SOURCE: Generalized from Green and Swets (1966).

Numerous experiments have shown that human observers change their thresholds in response to change in the relative costs of misses and false alarms. It is not unreasonable to speculate that in the IC, a highly publicized mistake of one kind changes the threshold or response bias in a direction to reduce the likelihood of the kind of error made and thereby increase the likelihood of the other kind of error. An obvious example is that the miss of 9/11 was soon followed by the false alarm of Iraq WMD. There are other similar, but less dramatic, examples. For instance, on May 17, 1987 (during the Iran–Iraq War), an Iraqi fighter jet fired two Exocet antiship missiles into the USS Stark. Although the Iraqi airplane was observed and tracked, it was not deemed hostile and was sent a routine warning. The radar systems on the USS Stark failed to detect the two incoming missiles that killed 37 sailors and injured 21 others. This was a dramatic miss that likely changed the response bias of commanders of ships in the Persian Gulf to err on the side of false alarms rather than misses. Subsequently, on July 3, 1988, the USS Vincennes, a guided-missile cruiser with sophisticated detection systems aided by Airborne Warning and Control System (AWACS) flying in the area, mistook an Iranian commercial airliner taking off from a nearby airport for an Iranian fighter jet on the ground at the same airport. The USS Vincennes shot down the airliner, killing all 290 civilians aboard. This was a serious false alarm.

Strong experimental evidence in other contexts shows that changing the costs of misses and false alarms changes response bias and hence the rates for misses and false alarms (e.g., Healy and Kubovy, 1978). It would be surprising if the IC as a whole and individual analysts did not change their response bias as a consequence to well-publicized misses and false alarms. Importantly, different parts of the IC may be receiving different feedback and therefore be changing their response bias in directions that differ from each other. For example, terrorist analysts learned (and relearned, after the 2009 Christmas day bombing attempt on a transatlantic flight) that avoiding blame for "missing" something is much more important than raising many false alarms, creating a systematic bias to overstatement. This may be reinforced by the military origins of the IC with its penchant for "worst case" analysis because it is better to overestimate the capabilities of an adversary than to underestimate them. On the other hand, those in the IC charged with warning about general problems, such as warning about WMD capabilities, learned the opposite lesson from the Iraq NIE fiasco and may not lean far enough forward in making calls lest they be accused again of exaggerating the evidence or distorting it for political reasons and/ or to avoid providing politicians with judgments that can easily be pushed beyond what analysts intended.

Effect of base rates Importantly, the above discussion omitted any consideration of a simple measure such as *percentage correct* as a measure of detection performance. This is because percentage correct is a function not only of the hit and false alarm rates, but also the base rate for occurrence of the signal. Base rate is the probability that the event of interest occurs in the population of events being examined. For example, when evaluating a medical screening test for, say, prostate cancer, the base rate—the proportion men screened who are expected to truly have prostate cancer—is critical for evaluating the performance of the screening test. Regardless of the detector's inherent quality, extreme base rates can have a profound effect on the percentage of events classified correctly as signal or noise. Many authors provide their favorite examples of the nonintuitive consequences of ignoring base rates (e.g., Heuer, 1999, pp. 157–160, adapts an example to an intelligence problem; National Research Council, 2008, pp. 39–40), and many empirical studies have demonstrated that human decision makers often ignore the effects of base rates (e.g., Kahneman and Tversky, 1973; Bar-Hillel, 1980). Here is an example of a detection problem that illustrates the substantial effects of base rates on percentage accuracy even when the hit rate is very high and the false alarm rate is very low.

> A company believes approximately 2 percent of its employees are drug users. The company administers a screening test to detect drug users. The test is very good with a hit rate of 95 percent and a false alarm rate of only 5 percent. Sara, selected at random for the screening test, receives a positive test result. What is the probability that Sara is actually a drug user?

Note that a drug test with such accuracy would represent extraordinary performance for a detector, represented by the most extreme (i.e., upper left corner) curve in Figure 4-3. For comparison, the detection performance of physicians diagnosing appendicitis or radiologists reading mammograms, for example, is not nearly as good. To answer the probability question for Sara, consider the expected frequencies in Table 4-2 of applying the screening test to 1,000 employees. With a base rate of only 2 percent, we would

TABLE 4-2 Expected Results for 1,000 People Screened by the Drug Test

		Truth:		
		Drug	Clean	Total
Drug Test:	"User"	19	49	68
	"Clean"	1	931	932
	Total	20	980	1,000

expect only 20 of the 1,000 to truly be drug users and the test would correctly identify 19 of those 20 (95 percent hit rate) as users. The remaining 980 employees are not drug users, but the test would incorrectly identify 49 of those 980 (5 percent false alarm rate) as drug users. The numbers in the table follow directly from the given base rate (2 percent), hit rate (95 percent), and false alarm rate (5 percent). Now consider the 68 employees who received positive drug test results. Of those 68, only 19 or 28 percent are truly drug users. Despite a highly accurate test, the probability that Sara (or anyone else with a positive test result) is truly a drug user is only 0.28. The low probability, despite a highly accurate test, is because the low base rate means the test is given many more opportunities (980 versus 20) to make a false alarm than to make a miss. The lesson is that even highly accurate detectors will produce many more false alarms than hits when detecting low base-rate events.

The important IC task of detecting hostile events toward the United States and its citizens is the task of detecting low base-rate events. Only a tiny fraction of all the passengers boarding airplanes or parking vehicles near Times Square are terrorists. Such detection systems will necessarily generate a large number of false alarms for each accurate detection of a terrorist. The signal detection model may be useful for communicating to IC customers and policy makers the inevitability of numerous false alarms in low base-rate detection situations.

Summary of Benefits of Signal Detection Theory

If one is going to keep score of prediction performance, signal detection theory provides an ideal framework. Its fundamental value is separating the effects of base rates, detector accuracy, and cut-point biases motivated by avoiding either false alarms or misses. In their abstract for a review chapter on clinical assessment, McFall and Treat (1999, p. 215) provide an excellent summary of the benefits of signal detection theory. One can read the following and substitute "intelligence assessment" for "clinical assessment."

> The aim of clinical assessment is to gather data that allow us to reduce uncertainty regarding the probabilities of events. This is a Bayesian view of assessment that is consistent with the well-known concept of incremental validity. Conventional approaches to evaluating the accuracy of assessment methods are confounded by the choice of cutting points, by the base rates of events, and by the assessment goal (e.g., nomothetic versus idiographic predictions). Clinical assessors need a common metric for quantifying the information value of assessment data, independent of the cutting points, base rates, or particular application. Signal detection theory (SDT) provides such a metric.

A rephrasing of the two last sentences appropriate for intelligence analysis might be:

> "Intelligence assessors need a common metric for quantifying the information value of intelligence data and inputs, independent of the threshold biases used to change a graded response into action, the base rates of the hostile event to be detected, and whether the goal is to make a decision in a specific instance (e.g., does Country X have stockpile of biological weapons?) or a general rule (e.g., a policy that all airline passengers with certain characteristics be subjected to secondary screening). Signal detection theory (SDT) provides such a metric."

An important benefit of using signal detection theory to evaluate and compare performance of individuals, teams, systems, procedures, and other factors is that it would require only a minimal, almost trivial, addition to the daily activities of the typical analyst. The only additional workload for the analyst would be to produce a probabilistic or categorical prediction of the future events being analyzed. Other researchers—not working analysts—could then subsequently assess the accuracy of those predictions in a signal detection analysis. That is, signal detection methods would not involve any immediate change in how the analysts did their work. Instead, SDT would be used by researchers to sift the wheat from the chaff among the methods and procedures analysts are already using or new ones that might be proposed.

BENEFITS OF KEEPING SCORE

A variety of measures might be used to score the performance of either individual analysts or more likely larger workgroups. A number of alternative, often mathematical, transformations of the traditional signal detection measures exist. For example, O'Brien (2002) uses similar measures—overall accuracy, recall, and precision—from the forecasting and text-retrieval literatures in an intelligence context to evaluate a pattern classification algorithm for predicting country instability. Studies in medicine often use closely related measures of sensitivity and specificity.

Regardless of whatever measures are used to keep score of prediction accuracy—even the less desirable percentage correct measure—studies in a number of contexts have shown that simply reporting scores as feedback have fostered improved performance without any other intervention. We all seem to be self-motivated to score better. An interesting example is an early study of probabilistic weather forecasting in the Netherlands (Murphy and Daan, 1984). In the first year, forecasters simply became acquainted with the process of making probabilistic forecasts. At the beginning of the second year, forecasters received feedback about their performance—they tended to overforecast. At the end of the second year, their accuracy had markedly improved. Murphy and Daan (1984, p. 413) attribute the performance improvement "to the feedback provided to the forecasters at the beginning of the second year of the experiment and to the experience in probability forecasting gained by the forecasters during the first year of the program." Although probabilistic forecasting and its improvement are almost surely more difficult in intelligence predictions than in weather predictions because of the quick and knowable feedback in weather forecasts, the IC might do well to study the history of probabilistic weather forecasts. Such forecasts were once rare (see Murphy's 1998 review of the early history) and resisted, but now have become commonplace and expected with customers making important decisions based on probabilistic information.

Another context in which public scorecards have had substantial benefits is in the hospital setting, where nosocomial infections may occur. The Centers for Disease Control[2] began the voluntary National Nosocomial Infections Surveillance (NNIS) system in 1970 with 20 hospitals. Now more than 300 hospitals participate (NNIS has recently been renamed National Healthcare Safety Network[3]). Hallmarks of the system are "standardized definitions, standardized surveillance component protocols, risk stratification for calculation of infection rates, and provided national benchmark infection rates for inter- and intra-hospital comparisons" (Jarvis, 2003, p. 44). Clearly the publication of infection rates has motivated hospitals to improve and increased searches for successful interventions, whose success in turn was monitored by changes in the published infection rates. In the 1990s, bloodstream infection rates declined 31–43 percent in intensive care units in hospitals participating in NNIS (Centers for Disease Control and Prevention, 2000). The rigorous definitions, careful monitoring, and especially the confidentiality of the NNIS system might provide a useful model for scorekeeping within the IC to improve performance.

EVIDENCED-BASED PRACTICE

Another obvious benefit of being able to keep score is the evaluation of innovations and even existing methods. Many methods used by or proposed to the IC have not been formally evaluated using randomized controlled trials. For example, intelligence analysis tradecraft not evaluated adequately include alternative competing hypotheses, PCASS, and even recent communication innovations such as Intellipedia and A-Space. The scientific literature is replete with examples of conventional wisdom, often based on observational data and anecdotes that turn out to be untrue when

---

[2]Now the Centers for Disease Control and Prevention.

[3]For more information, see http://www.cdc.gov/nhsn/ [accessed October 2010].

scientifically evaluated. Medicine is full of examples of drugs and procedures that medical practitioners firmly believed to be effective, but turned out not to be when evaluated with randomized clinical trials.

An example of the mismatch between practitioner beliefs and actual facts is the conventional wisdom in many disciplines that treatment practice must be tailored to the idiosyncratic characteristics of individuals receiving treatment. However, when tested, the benefits of such tailoring are seldom supported. The education literature has countless articles about learning styles and the importance of tailoring educational material to those styles. However, critical evaluations and meta-analyses (e.g., Pashler et al., 2008) find little or no benefit for tailoring to learning styles. That is, the same good educational techniques are good for everyone, regardless of their putative learning styles. Similarly, treatments for alcoholics were believed to be most effective when tailored to specific patient characteristics. However, Project MATCH, a multisite clinical trial of alcohol treatment funded by the National Institute on Alcohol Abuse and Alcoholism to promote and test this hypothesis, eventually concluded that tailoring treatment to client attributes had little or no benefit (Project MATCH Research Group, 1997, 1998). These specific examples probably have no direct relevance to intelligence analysis except that they demonstrate that many strong beliefs of practitioners, developed over many years of experience, are often not confirmed by scientific experimentation.

The frequent mismatch between beliefs of practitioners and actual verified effects has motivated a vast literature on evidence-based practice. Entering the term "evidence-based" in a Google search in January 2010 generated approximately 48.1 million page hits in fields as diverse as medicine, education, and policing. However, so far only a few instances of evidence-based intelligence analysis have been found. Again, a detailed how-to for evidence-based practice is not appropriate for this chapter.[4] Instead, I suggest by analogy how it might be useful in evaluating tradecraft practice in intelligence analysis. Evidence-based practice is not a panacea nor is it easy to implement, but the benefits of its application in other areas have been enormous.

A useful analogy might be the history of tonsillectomy (Grob, 2007) because it raises many issues similar to those faced in intelligence analysis. According to Grob, removing tonsils became popular once it became an easy surgery because it fit a contemporary disease model and because it stopped the recurrence of certain infections. However, there was no comparison of effectiveness relative either to a control group or to possible increases in other disease once the tonsils were removed. In fact, true randomized clinical trials would have been difficult or unethical because

---

[4]Useful how-to information includes the website http://www.cebm.net [accessed October 2010] of the Centre for Evidence Based Medicine and Straus et al. (2005).

true control groups would have required sham operations. Intelligence analysis may have similar problems implementing true randomized control trials. Only after innumerable tonsils had been removed were clinical trials begun in 1962. The hypothesis that the popularity of tonsillectomies might be motivated primarily by the pecuniary self-interests of the physicians is refuted by the fact that children of physicians had tonsillectomy rates as high or higher than those of other children (Bakwin, 1958). As tonsillectomies increased in frequency, they came to be expected and even demanded by the customers—parents of small children—and some argued for the prophylactic removal of tonsils in all children. Parents continued to request tonsillectomies even after enthusiasm waned among physicians. Only gradually have tonsillectomy rates declined, long after estimates of the benefits declined dramatically. The analogy of intelligence problems to the history of tonsillectomy is sobering. Evidence-based intelligence analysis is likely to be difficult and randomized trials may be nearly impossible (although simulated tournaments might be plausible substitutes). However, the history of tonsillectomy also suggests that evidence-based practice is possible with verified methods eventually supplanting conventional wisdom.

SUMMARY

Many fields akin to intelligence analysis, that is, those that make predictions and diagnoses in the face of uncertainty, have benefited from keeping score. Keeping score itself seems to motivate performance improvement without any specific interventions, presumably because units motivated to improve their scores relative to peers generate their own interventions. There is every reason to expect similar benefits of scorekeeping for intelligence analysis. Scorekeeping is also necessary to be able to implement evidence-based practice to evaluate scientifically existing and proposed tradecraft for intelligence analysis. Although many possible measures might be used as scores, those of signal detection theory seem naturally suited to the uncertainty problems facing the IC that involve problems of low base rates, fluctuating biases toward false alarms and misses, and detector accuracy.

REFERENCES

Bakwin, H. 1958. The tonsil–adenoidectomy enigma. *Journal of Pediatrics* 52(3):339–361.
Bar-Hillel, M. 1980. The base-rate fallacy in probability judgments. *Acta Psychologica* 44:211–233.
Centers for Disease Control and Prevention. 2000. *Hospital infection rates decline using CDC model program.* Press release. Available: http://premierinc.com/safety/topics/patient_safety/downloads/10_nnispress300.pdf [accessed May 2010].

Director of National Intelligence. 2007. *Intelligence community directive (ICD) 203: Analytic standards*. June 21. Available: http://www.dni.gov/electronic_reading_room/ICD_203.pdf [accessed May 2010].

Green, D. M., and J. Swets. 1966. *Signal detection theory and psychophysics*. New York: John Wiley & Sons.

Grob, G. N. 2007. The rise and decline of tonsillectomy in twentieth-century America. *Journal of the History of Medicine and Allied Sciences* 62:383–421.

Healy, A. F., and M. Kubovy. 1978. The effects of payoffs and prior probabilities on indexes of performance and cutoff location in recognition memory. *Memory and Cognition* 6(5):544–553.

Heuer, R. J., Jr. 1999. *Psychology of intelligence analysis*. Washington, DC: Center for the Study of Intelligence, Central Intelligence Agency.

Jarvis, W. R. 2003. Benchmarking for prevention: The Centers for Disease Control and Prevention's National Nosocomial Infections Surveillance (NNIS) system experience. *Infection* 31(Suppl. 2):44–48.

Kahneman, D., and A. Tversky. 1973. Psychology of prediction. *Psychological Review* 80(4):237–251.

Kent, S. 1964. Words of estimative probability. *Studies of Intelligence* 8(4). Available: https://www.cia.gov/library/center-for-the-study-of-intelligence/kent-csi/vol8no4/html/v08i4a06p_0001.htm [accessed May 2010].

Lusted, L. B. 1971. Signal detectability and medical decision-making. *Science* 171(3977):1217–1219.

McFall, R. M., and T. A. Treat. 1999. Quantifying the information value of clinical assessments with signal detection theory. *Annual Review of Psychology* 50:215–241.

McNichol, D. A. 2004. *A primer of signal detection theory*. London, UK: Allen and Unwin.

Murphy, A. H. 1998. The early history of probability forecasts: Some extensions and clarifications. *Weather and Forecasting* 13(1):5–15.

Murphy, A. H., and H. Daan. 1984. Impacts of feedback and experience on the quality of subjective probability forecasts: Comparison of results from the first and second years of the Zierikzee experiment. *Monthly Weather Review* 112(3):413–423.

National Research Council. 2003. *The polygraph and lie detection*. Committee to Review the Scientific Evidence on the Polygraph. Division of Behavioral and Social Sciences and Education. Washington, DC: The National Academies Press.

National Research Council. 2008. *Emerging cognitive neuroscience and related technologies*. Committee on Military and Intelligence Methodology for Emergent Neurophysiological and Cognitive/Neural Research Methods in the Next Two Decades. Division of Behavioral and Social Sciences and Education. Washington, DC: The National Academies Press.

O'Brien, S. 2002. Anticipating the good, the bad, and the ugly: An early warning approach to conflict and instability analysis. *The Journal of Conflict Resolution* 46(6):791–811.

Oliver, R., O. Bjoertomt, R. Greenwood, and J. Rothwell. 2008. "Noisy patients"—Can signal detection theory help? *Nature Clinical Practice Neurology* 4(6):306–316.

Pashler, H., M. McDaniel, D. Rohrer, and R. Bjork. 2008. Learning styles: Concepts and evidence. *Psychological Science in the Public Interest* 9:106–119.

Project MATCH Research Group. 1997. Project MATCH secondary a priori hypotheses. *Addiction* 92:1671–1698.

Project MATCH Research Group. 1998. Matching alcoholism treatments to client heterogeneity: Project MATCH posttreatment drinking outcomes. *Journal of Studies on Alcohol* 59(6):631–639.

Sorkin, R., C. Hays, and R. West. 2001. Signal-detection analysis of group decision making. *Psychological Review* 108(1):183–203.

Sorkin, R., S. Luan, and J. Itzkowitz. 2004. Group decision and deliberation: A distributed detection process. In D. J. Koehler and N. Harvey, eds., *Blackwell handbook of judgment and decision making* (pp. 464–484). Malden, MA: Blackwell.

Straus, S. E., W. S. Richardson, P. Glasziou, and R. B. Haynes. 2005. *Evidence-based medicine,* 3rd ed. London, UK: Churchill Livingstone.

Swets, J. A., R. M. Dawes, and J. Monahan. 2000. Psychological science can improve diagnostic decisions. *Psychological Science in the Public Interest* 1:1–26.

Tanner, W. P., Jr., and J. A. Swets. 1954. A decision-making theory of visual detection. *Psychological Review* 61(6):401–409.

Wickens, T. 2001. *Elementary signal detection theory.* New York: Oxford University Press.

5

Qualitative Analysis for the Intelligence Community

Kiron K. Skinner

WHAT IS THE ISSUE?

U.S. national security depends on the closely linked network of the data collector, the analyst, and the policy maker, or customer. The analyst, who serves as the bridge between the data collector and the policy maker, occupies a crucial position in this policy continuum (Barry et al., 1994; Davis, 1996; Director of National Intelligence, 2008). The magnitude of what the intelligence analyst faces regularly becomes clear when the range of the analyst's tasks is considered: Although collectors provide the analyst with data, the analyst is centrally involved in the data process. After reviewing the assembled data, the analyst may need to redirect the collector. The analyst is responsible for addressing a range of issues related to the quantity, quality, and reliability of the information on which his or her assessments must rest. In many situations, the analyst tries to make sense of a single case using qualitative methods, and must turn a point of view (the customer's, his or her own, or both) into testable hypotheses. Customers often request the completion of all of this work in a short time. Sometimes the intelligence officer has limited knowledge of part of a complex issue under investigation. Each factor adds a layer of difficulty that could inhibit systematic qualitative analysis. Yet qualitative analysis is an intelligence community (IC) mainstay.

These challenges have always been apparent to the IC and those who study its work and processes. Sherman Kent addressed many of the challenges facing the IC in *Strategic Intelligence for American World Policy* (1951). More than a decade later, in her 1962 study on the Japanese attack on Pearl Harbor, Roberta Wohlstetter wrote: "To discriminate significant sounds against this background of noise, one has to be listening for something or for one of several things. In short, one needs not only an ear, but a variety of hypotheses that guide observation" (Wohlstetter, 1962, p. 56). Similar suggestions run through the literature on the IC (Berkowitz and Goodman, 1989; Betts, 1978; Cooper, 2005; George and Bruce, 2008; Goodman et al., 1996; Heuer, 1999; Jervis, 2010; Johnston, 2005; Knorr, 1964; Lieberthal, 2009; Sims and Gerber, 2005; Turner, 2006). National commissions and government studies on intelligence failures also have advocated further analytic development of the intelligence tradecraft. For instance, in his assessment of the IC's lack of foresight on India's nuclear test in 1998, Admiral David Jeremiah endorsed the use of red-team analysis. Responding to the Jeremiah Report, Director of Central Intelligence (DCI) George Tenet called for an "institutionalized . . . system of subjecting our analysis to contrary views" (Tenet, 1998, p. 1).

A full complement of structured analytic techniques for qualitative assessments has been developed within the IC in the past several decades (e.g., Heuer and Pherson, 2010). The Analysis of Competing Hypotheses is a prominent method. It "demands that analysts explicitly identify all the reasonable alternative hypotheses, then array the evidence against each hypothesis—rather than evaluating the plausibility of each hypothesis one at a time" (U.S. Government, 2009, p. 14). The method also calls for "report[ing] all the conclusions, including the weaker hypotheses that should still be monitored as new information becomes available" (U.S. Government, 2009, p. 15). Other structured analytic techniques presented in tradecraft manuals include Alternative Futures, Chronologies and Time Lines, Description Detection, Devil's Advocacy, Force Field Analysis, High-Impact/Low-Probability Analysis, Hypotheses Generator, Indicators, Key Assumptions Check, Multiple Scenarios Generation, Outside-In Thinking, Pre-Mortem Assessment, Quadrant Crunching, Red Hat Analysis, Social Network Analysis, Structured Brainstorming, and Team A/Team B (Heuer and Pherson, 2010).

These methods have common characteristics. They challenge prevailing perspectives by providing alternative modes of thinking. Some are much more explicit about stating the assumptions and hypotheses than are the less formal, traditional methods. Researchers debate whether structured analytic techniques actually improve the analytic product, but the IC remains committed to refining these methods and teaching them in their training centers (Marrin, 2009).

One academic discipline that may offer analysts assistance in improving their analyses and forecasts is the study of political science. Over the years political scientists have developed a variety of qualitative methods that might be used by intelligence analysts either in real time to increase the usefulness and accuracy of their analyses or retrospectively to better assess previous reports. This chapter will focus on one such method in particular, the Strategic Perspective or SP (Bueno de Mesquita et al., 2003; Bueno de Mesquita, 2010). After a brief description of the approach, the chapter will offer two examples to illustrate how it might be used and the types of insights it can provide. Both examples are retrospective looks at what proved to be failures of intelligence analysis. The examples are offered with the understanding that hindsight is always sharper, and that what seems straightforward from the comfortable perspective of 25 years down the road is much less straightforward when the clock is ticking, lives are at stake, and the answer is highly uncertain. Nonetheless, it is hoped that these retrospective examples will provide an indication of how the Strategic Perspective may help analysts deepen their understanding of situations and perhaps improve the accuracy of their forecasts.

THEORETICAL GROUNDING:
THE STRATEGIC PERSPECTIVE

The international system poses ongoing dilemmas for statesmen, scholars, and policy analysts. Is the state, the nation, or some other entity the core unit of analysis? What should be the major dependent variables: war/peace, cooperation/discord, and so on? What are the major explanatory variables: international institutions, power, security, wealth, or a combination of these factors? On what level of analysis (international system, state level, individual level, or still others) should questions be raised and explanations offered? When and how should levels be combined for explanation and prediction?

The Strategic Perspective provides a theoretical perspective on state behavior, political leadership, and the connections between domestic politics and international relations. Its tenets regarding the relationship between a state's type of regime and its public policy have had a major effect on scholarly work in recent decades (among many others, see Bernauer and Koubi, 2009; Brown and Mobarak, 2009; Chhibber and Nooruddin, 2004; Chiozza and Goemans, 2004; Gelpi and Grieco, 2001; Goemans, 2000; Kilchevsky et al., 2007; Licht, 2009; McDonald, 2007; McGillivray and Smith, 2008; Peceny and Butler, 2004). This research can be particularly useful for IC analysts and policy makers because it is a theory about actual decision making as opposed to arguments about how structural arrangements at the international level determine outcomes and lead to fixed preferences for states. SP holds that the decision making of leaders determines or influences much of politics. In this theory, leaders, not nation-states, are the core unit of analysis. Leaders are uniquely situated in politics. As heads of government, they must respond to both domestic politics and international challenges. They must weigh how their domestic decisions affect international relations, and vice versa. As a result, the international political situation is strongly influenced by leaders' calculations about how their decisions on domestic and foreign policy will affect their necessary domestic coalitions, and how foreign challenges can be held at bay. In political systems with large winning coalitions, such as democracies, leaders perforce pursue public policies that satisfy millions of people. By contrast, in autocracies and other small-coalition countries, leaders can stay in power by dispensing private benefits to coalition members and do not need to consider the desires of the majority of the population.

The SP has a number of aspects that should make it valuable for use by the IC. The theory defines international relations as "the product of the cumulative impact of the foreign policies of the nations of the world. Foreign policies are always linked to and partially shaped by internal politics, especially domestic political concerns that influence a leader's prospects of retaining his or her job" (Bueno de Mesquita, 2006, p. 2). This definition removes the conventional distinction scholars have made between foreign policy and international relations (IR) as well as the division between security studies and political economy. Students of foreign policy typically write about specific decisions or crises, or they develop mid-range theories that apply to a small set of foreign-policy cases. IR specialists, on the other hand, often ignore specific foreign-policy decisions in an attempt to develop higher altitude explanations for state behavior. SP is a move toward developing a theory of politics that explains all public policy choices of leaders, but, in the case of foreign policy, it links leaders' choices to larger factors in the international system. The theoretical principles about the relationship between foreign policy and international outcomes apply to issues of both national security and political economy.

SP offers other scientifically useful tools as well. In locating explanation and prediction at the domestic and international levels (leaders calculate public policy based on what will both satisfy their domestic coalition and stave off foreign threats), the distinction between these two levels is swept away. In identifying coalition size as the key institutional feature that incentivizes and constrains leaders and organizes the polity, the noise of domestic politics is intellectually managed. The probable international effects of religion, culture, nationalism, and civil strife are filtered through the institutional feature of coalition size. Thus, researchers will find that no case is so unique that systematic analysis across a class of cases becomes impossible. Unlike structural theories, SP holds that preferences and behavior are not determined by a state's position in the international structure of bipolarity, multipolarity, or hierarchy. Rather, the theory contends that state behavior and preferences are fluid, determined in large measure by how leaders navigate domestic and international challenges to their survival. Because leaders are constantly speculating what their domestic and international adversaries will do, all decisions and interactions are strategic and contingent—a fact not captured in conventional IR theories. The Strategic Perspective is a formal theory that can be used in qualitative and quantitative analysis.

The National Intelligence Strategy has identified violent extremist groups, insurgents, and transnational criminal organizations as "non-state and sub-state actors . . . [that affect U.S.] national security" (Director of National Intelligence, 2009, p. 3). IR is primarily about people: how they interact across state borders and how their actions within borders affect what happens internationally. Structural theories and other traditional modes of thinking have recognized that people matter, but they have not acknowledged them operationally as the very fabric of international relations. The focus on political leadership in SP provides an organizing principle for thinking through the role of people (leaders and constituents). Why do leaders remain in power in countries dominated by public policies that support or produce kleptocracy, rent seeking, corruption, unsuccessful international wars, and/or civil unrest? Intelligence analysts and policy makers need explanations and possibilities for prediction that are empirically grounded from the bottom up. The current international system is as much about how internal challenges to state power simultaneously affect domestic politics and relations among states as it is about how nation-states interact.

The Strategic Perspective provides direction in uncovering the strategic interaction taking place in a specific case. When there are multiple hypotheses from which to choose, those that can best be turned into strategic interaction stories should have top priority. Such cases train attention on the key actors, the constraints they face, and the calculations they make in terms of their domestic and international rivals. These cases require the analyst to think through the policy trade-offs that political actors must make, their contemplations off the path of equilibrium, and, more generally, contingent behavior. Importantly, uncovering a strategic interaction story can be determined regardless of the amount of data readily available.

SP can and has been applied to scenarios other than the dilemmas faced by heads of government. All organizational leaders have constituency challenges, and SP is a theory about the policy choices that leaders make in light of such challenges and external threats. Among its numerous applications, SP can help explain and predict what business leaders and heads of terrorist organizations will do.

INSIGHTS FROM THE STRATEGIC PERSPECTIVE

The late Sen. Daniel Patrick Moynihan (D-NY) remarked, "If it seems simple in the archives, try it in the maelstrom" (Moynihan and Weaver, 1978, p. vii). Intellectual humility should be the attitude of anyone reviewing intelligence and policy scenarios, especially those undertaken in periods of high tension or major crises. The intelligence officer and the policy maker do not have the luxury of time or the positive benefits sometimes associated with hindsight. Similarly, "the lessons of hindsight do not guarantee improvement in foresight, and hypothetical solutions to failure only occasionally produce improvement in practice" (Betts, 1978, p. 62).

Tempered by these admonitions, the goal of this section is to show members of the IC how the Strategic Perspective can enhance description, explanation, and prediction. It will do so by offering a retrospective look at two well-known intelligence failures, the Iranian revolution of 1979 and India's nuclear tests in 1998, and indicating how the use of SP might have led analysts at the time to understand more clearly the forces that led to the eventual outcomes.

As described above, the central insight in the Strategic Perspective is that international relations and domestic issues are irretrievably linked, with this linkage arising from the fact that leaders act in such a way to stay in power. The necessary "coalition" is the collection of people and groups that a leader needs to stay in power. SP provides intellectual guidance in understanding how decisions on international issues are shaped by domestic considerations. Leaders will generally act in such a way as to remain in power; this requires that they maintain a coalition powerful enough to keep them in office, and to maintain this coalition, leaders must act in ways that satisfy the coalition.

The Iranian Revolution, 1979

The Strategic Perspective may be applied to Mohammad Reza Shah Pahlavi's fall from power in Iran. The shah's long rule came to an end in early 1979 amidst the emerging Iranian revolution. Among other factors, misunderstanding his domestic political base undermined the shah's reign and had major implications for international relations.

Starting in the 1960s, oil exports constituted the lion's share of government revenues for Iran. Between 1963 and 1977, oil revenues as a percentage of government income jumped from 45 to 77 percent (Parsa, 1989; Abrahamian, 1980). International demand for oil made the state dependent on international consumption. Thus, Iran's economy and government were deeply affected by global-market phenomena (Karshenas, 1990; Parsa, 1989). Oil exports produced extreme wealth for a small group of elites.

The shah undertook modernization projects that were flawed and highly dependent on Western technology (Keddie and Richard, 1981). These projects further deepened Tehran's dependence on the West. Development funds generally were used for a range of infrastructure projects and the financial realm. Funds oriented toward the private sector were targeted largely at urban professionals, leaving the poorest Iranians outside the pool of the emerging economic activity (Parsa, 1989). Iran's massive oil wealth was not creating a large political base for the shah.

The bazaaris were one social group that became alienated from the shah's policies, and they were an important political, social, and economic force. "By the time of the revolution, Tehran's central bazaar, the heart of the nation's trade, numbered close to 40,000 shops and workshops. . . . Despite a relative decline, bazaaris controlled most of the national trade in the 1970s, including more than two-thirds of the nation's domestic wholesale trade and more than 30 percent of all imports" (Parsa, 1989, pp. 92–93). The bazaaris benefitted from some of the shah's economic policies, and they generally supported his regime. For instance, during the shah's repressive response to the uprising by religious students in 1975, which reportedly left dozens of students dead and many others imprisoned, shop owners did not shut down in protest (Parsa, 1989).

The price controls the shah imposed in August 1975 began to be felt by shopkeepers, however, and many of them were subjected to government-led investigations or forced out of business by 1977. That year, the bazaaris joined forces with religious groups to protest the shah's policies and they closed their stores en masse (Parsa, 1989). Government policies combined with the global economic downturn helped to account for this change.

The shah's power base appeared to be the urban and oil elites who benefitted from his economic policies, based on oil exports as well as his foreign policy of close reliance on the United States. The elites he relied on for support and protection did not actually constitute a coalition of the sort that all leaders need to stay in power. Over time, groups like the bazaaris, which were part of Iran's domestic economic engine, found common cause with religious forces, including the exiled Ayatollah Khomeini. Their response to the shah, his policies, and his alliance with the West ultimately undermined the shah's reign. It was not just one economic segment or one religious faction that came to oppose the shah's regime. Homa Katouzian (1998, p. 36) writes, "there was a massive revolt, true to the ancient pattern, of the society against the state, almost irrespective of occupation, rank, wealth and income, education, or degree of religious commitment."

The Strategic Perspective directs the researcher, as well as the policy maker and the statesman, to identify the relevant coalition a leader needs to stay in power. The theoretical perspective does not contend that a leader will correctly perceive the relevant coalition or know how to satisfy that coalition with public or private benefits. It merely states that these factors are essential for political survival. The shah remained in power for a long time, but the domestic environment was evolving.

Furthermore, under President Jimmy Carter, the shah's international support coalition was falling away. On his New Year's visit to Iran in

1977–1978, the U.S. President toasted the shah, declaring: "There is no other head of state with whom I feel on friendlier terms and to whom I feel more gratitude" (cited by Tyler, 2009, p. 213). At the same time, President Carter's human rights approach to foreign policy made him less sympathetic than earlier U.S. presidents to the shah's internal predicament. He ultimately decided not to intervene, stating: "We have never had any intention and don't have any intention of trying to intercede in the internal political affairs of Iran. We primarily want an absence of violence and bloodshed. . . . We personally prefer that the shah maintain a major role in the government, but that is a decision for the Iranian people to make" (quoted in Sick, 1985, p. 128). Debate about supporting the shah raged within the Carter Administration. In hindsight, it seems clear that U.S. policy might have been somewhat different if there had been a better understanding of Iranian domestic politics and possible international outcomes resulting from Iran's internal crisis. At the least, SP analysis would have led to greater texture in U.S. policy.

India's Nuclear Tests, 1998

On May 11, 1998, Atal Bihari Vajpayee, the new prime minister of India, announced that earlier that day his government had tested three nuclear devices (Associated Press, 1998; India tests nuclear devices, 1998). Following the tests, Sen. Richard Shelby (R-AL), a member of the Senate Select Committee on Intelligence, called DCI George Tenet and asked what happened. Tenet replied, "Senator, we didn't have a clue" (Tenet and Harlow, 2008, p. 44). On May 13, the Indian government announced that it had undertaken a second round of nuclear tests. "I personally woke up this morning and I did not know about it," Robert J. Einhorn, deputy assistant secretary of state for nonproliferation, told the Senate Foreign Relations Committee on the day of the second tests (Einhorn, 1998, p. 16; Pincus, 1998; Richelson, 2006).

The Strategic Perspective sheds light on why India would risk international retribution and economic sanctions, among other things, by testing nuclear devices, which it had not done since 1974.

Vajpayee was a member of India's Bharatiya Janata Party (BJP), which won a plurality of the vote in 1996. Vajpayee took the oath of office on May 16, but needed a parliamentary confidence vote within 15 days. As soon as he took office, Vajpayee approved nuclear testing. U.S. intelligence noted the impending test, and the Clinton Administration pressured India to reverse course. In any case, the BJP lost the parliamentary vote on May 28 and was replaced by a United Front government (Perkovich, 1999). During his 1998 campaign, Vajpayee once again advocated nuclear testing (Perkovich, 1999).

Tenet appointed Admiral (Retired) David E. Jeremiah, former vice chairman of the Joint Chiefs of Staff, to lead an investigation of the intelligence lapse. One of Jeremiah's conclusions indicates that a core principle of the Strategic Perspective had been violated:

> [B]oth the intelligence and the policy communities had an underlying mindset going into these tests that the BJP would behave as we behave. For instance, there is an assumption that the BJP platform would mirror Western political platforms. In other words, a politician is going to say something in his political platform leading up to the elections, but not necessarily follow through on the platform once he takes office and is exposed to the immensity of his problem. The BJP was dead serious. . . . (Best and Cumming, 2007, p. 23)

Thus, even though the BJP had indicated it would quickly resume nuclear testing upon being elected, much of the analysis at the time downplayed the likelihood of the party following through on its pledge, or at least expected that the fulfillment of the pledge would not come nearly as soon as it did. But SP research has shown that during campaigns for office in the United States, the rhetorical commitments candidates make are often more than mere rhetoric. They are typically made to create or hold together a necessary coalition, and once in office the commitments can be binding (Skinner et al., 2007). SP unpacks domestic politics in ways that go against conventional thinking about domestic politics itself and how it affects foreign policy.

Ultimately, the link between domestic politics and international outcomes was not lost on the IC during its post mortem on India's nuclear testing. Testifying before the Senate Select Committee on Intelligence, DCI Tenet said: "[E]ven in the absence of robust collection, we should have questioned harder the potential impact the change in the Indian government would have on India's desire to advance its nuclear program and assert itself as a world power" (Tenet, 1998).

SP not only suggests that U.S. analysts and policy makers should have paid closer attention to the domestic and international implications of the Indian election, but it also provides a mechanism (the relationship between a leader and his core support coalition) for thinking through the implications of what was taking place in the election. As important as Tenet's insight is, it does not provide a precise mechanism for understanding the potential international effects of India's change in government. SP goes beyond saying that domestic politics matter.

What coalition was Vajpayee satisfying? Traditionally, the BJP has been a right-wing, nationalist Hindu party. The party campaigned on an inclusive platform, but the candidate had to walk a fine line between the right-wing base, which included many elites, and others. National security was one area in which the base could be satisfied, and it had the further advantage of not being a high-priority issue for the many nonelites BJP needed. Many elites wanted their country to be a full nuclear power. Campaigning on this issue made good political sense. It was a real issue (Perkovich, 1999). *The Economist* (India as a nuclear power, 1998, p. 20) discussed the matter soon after India's nuclear tests:

> The new coalition will be fractious. The compromises needed to govern will cramp the BJP's Hindu-nationalist style. But the nuclear issue is popular with voters proud of India's technological prowess. Building nuclear weapons could be one of the few policies the coalition can agree on and thus the easiest way for the BJP to trumpet its Hindu-nationalist pride.

Regional factors were also relevant. On April 6, 1998, Pakistan had tested the Guari Missile, a new ballistic missile. Pakistan could hit parts of India with these weapons (Perkovich, 1999). China became a nuclear power in 1966. There were long-standing tensions between the United States and former Soviet Union on border issues and relations with India and China (Synnott, 1999). In a letter to President Clinton on May 11, 1998, the day of the first set of tests, Vajpayee pointed a finger at China: "We have an overt nuclear-weapon state on our borders . . . a state which committed armed aggression against India in 1962" (Perkovich, 1999, p. 417). The claim here is not that the tensions India had with China, Pakistan, or both countries were fully responsible for the nuclear tests. Rather, if one took the campaign pledge seriously, then considering how external threats might make the pledge more or less credible would have been worthwhile.

CONCLUDING STATEMENT

The IC has committed substantial resources to developing structured analytic techniques and training its officers to use them. Although the face value of these techniques is not uniformly clear, astute researchers and practitioners contend that the techniques are an essential part of the intelligence officer's analytic toolkit, and work must be done continually to test and further develop the scientific rigor of the techniques (Heuer and Pherson, 2010; Pherson, 2008).

This essay has sought to reemphasize the importance of structured qualitative analysis in the IC by demonstrating how a major theoretical project in political science understands international politics and can be applied to qualitative analysis. Analysts in Afghanistan contend that unpacking the state is the most significant barrier to providing credible intelligence (Flynn et al., 2010). A background theory that helps researchers, analysts, and policy makers think systematically about subnational forces and how they affect state policy and international relations is especially important in the 21st century.

REFERENCES

Abrahamian, E. 1980. Structural causes of the Iranian revolution. *MERIP Reports No. 87: Iran's revolution: The rural dimension* (pp. 21–26). Washington, DC: Middle East Research and Information Project.

Associated Press. 1998. India explodes nuclear device: World community dismayed at testing. *Cincinnati Post,* May 12, A2.

Barry, J. A., J. Davis, D. D. Gries, and J. Sullivan. 1994. Bridging the intelligence–policy divide. *Studies in Intelligence* 37(5):1–8.

Berkowitz, B. D., and A. E. Goodman. 1989. *Strategic intelligence for American national security.* Princeton, NJ: Princeton University Press.

Bernauer, T., and V. Koubi. 2009. Effects of political institutions on air quality. *Ecological Economics* 68(5):1355–1365.

Best, R. A., and A. Cumming. 2007. *Open Source Intelligence (OSINT): Issues for Congress.* Washington, DC: Congressional Research Service. Available: http://www.fas.org/sgp/crs/intel/RL34270.pdf [accessed May 2010].

Betts, R. K. 1978. Analysis, war, and decision: Why intelligence failures are inevitable. *World Politics* 31(1):61–89.

Brown, D. S., and A. M. Mobarak. 2009. The transforming power of democracy: Regime type and the distribution of electricity. *American Political Science Review* 103(2):193–213.

Bueno de Mesquita, B. 2006. *Principles of international politics: People's power, preferences, and perceptions,* 3rd ed. Washington, DC: CQ Press.

Bueno de Mesquita, B. 2010. *Principles of international politics,* 4th ed. Washington, DC: CQ Press.

Bueno de Mesquita, B., A. Smith, R. M. Siverson, and J. D. Morrow. 2003. *The logic of political survival.* Cambridge, MA: The MIT Press.

Chhibber, P., and I. Nooruddin. 2004. Do party systems count? The number of parties and government performance in the Indian states. *Comparative Political Studies* 37(2):152–187.

Chiozza, G., and H. E. Goemans. 2004. International conflict and the tenure of leaders: Is war still *ex post* inefficient? *American Journal of Political Science* 48(3):604–619.

Cooper, J. R. 2005. *Curing analytic pathologies: Pathways to improved intelligence analysis.* Washington, DC: Center for the Study of Intelligence, Central Intelligence Agency.

Davis, J. 1996. The challenge of managing uncertainty: Paul Wolfowitz on intelligence–policy relations. *Studies in Intelligence* 39(5):35–42.

Director of National Intelligence. 2008. *Vision 2015: A globally networked and integrated intelligence enterprise.* Washington, DC: Office of the Director of National Intelligence. Available: http://www.dni.gov/reports/Vision_2015.pdf [accessed October 2010].

Director of National Intelligence. 2009. *The national intelligence strategy of the United States of America.* Washington, DC: Office of the Director of National Intelligence. Available: http://www.dni.gov/reports/2009_NIS.pdf [accessed May 2010].

Einhorn, R. 1998. U.S. Congress, U.S. Senate, Committee on Foreign Relations, Subcommittee on Near Eastern and South Asian Affairs. *Crisis in South Asia: India's nuclear tests; Pakistan's nuclear tests; India and Pakistan: What's next?* 105th Cong., 2nd Sess. May 13.

Flynn, M. T., M. Pottinger, and P. D. Batchelor. 2010. *Fixing intel: A blueprint for making intelligence relevant in Afghanistan.* Washington, DC: Center for New American Security. Available: http://www.cnas.org/files/documents/publications/AfghanIntel_Flynn_Jan2010_code507_voices.pdf [accessed May 2010].

Gelpi, C., and J. M. Grieco. 2001. Attracting trouble: Democracy, leadership tenure, and the targeting of militarized challenges, 1918–1992. *Journal of Conflict Resolution* 45(6):794–817.

George, R. Z., and J. B. Bruce, eds. 2008. *Analyzing intelligence: Origins, obstacles, and innovations*. Washington, DC: Georgetown University Press.

Goemans, H. E. 2000. Fighting for survival: The fate of leaders and the duration of war. *Journal of Conflict Resolution* 44(5):555–579.

Goodman, A. E., G. F. Treverton, and P. Zelikow. 1996. *In from the cold*. New York: The Twentieth Century Fund Press.

Heuer, R. J., Jr. 1999. *Psychology of intelligence analysis*. Washington, DC: Center for the Study of Intelligence, Central Intelligence Agency.

Heuer, R. J., Jr., and R. H. Pherson. 2010. *Structured analytic techniques for intelligence analysis*. Washington, DC: CQ Press.

India as a nuclear power. 1998. *The Economist*, March 28, 20.

India tests nuclear devices. 1998. *Austin American Statesman*, May 12, A1.

Jervis, R. 2010. *Why intelligence fails: Lessons from the Iranian revolution and the Iraq war*. Ithaca, NY: Cornell University Press.

Johnston, R. 2005. *Analytic culture in the U.S. intelligence community: An ethnographic study*. Washington, DC: Center for the Study of Intelligence, Central Intelligence Agency.

Karshenas, M. 1990. *Oil, state and industrialization in Iran*. New York: Cambridge University Press.

Katouzian, H. 1998. Problems in democracy and the public sphere in modern Iran. *Comparative Studies of South Asia, Africa and the Middle East* 18(2):31–37.

Keddie, N. R., and Y. Richard. 1981. *Roots of revolution: An interpretive history of modern Iran*. New Haven, CT: Yale University Press.

Kent, S. 1951. *Strategic intelligence for American world policy*. Princeton, NJ: Princeton University Press.

Kilchevsky, A., J. Cason, and K. Wandschneider. 2007. Peace and economic interdependence in the Middle East. *World Economy* 30(4):647–664.

Knorr, K. 1964. Failures in national intelligence estimates: The case of the Cuban missiles. *World Politics* 16(3):455–467.

Licht, A. A. 2009. Coming into money: The impact of foreign aid on leader survival. *Journal of Conflict Resolution* 54(1):58–87.

Lieberthal, K. 2009. *The U.S. intelligence community and foreign policy: Getting analysis right*. Washington, DC: Brookings Institution.

Marrin, S. 2009. Training and educating U.S. intelligence analysts. *International Journal of Intelligence and CounterIntelligence* 22(1):131–146.

McDonald, P. J. 2007. The purse strings of peace. *American Journal of Political Science* 51(3):569–582.

McGillivray, F., and A. Smith. 2008. *Punishing the prince*. Princeton, NJ: Princeton University Press.

Moynihan, D. P., and S. Weaver. 1978. *A dangerous place*. Boston, MA: Little, Brown.

Parsa, M. 1989. *Social origins of the Iranian revolution*. New Brunswick, NJ: Rutgers University Press.

Peceny, M., and C. K. Butler. 2004. The conflict behavior of authoritarian regimes. *International Politics* 41(4):565–581.

Perkovich, G. 1999. *India's nuclear bomb: The impact on global proliferation*. Berkeley, CA: University of California Press.

Pherson, R. H. 2008. *Handbook of analytic tools and techniques*. Reston, VA: Pherson Associates.

Pincus, W. 1998. 2 new tests again catch U.S. intelligence off guard. *Washington Post*, May 14, A28.

Richelson, J. T. 2006. *Spying on the bomb: American nuclear intelligence from Nazi Germany to Iran and North Korea*. New York: W. W. Norton and Company.

Sick, G. 1985. *All fall down: America's tragic encounter with Iran*. New York: Random House.

Sims, J. E., and B. Gerber. 2005. *Transforming U.S. intelligence*. Washington, DC: Georgetown University Press.

Skinner, K. K., S. Kudelia, B. Bueno de Mesquita, and C. Rice. 2007. *The strategy of campaigning*. Ann Arbor: University of Michigan Press.

Synnott, H. 1999. *The causes and consequences of South Asia's nuclear tests*. Adelphi Paper 332. London, UK: International Institute for Strategic Studies and Oxford University Press.

Tenet, G. 1998. U.S. Congress, U.S. Senate, Senate Select Committee on Intelligence, *Testimony on the Jeremiah Report by DCI Tenet*. June 2. Available: http://www.foia.cia.gov/browse_docs.asp?doc_no=0001380715 [accessed October 2010].

Tenet, G., and B. Harlow. 2008. *At the center of the storm: The CIA during America's time of crisis*, 1st ed. New York: Harper Perennial.

Turner, M. A. 2006. *Why secret intelligence fails*, revised ed. Washington, DC: Potomac Books.

Tyler, P. 2009. *A world of trouble: The White House and the Middle East—from the cold war to the war on terror*. New York: Farrar, Straus and Giroux.

U.S. Government. 2009. *A tradecraft primer: Structured analytic techniques for improving intelligence analysis*. Available: https://www.cia.gov/library/center-for-the-study-of-intelligence/csi-publications/books-and-monographs/Tradecraft%20Primer-apr09.pdf [accessed May 2010].

Wohlstetter, R. 1962. *Pearl Harbor: Warning and decision*. Stanford, CA: Stanford University Press.

Part III

Analysts

Analysis depends on the skills, training, and judgment of the analysts. The four papers in this section report and apply behavioral and social sciences research on individual reasoning, intuitive theories of behavior, group processes, and intergroup dynamics. Each topic was selected because it represents some of the most significant challenges to and opportunities for improving the way analysts perform their work.

In Chapter 6, Barbara A. Spellman describes some of the vast research on individual reasoning. Much of that research details systematic shortcomings and biases in reasoning. Spellman illustrates how recent theories explain such shortcomings as products of people's desire to seek causes and explanations of events, people's tendency to see each situation as unique, and the interaction between conscious and unconscious reasoning systems. Understanding these general reasoning processes, and how they may lead to errors, can contribute to improving analysis by improving the design of analysts' training, tasks, tools, and work environments.

In Chapter 7, Hal Arkes and James Kajdasz present the intuitive theories that guide individuals' interpretation of others' behavior, a fundamental task of intelligence analysts. They show how these intuitive theories are often wrong and how they can lead to erroneous inferences. As examples, they describe tendencies to attribute individuals' actions to personal characteristics, neglecting situational constraints; exaggerate confidence in the quality of one's assessments and predictions; underestimate the risk of relying on expertise; place unwarranted confidence in gathering additional information; and confuse the role of intuition in judgment. Arkes and

Kajdasz stress the critical importance of questioning and testing intuitive theories and assumptions.

In Chapter 8, Reid Hastie summarizes research into how analyses differ when carried out by groups and individuals. Understanding those differences provides opportunities to design more effective group processes. He notes that successful teams have been found to have four key features: (1) a clear, separate identity; (2) a clear purpose; (3) a structure appropriate to their tasks; and (4) a system of self-monitoring and regular feedback, allowing the team to learn from experience. Hastie notes, too, the inherent tensions between individuals and their groups—which often have both divergent and convergent goals—when trying to accommodate both the insights of individual opinions and the pressure for consensus. He shows how these tensions may be balanced differently depending on a group's analytical task.

In Chapter 9, Catherine H. Tinsley considers the effects of social categorization on collaboration within the intelligence community. She notes that efforts to increase collaboration among agencies face the well-documented tendency for the members of any group to accentuate differences with the members of other groups. Such grouping of people into social categories has both benefits and costs that must be recognized for effective organizational design. That recognition is often hampered by the subtle ways in which groups' culture and thinking shape their ability to understand and work with outsiders. Factors that intensify such intergroup biases include external pressures and strong or threatened group identification. Tinsley shows how awareness of these factors allows implementation of techniques that can improve collaboration, such as focusing on a higher-level group or minimizing group identification.

6

Individual Reasoning

Barbara A. Spellman

The job of an analyst is to make sense of a complicated mass of information—to understand and explain the current situation, to reconstruct the past that led to it, and to use it as the basis of predictions for the future.[1] To do so requires many types of sophisticated reasoning skills.

This chapter first describes a prominent historical characterization of overall individual human reasoning—that reasoning is filled with "irrationalities." The chapter then remarks on more recent characterizations of reasoning that try to uncover the judgment mechanisms that produce these irrationalities, including recognizing that human reasoning might best be thought of as involving both unconscious and conscious components that have different strengths and weaknesses. Finally, it describes two important characteristics of reasoning abilities: that people seek coherence, and that people are particularists (i.e., that we tend to emphasize the uniqueness of each situation). The chapter illustrates how these characteristics apply in several general tasks involved in analysis, including interpreting questions, searching for information, assessing information, and assessing our own judgments.

CHARACTERIZATIONS OF REASONING

Views about human rationality have differed widely over the years. In the mid-20th century, psychologists were optimistic about human

---

[1]Or, as Fingar states (this volume, Chapter 1), "to evaluate, integrate, and interpret information in order to provide warning, reduce uncertainty, and identify opportunities."

rationality and claimed that people were "intuitive statisticians" and "intuitive scientists." The heuristics and biases research program changed that perspective; current views that incorporate research on emotion, culture, and the unconscious have changed it yet again.

Heuristics and Biases Approach

Since at least the 1970s, psychologists and decision theorists have been documenting the many fallibilities and "irrationalities" in individual judgment. Countless examples show that people do not reason according to the rules of logic and probability, that we fail to recognize missing information, and that we are overconfident in our judgments. That list is just a small sample of what was discovered by the "Heuristics and Biases Program" (for an anthology of the classic works, see Kahneman et al., 1982; for a more recent update, see Gilovich et al., 2002). Lists of reasoning fallacies can be found in many places and, indeed, Heuer's (1999) classic work, *Psychology of Intelligence Analysis*, was an attempt to interpret those findings with respect to the intelligence analyst. Among the better known irrationalities are the availability and representativeness heuristics and the hindsight and overconfidence biases (all discussed below). However, creating lists of fallacies is not very useful; more are likely to be found, and when attempting to "repair" one such leak, others may emerge. To better understand, predict the occurrence of, and, perhaps, remedy such irrationalities, it is useful to understand when, why, and how they arise.

Perhaps the most important thing to know about reasoning errors is that the errors are not *random*. That observation (Tversky and Kahneman, 1974)—that the errors are systematic (or, as in Ariely's 2008 clever book title, *Predictably Irrational*)—is what makes such errors interesting, informative, and sometimes treatable. If such irrationalities are built into our reasoning, what in our cognitive system causes them?

Some theorists argued that many of the "irrationalities" were just laboratory tricks—specific to the presentation of the problems and the populations routinely used in such studies. Indeed, some errors may be reduced when minor changes are made to the presentation (e.g., when information is presented in frequency rather than probability format or when people see that a random generator was at work; e.g., Gigerenzer and Hoffrage, 1995). However, most errors cannot be made to disappear and most are (1) present in experts as well as novices and (2) resistant to debiasing attempts.

Attribute Substitution

One compelling account of many of these errors is that they are the result of "attribute substitution"—a kind of reasoning by proxy. People often have to make a judgment about some attribute—perhaps an external attribute such as how frequently some event occurs, or an internal attribute such as how happy you are. When the attribute is complicated because important information about it is unknown, the information is difficult to assess, or too much information is available, people substitute that attribute judgment with one that is simpler to make. Typically the simpler judgment is based on a related, but different, "attribute" at issue (Kahneman and Frederick, 2005). Take, for example, the "availability heuristic." Suppose you are asked: Do more countries in the United Nations begin (in English) with the first letter P or I or N? Because you do not have the current list embossed in your memory, and going through your mental map of the world would be tedious, you decide to think up the names of countries that begin with those letters and guess whether they are in the United Nations. Some examples easily pop into mind because of recent news stories; other might come to mind after cueing your memory with a question like: "From which countries do many Americans originate?" Note that in many situations, this technique will work because often things for which you can think of examples are actually more likely (e.g., Are more Americans named John or Nandor?). However, for the United Nations problem, substituting what you can think up for what is true is likely to lead you to fail.[2]

The Inside View

"Attribute substitution" explains many other reasoning biases. A common and important type of attribute substitution is the use of the "inside view"—that when asked to make judgments about various qualities, we query our own phenomenological experiences, or run our own mental simulations of events, and provide that as the "answer."

Imagining versus doing Consider this oft-told story by the Nobel-prize winning psychologist Danny Kahneman.[3] (It is an example of the "Planning Fallacy.") Kahneman was part of a group trying to develop a high school

---

[2]It is easy to think of the eight countries beginning with I: Iraq, Iran, India, and Israel are related to current U.S. issues in the Middle East and East Asia; many American families originate from Ireland and Italy; Iceland and Indonesia might also come to mind for various current events reasons. However, nine countries begin with "N" and "P" each. See http://www. un.org/en/members/index.shtml for a current list of United Nations member states [accessed August 2009].

[3]Kahneman won the Nobel Prize in Economics; there is no Nobel Prize in Psychology.

course and textbook on judgment and decision making. The group had been meeting for about a year and had written a few lessons and chapters. One day, Kahneman asked each group member to privately estimate how much more time each one thought would be needed to finish the book. The estimates ranged from 1.5 to 2.5 years. Then he asked the curriculum expert how long other groups like this one had taken finish a textbook. The expert seemed chagrined. He reported that about 40 percent of such groups never actually finished their books, and of those that did, completion times ranged from 7 to 10 years. (Completion ended up taking 8 years.) Such misestimates occur because when we consider how things will pan out, we think about how much work we could possibly get done in a period of time, and we think of the best case scenario (and forget to expect the usual unexpected types of distractions and delays). Judgments about the time needed to do a task are important to both the analysts' own work and in predicting the abilities and actions of others. For our own planning, we are usually better off with the "outside view"—comparing ourselves to a similar situation.

If we have actually performed a task ourselves, we may be good at judging how long others will take to do it—but the usefulness of that judgment can be destroyed. For example, suppose you are asked: How difficult is it to find the anagram for FSCAR? People who need to find the answer themselves are better at judging the relative difficulty of an anagram problem than people who solve it after having seen the answer[4] (Kelley and Jacoby, 1996). When you need to work out problems for yourself, you can use your own subjective difficulty as a good predictor for the subjective difficulty of others. However, if you have previously seen the answer, the informativeness of your subjective difficulty is ruined. In the study, those who had earlier seen the answer in a list of words (but didn't necessarily remember seeing it) solved the anagram faster. They then used their own speed as the basis for their judgments—making them bad at predicting the difficulty other people would have. Those who had seen the anagram and answer presented right next to each other knew not to rely on their own subjective experience in solving the anagram. Instead, they came up with hypotheses about why some anagrams should be more difficult to solve than others and made good predictions of other peoples' performance.

Hindsight bias The FSCAR example is related to the hindsight bias (or "Monday morning quarterbacking")—once we know something, we are bad at judging what we would have thought or done without that knowledge. In many studies (see Fischhoff, 2007, for a historical review), people read about the prelude to an obscure battle between the British and the

---

[4]Spoiler: Something you wear around your neck in winter.

Gurkhas. Some people were told that the British won, others that the Gurkhas won, and others were not told who was victorious. Then all were told to ignore the victor information. Later, asked to judge the probability of various outcomes or when asked to judge what others who did not know the outcome would think, people who read a particular outcome were more likely to respond that that particular outcome is the one that would have occurred or that others would guess.

This inability to forget or ignore what we know can be a pernicious problem in the courtroom. For example, judgments of negligence should reflect whether an injury was "foreseeable"; that is, whether someone should have known beforehand that the injury might have occurred. However, once an injury *has* occurred, the hindsight bias comes into play. Thus, although it might seem unlikely that people would badly misuse a consumer product, once it happens, jurors are likely to conclude that the use, and resulting injury, were foreseeable (Kamin and Rachlinski, 1995).

Indeed, once something has occurred, accusations of how something was "obvious" or could easily have been discovered or stopped beforehand are rife in the world of law enforcement and intelligence.

Assessing ourselves A very important judgment that analysts (and others) commonly have to make is how confident they are in what they know or in the predictions they have made. As described by Arkes and Kajdasz (this volume, Chapter 7, Intuitive Theory #2), people are typically overconfident in their judgments. For example, predictions made with 90 percent confidence are likely to happen less than 90 percent of the time. In addition, people are not always good at discriminating between events that should be believed with high confidence and those that should not.

Why might overconfidence occur? Correlations between beliefs (like predictions) and actuality typically go awry when the factors affecting the judgment are different from the factors affecting the reality. To make predictions about the likelihood of an event, we typically use the "inside view"—we run mental simulations and try to think of scenarios that will, or will not, lead to the predicted outcome. Like other mental processes that rely on the availability of "what comes to mind," we are likely to miss relevant information and be affected by ideas or events that are more recent or obvious. We thus end up with more confidence in outcomes that come to mind more easily.

A related problem in assessing ourselves is that we view ourselves as more fair and less biased than others. When we think about how we came to a conclusion, we don't *feel* ourselves being biased. We don't *feel* like we have been affected by our prior beliefs or by what we (or our boss) wanted the answer to be, or by the order in which information has been presented to us or by how difficult it was to get. But we are, and all of those affect our predictions. For a good review of the above work, see Dunning (2007).

Incorporating the Unconscious, Emotion, and Culture

During the past several decades, researchers broadened their investigations regarding the inputs to our reasoning, including examining the effects of unconscious knowledge, emotion, and culture. Emotion was long considered to be a detriment to reasoning, but current thinking suggests that emotion might give us accurate information and change our thinking strategies in ways appropriate to the situation (Clore and Palmer, 2009). Research on cultural effects on reasoning demonstrates a variety of differences in what might have been thought to be common human reasoning processes. An important recent article on that topic points out that nearly all of the research in psychology journals (including most of what is cited in this chapter) was conducted with U.S. participants, typically university undergraduates (although increasingly less so). The reasoning of these "WEIRD" people (white, educated, industrialized, rich, democratic) is different from that of people from other regions, groups, and cultures in many ways (Henrich et al., 2010). Thus, the research described herein is likely to characterize the reasoning of analysts themselves, but it might not characterize individuals from the various populations that analysts may consider.

Two Systems of Reasoning

A huge amount of research has been conducted during the past two decades on the role of unconscious thought, or "intuition," in reasoning. Malcolm Gladwell's (2005) bestselling book, *Blink*, described some of that research. Unfortunately, many people took the lesson from the book that intuition is always good and reliable. A better lesson is that sometimes intuition is good—but only when conditions are right. Gladwell did not specify what those conditions were, but a recent "debate" between Kahneman and Klein (2009) attempts to do so. In the past, on the surface, these authors seemed to disagree—Kahneman demonstrated that intuition (heuristics) can often give the wrong result, whereas Klein demonstrated that, especially in the hands of experts, intuition often yields the correct result. What Kahneman and Klein agree on is that intuition can be a good tool when: (1) the environment is predictable (so what happened previously is a good predictor of what will be likely to happen again); and (2) the person has had the "opportunity to learn the regularities of the environment" through repeated exposure and feedback. They also agree that a person's confidence in an intuitive judgment is not independently a good indicator of its accuracy.

Definitions of System 1 and System 2

The mind can be thought of as having two reasoning systems, often labeled System 1 and System 2 (Stanovich and West, 2002).[5] In broad strokes, System 1 is the "intuitive system"—it works unconsciously, reaches conclusions fast, engages emotion, and relies on heuristics—whereas System 2 works consciously and deliberately, comes to conclusions slowly, and uses logic.[6] When presented with a problem or decision, both systems engage. But System 1 comes up with an answer more quickly. Then System 2 might check and either approve or override that answer (Evans, 2008).

Consider, for example, the following problem:

> A bat and a ball cost $1.10 in total. The bat costs $1 more than the ball. How much does the ball cost?

Most people will initially think the answer is 10 cents; 10 cents was mentioned and it seems about the right size. However, if System 2 is engaged to check the math, seeing how that answer is wrong is simple.[7] Yet most people, most of the time, including students at the best universities, will report the answer as 10 cents. Note, however, that how people answer depends somewhat on various features of the situation—such as the time available for making the decision, the way the information is presented—and on various features of the individual—such as IQ and statistical training (Kahneman and Frederick, 2005).

At a global level, analysis is more a System 2 than a System 1 process. Even when decisions need to be made quickly, they do not need to be made instantly; there is time for System 2 to check the work of System 1. Still, the thoughts generated quickly by System 1 may serve as inputs (for better or worse) to later reasoning.

Interaction of reasoning systems

System 2 can play the "overriding" role in many ways. So, for example, in the classic irrationality findings in which System 1 makes an attribute substitution (e.g., substituting ease of retrieval for systematic counting), System 2 can slow things down to reach the correct answer (e.g., in the United Nations example above). Making people conscious of attribute substitutions that affect their judgments can often change judgments for

---

[5]Theorists debate not only about whether there are two (or more) reasoning systems, but also whether these two are really a dichotomy or represent ends of a continuum (see Evans, 2008).

[6]When I try to remember which system is which, my mnemonic is that ONE came first—it is thought to be evolutionarily older and shared with animals—whereas TWO is thought to be newer and require language.

[7]Spoiler: The answer is 5 cents. Check your work.

the better because people might then be able to use the real rather than the substituted attribute. For example, when researchers phone people and ask, "How happy are you?" the answers are affected by the weather at the time—when the weather is better, people report being happier. However, if the researchers preface the happiness question with a seemingly banal question about the weather, the weather—an irrelevant factor—no longer affects mood judgments; that is, people eliminate its influence (Schwarz and Clore, 1983). This result is similar to the FSCAR example above: When people are aware of something that could be throwing off their judgment, they may be able to set it aside and rely on different (possibly better) information when making the judgments.

However, just because System 2 has the labels "conscious" and "logical" as opposed to System 1's "unconscious" and "heuristic" does not mean that System 2 is always better. Becoming conscious of a factor that *is* relevant to an answer can cause that factor to be overweighted. So, when college students were asked the following two questions—"How happy are you with your life in general?" and "How many dates did you have last month?"—the order in which they answered the questions made a huge difference in the relation between the answers. When the "general" question was answered first, the two answers showed little relation; however, when the "date" question was answered first, there was a huge positive correlation between the answers, suggesting that the students used the simple numerical answer to the dating question as a proxy for the answer to the more amorphous question about happiness (Strack et al., 1988). Indeed, with complex multidimensional problems, System 1 may be valuable for considering multiple factors proportionally and finding the most coherent story.[8]

Embodied Cognition

An even more recent line of theorizing broadens the factors that influence thinking to include the human body. This line points out that reasoning is not a disembodied activity; rather, it takes inputs from human sensory systems, occurs in brains molded by evolution to fit human needs, and serves the goal of facilitating human action. The range of findings show how our moods and emotions, our bodily states (e.g., being tired), our physical environment (e.g., being hot or cold), and our social environment

---

[8]Much debate is happening about the "deliberation without attention" effect—the finding that when solving complex problems, people whose attention was distracted made better choices and decisions than people who were continuously focused on the problem (see Lassiter et al., 2009, for a critique).

(e.g., in the presence of friends or enemies) can affect how we reason (see Spellman and Schnall, 2009, for a review).

CHARACTERISTICS OF REASONING I:
PEOPLE SEEK COHERENCE

People actively try to understand and make sense of the world. Among the important relevant properties of human reasoning are that we seek patterns and explanations, that we use both top-down and bottom-up processing, and that our imaginations are often constrained by reality. These characteristics of reasoning have important implications for various analytic tasks.

People Seek Patterns

People are adept at finding patterns in the world, even when such patterns are not "real." These days we look up at the constellations Ursa Major and Ursa Minor[9] and wonder, what were second-century astronomers thinking? Did they really see bears in those patterns of stars? Yet giving a name to what would otherwise be a scattered collection helps us to identify, describe, and use it when it is helpful.

Although people are good at finding patterns, we are bad at both detecting and generating randomness. For example, it is commonly believed that basketball players have "hot streaks"— short bursts when their performance is better than what would be predicted by chance and their baseline level of ability. Yet Gilovich et al. (1985) showed that such streaks in performance are what would be generated by chance.

People also typically think randomness should "look more random" than it actually does. In a classic demonstration of the representativeness heuristic, people are asked to decide which was a more likely string of tosses of a fair coin (where H = heads and T = tails): HHHTTT or HTTHTH. People more often choose the second string even though they are equally likely. Similarly, people commonly commit the "gambler's fallacy"—believing that after a coin is tossed and comes up H, H, and H again, the chance of tails on the next toss is much greater than 50 percent when, in fact, it is the same 50 percent as always. Randomness sometimes generates long sequences of the same thing. When people are told to generate something at random themselves—for example, to write down "heads" and "tails" as if flipping a fair coin—they will have more switching back and forth

---

[9]In Latin, Ursa Major and Ursa Minor mean Great Bear and Little Bear, respectively. The seven brightest stars of Ursa Major form the Big Dipper and of Ursa Minor form the Little Dipper.

between heads and tails and fewer long sequences than an actual fair coin. Note that this inability to be random can yield important information when one is trying to detect whether something has happened by chance (e.g., a series of fires, several train crashes) or by human design. (See Oskarsson et al., 2009, for a review.)

Patterns in Deception

The patterns that come from deceptive sources of information are likely to be different from the patterns that do not—but those differences are likely to be difficult to detect. There is a vast literature on "detecting deception"—the cues that people use when trying to determine whether someone is lying to them while speaking (e.g., shifting gaze, fidgeting, etc.) (Bond and DePaulo, 2006). But there is little psychology research on how people determine whether a pattern of behavior is likely to be deceptive and how information about such suspected behavior is used.

Suppose you are given a choice: You can take the advice of someone who has always said accurately in the past that five coins were behind door A or take the advice of someone who has been correct only 80 percent of the time in the past that seven coins are behind door B. People vary on which they choose, but that is not what is at issue.[10] Suppose you believe the person with the 80 percent accuracy rate is really trying to help you—he or she does not benefit from your errors and apologizes when he or she cannot deliver. Contrast that person ("uncertain") to another person ("deceptive") who has also been 80 percent reliable in the past, but whom you know benefits from your errors and who takes delight when you wrongly choose his door. Although overall the odds are the same with the uncertain and deceptive informants, people are much more cautious about taking the gamble (whether or not it is rational to do so) when the 80 percent informant is deceptive rather than uncertain.

Of course, truly deceptive people would never advertise themselves as such. But can individuals pick up on patterns of deception? Suppose you can now choose between believing someone who has been 70 percent accurate in the past or someone who has been 80 percent accurate in the past. Whom do you choose? The answer should be: It depends. Table 6-1 depicts the accuracy of information provided by two informants (e.g., 9/10 means that of 10 pieces of information, 9 were accurate). You can see that for both low- and high-value information, Informant A is more accurate (in terms of percentages) than Informant B. Yet overall, Informant B is more accurate. (This seeming contradiction is called Simpson's paradox and is explained in

---

[10]Yes, the expected value of the "sure thing" is 5 and of the "gamble" is $0.8 \times 7 = 0.56$. So it is rational to take the gamble. But that is not the important comparison here.

TABLE 6-1 Information and Accuracy of Two Informants

	Low-Value Information (easy to uncover)	High-Value Information (difficult to uncover)	Overall Total
Informant A	9/10 = 90%	5/10 = 50%	14/20 = 70%
Informant B	87/100 = 87%	1/10 = 10%	88/110 = 80%

another context by Zegart, this volume, Chapter 13.) Informant B is exhibiting a deceptive pattern—giving away lots of low-stakes information, but being deceptive on high-stakes issues. However, in a study with a similar structure, unwary participants thought Informant B was more reliable and less deceptive than Informant A—presumably because he was correct more often overall.

Of course, analysts are wary of the possibility of deception. Having the motivation to look for such patterns or the belief that they might exist (i.e., top-down knowledge; see the next section) will help one to discover such patterns (Spellman et al., 2001). But if information about source behavior is not effectively collected, collated, and provided, trying to discriminate deceptive from uncertain sources will be difficult.

People Use Both Top-Down and Bottom-Up Processing

People do not come to every new situation with a blank mind; we obviously already know or believe many things about how the world is likely to work. Thus, when perceiving something new, we use two kinds of information: "bottom-up" information is the information contained in the stimulus and "top-down" information is what we already know. Top-down and bottom-up processing work in parallel to help us make sense of information. A simple perceptual example is found in Figure 6-1. Assume that some blobs of ink have fallen on a manuscript and you have to decide what it says. What most English-speaking people see are the words THE CAT. Now look more carefully at the middle letters in each word. They are printed exactly the same, but we interpret them differently—one as an H and one as an A—because of our top-down knowledge of English words.

FIGURE 6-1 Ink blobs.

Users of other writing systems or non-English speakers might see them as the same. The fact that top-down knowledge affects interpretation means (among other things) that two people with the same information—be it a low-resolution satellite photograph or the incomplete facts surrounding a death—can logically interpret it differently given different prior knowledge.

People Seek Explanations and Causes

From telling stories about the gods of Mount Olympus to examining the tiniest bits of matter, people try to make sense of the world by figuring out the causes of events. The causal stories allow us to explain, and we hope to predict or even control, our world.

The desire to find patterns and the use of top-down knowledge combine in the quest for finding causal explanations. When events co-occur we may "see" a cause–effect pattern that really is not there. For example, when people are asked to push buttons and then decide whether they are causing a variable light to turn on and off, they often overestimate the control they have over the light (see Alloy and Tabachnik, 1984[11]). When people read stories in which a sequence of events occur, but no causal words are used (e.g., "John held the glass" and "The glass broke"), people are likely to misremember hearing causal links that were never stated (e.g., "John broke the glass"; see Fletcher et al., 1990). Furthermore, when people hear complex, competing information about how an event occurred—the kind of information a juror (or analyst) might hear—they try to extract the most complete and coherent explanation they can from the information. Once they are set on one story, however, they tend to devalue and misremember information that is inconsistent with the explanation they believe is best (Pennington and Hastie, 1986).

Analysts often try to assess causation. They have the important tasks of seeking information, reaching and explaining judgments, and assessing the quality of the information and their confidence in those judgments.

Searching for Information

Whether to answer a specific question or to keep abreast of current conditions (and thus know whether there is something that should be told), analysts must be aware of vast amounts of information. Years ago, analysts often suffered from a dearth of information; now, there is often too much information—and it becomes difficult to sift what is relevant and reliable out of all the noise.

---

[11]This article provides an old, but excellent, review of the findings regarding the interacting influences of top-down and bottom-up knowledge on causal judgments.

Looking at a mass of information and making sense of it is nearly impossible without a question in mind. Yet when people are too focused on one question, they may miss important information that is right in front of them. Everyone has been to a restaurant, interacted with a waiter, then, later, when it was relevant, failed to remember what the waiter looked like. A fabulous demonstration of a failure to notice things can be seen at http://viscog.beckman.illinois.edu/flashmovie/15.php [accessed August 2009]. The watcher is supposed to count the number of times that the players in white shirts pass the basketball. When people are intent on doing that, they miss the unusual event in the scene. (Try it before reading this footnote.[12])

When people have a particular answer to a question or a particular hypothesis in mind, they may suffer from "confirmation bias." Much has been written about confirmation bias in the analysis literature and, indeed, many analytic tools have been developed to address different aspects of it. The term has been used to describe various flaws in reasoning that, although often lumped together, are distinct. They include (1) only searching for information that is consistent with one's favored hypothesis, and (2) devaluing, ignoring, or explaining information that is not consistent with one's favored hypothesis.

The suggestion that people only search for information that is consistent with their hypotheses, even if true, may not be as bad as it appears. When searching for information to support a hypothesis, you are also likely to find information that will undermine your hypothesis (Klayman and Ha, 1987). Suppose, for example, you suspect a country is developing various types of weapons of mass destruction (WMDs). You search, but find no evidence of anything related to creating nuclear weapons. However, you do find evidence for some enhanced biological research activities. Thus, in looking for evidence to support your broader theory (of developing all types of WMDs), you have disconfirmed it. With the new evidence you might decide to revise and narrow your theory to believing the country is only creating biological WMDs. (Of course, you might form a new theory that it is trying to upgrade its medical technology, or you might keep your initial theory but add the assumption that it has managed to hide the other evidence.)

Therefore, whether looking for information to confirm a hypothesis is bad depends on the relationship between the hypotheses and the true state of the world (which is, of course, unknown). However, other processes that fall under the term "confirmation bias" have more insidious effects, as described below.

---

[12]Spoiler: There is a person dressed in a gorilla suit walking through the game. Once you know it, you can't fail to see it.

Revaluing and Rejecting Information

Sometimes information that is discovered must be revalued or ignored. The following are two examples of real-world situations that cause people to revalue or ignore information.

Duplicate sources A problem that arises when there is too much information comes from the duplication of information from the same, rather than independent, sources. Information that is repeated will be overweighted even if the repetition does not add independent verification because it comes from a redundant source. When people learn, for example, that three pieces of information come from the same source, they can devalue it appropriately, but only if they learn that it comes from the same source before they are exposed to the information. Once it is integrated with other knowledge it is difficult to devalue. (See Ranganath et al., 2010, for a review regarding information sources.)

Hidden information Consider the (classic television) courtroom situation in which a witness blurts out some incriminating evidence and the judge instructs the jury to disregard it. Results from numerous studies on this issue are consistent with intuitions—typically jurors don't fully disregard that information. But why? Some explanations are cognitive (e.g., that jurors can't forget information that has been woven into the causal explanation of the case); other explanations are more social (e.g., they don't want to let a guilty person go free).[13] Sometimes jurors who are told to disregard a piece of information pay even more attention to it than jurors who are not told to disregard it. (See Steblay et al., 2006, for a review.) An additional hypothesis suggests that jurors pay more attention to information they believe people are trying to hide (Walker-Wilson et al., unpublished).

Regardless of whether sources are trying to hide information, it is likely that people treat information that takes longer to find as more valuable than information that is obvious or easy to find. In addition, anecdotal evidence from analysts suggests that more highly classified information may be treated as more valuable information—despite not necessarily being either more relevant or reliable. (This effect sounds like an attribute substitution effect.)

Explaining Judgments

After searching and evaluating information, an analyst must come to a conclusion—often before he or she feels ready to do so. It has long been

---

[13]But note that even judges (who could be considered "experts") may be influenced by information they know they should not consider (Wistrich et al., 2004).

known that when there are no good reasons for a decision (or equally good reasons for all decisions), people will make up reasons. For example, when people are presented with four products of identical quality and asked to pick which one they prefer, they will pick one (most often the right-most one) and proclaim that it was best because of some made-up difference (Nisbett and Wilson, 1977). More importantly, even when there are good reasons for a decision, people often cannot explain why they made a judgment, and they make up explanations. Worse yet, by articulating some reasons, they may overweight those reasons and lose access to other reasons.

The examples of how asking about dating or the weather first influences subsequent judgments of happiness described earlier illustrate how thinking about some reasons causes overweighting of those reasons. Illustrations of how articulating only some knowledge or reasons that can impair decision making come from the "verbal overshadowing" literature. Suppose you and a friend have witnessed a truck bombing and suspects running from the scene. You are asked to describe the suspects' faces, but your friend is not. Later you are both shown pictures of faces similar to the suspects. Who will be more accurate at picking out the suspects? Your friend. Faces are made up of many features and some of them are holistic. When you described the faces, you described some features and not others; your later memory is biased toward the features you described. This problem may be eliminated if you talk to someone else who gave a different description (Dodson et al., 1997).

Of course, in intelligence, *not* explaining reasoning is not an option. But we should be aware that explaining after the fact is not always complete or accurate, that the act of explanation can change memory, and that previous potential influences on judgment should be recorded and considered.

Assessing Information

Another important judgment that analysts must make is about the quality of information and its value in supporting a potential conclusion.

Fluency Consistent with the research on the "inside view," people believe that answers or judgments that more easily come to mind are more sound. But ease (also known as "fluency") can be simply manipulated, and the confidence based on such ease isn't warranted. So, for example, recall the bat and ball problem for which people often give the incorrect answer of 10 cents. People who see the problem in a hard-to-read font (thus making the problem seem more difficult) are more likely to get the correct answer of 5 cents—presumably because they did not have the same sense of ease in solving the problem so they are more likely to check their own work (Oppenheimer, 2008).

Disconfirming hypotheses The second set of types of confirmation bias (devaluing, ignoring, or explaining away conflicting information) occurs when assessing information and can have disturbing effects. See Arkes and Kajdasz (this volume, Chapter 7, end of Intuitive Theory #5). For example, people take more seriously (and find fewer flaws) in information consistent with their own hypotheses regardless of whether they are ultimately correct (Lord et al., 1979).

A common mistaken belief is that not only can a hypothesis never be proven no matter how many confirming instances are found (this is accurate), but also that one disconfirming instance can disprove a hypothesis (this is generally inaccurate). For example, in high school physics, our class was told to drop a ball in a vacuum tube, measure how long it took to drop, then calculate the earth's gravitational force. Our answer was 7.8 m/s^2 (rather than the "more traditional" 9.8 m/s^2). Did we tell the teacher that on a Tuesday afternoon, in a small town in New York, gravity had changed? No, my lab partner and I checked the stopwatch, checked the vacuum, remeasured the tube, redid our calculations, blamed each other, and duly reported our answer as 9.4 m/s^2.[14] One moral of this story is that disconfirmation information in itself is often not sufficient to disprove a theory (particularly a well-established theory—and rightly so). Information comes with "auxiliary assumptions" (Quine, 1951), and when those are attacked so is the value of the information. Another moral, however, is that people are more likely to find such problems in the information when they are motivated to search for them—that is, when the information is inconsistent with their preferred hypothesis. If we had originally gotten an answer we wanted (of about 9.8 m/s^2), we would never have checked for faulty equipment or faulty logic.

Note that in the physics classroom, the answer we wanted to get was also the answer we knew (from reading ahead in the textbook) was objectively correct. When people reason they usually have one of two goals: one is to try to find the most accurate answer, and the other is to find a particular answer. The goal will affect the reasoning strategies chosen; the strategies chosen will affect what is concluded (see Kunda, 1990, for an excellent description of the strategies and processes involved). However, when people are motivated to find a particular answer (whether by internal or external pressures), they are more likely to do so, regardless of the accuracy of that answer.

Of course, sometimes people do not have an initial preferred answer. When choosing between two equally novel and appealing products—or hypotheses—people are more influenced by information learned early

---

[14]Of course, we didn't report the exact answer. Then the teacher would have been sure we had faked it.

rather than later. Then, once there is a preferred alternative, people bias their interpretation of later incoming information to be consistent with that initial preference, perhaps to maintain consistency (Russo et al., 2008).

Imaginations Stick Close to Reality

Our reasoning and imagination often stick very closely to reality. For example, when children are asked to draw creatures from another planet, the aliens almost always have an even number of limbs and exhibit bilateral symmetry (as do most terrestrial animals) (Karmiloff-Smith, 1990). When adults read a story in which a bad outcome occurs and they are asked to change the story so that the outcome would be different, the responses ("counterfactuals") they generate tend to converge on certain minimal changes of reality. For example, people may read about Mr. Jones, who decides to take the scenic route home from work one day, brakes hard to stop at a yellow light, and is hit by a drunk driver. When asked to change the story so that the outcome would be different, most people suggest not taking the unusual route, or not braking at the light, or the driver not being drunk. Few people suggest considering what would have happened if Mr. Jones had not gone to work that day at all or if the driver did not own a car. No one suggests considering what if cars were made of rubber or gravity had been suspended (e.g., Mandel and Lehman, 1996).

Generating counterfactuals helps us figure out the causes of events. The fact that our counterfactuals tend to be narrow can impede our considerations of the possible consequences of actions—an important skill for individuals and analysts (see papers in this volume by Fingar, Chapter 1, and Bueno de Mesquita, Chapter 3).

In addition, people often display "functional fixedness"—the inability to break free of conventional procedures or uses of objects. A standard functional fixedness task asks how one might attach a lighted candle to a wall so it does not drip on the floor. You are given a candle, a box of matches, and some thumbtacks.[15] One must overcome functional fixedness to see fertilizer as an ingredient for explosives or to view airplanes as potential missiles—or to stay one step ahead of people who will do so.

CHARACTERISTICS OF REASONING II: PEOPLE ARE PARTICULARISTS

A second important characteristic of human reasoning is that people can be both generalizers and particularists, depending on context. What

---

[15]The task is difficult because it requires each object to be used unconventionally: open the box, thumbtack the side of the bottom piece to the wall, then place the lit candle in it.

does that mean? As generalizers we see things as alike and treat them as alike. So, for example, we have general knowledge structures such as categories (groups of objects that we know are different, but treat as the same for some purposes) and scripts (general outlines of what to do in a situation similar to previous situations). When we meet a new dog, we know it might bite; when we enter a new fast food restaurant, we know to go to the counter to order, pay, and pick up our food.[16]

Yet, of course, we also know how to distinguish members of categories from each other. As particularists we see individuating characteristics in objects of interest, and often use those to make judgments in individual cases. Yes, some pit bulls are easily provoked, but not the one lovingly raised by your sister (or so you thought). Which takes precedence in decision making—treating things as similar and relying on category information, or treating things as different and relying on particular information? As for so many types of reasoning, what people do depends on the context. But in many analysis-related contexts, people may too often focus on the unique features of a situation and fail to rely on important similarities to other situations.[17]

Seeing Similarities and Differences

On first thought it seems as though similarity and difference are simply opposites—the more things are similar, the less they are different (and vice versa). However, whether, how, and how much things are judged as similar or different depends on both the context and the judge.

In a classic cold war example, Tversky (1977) asked some people which pair was more *similar*: (1) West Germany and East Germany, or (2) Ceylon and Nepal; 67 percent picked the former. Other people were asked which pair was more *different*; 70 percent picked the former. How can the same pair be both more similar and more different? Tversky argued that people knew more about the former countries than the latter countries. When asked about similarity, they weighted the similar features more; when asked about differences, they weighted the different features more—thus resulting in the seemingly contradictory answers.

Of course, the most important issue in assessing similarity is keeping

---

[16]See Arkes and Kajdasz (this volume, Chapter 7, Intuitive Theory #3) for a discussion of schemas, which are another type of generalized knowledge.

[17]Relevant findings include the classic research on the failure to use base rates when given individuating information (e.g., Tversky and Kahneman, 1973) and on the superiority of actuarial to clinical judgments (see Arkes and Kajdasz, this volume, Chapter 7, Intuitive Theory #3, and the discussion of experts versus algorithms). People are also particularists in legal settings when they agree that some law is good in general, but don't like it to be applied to a particular case at hand.

the question in mind: Similar with respect to what? Which pair is more similar: (1) United States and China, or (2) United States and Italy? The answer differs depending on whether the question is about production capabilities or how the government is likely to respond to protests against it.

Thus, how we judge similarity (of people, events, situations) depends on time, context, the question asked, and the judge's knowledge (Spellman, 2010). How similar we judge two situations to be affects how relevant we will believe one is to understanding or predicting the other. Assumptions about the level of analysis (categories or individuals) and about the relative importance of similarities and differences are key to how an analyst might interpret and answer questions.

Interpreting Questions

As described by Fingar (this volume, Chapter 1), one job of analysts is to answer direct questions from customers. Other jobs mentioned include providing warning and assessing current developments and new information. Each of those is also like answering a question—but the less specified question: "Is there something that should be told?"[18]

Level of categorization Answering a question depends very much on understanding why the question was asked and the appropriate level of categorization. The level at which a question is asked and answered can affect estimations. For example, experiment participants were told that each year in the United States, about 2 million people die. Some were asked to estimate the probability of people dying from "natural causes"; the average was 58 percent. Others were asked to estimate the probability of dying from "heart disease, cancer, or some other natural cause"; the average was 73 percent. These questions asked for exactly the same information—the difference was whether the category ("natural causes") was decomposed into subcategories (Tversky and Koehler, 1994). Of course, in this example, numbers can be looked up, but often they cannot be (e.g., how many insurgents does Country Z have?). This phenomenon ("subadditivity"—in which the whole is less than the sum of the parts) is even exhibited by political historians when asked about potential counterfactual outcomes to the Cuban missile crisis (Tetlock and Lebow, 2001). It importantly illustrates that when people think about a general category, they often don't "unpack" it into all of the relevant subcategories.

---

[18]That broad question includes the following types of other questions: Have we learned something new and important? Has something important changed? Has something unexpected happened? Is something now relevant to the current situation that wasn't relevant in the past?

Compared to what? The issue of "compared to what" is implicit in nearly every question. An American colleague recently took a year-long prestigious British fellowship and was often asked: "Why are you here?" Depending on who asked, he would answer: "Because I could take time off this year rather than next year," or "Because it's nicer here than at that other British university," or "Because they couldn't get Antonin Scalia." Each is an answer to the question—but a different implicit part of the question (why now rather than the future, why here rather than there, why him rather than someone else). In analysis it is essential to get the "compared to what" correct (e.g., "Why is this country taking that action now?" could be answered with regard to the country, the action, or the timing).

Note that when people ask themselves multiple questions, the order in which the questions are asked can affect the answers because different questions will bring to mind different features and comparisons (recall the weather, dating, and happiness examples). Like the other processes described earlier, how people answer a question will depend not only on what they already know and what the context is, but also on assumptions about what is relevant to the questioner. Those assumptions can easily be wrong.

Analogy: Using the Past to Understand the Present

An important and useful reasoning skill for analysis that uses similarities and difference is analogy. People use analogies when trying to make sense of what to do with a new problem; they find past similar problems that are better understood ("source analogs") and may use the relevant similarities to help them solve the current problem. Analogies can be used to help understand a situation, to predict what will happen, and to persuade others. For example, nearly every time the United States considers a new global intervention, the two great source analogs emerge in popular debate: World War II (the necessary, well-fought, victorious war) and Vietnam (the questionable, poorly fought, lost war).[19] When the first President Bush considered military action against Iraq in 1991, those two analogies were often discussed. The World War II analogy won (Saddam Hussein was like Hitler, he had already annexed Kuwait, he would move against other countries in the region, he needed to be stopped) and the United States went to war. The situation in Iraq in 2003 did not provide a good analogy to World War II and Persian Gulf War II did not garner the public and international support of Persian Gulf War I.

What makes a good analogy? The key is finding *relevant* similarities—typically similarities that matter to causal relationships—between the two

---

[19]These are the popular press characterizations.

situations. For example, in drawing an analogy, does it matter whether countries are large or small, have the same climate or geography, are similar in population, major religion, or type of government? That depends on the question. An important distinction to make when using analogies is between superficial and structural similarities. Superficial similarities are usually observable attributes (e.g., that a country is poor) that situations have in common. Structural similarities are underlying relationships (e.g., that one country attacked another) that situations have in common. These latter relational similarities are typically more important when using analogy for understanding and prediction (Holyoak and Koh, 1987).

When retrieving potential source analogs from memory, people typically first think of situations that share superficial similarities. For example, in 1991 college students were asked to "fill in" the analogy: "People say Saddam is like Hitler. If so, who/what would they say is: Iraq? George H. W. Bush? The United States? Kuwait?" Most students said that President Bush was like Franklin Delano Roosevelt and the United States (in 1991) was like the United States of World War II (U.S. WWII). That analogy has a high degree of superficial similarity—U.S. 1991 is in many ways like U.S. WWII and a current president is like a past one. However, when students read brief passages about World War II before filling in the analogy, depending on the passage, many of them preferred to say that U.S. 1991 was like Great Britain of World War II and President Bush was like Churchill.[20] That mapping has less superficial similarity, but more structural similarity in that it captures the relations and forces at work (Spellman and Holyoak, 1992).[21]

Note that when under time pressure, the more obvious superficial features of a situation are processed more quickly and may form the basis of similarity/analogy decisions (Medin et al., 1993) even though structural similarity is usually more important to understanding a situation.

Experts' Use of Analogy

When using analogies, experts are better at ignoring superficial similarities and using structural similarities; indeed, part of developing expertise is learning about the important underlying structures of information. For example, novice and expert physicists were given cards with illustrations of physics problems and asked to sort them. Novices sorted them by the simple machines involved (e.g., pulleys, axles, levers) whereas experts

---

[20]The various passages were all historically accurate, but emphasized different aspects of World War II.

[21]For example, Great Britain actively went to war over Germany's actions in Eastern Europe whereas the United States did not declare war against Germany until after Pearl Harbor.

sorted them by the underlying principles involved (e.g., conservation of momentum) (Chi et al., 1981). Thus, an important part of expertise in any field is having a base of experiences from which to extract the information relevant to the present situation.

Analogies at War (Khong, 1992) describes the many analogies the United States considered informative as it became involved in Vietnam in the 1960s. The book illustrates how what one sees as the important similarities between two situations will not only affect the judgments made based on the similarities, but also the lessons learned. The war in Vietnam has left us with two contradictory lessons that continue to frame foreign policy debates. The phrase "no more Vietnams" meant for some people "that the United States should abstain from intervening in areas of dubious strategic worth, where the justice of both the cause and of the means used are likely to be questionable, and where the United States is unlikely to win" (p. 258); it meant for others "that is was the imposition of unrealistic constraints on the military by civilians unschooled in modern warfare that led to the defeat in Vietnam" (p. 259) and that in the future the military should be allowed to do whatever it needs to do to win.

But, indeed, whether any lessons learned are applied to future situations depends on whether the past examples are viewed as sufficiently similar to be relevant. Experts may be especially prone to particularizing situations rather than generalizing them precisely because of their extra knowledge, information, and expertise. On the one hand, the more potential source analogs someone is aware of, the more easily he or she will be able to access them from memory, and find one that seems relevant to the present situation. On the other hand, the more one knows about the past and present, the easier it is to find features that distinguish the current situation from other situations. It is well documented that experts in a variety of fields rely too much on what they see as special circumstances of the present case rather than relying on the common features of a case.[22]

Especially important in the context of analysis, there may be a reward structure in place that values characterizing current situations as different from past ones. For example, an expert might "get credit" for expertise when pointing out how a new situation is different from the past rather than saying, as any non-expert could, that it is the same as the past. Such a reward structure would accentuate looking for and more highly weighting differences—which will then be found—rather than the relevant similarities.

Thus, experts are both best poised to use analogies (because they can identify the important underlying structural similarities between situations), but also best poised to (mistakenly) dismiss them even when relevant.

---

[22]See Arkes and Kajdasz (this volume, Chapter 7, Intuitive Theories #3 and #4).

CONCLUSION

Just as much has changed in the world of intelligence in the past 25 years, so has much changed in theorizing about how humans think and reason. The list of "irrationalities" has grown longer, but we now have more insights into what they have in common and how they arise. Such knowledge can help us design ways to improve the products of individual reasoning.

REFERENCES

Alloy, L. B., and N. Tabachnik. 1984. Assessment of covariation by humans and animals: The joint influence of prior expectations and current situational information. *Psychological Review* 91:112–149.

Ariely, D. 2008. *Predictably irrational.* London, UK: HarperCollins.

Bond, C. F., Jr., and B. M. DePaulo. 2006. Accuracy of deception judgments. *Personality and Social Psychology Review* 10(3):214–234.

Chi, M. T. H., P. J. Feltovich, and R. Glaser. 1981. Categorization and representation of physics problems by experts and novices. *Cognitive Science* 5:121–152.

Clore, G. L., and J. Palmer. 2009. Affective guidance of intelligent agents: How emotion controls cognition. *Cognitive Systems Research* 10:21–30.

Dodson, C. S., M. K. Johnson, and J. W. Schooler. 1997. The verbal overshadowing effect: Why descriptions impair face recognition. *Memory and Cognition* 25(2):129–139.

Dunning, D. 2007. Prediction: The inside view. In A. W. Kruglanski and E. T. Higgins, eds., *Social psychology: Handbook of basic principles*, 2nd ed. (pp. 69–90). New York: Guilford Press.

Evans, J. S. B. T. 2008. Dual-processing accounts of reasoning, judgment, and social cognition. *Annual Review of Psychology* 59:255–278.

Fischhoff, B. 2007. An early history of hindsight research. *Social Cognition* 25:10–13.

Fletcher, C. R., J. E. Hummel, and C. J. Marsolek. 1990. Causality and the allocation of attention during comprehension. *Journal of Experimental Psychology: Learning, Memory, and Cognition* 16:233–240.

Gigerenzer, G., and U. Hoffrage. 1995. How to improve Bayesian reasoning without instruction: Frequency formats. *Psychological Review* 102:684–704.

Gilovich, T., R. Vallone, and A. Tversky. 1985. The hot hand in basketball: On the misperception of random sequences. *Cognitive Psychology* 17:295–314.

Gilovich, T., D. Griffin, and D. Kahneman. 2002. *Heuristics and biases: The psychology of intuitive judgment.* New York: Cambridge University Press.

Gladwell, M. 2005. *Blink: The power of thinking without thinking.* New York: Little Brown.

Henrich, J., S. J. Heine, and A. Norenzayan. (2010). The weirdest people in the world? *Behavioral and Brain Sciences* 33:61–83.

Heuer, R. J., Jr. 1999. *Psychology of intelligence analysis.* Washington, DC: Center for the Study of Intelligence, Central Intelligence Agency.

Holyoak, K. J., and K. Koh. 1987. Surface and structural similarity in analogical transfer. *Memory and Cognition* 15:332–340.

Kahneman, D., and S. Frederick. 2005. A model of heuristic judgment. In K. J. Holyoak and R. G. Morrison, eds., *The Cambridge handbook of thinking and reasoning* (pp. 267–294). New York: Cambridge University Press.

Kahneman, D., and G. Klein. 2009. Conditions for intuitive expertise: A failure to disagree. *American Psychologist* 64:515–526.

Kahneman, D., P. Slovic, and A. Tversky, eds. 1982. *Judgments under uncertainty: Heuristics and biases*. New York: Cambridge University Press.

Kamin, K. A., and J. J. Rachlinski. 1995. Ex post ≠ ex ante: Determining liability in hindsight. *Law and Human Behavior* 19:89–104.

Karmiloff-Smith, A. 1990. Constraints on representational change: Evidence from children's drawing. *Cognition* 34:57–83.

Kelley, C. M., and L. L. Jacoby. 1996. Adult egocentrism: Subjective experience versus analytic bases for judgment. *Journal of Memory and Language* 35(2):157–175.

Khong, Y. F. 1992. *Analogies at war: Korea, Munich, Dien Bien Phu, and the Vietnam decisions of 1965*. Princeton, NJ: Princeton University Press.

Klayman, J., and Y.-W. Ha. 1987. Confirmation, disconfirmation, and information in hypothesis testing. *Psychological Review* 94:211–228.

Kunda, Z. 1990. The case for motivated reasoning. *Psychological Bulletin* 108:480–498.

Lassiter, G. D., M. J. Lindberg, C. Gonzalez-Vallejo, F. S. Belleza, and N. D. Phillips. 2009. The deliberation-without-attention effect: Evidence for an artifactual interpretation. *Psychological Science* 20:671–675.

Lord, C. G., L. Ross, and M. R. Lepper. 1979. Biased assimilation and attitude polarization: The effect of prior theories on subsequently considered evidence. *Journal of Personality and Social Psychology* 37:2098–2109.

Mandel, D. R., and D. R. Lehman. 1996. Counterfactual thinking and ascriptions of cause and preventability. *Journal of Personality and Social Psychology* 71:450–463.

Medin, D. L., R. L. Goldstone, and D. Gentner. 1993. Respects for similarity. *Psychological Review* 100(2):254–278.

Nisbett, R. E., and T. D. Wilson. 1977. Telling more than we can know: Verbal reports on mental processes. *Psychological Review* 84(3):231–259.

Oppenheimer, D. O. 2008. The secret life of fluency. *Trends in Cognitive Sciences* 12:237–241.

Oskarsson, A. T., L. Van Boven, G. H. McClelland, and R. Hastie. 2009. What's next? Judging sequences of binary events. *Psychological Bulletin* 135:262–285.

Pennington, N., and R. Hastie. 1986. Evidence evaluation in complex decision making. *Journal of Personality and Social Psychology* 51:242–258.

Quine, W. V. O. 1951. Two dogmas of empiricism. *The Philosophical Review* 60:20–43. Reprinted in W. V. O. Quine. (1953). *From a logical point of view: Nine logico-philosophical essays*. Cambridge, MA: Harvard University Press.

Ranganath, K. A., B. A. Spellman, and J. A. Joy-Gaba. 2010. Cognitive "category-based induction" research and social "persuasion" research are each about what makes arguments believable: A tale of two literatures. *Perspectives on Psychological Science* 5(2):115–122.

Russo, J. E., K. A. Carlson, M. G. Meloy, and K. Yong. 2008. The goal of consistency as a cause of information distortion. *Journal of Experimental Psychology: General* 137(3):456–470.

Schwarz, N., and G. L. Clore. 1983. Mood, misattribution, and judgments of well-being: Informative and directive functions of affective states. *Journal of Personality and Social Psychology* 45(3):513–523.

Spellman, B. A. 2010. Judges, expertise, and analogy. In D. Klein and G. Mitchell, eds., *The psychology of judicial decision making* (pp. 149–164). New York: Oxford University Press.

Spellman, B. A., and K. J. Holyoak. 1992. If Saddam is Hitler then who is George Bush? Analogical mapping between systems of social roles. *Journal of Personality and Social Psychology* 62:913–933.

Spellman, B. A., and S. Schnall. 2009. Embodied rationality. *Queen's Law Journal* 35(1): 117–164.

Spellman, B. A., C. M. Price, and J. M. Logan. 2001. How two causes are different from one: The use of (un)conditional information in Simpson's paradox. *Memory and Cognition* 29:193–208.

Stanovich, K. E., and R. West. 2002. Individual difference in reasoning: Implications for the rationality debate? In T. Gilovich, D. Griffin, and D. Kahneman, eds., *Heuristics and biases: The psychology of intuitive judgment* (pp. 421–440). New York: Cambridge University Press.

Steblay, N., H. M. Hosch, S. E. Culhane, and A. McWethy. 2006. The impact on juror verdicts of judicial instruction to disregard inadmissible evidence: A meta-analysis. *Law and Human Behavior* 30(4):469–492.

Strack, F., L. L. Martin, and N. Schwarz. 1988. Priming and communication: The social determinants of information use in judgments of life satisfaction. *European Journal of Social Psychology* 18:429–442.

Tetlock, P. E., and R. N. Lebow. 2001. Poking counterfactual holes in covering laws: Cognitive styles and historical reasoning. *American Political Science Review* 95(4):829–843.

Tversky, A. 1977. Features of similarity. *Psychological Review* 84(4):327–352.

Tversky, A., and D. Kahneman. 1973. On the psychology of prediction. *Psychological Review* 80:237–251. Reprinted in D. Kahneman, P. Slovic, and A. Tversky, eds. (1982). *Judgments under uncertainty: Heuristics and biases* (pp. 48–68). New York: Cambridge University Press.

Tversky, A., and D. Kahneman. 1974. Judgment under uncertainty: Heuristics and biases. *Science* 185(4157):1124–1131. Reprinted in D. Kahneman, P. Slovic, and A. Tversky, eds. (1982). *Judgments under uncertainty: Heuristics and biases* (pp. 3–20). New York: Cambridge University Press.

Tversky, A., and D. J. Koehler. 1994. Support theory: A nonextentional representation of subjective probability. *Psychological Review* 101(4):547–567.

Walker-Wilson, M., B. A. Spellman, and R. M. York. (unpublished manuscript). *Beyond instructions to disregard: When objections backfire and interruptions distract.* Available: https://public.me.com/bobbie_spellman [accessed January 2011].

Wistrich, A. J., C. Guthrie, and J. J. Rachlinski. 2004. Can judges ignore inadmissible information? The difficulty of deliberately disregarding. *University of Pennsylvania Law Review* 153:1,251–1,345.

7

Intuitive Theories of Behavior

Hal R. Arkes and James Kajdasz

In 1972, the U.S. Supreme Court ruled in *Neil* v. *Biggers* (409 U.S. 188 1972) that jurors may use a witness's confidence in assessing the witness's accuracy. The justices' entirely reasonable assumption was that more confident witnesses are necessarily more accurate. However, substantial research over the past 40 years suggests that this intuitive theory is incorrect: Confidence is not closely related to accuracy.

For many years the *Wall Street Journal* ran contests to determine the accuracy of stock movement when predicted by dartboards versus expert stockbrokers. A panel of stockbrokers picked stocks they thought would appreciate in value. Competing against them were *Wall Street Journal* staff members who threw darts at a listing of stocks. The stocks on the list that were punctured by the darts were the stocks "chosen" by the staffers. After several months, the stock prices of the two sets of stocks were compared. The intuitive theory was that the expertise of the stockbrokers would easily swamp the darts' total ignorance. The contest was eventually stopped, probably because the superiority of the stockbrokers was so embarrassingly minimal.

We all have intuitive theories regarding appropriate reasons for high confidence, the benefits of expertise, and other judgment and decision-making topics. However, many of these theories have required substantial alteration due to research findings over the past 40 years. The goal of this chapter is to present these intuitive theories and outline their shortcomings. Because research suggests that mere awareness of these shortcomings is not sufficient for the avoidance of their negative influence, some education or training may be required to prevent these intuitive theories from interfering with sound intelligence tradecraft.

INTUITIVE THEORY #1:
WHY PEOPLE BEHAVE IN PREDICTABLE WAYS

Richard Nixon was known as a fierce anticommunist. His congressional and national campaigns were characterized by severe condemnations of those whom he accused of being "soft." Yet President Nixon visited China in 1972, a trip that began to thaw the long-frozen relations between the two countries.

Anwar Sadat authorized the Yom Kippur War against Israel in 1973. This was another in a series of hostile events between Egypt and Israel that had begun with the founding of Israel 25 years earlier. Yet in 1977 Sadat visited Israel, a trip that led to a comprehensive peace agreement 2 years later between the formerly bitter enemies.

These two examples plus many others illustrate that predicting the behavior of individuals who have previously exhibited consistent behavior is not an easy task. The mistaken belief that people have a stable personality that manifests itself in consistent behavior was criticized many years ago by David Fischer (1970) in his classic book, *Historians' Fallacies*. He termed the error in question "the fallacy of essences," which is predicated on the belief that every person, nation, or culture has an essence that governs much of the behavior of that entity. Fischer was particularly blunt in his derogation of the fallacy of essences: "This most durable of secular superstitions is not susceptible to reasoned refutation. The existence of essences, like the existence of ghosts, cannot be disproved by any rational method" (p. 68). Referring to those people who endorse this fallacy as "essentialists," Fischer continues, "The essentialist's significant facts are not windows through which an observer may peek at the inner reality of things, but mirrors in which he sees his own a priori assumptions reflected" (p. 68). Of course, analysts must be on guard not to let their conclusions be nothing more than mere depictions of a priori assumptions.

Contemporaneous with Fischer's book were a pair of psychological research programs. One of the most famous controversies in the history of psychology was largely engendered by the research of Walter Mischel (1973), who pointed out convincingly that the cross-situational consistency of any person's behavior was surprisingly low. For example, extroverts did not seem to behave in a gregarious manner in all situations, and introverts did not seem to behave in a reserved manner in all situations. Mischel emphasized that the situation exerted far more influence on a person's behavior than personality theorists had previously thought. Aggressive children may be obedient at school, but defiant at home. Conscientious people may work hard on the job, but be sloths at home. Factors such as rewards, punishments, and other contingencies must be taken into account in predicting behavior, and when they are considered, predictability of behavior is markedly enhanced. For example, Vertzberger (1990) attributed some of Israel's failure to anticipate the Yom Kippur War as due to the Israeli military's underestimation of the domestic and external pressures on Sadat to initiate military operations. Instead, Vertzberger concluded that the Israeli military relied on negative stereotypes about the Arab armies. This is the crux of the fallacy of essentialism: attributing cause to stable internal factors and disregarding the powerful influence of situational external factors.

The second highly relevant psychological research program contemporaneous with Fischer's book pertains to "the fundamental attribution error" (Ross, 1977, p. 183), which is defined as the tendency " . . . to underestimate the impact of situational factors and to overestimate the role of dispositional factors in controlling behavior." A dispositional factor would be one's personality, for example. In a famous study, undergraduates concocted and then asked esoteric questions to other undergraduates in a mock quiz game. The questioners knew the answers to these questions because they created them. The questions were in areas of interest or expertise of the questioner, which meant that the respondents performed poorly in answering them. Observers who witnessed this mock quiz show and were aware of the drastically different roles of the questioners and responders nevertheless rated the former as far more knowledgeable than the latter. This result seems grossly unfair. The superior "knowledge" of the questioners was because their role gave them a tremendous advantage. The poor performance of the respondents was because their role put them at a tremendous disadvantage. Yet observers did not take this external factor of assigned role into account, instead attributing differing impressions of the two members of the pair to an internal factor—knowledge. Observers' overattribution of cause to internal factors is the fundamental attribution error (Ross et al., 1977). Ross and others do not deny the existence of personality factors. Their point is simply that observers overemphasize such internal factors, which results in less accurate predictions and judgments.

Why does the fundamental attribution error occur? Observers are simply not aware of many (or sometimes any) of the situational factors that might influence an actor's behavior. As a result the observer is left with an internal attribution by default: "It's his personality." "He's an anticommunist." "He's militarily incompetent." The actor, on the other hand, is more aware of the external factors influencing his or her behavior, so external attributions are more likely, and the fundamental attribution error is therefore less prevalent among actors than among observers (Storms, 1973).

As another example, Robert F. Kennedy and A. Schlesinger's recollection (1969), *Thirteen Days: A Memoir of the Cuban Missile Crisis,* led to a much different view of that time period than the prevailing view when the crisis occurred 7 years earlier. Immediately following the confrontation with the Soviets, the general view of the American public was that the Kennedy brothers had behaved with bravery and intelligence. These were very positive internal attributions by the public, who were in the position of observers. However, Robert Kennedy's rendition of the events seemed to imply that the President and his advisers were responding with what they perceived as an extremely constrained set of options available to them. In other words, Robert Kennedy asserted that external factors were largely responsible for the actions they took. Again, although observers make internal attributions ("He's brave"), actors are more likely to make external ones ("Krushchev said he'd do this, so we just had to respond accordingly."). Of course, intelligence analysts are in the role of observers who may or may not be aware of the external factors that may be influencing an actor's behavior, so it is understandable why the fundamental attribution error might be a temptation.

A factor that tends to foster reliance on internal, stereotypic explanations is cognitive load. Researchers found that people who were trying to remember a difficult 8-digit number while viewing a conversation tended to rely more on the stereotype they had of the conversation's participants than people who had to remember an easy 2-digit number. For example, cognitively busy people who watched a conversation between a doctor and a hairdresser tended to remember the former as more intelligent, stable, and cultured, whereas the latter was remembered as more extroverted, talkative, and attractive, even if the stereotype-congruent traits were not actually present in the appropriate conversation participant (Macrae et al., 1993). Relying on a stereotype is an internal attribution: "She is a doctor, so that's why she is likely to be intelligent." Of course, being a physician and being intelligent are indeed highly related. However, relying on such associations will serve as a " . . . mirror in which . . . one sees . . . [one's] own a priori assumptions reflected," as Fischer warned (1970, p. 68). In other words, contrary evidence is likely to be disregarded when cognitive load is high and stereotypic explanations are available.

Essentialism or the fundamental attribution error comprises an intuitive theory that is eminently sensible. If an observer cannot perceive the external causes, it is reasonable to default to an internal attribution that would have cross-situational consistency. After all, essential personality factors or other stable causes persist from one situation to another. However, the evidence is that external causal factors account for far more causal influence than we generally appreciate (Ross, 1977).

INTUITIVE THEORY #2:
HIGH-CONFIDENCE PREDICTIONS ARE LIKELY TO BE CORRECT

An intuitive theory probably endorsed by most people and officially endorsed by the Supreme Court is that predictions or judgments made with high confidence are more likely to be correct than predictions or judgments made with low confidence. However, research suggests that even expert decision makers such as physicians can lack a strong relation between confidence and accuracy. Before inserting a right-heart catheter, physicians were asked to estimate three separate indexes of heart functioning. The 198 physicians who participated in this research were also asked to state their confidence in each estimate. After each catheter was inserted and "read," the researchers could assess the relation between the accuracy of each physician's estimate and his or her confidence in that estimate. The relation was essentially zero! Like intelligence analysts, these physicians were bright, dedicated, and conscientious. They were confronted with a relatively high-stakes situation in which getting the right answer was exceedingly important. Yet the estimates in which they expressed high confidence were no more likely to be correct than those in which they expressed low confidence (Dawson et al., 1993).

Research highly relevant to the everyday tasks confronting the intelligence analyst is that of Philip Tetlock (2005), who posed forecasting problems to 284 professionals over the course of several years. These professionals were highly educated persons who had advanced training or graduate degrees in their field of expertise. They were employed in government service, by think tanks, in academia, or in international institutions. They were asked questions concerning issues such as the longevity of apartheid, the secession of Quebec, and the demise of the Soviet Union. Two indexes were used primarily to assess the accuracy of their forecasts. "Discrimination" refers to the ability to assign different probability to events that eventually do occur from events that do not occur. Figure 7-1a contains the data for a forecaster with perfect discrimination and one with poor discrimination. Forecasters' discrimination accounted for only 16 percent of the variance, leaving 84 percent of the variance unexplained.

The second index relating accuracy and confidence is "calibration," which pertains to the tendency to assign higher probabilities to higher objective frequencies of occurrence. For example, if I assign an estimated probability of occurrence of 90 percent to 10 separate events, I am well calibrated if 9 of those 10 events do actually occur. Similarly, if I assign an estimated probability of occurrence of 60 percent to 10 separate events, I

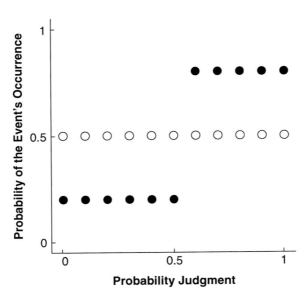

FIGURE 7-1a Low- and high-discrimination forecasters.
NOTE: The forecaster depicted by the open circles has very poor discrimination.
The forecaster depicted by the filled circles has excellent discrimination.

am well calibrated if 6 of those 10 events do actually occur. Good calibration denotes a good match between confidence and proportion correct. Figure 7-1b contains the data for a forecaster with perfect calibration and one with poor calibration. In general, Tetlock's forecasters expressed levels of confidence that were approximately 15 percent removed from reality. Forecasters did give lower confidence ratings to those events that did not occur, but their confidence was not sufficiently low. They did give higher confidence ratings to events that did occur, but their confidence was not sufficiently high. In other words, confidence and accuracy were related, but the magnitude of the relation was small. As a comparison, weather forecasters have near-perfect calibration (Murphy and Winkler, 1984), despite public perception to the contrary.

Mandel (2009) reported a research study done with Canadian intelligence analysts making predictions about upcoming political events. Their discrimination and calibration were far superior to those of Tetlock's participants. Here the application of the intuitive theory relating confidence and accuracy would be much more justified. What might account for the relatively better performance among the Canadian sample? Two factors are most likely. First, the Canadian participants were asked questions about

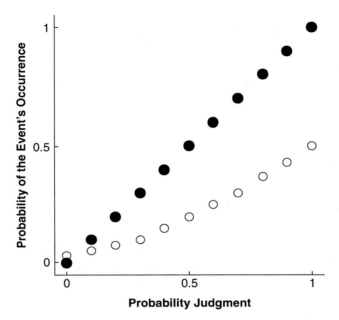

FIGURE 7-1b Low- and high-calibrated forecasters.
NOTE: The forecaster depicted by the open circles has poor calibration. The forecaster depicted by the filled circles has excellent calibration.

specific events in the Middle East or Africa that would or would not occur within the subsequent year. In general, these were specific strategic intelligence issues that the analysts had been thinking about for an extended period of time rather than questions posed "on the spot." Second, the judgments made by the Canadian participants were subject to scrutiny by their peers and superiors before the judgment was finalized. The judgments made by Tetlock's participants would not be evaluated by persons other than the researchers. The accountability such as that imposed on the Canadians has been shown to improve calibration and discrimination, as well as the complexity of the ensuing description of the raw data (Tetlock and Kim, 1987).

Other factors are also important in improving the accuracy–confidence relation from that manifested by Dawson and colleagues' (1993) physicians to that manifested by Mandel's Canadian analysts. One is the role of feedback. Physicians normally insert the catheter, obtain the results, and then apparently conclude that the results are pretty much what they would have anticipated. This "confirmation" of their nonexistent prediction is simply a manifestation of hindsight bias, which is defined as the tendency after an event has occurred to exaggerate the extent to which we think we could have predicted it beforehand (Fischhoff, 1975). With no actual prediction with which to compare the outcome data, we are free to assume that we would have made a high-quality forecast. To maximize one's learning, one needs to make a prediction and then obtain feedback. The physicians in the Dawson et al. (1993) study had never been forced previously to make an a priori prediction to which they could have compared the catheter data. Mandel's participants, on the other hand, were asked to make a binary prediction about the occurrence or nonoccurrence of an event during a specified time period. At the end of the period, the event either had or had not taken place. This was perfect feedback that could then be compared to the forecast. The bases for the matches and mismatches could then be discussed with the analyst—an ideal learning opportunity likely to improve the confidence–accuracy relation.

The second factor important in tightening the confidence–accuracy relation is to consider contrary evidence. In one exemplary study control group, participants were asked to answer two-option multiple-choice questions and indicate their confidence in their chosen answer. As usual, the confidence–accuracy relation was similar to that found by Tetlock: confidence exceeded accuracy. A second group was asked to provide a reason supporting the alternative it selected as the correct one, and another group was asked to generate a reason that supported the alternative choice—the option not selected. This study by Koriat and colleagues (1980) had two interesting findings. First, the group providing the supporting reason had the same elevated confidence as the control group, suggesting that people left to their own devices generate reasons supporting their choice. Second, being forced to generate a contrary reason markedly improved the confidence–judgment relation. The structured analytic technique known as "analysis of competing hypotheses" (ACH) fosters consideration of evidence contrary to the hypothesis tentatively being favored. This technique exploits the motivation behind the Koriat et al. study, although the efficacy of ACH in intelligence tradecraft has not been extensively tested. (However, see Folker, 2000, and Lehner et al., 2008.)

Another technique designed to prevent one's concentration largely on supporting evidence has been advocated by Neustadt and May (1986), who taught a course at Harvard entitled "The Uses of History." Neustadt and May recommended that decision makers who confront an uncertain situation list those factors that are known, those that are presumed, and those that are unclear. The list of factors in that third column might help keep overconfidence under control and improve the confidence–judgment relation. Without the entries in that column, people would generate primarily supporting reasons, which would in turn inflate confidence, which would then cause an unwarranted belief that their prediction would be highly accurate.

INTUITIVE THEORY #3:
EXPERTISE HAS ONLY BENEFITS, NOT COSTS

We'll use a definition of "experts" proposed by Shanteau (1992, p. 255): " . . . those who have been recognized within their profession as having the necessary skills and abilities to perform at the highest level." Expertise obviously has enormous advantages over naïveté. However, expertise has some surprising pitfalls that need to be recognized and avoided. The problem is that experts may know many facts within a particular domain, but may not necessarily make good decisions within that domain.

Consider again the study in which physicians were asked to estimate three measures of cardiac functioning before they inserted a right-heart catheter into a patient (Dawson et al., 1993). Although more experienced physicians' estimates were no more accurate than those of their less experienced colleagues, the veteran physicians were significantly more confident. In one sense these results should not have been surprising, because Einhorn and Hogarth (1978) showed more than 30 years ago that merely rendering more decisions within a domain ineluctably leads to more confidence in those decisions. Of course, experts do have more experience than rookies.

Experts Versus Algorithms

A second possible comparison is not between experts and nonexperts, but between experts and simple algorithms. An example of a simple algorithm is to predict the probability of an event in the next 5 years to be equal to the relative frequency of that event in the past 5 years. What is the probability that Quebec will vote to secede from Canada? The answer is simply to report the consistent results of the last such referendums. Tetlock's 284 professionals who participated in his research exhibited substantially inferior calibration and discrimination compared to the algorithms (Tetlock, 2005). This is an extremely common finding (Grove et al., 2000), which is troubling. Experts are indisputably much more knowledgeable than novices and cognitively vacuous algorithms. What factors are impeding the experts' performance?

The first factor is that in a rich data source, an expert can find some evidence to support nearly any prediction or conclusion. In this sense experts are *too* adroit. In one research study undergraduates and graduate students in finance were asked to make predictions about the fate of various companies' stocks. Both groups of participants were given background and financial information for each company. Despite their vastly superior knowledge, the finance graduate students actually performed worse. A major problem in their predictions is captured by the statistical index known as "scatter," which is an amalgamation of multiple standard deviations. The finance students were aware of far more potential predictors than were the novices, so their predictions flitted from reliance on one cue to another as each company's complex financial information was presented for evaluation. This inconsistency led to high scatter, which led to poor prediction performance. The undergraduates who knew much less than the experts based their predictions on the few cues they were able to apprehend. Their scatter was lower, which improved their prediction performance (Yates et al., 1991).

The greater consistency of algorithms is also what gives them an advantage over experts. Simple algorithms are boringly consistent. Plug some predictors into a simple algorithm that forecasts political instability, and you will get an answer. Plug it in again, and you will get the same answer. This is not so with humans, who can be inconsistent, overworked, and otherwise distracted. Humans are needed to create the algorithms, and only humans can perform the absolutely essential task of identifying the potentially relevant cues. However, Tetlock (2005) showed that in making the actual predictions, the algorithms bested their creators.

The cognitive adroitness with which experts are blessed can pose an additional problem. Given a rich data source such as those commonly found in the intelligence community, an expert can generally find a "broken leg cue" that can be used to override an algorithm or any other prediction. To use an example based on Meehl (1954), consider the task of predicting whether a professor will see a movie today. Our algorithm employs factors such as the day of the week and the type of movie available to make its prediction. However, the prediction fails because the algorithm cannot consider the fact that the professor cannot leave the house because he has a broken leg, a condition that negates the normally accurate forecast made by the algorithm.

Experts are able to find broken leg cues in a rich data source. Whether such a cue truly *should* override a prediction is highly problematic. In general, allowing people to override a prediction based on what they *think* is a genuine broken leg cue causes a decrease in the accuracy of the prediction (Lawrence et al., 2002) because people are prone to attribute more diagnosticity to such cues than they actually deserve. Note the irony of this situation. Novices are less likely to presume that they know enough to override the prediction (Arkes et al., 1986), and they perceive fewer candidate cues that could signify a broken leg. Thus they do not override the prediction, and therefore can perform better. Due to their understandably higher level of confidence, experts are more likely to presume that they do know enough to override, and they thus can perform worse.

Schema-Based Reasoning

A second important cost of expertise is that experts have the background knowledge with which they can fill in knowledge gaps with concocted data. Students in a hearing and speech science class were shown four symptoms of Down's syndrome. Approximately half the students were able to make the diagnosis. Half were not. Twelve days later these same students were shown 12 symptoms, 4 of which were the ones shown previously, 4 of which were symptoms of Down's syndrome that had *not* been shown before, and 4 of which were unrelated to Down's syndrome. All subjects indicated whether they had seen each symptom 12 days earlier. Those students who had not been able to make a diagnosis during the first presentation relatively confidently (and correctly) deemed all eight of the new symptoms as not having been shown earlier. However, those students who had been expert enough to make the diagnosis of Down's syndrome were uncertain whether the "new" symptoms related to Down's syndrome had been shown 12 days before. They were quite certain that the symptoms *un*related to the syndrome were new, but those new related ones were problematic. "I know that a fissured tongue is characteristic of a child with Down's syndrome, and I know that this child has Down's syndrome. So I wonder if I may have seen it 12 days ago when the child's symptoms were presented." This indecision is caused by the fact that the knowledge base of the better students led them to suspect that data consistent with their diagnosis might have been seen. The less knowledgeable students had a more impoverished database—they could not make a diagnosis—so this identification problem was not present for them. The benefit of expertise was manifested in the finding that the students who could make the correct diagnosis were highly confident that the old symptoms consistent with Down's syndrome actually had been shown the week before, and they were also highly confident that the new symptoms inconsistent with Down's syndrome had not (Arkes and Harkness, 1980).

A related study was done by Arkes and Freedman (1984). Baseball experts know that if (1) there is one out and men on first and third, (2) the team in the field attempts a double play, and (3) a run is scored, then it may be inferred that the batter was safe at first. Baseball experts and nonexperts read exactly this scenario and were later asked to state whether various sentences had appeared in the story. One such sentence was "The batter was safe at first," a sentence that never appeared. Experts mistakenly thought that it had. Nonexperts correctly deemed it "new."

The results of both the Down's syndrome and the baseball inference studies can be explained by use of the concept of a schema (plural is "schemata"). Schemata are " . . . mental structures—units of organized knowledge that individuals have about their world" (Moates and Schumacher, 1980, p. 17). For example, I have a schema concerning the layout of a particular traffic intersection near my home. I have a schema concerning how to fix a flat tire. The hearing and speech science students who were able to make a diagnosis imposed their schema of Down's syndrome onto the collection of symptoms they were shown. Two weeks later they could recall that schema, but they no longer had a crisp memory of the evidence that had instantiated the schema in the first place. As a result they were unable to determine whether "fissured tongue" was an old or new stimulus. It was consistent with the schema, which may have tempted the respondents into saying "old." However, they had no actual memory of its presentation, which should have fostered the decision to call it "new." Students who were not able to impose the schema of Down's syndrome on the original set of symptoms had no such problem because there was no basis for incorrectly deeming it to be "old." Thus they could confidently deem it "new."

Similarly, the baseball experts could easily infer that the batter was safe at first because the attempt at the double play must have failed if the runner on third had scored. This inference composed the test sentence, so experts were prone to think this sentence had been presented. Their schematic knowledge concerning the rules of baseball usually confers a benefit. However, in this case it constituted a cost. Nonexperts could not make an inference about the fate of the batter, so there was no reason for them to think that the new sentence had been presented earlier.

Experts have highly structured schematic knowledge. Organizing knowledge into schemata is generally highly adaptive. When Jones is seen during a follow-up visit, the physician does not have to recall every symptom Jones had during the first visit. The doctor just needs to recall the diagnosis, which comprises a cognitively economical way of capturing all of the characteristics of the patient's medical situation.

In their analysis of the failure of the Israeli Directorate of Military Intelligence (AMAN) to anticipate the Yom Kippur attack in 1973, Bar-Joseph and Kruglanski (2003) point out that the lack of information was not the cause of intelligence failures. It was the " . . . incorrect comprehension of the meaning of available information before the attack . . ." (p. 77) that caused the failure. Information consistent with the prevailing schema is accepted or inferred, but questionable data are mistakenly thought to be veridical, and inconsistent information is rejected. Kruglanski and Webster (1996) refer to this situation as "seizing and freezing." An incorrect hypothesis—a schema of the situation—is seized. This schema freezes out contrary information. The incorrect schema persists. Those who do not share this overarching schema are less likely to freeze out the contrary information, a point we will return to when we discuss the dangers of premature closure of hypothesis generation.

Cognitive Styles

Tetlock (2005) divided his experts into two gross categories—hedgehogs and foxes, based on the dichotomy invented by Isaiah Berlin. The hedgehogs have one large, overriding schema, such as "axis of evil," with which they parsimoniously analyze world affairs. Foxes are less wedded to one overarching world view and instead "improvise ad hoc solutions" (p. 21) to explain and forecast individual events. We would say that hedgehogs are more schematic than foxes are, and Tetlock's data illustrate the costs of such schemata. First, hedgehogs do not change their minds as much as foxes do when disconfirming data occur, the point made by Bar-Joseph and Kruglanski (2003). AMAN knew that the Egyptian military exercises seemed "unusually realistic" in the days preceding the Yom Kippur War, but that datum was interpreted to be consistent with the prevailing schema that this was the usual time for Egypt's annual exercises. Hedgehogs more than foxes see the world in schematic terms, so hedgehogs are more likely to distort the data to fit the schema.

Second, their lower propensity to perform such data "management" may be the one reason why foxes have superior calibration and discrimination compared to hedgehogs. Because they can assume multiple perspectives rather than rely on one overarching perspective, foxes can more accurately distinguish what did and did not occur and can assign confidence levels more appropriately. These tasks are the essence of calibration and discrimination.

Third, hedgehogs are more likely than foxes to invoke "close-call counterfactuals" in explaining away their forecasting failures. "Sure, I predicted that Soviet hardliners would prevail, but if the conspirators had been just a little less inebriated, they would have succeeded in ousting Gorbachev." To explain away a forecasting failure means to disregard important feedback, which might impair future judgments.

Related to this is a fourth point. Hedgehogs, more than foxes, are biased in their interpretation of evidence consistent and inconsistent with their opinion. Hedgehogs seem relatively unapologetic about denigrating contrary evidence and accepting consistent data, which is to be expected if their knowledge is more schematic than that of foxes. Table 7-1 summarizes some of the differences Tetlock hypothesizes between hedgehogs and foxes.

As a final example of the cost of expertise, consider some research that was motivated by the fact that delays in diagnosing celiac disease average an unbelievable 13 years! (Celiac disease is a digestive disorder resulting from intolerance to the protein gluten.) The researchers presented 84

TABLE 7-1 Hedgehogs Versus Foxes

Hedgehogs	Foxes
More schematic thinking	Less schematic thinking
Less responsive to disconfirming data	More responsive to disconfirming data
Inferior calibration	Superior calibration
Inferior discrimination	Superior discrimination
More likely to explain away disconfirmed forecasts	Less likely to explain away disconfirmed forecasts

SOURCE: Adapted from Tetlock (2005).

physicians with a scenario consistent with celiac disease; 50 physicians misdiagnosed the condition! Thirty-eight of these 50 then underwent a "stimulated recall" in which they were asked to report their thoughts as the researchers and physicians jointly went back through the physicians' information gathering that had occurred during the original diagnosis exercise. One conclusion was the following (Kostopoulou et al., 2009, p. 282): "Information inconsistent with the favorite irritable bowel syndrome diagnosis was overlooked." Once an incorrect schema is substantiated, consistent evidence is noted, and inconsistent evidence is not. Physicians are exceptionally intelligent people who are trying their utmost to "get it right." They are experts in their field. But experts are expected to impose a schema, which in the case of medicine is a diagnosis. Do we want our physicians to be capable of generating a diagnosis? Of course! But this expertise has a cognitive cost.

To counteract this cost, Vertzberger (1990, p. 355) suggested a "two-tiered system" of analysts, " . . . one tier to deal with current information on a daily basis, the other to deal with information patterns and processes that emerge over time. . . . A two-tiered system is also needed because of the effects of incrementalism and preconceptions that cause discrepant information to be assimilated into existing images. . . . To overcome the effects of both incrementalism and preconceptions, a new team of analysts (in addition to those permanently on the job) should be inexperienced in the specific issue area because experience can be counterproductive due to preconceptions."

Vertzberger (1990) suggests the second tier of analysts should be inexperienced in the topic being analyzed! Because inexperienced analysts have no schema, they do not have the disadvantage of preconceptions, which can damage the unbiased consideration of incoming data. Of course, the experienced analysts have greater domain expertise, which is an essential benefit. But expertise has some costs, which the second tier of analysts might be able to minimize.

This second tier of analysis is similar to the technique of "Devil's

Advocacy," a popular technique used in organizations and a "Structured Analytic Technique" used in the intelligence community. This strategy involves assigning a group the task of criticizing a plan or suggestion in order to expose its weaknesses. The effectiveness of this strategy has been justifiably questioned, although research seems to indicate that if the devil's advocate exhibits authentic disagreement with the plan rather than merely fulfilling a role of being a contrary individual, the technique is significantly more effective (Nemeth et al., 2001).

INTUITIVE THEORY #4:
MORE INFORMATION IS ALWAYS BETTER

This intuitive theory seems unassailable. However, we have already presented a hint suggesting that this theory might not be correct. The graduate students in finance in the Yates et al. (1991) study would have been able to discern and use much more of each company's financial information than would the undergrads. Yet the finance graduate students predicted the future stock prices less accurately. As was pointed out earlier, the scatter of the finance students' predictions was higher because they based their forecasts on varying amalgamations of the various available cues. Higher scatter means less consistent judgments.

A second reason why more information may be detrimental is that the extra information may be of low quality and may dilute the diagnosticity of the earlier information. Fifty-nine graduate students in social work were asked to read information about 12 clients and provide ratings indicating how likely it was that each client was a child abuser. In the personality profiles of most interest to this discussion, some clients' descriptions had either one or two pieces of information that pretest subjects had indicated were highly diagnostic of being a child abuser, such as "He was sexually assaulted by his stepfather." The researchers inserted into various profiles zero, two, four, or eight pieces of information that pretest subjects had indicated were nondiagnostic, such as "He was born in Muskegon." The most important finding was that adding completely nondiagnostic information had a pronounced effect of diminishing the impact of the diagnostic information. "Dilution effect" is the apt name the researchers gave to this phenomenon (Nisbett et al., 1981). The additional information should have been disregarded. Instead it played a detrimental role with regard to the judge's performance.

Graduate students in social work are not stupid or careless people. However, their predictions seemed to be based on a type of averaging rule or similarity judgment rather than on normative Bayesian reasoning. The more nondiagnostic information one has, the less the target person bears some similarity to the category into which he or she might be a candidate.

The average diagnosticity of the various pieces of information to the stereo-type of a child abuser diminishes the more nondiagnostic information one has. Being born in Muskegon and working in a hardware store do not seem to be diagnostic of a child abuser, so when these two pieces of informa-tion are added to being sexually assaulted by one's stepfather, the average diagnosticity is reduced compared to the scenario in which the diagnostic piece of information is not diluted. Of course, this averaging strategy is not normative. Here is a case in which more information, if not combined properly, will lead to worse judgments.

Perhaps the most prominent research program devoted to the use of a small number of predictors is that of Gerd Gigerenzer, who suggests that people use "fast and frugal" heuristics to make judgments. One such heu-ristic is called "Take the Best," in which a judge " . . . tries cues in order, one at a time searching for a cue that discriminates between the two objects in question" (Gigerenzer et al., 1999, p. 98). For example, who is more likely to succeed Castro, person A or person B? A forecaster who uses the Take the Best (TTB) heuristic will first think of the best cue that would help answer this question, such as whether person A or person B is a blood relative of Castro. If one person is and the other is not, then the forecast is based on this single factor. If both persons are or are not blood relatives, then this cue cannot distinguish between the two candidates, and the next best cue is used, such as the number of years he or she has been prominent in the Cuban government. The judgment is made when the decision maker finds a cue that can discriminate between the two candidates. Note that this heuristic uses few cues, whereas a statistical technique such as multiple regression, for example, generally uses more cues. Gigerenzer and his col-leagues have shown that TTB does approximately as well as, and sometimes better than, multiple regression in making accurate judgments on tasks such as predicting a high school's drop-out rate or a professor's salary. In other words, the extra information needed to feed a multiple regression equation is often not worth the effort. How can this be?

Because analysts do not think in a way that mimics a multiple-regression equation, and because most problems that confront analysts cannot be ana-lyzed using such an equation, our consideration of this question should be directed at the high performance of TTB rather than its relative accuracy compared to that of multiple regression. One reason for its high perfor-mance is that TTB is not likely to succumb to the dilution effect. Few cues are scanned and only one is used, so there is less danger of dilution in TTB. Second, such problems are likely to have flat maxima; once the best cue or cues are considered, modest changes in the weights placed on those cues or the addition of cues with negligible validity will have only a small effect on accuracy. So TTB, which uses few cues and does not even address the issue of weights, is not going to suffer much of a diminution in its accuracy by disregarding some potentially relevant cues. Third is the problem of "overfitting." If I have developed a regression equation that predicts political instability in nations, I must have used some historical cases to develop that algorithm. My equation may fit the historical data quite well, but will it fit new cases, because they may differ in some important way from the countries I used to create the equation? In other words, the equation may fit the prior data that generated it better than the new data that it attempts to predict. Gigerenzer and colleagues (1999) provide examples that show that this shrinkage in fit may be smaller when going from an old to a new dataset when TTB is used than when multiple regression is used. The point is that once a decision maker appropriately employs a small number of diagnostic cues, the time, effort, and possibly the danger of obtaining the additional cues may not be worth the extra cost. More information is not necessarily better.

We will use a final study to drive home this point (Arkes et al., 1986). People who participated in this research were shown the grades that each of 40 University of Oregon undergraduates received in three courses taken during their senior year. The participants' task was to decide on the basis of this evidence whether each of the 40 undergraduates had graduated with honors. Each participant was given a table accurately indicating that if the student in question received three grades of A, then the probability of graduating with honors was 79 percent; with two A's it was 62 percent, with one A it was 39 percent, and with no A it was 19 percent. This experiment investigated two important factors. The first was incentive. Some participants were paid nothing; some were paid 10 cents per correct answer; some were told that the person who predicted correctly the highest number of times would get $5. The second factor was the type of instructions. Two groups of subjects—the control group and the "no-feedback" group—were both told that 70 percent correct was about as well as anyone could hope to do on this task. The former group, but not the latter, received feedback on every trial as to whether their prediction was correct. A third group—the "innovate" group—was told about this 70 percent expectation, but was also told " . . . we think that people who are extremely observant might be able to beat the 70 percent level. Give it a try." The fourth and final group—the "debiasing" group—was told that people who try to beat the 70 percent expectation actually do worse. "So just follow an obvious strategy that will allow you to get most of the answers right" (Arkes et al., 1986, p. 97).

The results were highly instructive. First, both of the groups incentivized with money performed more poorly than did the group whose members received no money. Second, the control and "innovate" groups had nearly identical data. Third, the debiasing group did the best, with the no-feedback group close behind. Both performed significantly better than did the control group subjects. These results teach us several lessons.

First, extra incentive can reduce performance! People who are highly motivated to "get it right" are not satisfied with using a rule that results in only a 70 percent accuracy level. Even though the task is probabilistic and not deterministic, that is, even though the correct answer cannot be known with certainty, decision makers who are highly motivated will want to squeeze out every iota of error variance. Who can blame them? If accuracy is very important, then this seems like a reasonable goal. However, if the task is probabilistic, then it is not possible to eliminate all error, and one must be satisfied with the best, albeit imperfect, prediction strategy. In this study those with high incentives were less likely to heed the obvious rule of "Choose 'honors' if the person had 2 or 3 A's, choose 'not honors' otherwise." They wanted to beat 70 percent, so they used highly creative, but invalid, strategies to try to maximize their performance.

Second, the fact that the control and "innovate" groups had nearly identical data suggests that people who are given no special instructions to "innovate" do so anyway. The strategies used by these participants were inventive, but invalid.

Third, debiasing worked in that people who were told to curb their attempts to beat the obvious strategy were able to restrain themselves and thus performed better than the two worst groups.

Fourth, being given no feedback about the correctness of their predictions resulted in relatively high performance. How can this be?! Consider what happens when a person uses the optimal strategy and is told that the prediction is incorrect. That person is tempted to abandon the current strategy and search for one that can squeeze out a higher proportion of correct answers. Because the strategy one would shift to in this situation must be inferior to the optimal strategy, performance would suffer. However, if one uses the best strategy and is not told that the prediction is incorrect, there is no temptation to abandon it.

This experiment plus the follow-up study, which showed that experts are most prone to abandon the best strategy, have some direct implications for persons in high-stakes situations. In most forecasting tasks performed by an intelligence analyst, eliminating all uncertainty would be impossible. Should a responsible analyst continue to search for more information? If the task truly is probabilistic, one cannot guarantee that the best option can ever be discerned or that the best option would accomplish the desired result. Hence further information gathering may be futile. Second, more cues might mean less valid cues, which may in turn inappropriately dilute the impact of the valid ones. Third, more cues may lead one to attend to bogus broken leg cues, which can tempt one to disregard the conclusions of a very good strategy. In a profound article, Einhorn (1986) pointed out that one has to accept error to make less error. By this he meant that in a probabilistic task, one has to accept the fact that some error is inevitable. If one does not accept that and instead tries to convert the task to a deterministic task in which there is no error, then one will make more error by incorporating worthless cues and adopting suboptimal strategies. When the stakes are high, there is understandable reluctance to decide that all of the predictability has already been squeezed out of the situation. Indeed, accepting error is politically and pragmatically more difficult in some domains than in others. But consider the fact that even with X-rays, computed tomography (CT) scans, and an arsenal of lab tests, diagnosing a disease is not always possible. Is human behavior more predictable than a medical condition?

INTUITIVE THEORY #5:
ACCURATE, QUICKEST—AND DANGEROUS

Experts, one would hope, are able to quickly size up a situation, make superior assessments, and execute better quality decisions compared to novices who appear indecisive and seem to flail about as they attempt to comprehend the situation. Evidence for the quick and accurate expert can be found, for example, in the game of chess. Players rated as chess masters were compared to lower ranked class B players. The quality of the moves the players made during games was evaluated by a group of highly rated grand masters on a 5-point scale, where 5 = outstanding move and 1 = blunder. Regulation play is relatively slow paced, with approximately 2.25 minutes per move. In regulation play the average move quality of master players was nearly identical to the average move quality of class B players. The disparity between expert and novice became more apparent when speed of play was increased. In blitz play the time is highly restricted, giving players on average only 6 seconds per move. Under these conditions the novice B players made more blunder moves, increasing from 11 percent in regulation play to 25 percent blunders in blitz play, and their average move quality dropped to 2.68. The masters were able to maintain their average move quality at 3.02, with no increase in blunders observed. "[T]he move quality of master games was virtually unaffected by vastly increased time pressure" (Calderwood et al., 1988, p. 490). Klein (1998) observed similar quick and accurate decision-making performance in other experienced professionals. Fireground commanders were able to rapidly visualize how the fire was moving inside a building and choose an appropriate strategy. Nurses in the neonatal intensive care unit were able to look at a premature infant and know if the infant had become septic from infection, even though the less experienced could see no indication. The experts in these examples do not spend time comparing various alternatives, Klein argued.

Rather, based on their broad experience base, they simply know the correct, or at least reasonable, course of action to take. "Skilled decision makers make sense of the situation at hand by recognizing it as one of the prototypical situations they have experienced and stored in their long-term memory. This recognition match is usually done without deliberation" (Phillips et al., 2004, p. 305).

It's not surprising, then, that rapid decisions are sometimes taken as a signal for expertise. However, to achieve high levels of accuracy, decision makers must know when to slow down the assessment and decision process. When a situation presents a novel scenario that does not map well onto past scenarios, the best decision makers recognize that quick and accurate assessment may not be possible. "Sometimes the decision maker runs up against a situation that is ambiguous or unfamiliar. The expert must then deliberate about the nature of the situation, often seeking additional information to round out the picture" (Phillips et al., 2004, p. 305).

Expertise is easier to acquire in some domains than others. According to Shanteau (1992), the characteristics of the domain dictate how easily expertise can be gained over time. He suggests that gaining expertise in a given domain is more difficult if (1) the domain is fluid and has changing conditions, (2) we have to predict human behavior as opposed to physical states, (3) we have less chance for feedback, (4) the task does not have enough repetition to build a sense of typicality, or (5) we confront a unique task. This is a discouraging list. The domain of intelligence analysis seems to contain many (if not all) of these limitations. Let's consider each limitation in turn.

The firefighter, neonatal nurse, chess master, and intelligence analyst are all working in a domain that is, to some degree, fluid and changing. However, the infant's body will not suddenly abandon one disease in favor of another. An intelligence target, on the other hand, can abandon one strategy in favor of another.

The firefighter and neonatal nurse are observing and predicting the physical state of a burning building or an infant's biological system. Only the chess master and intelligence analyst are predominantly predicting human behavior. However, the behavior that can be exhibited on a chess board is highly restricted by a codified set of rules. This simplifies the task of the chess master by constricting the range of possible human behavior that must be considered. This restricted range makes it more likely that any given behavior has been observed before.

Repeated behavior allows the chess master to draw on feedback received during those past games. The firefighter also has encountered enough burning buildings to develop a sense of what is typical when a fire consumes a building. The neonatal nurse acquires a sense of how a typical infant should look and act. An intelligence analyst can develop a sense of what typical message traffic is like. However, there is an important difference between the analyst and the other professionals when an atypical situation occurs. The experienced nurse or firefighter is likely to have encountered such a situation before, allowing them to draw on experience. The experienced intelligence analyst, some might argue, is more likely to deal with a turn of world events that has no precedent. Furthermore, the "real answer" to the analytic question may never be known, or may be debated by historians for decades. When taking an action to control a fire, the firefighter can see the fire's response to that action. The neonatal nurse later learns the outcome of the patient. The chess master wins or loses the game. These professionals will benefit from feedback; the analyst often will not receive feedback.

Because the nature of intelligence analysis often denies us the ability to make the quick, accurate assessments that experts in some other domains can make, a slower, more careful comparison of options is the only alternative. Herek et al. (1987) offer a picture of what careful analysis looks like and the better decisions it facilitates. The authors studied the policy decisions made by U.S. Presidents during 19 international crises. They suspected that the most effective policy makers were those who engaged in a careful search for relevant information, made a critical appraisal of viable alternatives, performed careful contingency planning, and exercised caution to avoid mistakes. They were interested in seeing whether such quality processes were observed to lead frequently to higher quality outcomes. They defined a poor-quality process as one exhibiting defective symptoms such as (1) gross omissions in surveying alternatives, (2) gross omissions in surveying objectives, (3) failure to examine major costs and risks of preferred choice, (4) poor information search, (5) selective bias in processing information at hand, (6) failure to reconsider originally rejected alternatives, and (7) failure to work out detailed implementation, monitoring, and contingency plans. A favorable outcome to the United States was one that did not increase international conflict or lead to military confrontation, escalation, or risk of nuclear war (rated separately by both conservative and liberal judges). In their study Herek et al. (1987) found that high-quality processes (e.g., careful survey of various alternatives, etc.) were much more likely to result in high-quality outcomes ($r = 0.64$). This is a very impressive statistic.

Ramifications of the Hasty Assessment

The consideration of various alternatives sometimes will involve a search for objective diagnostic indicators that favor one hypothesis over others. There may be pressure to make an assessment as quickly as possible. Thus there is the temptation to arrive at a conclusion after evaluating only a minimum of indicators. Accepting a hypothesis has unfortunate implications when it is done prematurely. For example, physicians may request no more tests if they believe they have reached a diagnosis, when in fact that diagnosis is erroneous.

A possible strategy to counteract premature closure to a hypothesis might be to deem the current hypothesis as only tentative. Theoretically a tentative hypothesis can be revised as additional information is obtained. Unfortunately the very act of creating even a tentative or "working" hypothesis can have negative cognitive ramifications. The initial hypothesis, once formed, is resistant to change. Additional information is processed in a biased manner so that we are "apt to accept 'confirming' evidence at face value while subjecting 'disconfirming' evidence to critical evaluation, and as a result [we] draw undue support for [the] initial position from mixed or random empirical findings" (Lord et al., 1979, p. 2,098). This effect has been observed in a number of psychological studies.

In one experiment, a series of fictitious crime studies was created. The results showed mixed support for the effectiveness of capital punishment as a deterrent. People who had previously supported the death penalty interpreted the mixed results as supporting their view. Others who opposed the death penalty believed the same results supported their view (Lord et al., 1979)! In another study, supporters of nuclear deterrence believed the factual descriptions of near accidents showed that current safeguards were adequate. Supporters of nuclear disarmament believed the existence of such near accidents indicated just how possible a more serious accident was (Plous, 1991).

Why do we process this post-hypothesis information in a biased manner? Kruglanski and Webster (1996) argue that individuals exhibit a tendency toward cognitive permanence—a need to preserve past knowledge. Consolidating a hypothesis gives us understanding (or at least the illusion of understanding) of the world around us. This understanding allows a degree of predictability to guide us in our future actions. A lack of closure fosters an uncomfortable state; we are forced to revaluate previous knowledge we thought we could accept.

Bar-Joseph and Kruglanski (2003) offer an example of how the need for quick closure and the desire to make such closure permanent can hinder intelligence analysis. These authors believe that such factors contributed to the Israeli surprise during the 1973 Yom Kippur War. Two of the most influential intelligence analysts for Israel leading up to the war were Major General Eli Zeira (Director of Military Intelligence) and Lieutenant Colonel Yona Bandman (Israel's lead analyst for Egyptian issues). Zeira and Bandman assessed the chance of an attack from Egypt across the Suez Canal as being "close to zero" as long as Egypt lacked a fighter force capable of challenging the Israeli Air Force and ballistic missiles with enough range to threaten greater Israel. Zeira and Bandman, according to Bar-Joseph and Kruglanski, exhibited behavior consistent with a high need for cognitive closure. Such characteristics include a reluctance to interpret new information that might conflict with their views, discomfort with a plurality of opinions, and an authoritarian style of leadership (Bar-Joseph and Kruglanski, 2003, p. 84):

> Both exhibited a highly authoritarian and decisive managerial style. Both lacked the patience for long and open discussions and regarded them as "bullshit." Zeira used to humiliate officers who, in his opinion, came unprepared for meetings. At least once he was heard to say that those officers who estimated in spring 1973 that a war was likely should not expect a promotion. Bandman, although less influential . . . than Zeira, used to express either verbally or in body language his disrespect for the opinion of others. He was also known for his total rejection of any attempt to change a single word, even a comma, in a document he wrote.

It is not surprising, then, that Bandman and Zeira failed to revise their original estimate of the potential for an Egypt attack even though "In the days that preceded the Yom Kippur War, the Research Division of Military Intelligence had plenty of warning indicators which had been supplied (to them) by AMAN's Collection Division and by the other Israeli collecting agencies" (Agranat, 1975, as cited in Bar-Joseph and Kruglanski, 2003, p. 76).

Earlier we mentioned the course taught by Neustadt and May that is the basis for their 1986 book, *Thinking in Time*. Their book advocates use of "Alexander's Question," which is named after Dr. Russell Alexander. This public health professor was a member of the advisory committee that met before the March 1976 decision to immunize the U.S. citizenry against the swine flu. He asked what new data might convince his colleagues that the nation should not be immunized against the flu. His query was not answered, according to Neustadt and May. What if Israeli intelligence officers Bandman and Zeira had been asked Alexander's Question: "What information would make you revise your current view that the Egyptian army isn't going to attack?" To answer that reasonable but pesky question, Bandman and Zeira would have had to state a priori what would constitute disconfirming evidence. If any such data subsequently occurred, then premature closure and distortion of new information would both be avoided because such data previously had been deemed to be highly informative.

Note that "Alexander's Question" explicitly requests a decision maker to state what disconfirmatory evidence would be highly diagnostic. This request bears some similarity to structured analytic techniques currently advocated by some intelligence agencies. For example, ACH requires that analysts provide evidence supporting hypotheses contrary to the one currently being favored. Red Team Analysis requires that a subset of analysts take the role of an adversary in order to mimic what an actor within a different cultural and political environment would do. Team A/Team B is a technique that pits two or more competing hypotheses against each other. All of these techniques are designed to give contrary views a fair hearing.

CONCLUDING COMMENTS

A problem with intuitive theories is that they remain unchallenged due to their apparent validity. The study of judgment and decision making is a relatively recent phenomenon, so it is understandable why intuitive theories have not been challenged much earlier. We are not under the illusion that mere awareness of the evidence we have presented will eliminate any detrimental influence of these theories on intelligence tradecraft. However, we have suggested some debiasing strategies that should make their negative sway less powerful. "Alexander's Question," Koriat and colleagues' (1980) suggestion that reasons be provided for alternative courses of action, and the results from Tetlock and Kim (1987) and Mandel (2009) suggesting that instantiating accountability may improve judgment, are all potential affirmative steps one can take to introduce debiasing techniques into day-to-day intelligence tradecraft. Some research has already been performed to test the efficacy of structured analytic techniques (e.g., Folker, 2000; Lehner et al., 2008). The mixed results from these initial studies suggest that the techniques may be more effective with some tasks than others and with some participants than others. However, the results must be considered preliminary given the small number of tests with a limited number of participants. We suggest that further research be done in as realistic a manner as possible. This will allow testing of structured analytic techniques to determine if they do indeed improve intelligence performance and reduce reliance on tempting, but inaccurate, intuitive theories.

REFERENCES

Agranat (Investigation committee, Yom Kippur War). 1975. *The report of the Agranat commission*. Tel Aviv, Israel: Am Oved.

Arkes, H. R., and M. R. Freedman. 1984. A demonstration of the costs and benefits of expertise in recognition memory. *Memory and Cognition* 12:84–89.

Arkes, H. R., and A. Harkness. 1980. The effect of making a diagnosis on subsequent recognition of symptoms. *Journal of Experimental Psychology: Human Learning and Memory* 6:568–575.

Arkes, H. R., R. M. Dawes, and C. Christensen. 1986. Factors influencing the use of a decision rule in a probabilistic task. *Organizational Behavior and Human Decision Processes* 37:93–110.

Bar-Joseph, U., and A. W. Kruglanski. 2003. Intelligence failure and need for cognitive closure: On the psychology of the Yom Kippur surprise. *Political Psychology* 24:75–99.

Calderwood, R., G. A. Klein, and B. W. Crandall. 1988. Time pressure, skill, and move quality in chess. *American Journal of Psychology* 101:481–493.

Dawson, N. V., A. F. Connors, Jr., T. Speroff, A. Kemka, P. Shaw, and H. R. Arkes. 1993. Hemodynamic assessment in the critically ill: Is physician confidence warranted? *Medical Decision Making* 13:258–266.

Einhorn, H. 1986. Accepting error to make less error. *Journal of Personality Assessment* 50: 387–395.

Einhorn, H. J., and R. M. Hogarth. 1978. Confidence in judgment: Persistence in the illusion of validity. *Psychological Review* 85:395–416.

Fischer, D. H. 1970. *Historians' fallacies: Toward a logic of historical thought.* New York: Harper.

Fischhoff, B. 1975. Hindsight is not equal to foresight: The effect of outcome knowledge on judgment under uncertainty. *Journal of Experimental Psychology: Human Perception and Performance* 1(3):288–299.

Folker, R. D., Jr. 2000. *Intelligence analysis in theater joint intelligence centers: An experiment in applying structured methods.* Occasional Paper No. 7. Washington, DC: Joint Military Intelligence College.

Gigerenzer, G., P. M. Todd, and the ABC Research Group. 1999. *Simple heuristics that make us smart.* Oxford, UK: Oxford University Press.

Grove, W. M., D. H. Zald, B. S. Lebow, B. E. Snitz, and C. Nelson. 2000. Clinical versus mechanical prediction: A meta-analysis. *Psychological Assessment* 12:19–30.

Herek, G. M., I. L. Janis, and P. Huth. 1987. Decision making during international crises: Is quality of process related to outcome? *Journal of Conflict Resolution* 31:203–226.

Kennedy, R. F., and A. Schlesinger, Jr. 1969. *Thirteen days: A memoir of the Cuban missile crisis.* New York: Norton.

Klein, G. A. 1998. *Sources of power: How people make decisions.* Cambridge, MA: The MIT Press.

Koriat, A., S. Lichtenstein, and B. Fischhoff. 1980. Reasons for confidence. *Journal of Experimental Psychology: Human Learning and Memory* 6:107–118.

Kostopoulou, O., C. Devereaux-Walsh, and B. C. Delaney. 2009. Missing celiac disease in family medicine: The importance of hypothesis generation. *Medical Decision Making* 29:282–290.

Kruglanski, A. W., and D. M. Webster. 1996. Motivated closing of the mind: "Seizing" and "freezing." *Psychological Review* 103:263–283.

Lawrence, M., P. Goodwin, and R. Fildes. 2002. Influence of user participation on DSS and decision accuracy. *Omega* 30:381–392.

Lehner, P. E., L. Adelman, B. A. Cheikes, and M. J. Brown. 2008. Confirmation bias in complex analyses. *IEEE Transactions on Systems, Man, and Cybernetics—Part A: Systems and Humans* 38:584–592.

Lord, C. G., L. Ross, and M. R. Lepper. 1979. Biased assimilation and attitude polarization: The effects of prior theories on subsequently considered evidence. *Journal of Personality and Social Psychology* 37:2098–2109.

Macrae, C. N., M. Hewstone, and R. J. Griffiths. 1993. Processing load and memory for stereotype-based information. *European Journal of Social Psychology* 23:77–87.

Mandel, D. 2009. *Applied behavioral sciences in support of intelligence analysis.* Presentation at the public workshop of the National Research Council Committee on Behavioral and Social Science Research to Improve Intelligence Analysis for National Security, Washington, DC, May 15.

Meehl, P. E. 1954. *Clinical versus statistical prediction: A theoretical analysis and a review of the evidence.* Minneapolis: University of Minnesota Press.

Mischel, W. 1973. Toward a cognitive social learning reconceptualization of personality. *Psychological Review* 80:252–283.

Moates, D. R., and G. M. Schumacher. 1980. *An introduction to cognitive psychology.* Belmont, CA: Wadsworth.

Murphy, A. H., and R. L. Winkler. 1984. Probability forecasting in meteorology. *Journal of the American Statistical Association* 79:489–500.

Nemeth, C., K. Brown, and J. Rogers. 2001. Devil's advocate versus authentic dissent: Stimulating quantity and quality. *European Journal of Social Psychology* 31:707–720.

Neustadt, R. E., and E. R. May. 1986. *Thinking in time: Uses of history for decision makers.* New York: Free Press.

Nisbett, R. E., H. Zukier, and R. E. Lemly. 1981. The dilution effect: Nondiagnostic information weakens the implications of diagnostic information. *Cognitive Psychology* 13:248–277.

Phillips, J. K., G. Klein, and W. R. Sieck. 2004. Expertise in judgment and decision making. In D. Koehler and N. Harvey, eds., *Blackwell handbook of judgment and decision making* (pp. 297–315). Malden, MA: Blackwell.

Plous, S. 1991. Biases in the assimilation of technological breakdowns: Do accidents make us safer? *Journal of Applied Social Psychology* 60:302–307.

Ross, L. 1977. The intuitive psychologist and his shortcomings. In L. Berkowitz, ed., *Advances in experimental social psychology*, vol. 10. (pp.173–220). New York: Academic Press.

Ross, L., T. M. Amabile, and J. L. Steinmetz. 1977. Social roles, social control, and biases in social-perception processes. *Journal of Personality and Social Psychology* 35:485–494.

Shanteau, J. 1992. Competence in experts: The role of task characteristics. *Organizational Behavior and Human Decision Processes* 53:252–266.

Storms, M. D. 1973. Videotape and the attribution process: Reversing actors' and observers' point of view. *Journal of Personality and Social Psychology* 27:165–175.

Tetlock, P. E. 2005. *Expert political judgment: How good is it? How can we know?* Princeton, NJ: Princeton University Press.

Tetlock, P. E., and J. I. Kim. 1987. Accountability and judgment processes in a personality prediction task. *Journal of Personality and Social Psychology* 32:700–709.

Vertzberger, Y. Y. I. 1990. *The world in their minds: Information processing, cognition, and perception in foreign policy decisionmaking.* Stanford, CA: Stanford University Press.

Yates, J. F., L. S. McDaniel, and E. S. Brown. 1991. Probabilistic forecasts of stock prices and earnings: The hazards of nascent experience. *Organizational Behavior and Human Decision Processes* 49:60–79.

8

Group Processes in Intelligence Analysis

Reid Hastie

WHAT DO INTELLIGENCE TEAMS DO?

"The mission of intelligence analysis is to evaluate, integrate, and interpret information in order to provide warning, reduce uncertainty, and identify opportunities," Fingar writes in Chapter 1 of this volume. Intelligence analysis encompasses a vast variety of intellectual tasks and aims to achieve these objectives. Most analyses are performed in a social context with analysts interacting face to face or electronically in formal or informal teams to create estimates, answer questions, and solve problems that serve the interests of diplomatic, political, military, and law enforcement customers (see this volume's Fingar, Chapter 1, and Skinner, Chapter 5).

To idealize some role assignments, analysts occupy an organizational niche located between *collectors* and *policy makers*. Collectors are responsible for acquiring and initially processing "raw" intelligence information, described by a veritable dictionary of acronyms (e.g., HUMINT, SIGINT, MASINT). One reason for the separation of roles between collector and analyst is because collection often involves highly specialized technical skills (e.g., monitoring a telecommunications channel or maintaining an electronic system that transmits satellite images). Another reason is to protect the original sources from exposure in case, for example, the product of an analysis is acquired by an adversary. On the other side of the chain, analysts and policy makers are separated to protect the analyst's objectivity and single-minded focus on "what is true," without considerations of what is desirable or politically expedient. This unusual, insulated role is central to intelligence analysis, and there are no other close organizational analogues (Zegart, this volume, Chapter 13). Of course, these distinctions are not quite as sharp in practice as they sound from this description because analysts are often involved in the collection process and work in a close relationship with policy makers in order to provide the most relevant information and to communicate effectively.

The typical product of an analysis is a written document that describes the conditions in a politically significant situation, sometimes with evaluations of more than one interpretation of the true situation. The best known products of American intelligence analysis, the President's Daily Brief and National Intelligence Estimates, often look like news reports. However, they are likely to be more forward looking and include predictions of significant events, dissenting views, and confidence assessments (customarily expressed on a verbal scale indexed by terms such as "remote, unlikely, even chance, probably likely, and almost certainty"). Some estimates provide answers to specific questions (e.g., How many armed Taliban insurgents are present today in Kabul?), and many aim to provide a more comprehensive understanding of a situation (e.g., How is Israel likely to respond to Iran's increased nuclear weapons capacity?).

Analytic activities vary along many dimensions. Some involve immediate, in-person interactions among analysts, while others involve indirect, usually electronically mediated, interactions among individuals in remote geographical locations; some involve one-shot, time-intensive interactions, while others involve sustained, long-term interactions; some involve integrating information from several sources into a summary description, while others involve complex inferences about events that might occur under alternate uncertain scenarios; and still others require the generation of innovative responses to diplomatic, economic, or political problems. This heterogeneity creates a challenge for someone who attempts to give prescriptive advice to improve the many different processes. I address that challenge by focusing on one idealized analysis task and then generalizing from that example to other analysis tasks.

Distinguishing among three idealized, truth-seeking analytic tasks is useful, with the following scenarios provided as examples:

1. **Judgment and estimation tasks** involve integrating information from several sources into a unitary quantitative or qualitative estimate or descriptive report of a specific or general situation: Provide a best estimate of the date when Iran will have the capacity to launch a nuclear warhead missile strike on Israel (if its development of nuclear capacities continues at the current rate);

2. **Detection tasks** involve the detection of a signal that a change has occurred, that there is a pattern of interrelated events occurring, or

that "something funny" is happening: Has the opium production rate changed in Faizabad during the past few months? Has Kim Jong-Il's control of the government of North Korea changed at all during the past week?

3. **Complex problem-solving tasks** require generating and applying novel solutions in a specified context: Will the current regime in Pakistan stay in power for the next 12 months? What is the likeliest scenario that would result if the current regime fails?

WHAT IS DISTINCTIVE ABOUT INTELLIGENCE ANALYSIS?

Of course, these dimensions also describe aspects of many other important team performance situations in business, science, and government settings. But several conditions converge in intelligence analysis to create a distinctive, if not unique, situation:

- First, as noted above, analysts have a special, indirect connection to many sources of their intelligence—the front line of collectors acquire information, then pass it on to the analysts. This means there are special challenges in evaluating the validity and credibility of information because the analyst is not directly involved in the initial acquisition (see Schum, 1987, for a discussion of the special problems of cascaded and hierarchical inference that arise in intelligence and forensic contexts).

- Second, more than in any other domain, denial and deception must be considered when evaluating the credibility and validity of information. In many analytic situations, adversaries are present and trying to undermine and defeat the analysis.

- Third, many outcomes of intelligence analysis involve low-probability, high-impact consequences that can mean life or death for thousands of people. Furthermore, analysts must anticipate and infer what policy makers will want to know and even how they are likely to weight multifaceted outcomes, including the inevitable trade-offs between false alarms (e.g., weapons of mass destruction) and misses (e.g., 9/11) that are inherent in every policy decision.

- Fourth, the organizational relationship between the analysts and their customers can include the temptation to bias answers to fit what the customer wants to hear.

- Fifth, as in any complex collection of interdependent organizations, some of these activities occur in the intelligence community's fragmented, "siloed" organizational terrain with 16 loosely connected agencies attempting to cooperate while they simultaneously pursue sometimes conflicting and nonaligned objectives.

- Finally, feedback is especially rare and unreliable. For many important analytic estimates, outcomes remain unknown for a long time or cannot ever be known. Furthermore, often the U.S. government itself or another party will take an action that changes the outcomes that were the subject of the original analysis, making learning from feedback even more difficult.

The difficulty of learning from feedback is compounded by the intense scrutiny and criticisms in hindsight of every visible intelligence failure, while successes are rarely attributed to the analysts and, under many conditions, are unobserved (see Bruce, 2008, for a catalog of publicized failures, but see Jervis, 2006, for a defense of achievements of the intelligence community). There will always be room for improvement, but there is ample evidence for the high levels of professionalism and dedication in intelligence analysis (cf., Dawes, 1993; Fischhoff, 1975; Gladwell, 2003). One essential means to improving intelligence analysis is to develop systematic methods to evaluate the validity and accuracy of estimates (cf., Tetlock, 2006; Arkes and Kajdasz, this volume, Chapter 7; McClelland, this volume, Chapter 4) and then to apply these criteria to identify and reward best practices.

In this paper, I will focus on short-range, tactical intelligence estimates in the international domain, made by small teams of three to seven analysts working together face to face or through electronic communication. I will restrict the discussion to tasks for which the goal is to achieve the highest possible levels of accuracy in describing or forecasting a state of the external world. Our knowledge of how teams perform such tasks comes from all of the social sciences, sociology, social psychology, economics, political science, and anthropology as well as from composite fields of study, such as management science and cognitive science, although social psychology is the primary source for the current conclusions about truth-seeking group judgments.

FOUR ESSENTIAL CONDITIONS FOR EFFECTIVE TEAMWORK

In the most general terms, four basic conditions must be met if a team is to perform effectively in a larger organizational context (Hackman, 2002; Wageman, 2001). First, the team must have an identity as a distinct social unit in the larger organization (Tinsley, this volume, Chapter 9). It must be recognized as autonomous and be given a well-defined, organizationally significant set of objectives. It must be given the essential resources to achieve those objectives, including effective channels of communication with other units in the larger organization, especially the agent outside the team who oversees the team's activities. Under some conditions, the team should have a distinctive identity and even a "subculture" appropriate for its task within the larger organization (Tinsley, this volume, Chapter 9). In general terms, the more distributed and independent the team's *later* working procedures will be, the more important it is to establish a distinctive identity *at the beginning* (Moreland and Levine, 1982).

Second, the team must have a compelling direction, with clear, challenging, and consequential objectives. Its members should be autonomous, and individual activities should not be micromanaged by team leaders or organizational authorities outside of the team. Each member's personal goals must, to some extent, be subordinate to and aligned with the team's organizationally defined objectives. This means that both tangible incentives (e.g., financial or status rewards) and intrinsic incentives (e.g., social recognition, positive internal feelings) should be conditional on achievements relevant to the team's goals.

Third, the team must have an "enabling design" that provides the proper individual composition (skills, diversity, size), specialized role assignments if appropriate to the larger task, and plans and technological support for intermember communication, coordination, and a "group memory" of task-relevant information (Fiore et al., 2003).

Finally, the team must have a self-conscious, meta-level perspective that is constantly monitoring and correcting member motivations; refining operating procedures; and providing short-term feedback and eventual evaluation to allow members and the team to learn from experience performing the task.

BREAKING THE OVERARCHING ANALYTIC TASK INTO SUBTASKS

Each of these four conditions is essential for teams performing any task, but the specific manner in which each is accomplished depends on the task type. Each of the analytic tasks—integration, detection, and problem solving—can be described in terms of a stylized process model that breaks the larger task down into its component subtasks. This conceptual breakdown describes the task as it might be performed by an individual, a team, or even by an automated software system. What is distinctive about the performance of a team is the collection of special motivation and coordination problems that arise when independent agents collaborate on the task. Two closely related tensions describe the essential dilemma for effective teamwork: (1) individualistic-selfish motives versus collective-organizational motives; and (2) promotion of diversity and independence versus promotion of consensus and interdependence. Good team performance depends on addressing these tensions flexibly and effectively. The second requires the design of explicit incentives that will motivate individual members to work for the good of the team and the organization in which it is embedded. Implicit incentives, often attributed to the team and organizational "culture," are also important. The second requires careful oversight by the team's leader (or external manager) so that when certain subtasks are performed, independence is promoted; in other subtasks, consensus-conformity is promoted, appropriate to the local objectives of each subtask. (This last motivational problem is what economists call the *principal-agent problem*. There is a large literature on the subtle solutions to the problem, including discussions of conditions that seem to have no known theoretical solution; see Baron and Kreps, 1999, and Chen et al., 2009, for discussions of methods of motivating individuals in teams.)

Judgment and simple estimation tasks can be described as an ideal analytic process in terms of five component activities: Subtask 1, define the problem; Subtask 2, acquire relevant information; Subtask 3, terminate the information acquisition process; Subtask 4, integrate the information into a summary statement (estimate of a state of the past, present, or future world; descriptive summary report); and Subtask 5, generate an appropriate response (see Hinsz et al., 1997, for a similar discussion of "groups as information processors"; see Lee and Cummins, 2004, for a similar task analysis). (In the case of intelligence analysis, the "response" is nearly always the provision of information to a policy maker or a military actor, who decides on an appropriate action based on the intelligence.) The primary advantages of teams over individuals in performing such tasks are the teams' capacity for acquiring and pooling more information than any individual can contribute, and the teams' ability to "damp errors," as different views counterbalance one another, yielding a central consensus belief in discussion when integrating information and opinions from several sources.

The potential advantages of performing tasks requiring information integration and estimation with a team are derived from the greater store of information (including analytic skills) available to a team of several people and from the capacity of the group to leverage diverse perspectives to damp errors and converge on a sensible central value or solution. This implies that in the early stages of the team process, care must be taken to promote diversity in information acquisition; in the middle stages, coordinated information pooling; and in the later stages, convergence on a unitary "solution" or consensus response. Let's look at the requirements for effective team performance of each component subtask of the larger judgment process (for complementary analyses, also see Heuer, 2007; Kozlowski and Ilgen, 2006; and Straus et al., 2008).

Team Composition

Several affirmative suggestions can be made about how to design effective teams before they begin work on their analytic tasks (see Hackman,

2002, for similar advice). First, there are organizational issues: The team needs to be embedded appropriately in the larger organization in which it functions. This means effective lines of communication must define the team's operational goals in terms of the organizational objectives. In other words, the team needs to know what its task, goals, and performance criteria are in terms of what would help the organization. The team also needs resources from the larger organization and needs to be insulated from interference from the larger organization (e.g., to prevent micromanagement or undue influence from the organizational manager to whom the team reports).

Teams are usually composed of members from a larger organization or individuals recruited by that organization to support the team's performance (Kozlowski, this volume, Chapter 12). Team composition is obviously significant, although it is difficult to specify useful selection criteria that are general across tasks. Three conditions seem essential: (1) task-relevant diversity of knowledge and skills; (2) a capacity for full, open, and truthful exchange (i.e., communication skills); and (3) a commitment to the team's goal (the capacity or willingness to align one's own interests with the team goal to produce an accurate estimate). Composition depends on the task contents, so formulating more specific prescriptions for good practice is difficult.

Two generalities emerge from the behavioral literature: In practice, teams are usually too large (Hackman and Vidmar, 1970) and not diverse enough (Page, 2007). Of course, there is a paradox posed by the fact that smaller teams (e.g., an implication of much of the behavioral literature is that a typical analysis team should be composed of about five members) must be less diverse than larger teams. Part of the paradox arises from the fact that larger teams have more resources of all types than smaller teams, but larger teams also suffer from more "process losses" than smaller teams (Steiner, 1972). Process losses include the variety of conditions that impede group productivity in any goal-directed task: difficulties in communication and coordination; within-group social conflicts; lower cohesion; and confusions about group identity, to name the most obvious problems.

Note that the term "diversity" refers to task-relevant diversity in terms of knowledge, skills, perspectives, and opinions that promote variety in the types of task-relevant information and solutions that contribute to the team's performance. This kind of task-relevant diversity is likely to be correlated with differences in gender, cultural background, or personality, but not necessarily so. Page (2007) has provided the most comprehensive research-based argument for the advantages of task-relevant diversity over raw expertise in team problem solving. Some of his proofs take the form of abstract theoretical analyses of the capacities for multiple idealized interacting agents to solve mathematical problems. These results are abstract, but support strong claims for the advantages of task-relevant diversity. He also reviews sociological analyses of diverse versus homogeneous groups in behavioral experiments and natural settings, and again finds support for the value of diversity. Mannix and Neale (2005) have also reviewed the behavioral literature and reach pessimistic conclusions with regard to the effects of increased social diversity (race, gender, age) on team performance. Like Page, they note the potential value of task-relevant diversity (knowledge, skills, social-network resources), especially in performing tasks that involve information seeking, information evaluation, and creative thinking. But they also conclude that social diversity inevitably increases process losses through interpersonal conflict, communication problems, and lowered cohesion. Another aspect of this trade-off was pointed out by Calvert (1985) in a theoretical analysis of how a rational decision maker should weight biased information. One of the counterintuitive implications of his rational analysis was that, under many conditions, teammates who are biased to agree with you are more reliable sources of divergent information than those who are biased to disagree with you.

On the basis of current scientific results, it is impossible to spell out specific prescriptions for recruiting members with productively diverse characteristics without knowing something about the details of the team's task and the context in which it performs. Nonetheless, a good practice is always to oversample for diversity when a team is composed because the common tendency is to err in the direction of uniformity. At a minimum, a priori differences of opinion on the correct solution improve the performance of most problem-solving groups (Nemeth, 1986; Schulz-Hardt et al., 2006; Winquist and Larson, 1998). Several behavioral studies demonstrate the importance of member diversity, but also of the necessity that members know the specialties of other members, so that appropriate role assignments and coordination are supported (Austin, 2003; Moreland et al., 1996; Stasser et al., 1995). Hackman and colleagues (2008) provide a thoughtful discussion of team composition in intelligence analysis that promotes the design of teams that balance members' diverse cognitive skills (see also Pashler et al., 2008, for a discussion of the concept of cognitive styles). They also report a behavioral study that demonstrates the importance of aligning individual differences in skill sets (visual versus verbal thinking styles) with matching role assignments (navigation versus acquisition of targets) to maximize the contribution of member diversity to team performance.

To repeat, subtle trade-offs are always present between independence and conformity with the ultimate impact on team productivity (Mannix and Neale, 2005). With too much independence and diversity, team performance suffers because of loss of identification, decreased motivation, and simple coordination problems. Too much dependence and uniformity undermine the team's ability to perform components of the overall task that require divergent thinking. This balancing problem has no simple "fixes." This problem, of course, highlights the need for more rigorous research on analytic teamwork, based on objective measures of team performance.

Subtask 1: Defining the Problem

When the team initiates its performance on an analytic task, an essential step is to thoughtfully execute each of the subtasks of the overarching task. Completion of each subtask, in some manner, is necessary to produce a good solution, but many teams perform component subtasks in a perfunctory manner. Many teams fail to verify that every member understands and agrees on the target of the estimate, including criteria for a successful solution and a sense of cost–benefit trade-offs. The decision to terminate information search is next most likely to be performed in a careless manner; the most common postmortem evaluation of a poor team judgment is that information was not acquired or pooled effectively.

The first subtask of team performance, defining the problem, requires a mixture of independence and consensus (cf., Eisenhardt et al., 1997). During this stage, each team member grasps the goal state or target of the judgment and other relevant criteria for a successful or accurate response. This discussion should include consideration of the costs and benefits associated with potential errors (over- and underestimates or false alarms and misses). These criteria need to be shared with other team members; as the old saying goes, the team will fail if some members are headed for Los Angeles, when the primary destination is San Francisco. Each member also assesses "the givens," the information that is in hand or needs to be acquired to make a good estimate. At this point, independence and member diversity are probably best in the sources of information or evidence that will be used. The notion here is that "triangulation" based on independent sources of information (given a shared judgment objective) will promote innovation, error damping, and robustness in the final estimate.

Subtask 2: Information Acquisition

The second subtask, information acquisition, is the one for which independence and diversity of perspectives count the most. Team judgments have two major advantages (compared to individual judgments): Teams have more information than any one member and teams can damp errors in individual judgments and converge on an accurate "central tendency" (Sunstein, 2006, and Surowiecki, 2004, provide popularized accounts of these principles). Several devices can be used to achieve independence and diversity: recruiting a diverse set of perspectives and expertise sets when team members are selected; working anonymously and in dispersed settings during the information acquisition (and pooling) subtask; and cycling back and forth between searching for and pooling information, so that information from other members can stimulate new directions in search for each member.

Information acquisition (Subtask 2) and information pooling (Subtask 4) are probably most effectively promoted by careful design of the team's composition—by having a good mix of members with diverse information, backgrounds, and skill sets. At least two negative conditions, discussed below, need to be avoided (also see the discussion of Groupthink, below).

Association Blocking

If members interact with one another when they seek or pool information, *association blocking* can occur. Association blocking refers to a condition that occurs when individual team members get "locked into" a whirlpool of similar associations, and individual capacities for divergent thinking are impaired as they naturally respond associatively to one another's communications. For example, when a first interpretation concludes that certain aluminum tubing is likely to be used for uranium enrichment, then the mind is primed automatically to retrieve and interpret additional information as relevant to nuclear weapons, rather than, for example, ordinary military rockets. The phenomenon is most apparent when people try to generate unrelated, novel solutions to an innovation problem while interacting in person (Diehl and Stroebe, 1987; Nijstad et al., 2003; Paulus and Yang, 2000).

Several interaction process solutions to association blocking involve isolating members and promoting independent thinking. One method is to cycle between independent individual analysis and social interaction, and to have individuals acquire information separately; or in the case of pooling, each individual should pool information separately. The best practice is to start independently, share ideas, then return to independent search or generation, then back to social interaction. Several "unblocking" techniques, borrowed from group brain-storming practices, are available to promote novel search and generation by introducing haphazard or new directions (Kelley and Littman, 2001). Another method is to vary the composition of the group by adding new members (Choi and Thompson, 2005).

Information Pooling and the Common-Knowledge Effect

Beyond association blocking there is also a tendency to focus discussion on shared information and its implications, while neglecting to pool unshared information. This phenomenon has been observed most dramatically in "hidden profile" tasks (Larson et al., 1994; Stasser and Titus, 1985, 2003) and was dubbed the "Common Knowledge Effect" by Gigone and Hastie (1993, 1997). The Hidden Profile method was invented by Stasser and Titus and provides a powerful test bed to evaluate team performance on elementary inference and judgment tasks. The basic method involves designing a judgment task that provides an opportunity for high levels of achievement by individuals and groups who have been *provided with full information relevant to the judgment.* However, to create hidden profiles, the researcher distributes the information to members of the to-be-tested team in a way that no member has sufficient information to perform at a high level of isolation, although the team has all of the relevant information—albeit dispersed in a manner that provides a stiff challenge to the information-pooling capacity of the team. Of course, cases of widely distributed and vastly unshared information are the norm in intelligence analysis. Adding to the difficulty is the fact that often analysts with different regional or technical specialties must communicate with one another to converge on the truth. For example, regional experts, satellite image technicians, and nuclear scientists were all involved in the effort to determine if Saddam Hussein was developing nuclear weapons.

In its most diabolical form, the Hidden Profile method capitalizes on two fundamental human weaknesses to create a nearly insurmountable challenge. First, in the extreme form of the task, each member has an incorrect impression of the correct solution. The full set of information is distributed, so that the individual member subsets each favor a nonoptimal solution—in other words, a reasonable person begins the task with the wrong answer in mind. This creates a strong cognitive bias toward confirmatory thinking, and many naïve teams begin discussion by eliminating the correct solution because, after all, no individual member believes it might be the solution. Intelligence analysis, which involves many verified cases in which one party attempts to deceive another party by seeding communications with false and misleading information, represents one situation in which the diabolical forms of "hidden profiles" occur in naturally occurring contexts (others are cases of corporate strategic deception and some personnel matters in which individuals attempt to deceive others about professional qualifications). Furthermore, there are the social biases to underpool unshared information and overpool shared information, which if not resisted, amplify the bias against the correct solution. Finally, time pressure increases the negative effects of the confirmatory thinking and information-pooling challenges (Lavery et al., 1999).

Qualitative analysis of the content of group discussions shows that when shared information is mentioned, it is likely to be followed by affirmative statements and relevant discussion (Larson et al., 1994). When unshared information is mentioned, reactions are usually less responsive and the subject of discussion is likely to shift to another topic. Finally, the problem of pooling unshared information is exacerbated when other stages of the judgment process are mixed with information acquisition. For example, when members are both acquiring and sharing information *and* proposing answers to the current problem or estimate, the acquisition process is undermined by confirmatory thinking, and sharing disconfirming information is inhibited.

Several social procedures can increase the chances that a team will solve a hidden profiles problem. First, as noted before, if different members favor different solutions at the outset of discussion, dissent can promote more effective information pooling (Nemeth, 1986; Schulz-Hardt et al., 2006; Winquist and Larson, 1998). Second, if individual team members are assigned task-relevant roles (e.g., one is the HUMINT expert, one is the SIGINT expert, etc.), the team is likelier to succeed (Stasser et al., 1995; and see discussion of "Shared Mental Models" below). Finally, any other method that promotes more vigorous discussion is likely to improve performance to some degree, such as creating adversarial subteams or assigning one member to the social facilitator role (Kramer et al., 2001; Oxley et al., 1996).

Another well-defined method for promoting effective pooling is the Nominal Group Technique, which involves alternating between isolated individuals and interacting groups for task performance. The first cycle of information acquisition and recording is carried out individually, in isolation, followed by group information pooling in a round-robin procedure or by facilitated pooling (e.g., over a local network) to ensure that everyone is prompted to fully share their individual contributions. In some applications, this cycle is repeated several times. Rohrbaugh (1981) conducted an evaluation of the Nominal Group Technique in a simple estimation task (predicting the outcomes of horse races) and found that the Nominal Group Technique performed at about the level of the most proficient team member, who might not prevail in an interacting face-to-face group. Plous (1995) found that Nominal Groups were better calibrated, assigning more appropriate confidence intervals around quantitative estimates than individuals or interacting groups. Another method with a demonstrated record of success, the Advocacy Method, involves assigning members to roles to advocate one solution or another; this method is most likely to be successful if the roles are reassigned several times and if the team has practiced the advocacy method before (Greitemeyer et al., 2006).

Versions of these methods have been applied in intelligence analysis and are taught as "tradecraft" at the Sherman Kent School (U.S. Government, 2009). Furthermore, high-tech, electronic network-based facilities such as A-Space and Intellipedia were designed to solve these types of information pooling and networking problems and are receiving good reviews from practitioners (Yasin, 2009). Although primarily journalistic, other accounts support these methods in industry settings as remedies for the same information-pooling problems (e.g., Sunstein, 2006; Surowiecki, 2004; Tapscott and Williams, 2006).

Subtask 3: Terminating Information Acquisition

The third subtask involves a decision to terminate information acquisition and move to the information integration subtask. In practice, this subtask is often not explicitly recognized and acquisition simply stops when time runs out or when the flow of new information runs dry. In a well-defined mathematical estimation problem, it is possible to prescribe optimal stopping rules, but this requires exact knowledge (or assumptions) of the costs and benefits of the solution (and errors) and the value and probability of acquiring information items (De Groot, 1970). But information to compute optimal stopping solutions is usually lacking in practical analytic tasks. What can be done is to recognize that a decision to terminate acquisition is implicitly or explicitly inevitable and to deliberately plan a team process with that limit in mind.

Subtask 4: Information Integration

The process in the fourth subtask, information integration, depends on the nature of the product format, originally learned in the first subtask. If the estimate is a unitary numerical or category-membership judgment, the process often takes the form of an oral discussion, perhaps with calculation or voting on proposals for the solution. For example, a team might review members' estimates for a quantity such as the number of troops massed at a border location or a "category" such as the voting intention of a United Nations Security Council member and then select an answer based on an informal average or vote. If the product is a summary report, the process usually takes the form of drafting a written document, often with subpart assignments to member subject matter experts, followed by discussion to combine the pieces into a unitary product.

Assuming that information acquisition and pooling have been executed effectively, information integration is best served by vigorous discussion and debate. The basic problem is to avoid overconformity to an early solution that interferes with thorough evaluation of alternate solutions the team has generated (i.e., avoid confirmatory thinking). After Congress reviewed the National Intelligence Estimate that was in error on the extent to which weapons of mass destruction were available to Saddam Hussein in Iraq around 2003, there has been an obsession with avoiding Groupthink and confirmatory thinking in the analytic process.

The most basic precept is that all discussions should focus on tasks, and be uninhibited and vigorous. Many methods can be used to "have a good fight" in team discussions (Tinsley, this volume, Chapter 9). Eisenhardt and colleagues (1997; see also Okhuysen and Eisenhardt, 2002) studied several problem-solving teams in engineering- and biotechnology-oriented companies and identified some differences that predicted the performances of the more successful and less successful teams. They list some of the most important conditions for vigorous team problem solving: First, shared goals; second, a rich (diverse) information acquisition and pooling process; third, emphasis on data-driven analysis and dispute resolution; fourth, well-defined role assignments so it is always clear how discussion will proceed and how contingent decisions will be made; and finally, a willingness to decide with dissent or based on "consensus with qualification." Of course, group facilitation techniques, where one member focuses mostly on promoting an effective process (and is usually disengaged from substantive contributions), are helpful, even simply requiring a team to pause and deliberately plan a process (Larson et al., 1996). All of the effective solutions are enhanced if the team is embedded in a productive organizational culture that promotes candid, but not ad hominem evaluations of proposed solutions.

Subtask 5: Response Generation

The final subtask in performing a judgment task is to express the response in an appropriate format to satisfy the original objectives of the assignment. For most intelligence products, this means designing a summary of information—evidence and conclusions—in a form that is readily comprehended by the customer. The primary concerns are clarity, completeness, and transparency of expression (Fischhoff, this volume, Chapter 10). At this time, the costs of possible errors (over or under; false alarms or misses) should be considered and expressed.

The fifth subtask often involves compromises, where individuals with divergent views agree to subordinate their opinions to the consensus opinion. The report should include a summary of the degree of consensus among analysts on the team, including, if appropriate, a "dissenting opinion." The expectation that dissent will be reported can increase the efficacy of the analytic process in some prior stages of the task—especially the rigor of the information integration process (Hackman, 2002). Furthermore, the major conclusions in the report should be accompanied by systematic, ideally quantitative expressions of the team's confidence in those conclusions.

Again, simply requiring such an assessment can enhance performance of earlier stages in the overall team process.

Groupthink and Overconformity

One condition that definitely undermines the team analysis process is overconformity or Groupthink. Irving Janis popularized the term Groupthink in an influential book, *Victims of Groupthink* (1972), in which he reviewed several American policy decisions that led to bad outcomes (e.g., Bay of Pigs invasion of Cuba; failure to anticipate the surprise attack on Pearl Harbor; escalation of military commitment in the Vietnam War, see also Janis, 1982). The term appears to have been introduced into popular culture by William H. Whyte in 1952 (see also William Safire's editorial comment on the Senate Select Committee on Intelligence's Report on the U.S. Intelligence Community's Prewar Assessments on Iraq, 2004). Janis proposed that a systematic social pathology could explain these fiascos. The central explanatory concept was overconformity to the course of action favored by a charismatic or dominating leader, especially when other conditions produced a high degree of social cohesion among team members.

The details of Janis's analysis have not fared well as a coherent scientific claim. For example, experimental tests have not found that his "recipe" for Groupthink or consistently produced the effects he attributed to his historical examples. But Janis's basic insight that overconformity to powerful leaders or to the wishes of a customer can undermine good judgment seems indisputable and important (Baron, 2005; Kerr and Tindale, 2004; Paulus, 1998; Turner and Pratkanis, 1998; Whyte, 1998).

This general sense of the term "Groupthink" was referred to in the 2004 Senate Select Committee on Intelligence report (p. 18): " . . . [a] group think dynamic led intelligence community analysts, collectors, and managers to both interpret ambiguous evidence as conclusively indicative of a WMD [weapons of mass destruction] program as well as to ignore or minimize evidence that Iraq did not have active and expanding weapons of mass destruction programs." Political scientist Robert Jervis (2006, pp. 20–21) comments: "Taken literally, this is simply incorrect. Groupthink is, as its name implies, a small group phenomenon. . . . Intelligence on Iraq was not developed by small groups, however. A great deal of work was done by individuals, and the groups were large and of shifting composition. In fairness to the SSCI [Senate Select Committee on Intelligence], it is using the term Groupthink in a colloquial rather than a technical sense. What is claimed to be at work are general pressures of conformity and mutual reinforcement. Once the view that Iraq was developing WMD was established there not only were few incentives to challenge it, but each person who held this view undoubtedly drew greater confidence from the fact that it was universally shared."

In intelligence analysis, the pressure to conform to a premature conclusion can come from many sources, from a team leader or other senior analyst, from a coalition of team members who share a commitment to an answer or to an analytic approach that leads myopically to one answer, or from the wishes of a customer who favors a particular answer to the analytic question (cf., Davis, 2008). Good leaders seem to anticipate the problem and design team processes to avoid it, especially at the earliest stages of performance when selecting members and instilling a "team culture" (e.g., Goodwin, 2005). Groups in which there are sincere differences of opinion, represented in coalitions with more than one member, do seem to be less likely to exhibit signs of confirmatory thinking or overconformity (Schwenk, 1988). But introducing contrived dissent, using methods like assigning an individual to the role of a devil's advocate, has not produced consistent improvements in team judgments or decisions (e.g., Nemeth et al., 2001; Schweiger et al., 1986; Schwenk, 1990). Unfortunately, there seem to be no scientific evaluations of more vigorous adversarial role assignment methods such as red team/blue team exercises (e.g., where three-member subteams are created to develop alternate perspectives on a solution or strategy), although there is considerable informal enthusiasm for such exercises (Gold and Hermann, 2003). Another method to remedy Groupthink, with considerable face-validity (though untested scientifically), is to adapt Structured Analytic Techniques, such as the Analysis of Competing Hypotheses, for collaborative applications (see Heuer, 2008, for the argument in favor of collaborative Structured Analysis).

Polarization and Overconfidence

Two general properties of the solutions generated by groups making simple estimates were not reviewed in detail in this chapter: attitude polarization (Tinsley, this volume, Chapter 9) and overconfidence (Arkes and Kajdasz, this volume, Chapter 7). Several commentators have expressed concern about the nearly universal tendency for group discussions (or just individual expressions of opinions, without discussion) to produce polarization of individual opinions (e.g., Sunstein, 2009). For example, when a group of like-minded citizens meet and discuss a controversial issue such as affirmative action policies, gay civil unions, or the right to own guns, their individual postdiscussion views are more extreme in the direction of the average (or median) initial inclination. Thus, a group of liberals discussing those issues would conclude "more liberal" after discussion; a group of conservatives would shift away from neutrality and become "more conservative" (e.g., Schkade et al., 2007). Thoughtful political analysts, like

Sunstein, are concerned that these very general perceptual and behavioral tendencies will produce an "enclaving" phenomenon in a large heterogeneous society. Subgroups of like-minded citizens will form (the tendency to associate with similar others is also a universal tendency), they will discuss political issues, and individuals will move toward consensus *and* toward the extremes on opinion dimensions (again, the two movements—toward one another and toward the extreme—are universal tendencies). Furthermore, these potentially negative intragroup effects typically are accompanied by tendencies to view an opposing group as more extreme and inferior (cf., discussion of intergroup dynamics by Tinsley, this volume, Chapter 9). The result would be many local groups of extremist, antagonistic citizens— leading to indecision, intergroup conflict, and a degraded democratic process at the societal level.

Polarization is certainly likely to degrade intergroup relationships, such as those among intelligence agencies. However, at the team level, little behavioral evidence shows polarization in truth-seeking groups (e.g., intelligence teams whose primary goal is to make accurate estimates). Virtually all demonstrations of polarization involve bipolar attitude or evaluative dimensions. (But there are a few suggestive results, and polarization is expected to occur when the group is assessing beliefs as well as values.) It is also unclear that polarization in a truth-seeking group is a bad property of the process if the group is doing its task effectively and correctly zeroing in on the truth. In fact, the repeated advice to compose teams and design procedures to preserve task-relevant diversity is the best practice known to avoid mindless polarization. The common result of discussion in groups that include diverse attitudes or beliefs is depolarization, not polarization.

Overconfidence would seem more worrisome than polarization, although the author is unaware of any published studies that clearly demonstrate groups are more overconfident than individuals (see Sniezek, 1992, for a thoughtful discussion of hypotheses about group confidence). A frequently cited study by Puncochar and Fox (2004) measured confidence in student answers to questions about psychology course materials. The study found that groups of three to four students were more confident than individual students on both correct and incorrect answers. However, this study does not actually demonstrate *relative overconfidence* because groups were also more likely to be correct, so the higher confidence ratings might represent the same degree of calibration as for individuals. (Furthermore, participants answered individually and then in small groups in all experimental conditions. Thus, the study did not provide a clean individual versus group performance comparison, as the group task was confounded with performing the task for the second time.) In another frequently cited study, Zarnoth and Sniezek (1997) found that more confident individuals within a group have a greater impact on the group's answer to general-knowledge questions, but this also does not demonstrate *relative overconfidence* for groups. Rather, it reaches a conclusion about individual impact on group solutions. As with polarization, it is not clear that the overconfidence effect does not occur in teams, only that reliable research has not yet demonstrated such an effect. Also as with polarization, I believe the prescriptions outlined above for effective team performance include advice on the best practices currently supported by behavioral research.

"Group Cognition"

Cognitive scientists, usually working in multidisciplinary teams of engineers, psychologists, and mathematicians, have made a substantial contribution to our understanding of teamwork, with a focus on distributed workgroups that do not meet in person, and on the selection and training of team members (Kozlowski, this volume, Chapter 12; Fiore et al., 2003; Paris et al., 2000). The aspirations of these researchers are high, to create a practical theory that synthesizes most of the topics covered in the present chapter, adding selection and training of team members and the design of software systems to support and enhance teamwork. But the achievements are still modest. Much of the research involves pioneering observational studies (e.g., Klein and Miller, 1999), and many conclusions are in the form of useful conceptual frameworks (e.g., Bell and Kozlowski, 2002; Fiore et al., 2003; Klein et al., 2003). These foundations are critically important for the development of a comprehensive scientific analysis, but are in their infancy; they are useful as the source of hypotheses and research questions, but not a fount of practical advice or empirically verified conclusions.

For present purposes, the major contribution of these research programs has been the development of the concept of shared cognition or shared mental models (see Rouse and Morris, 1986; Wilson and Rutherford, 1989, for background on the concept of mental models). These are concepts about "interrelationships between team objectives, team mechanisms, temporal patterns of activity, individual roles, individual functions, and relationships among individuals" (Paris et al., 2000, p. 1055). As implied by this broad definition, it is difficult to provide a precise specification for a theoretical representation of a shared mental model, and the operational measurement of shared mental models appears to be ad hoc and varies from study to study. Nonetheless, the notion of a shared mental model and practices that will support effective mental representations of "the team" seem to be an important element of any effort to improve team performance.

For example, Mathieu et al. (2000) studied the performance of college student dyads completing missions "flying" a simulated F-16 fighter plane. Mathieu and colleagues measured individual mental models as ratings of the perceived relationships between operational components of operating the aircraft (e.g., banking and turning, selecting and shooting weapons), then used a correlation coefficient as the index of the degree to which mental models *of the situation* (not *team member interrelationships*, as in the definition quoted above) were shared. The shared mental model index was correlated at moderate levels with performance of the flying missions (correlations ranging from 0.05 to 0.38), increasing over time on the task.

The most tangible advice, based on the notion that enhancing shared mental models will improve team performance, is the suggestion to train teammates together (Hollingshead, 1998; Moreland and Myaskovsky, 2000). Providing specific role assignments and fully informing team members of one another's primary capacities and duties in performing a collective task is the most effective remedy for information-pooling inefficiencies in Hidden Profiles problems (Stasser and Augustinova, 2007; Stasser et al., 1995; discussed above in the section on "Information Pooling and the Common-Knowledge Effect").

High-Tech Alternatives to Face-to-Face Teamwork

Importantly, several usually web-based techniques are available for performing simple estimation and categorization tasks. Surowiecki (2004) and Sunstein (2006) review several of these methods, all of which have been used in intelligence analysis (Kaplan, this volume, Chapter 2). The simplest methods involve mechanically combining individual judgments into a summary solution—usually some kind of average value or election winner.

Delphi Method

The Delphi Method relies on a systematic social interaction process to find a central tendency in individual estimates (invented at the RAND Corporation in the 1950s by Helmer, Dalkey, Rescher, and others [see Rescher, 1998, for review of the method and its invention], cf., Linstone and Turoff, 1975). In its simplest form, the Delphi Method participants (usually selected for subject area expertise) make a series of estimates and reestimates anonymously, with a requirement to adjust on each round toward the center of the distribution of estimates from the prior round (e.g., each estimate must be within the interquartile range of the previous estimates). Some versions of the method also require participants to provide reasons for their estimates and adjustments. Although the method has been widely used in the intelligence community, few vigorous evaluations of its merits have been conducted. It does seem to outperform simple statistical aggregation methods (e.g., taking averages or even averages weighted by estimators' confidence; e.g., Rowe and Wright, 1999). But, there are no definitive comparisons of the Delphi Method against the performance of expert in-person teams, although it compares favorably with procedures based on statistical learning with feedback (a version of Social Judgment Theory; Cooksey, 1996; Hammond et al., 1977) and with prediction markets (Green et al., 2008; Rohrbaugh, 1979).

Prediction Markets

Another popular method, prediction markets, has participants buy and sell shares in an estimate (usually a forecast) that is paid off when the true outcome is revealed (e.g., Hanson et al., 2006; Wolfers and Zitzewitz, 2004). In applications to predict the outcomes of events (e.g., elections, sports contests), the prices of the estimates can be converted into probability-of-occurrence assessments. The method is used in many business and popular culture applications (e.g., predicting the outcomes of media awards and political elections) and has substantial journalistic evidence for accuracy. Nonetheless, a prediction market is just a market, and markets were designed to assess aggregate *values*, not true states of the world. Markets have many demonstrated weaknesses, even as "evaluation devices." Most published evaluations of prediction markets are theoretical and make arguments based on economic *models*, not on empirical data, for the efficacy or limits of the method (e.g., Manski, 2006; see Erikson and Wlezien, 2008, for an empirical evaluation of political election markets). Graefe and Weinhardt (2008) provide a "soft" evaluation that concludes that prediction markets and the Delphi Method perform at comparable levels of accuracy.

Following the negative public reaction to the Defense Advanced Research Projects Agency–sponsored Policy Analysis Market, the use of prediction markets in government agencies has been reduced, but not eliminated. (The original Policy Analysis Market was attacked by some members of Congress for promoting betting on assassinations and terrorist events, and the project was cancelled. See *Congressional Record*, 2003, and Hulse, 2003, for more information.) Note that prediction markets are restricted to applications in which a well-defined outcome set to occur in the near future can be verified. Furthermore, no market can be expected to perform efficiently without a substantial number of participants with different views on the "values" of the commodities being traded. Prediction markets are yet another tool for intelligence analysis that merit further exploration accompanied by hard-headed evaluations of efficacy (Arrow et al., 2007).

The Delphi Method does not have this restriction to verifiable outcomes and is more generally applicable. The requirement for verification is especially restrictive in intelligence applications. One caveat is that users of a partly mechanical system need to think carefully about the impact of the method on information pooling. Recall that a major failing of socially interacting teams is to thoroughly acquire and pool relevant information. A method is needed that encourages participants to share information relevant to the estimates as well as opinions on the correct solution. Some versions of the Delphi Method partially achieve this by requiring that on each round, each participant report an estimate and provide at least one item of information that he or she believes is an important cue to the solution. Similarly, prediction markets are often accompanied by chat room bulletin boards on which participants are encouraged to share relevant arguments about the information they used. (Note that some market mechanisms—e.g., posted bid double auctions—promote sharing information [participants want others to value investments they themselves have chosen], whereas others—e.g., parimutuel betting markets—promote secrecy.)

Detection and Problem-Solving Tasks

To summarize, the first general admonition for good performance is to make solid plans and be self-conscious about the team process, to understand the nature of the task you are performing, and to deliberately balance subtask demands for independence and consensus. Second, for estimation tasks, many research-supported suggestions are available on how to execute each subtask most effectively. Early subtasks tend to demand more independence and to profit most from task-relevant diversity. Later subtasks demand more interdependence, coordination, and even conformity. But what if a team is performing another task type? The best advice is to begin by analyzing the task, breaking it down into subtasks, and then figuring out what properties of the team process are demanded by the subtasks. Below are two additional subtask breakdowns for the next most commonly performed analytic tasks.

The second major task performed by intelligence teams is the detection of informative signals in the vast spectrum of noise produced by collectors and sources at an incredible rate. Probably the most common individual analyst task is to forage through the morning's incoming flood of electronic and other media. For a prototypical analyst, this usually involves searching various e-mail and news sources for something on a specific topic (e.g., Is anything relevant to the objective of detecting a local terrorist plan to attack a major U.S. target during the visit from a head of state?), or just for something out of place, strange, or anomalous (e.g., What does the sudden appearance of references to "nail polish remover" in e-mails intercepted between two suspected conspirators mean?). For such detection tasks, the research supports a six-subtask process model: (1) sample information; (2) construct an image or mental model of the "normal" or "status quo" conditions; (3) sample more information; (4) detect a difference (or not) that is "large enough" or "over criterion" to explore further; (5) interpret the difference—important or not; and (6) generate an appropriate response.

The analysis and performance of detection tasks is helped greatly by the availability of an optimal model for the detection decision, such as Signal Detection Theory (McClelland, this volume, Chapter 4). Even if the actual Signal Detection calculations cannot be performed, the model provides a useful organizing framework. Hundreds of concrete applications of the model have been reported in well-defined, real-world detection problems in medicine, meteorology, and other domains of practical activity. (Research by Sorkin and his colleagues is at the cutting edge of knowledge on team performance of detection tasks, e.g., Sorkin et al., 2001, 2004.)

For problem-solving and decision-making tasks, there is also an idealized subtask breakdown (although no model for optimal performance): Subtask 1, comprehending the problem and immersion in the relevant knowledge domains; Subtask 2, hypothesis (solutions) generation; Subtask 3, solution evaluation and selection; and Subtask 4, solution application and implementation. Again, the sheer volume and diversity of information offer many advantages that can be brought to bear on a solution by a team compared to an individual. The immersion, selection, and implementation subtasks can all be enhanced as more team members are included in a project. Something analogous to error damping can occur in the selection subtask, when diverse critical perspectives are focused on selecting the best generated solution. Furthermore, effectively deployed teamwork can increase the variety and quantity of different solutions that are produced in the innovative solution generation subtask. (Laughlin's research on "collective induction" is the best starting place, e.g., Laughlin, 1999.)

Learning from Experience in Teams

Including opportunities to learn from experience is essential for team performance. Effective leaders make sure that individuals receive feedback and coaching to improve both individual problem-solving skills and social teamwork skills. Ideally, when a team completes a task (e.g., by successfully executing the five subtasks that compose an information integration estimation task), a final subtask would be executed to evaluate the team's achievements and to extract lessons at the team and individual levels to improve future performance. To some extent objective feedback on the quality of the product will be of use (e.g., the accuracy of an estimate). But outcome feedback also provides indirect and partial information about the quality of the team process.

WHY TEAMWORK IS IMPORTANT
IN INTELLIGENCE ANALYSIS

Why have teams performed judgment, problem-solving, or decision-making tasks at all? Why not simply find the best individuals and have them perform all of the tasks? This question is often asked in the academic literature on small-group performance. A common answer is that there is no good reason to use teams or at least face-to-face teams (e.g., Armstrong, 2006). The reasoning is that in most controlled laboratory analyses that provide clear comparisons of group versus individual performance, groups perform at lower levels than the best individuals. Loosely speaking, teams perform between the median and the best member, usually closer to the median (Gigone and Hastie, 1997; Hastie, 1986). So, why not focus on methods to identify the most effective individuals or, at least, move to software-supported collaboration systems that do not require face-to-face meetings? The problem with this advice is that it is unrealistic and derived from scientifically valid studies, but studies of relatively simple, controlled tasks; these are tasks that can be performed effectively by both individuals and groups. But, in the real world of intelligence analysis, many tasks cannot be performed by one individual acting alone. There is no plausible comparison between individual and team performance, because unaided individuals cannot do the tasks. In many areas of intelligence analysis, teamwork is not an option, it is a necessity.

REFERENCES

Armstrong, J. S. 2006. How to make better forecasts and decisions: Avoid face-to-face meetings. *Foresight: The International Journal of Applied Forecasting* 5:3–8.

Arrow, K. J., S. Sunder, R. Forsythe, R. E. Litan, M. Gorham, E. Zitzewitz, R. W. Hahn, R. Hanson, D. Kahneman, J. O. Ledyard, S. Levmore, P. R. Milgrom, F. D. Nelson, G. R. Neumann, M. Ottaviani, C. R. Plott, T. C. Schelling, R. J. Shiller, V. L. Smith, E. C. Snowberg, C. R. Sunstein, P. C. Tetlock, P. E., Tetlock, H. R. Varian, and J. Wolfers. 2007. *Statement on prediction markets.* Pub. No. 07-11. Washington, DC: Brookings Institution.

Austin, J. R. 2003. Transactive memory in organizational groups: The effects of content, consensus, specialization, and accuracy on group performance. *Journal of Applied Psychology* 88(5):866–878.

Baron, J. S., and D. M. Kreps. 1999. *Strategic human resources: Frameworks for general managers.* New York: John Wiley and Sons.

Baron, R. S. 2005. So right, it's wrong: Groupthink and the ubiquitous nature of polarized decision making. *Advances in Experimental Social Psychology* 37:219–253.

Bell, B. S., and S. W. J. Kozlowski. 2002. A typology of virtual teams: Implications for effective leadership. *Group and Organizational Management* 27(1):12–49.

Bruce, J. B. 2008. The missing link: The analyst–collector relationship. In R. Z. George and J. B. Bruce, eds., *Analyzing intelligence: Origins, obstacles, and innovations* (pp. 191–210). Washington, DC: Georgetown University Press.

Calvert, R. L. 1985. The value of biased information: A rational choice model of political advice. *Journal of Politics* 47(2):530–555.

Chen, G., R. Kanfer, R. P. DeShon, J. E. Mathieu, and S. W. J. Kozlowski. 2009. The motivating potential of teams: Test and extension of Chen and Kanfer's (2006) cross-level model of motivation in teams. *Organizational Behavior and Human Decision Processes* 101(1):45–55.

Choi, H.-S., and L. Thompson. 2005. Old wine in a new bottle: Impact of membership change on group creativity. *Organizational Behavior and Human Decision Processes* 98(2):121–132.

Congressional Record. 2003. (Senate), July 29, pp. S10082–S10083. Available: http://www.fas.org/sgp/congress/2003/s072903.html [accessed June 2010].

Cooksey, R. W. 1996. *Judgment analysis: Theory, methods, and applications.* San Diego, CA: Academic Press.

Davis, J. 2008. Why bad things happen to good analysts. In R. Z. George and J. B. Bruce, eds., *Analyzing intelligence: Origins, obstacles, and innovations* (pp. 157–170). Washington, DC: Georgetown University Press.

Dawes, R. M. 1993. Prediction of the future versus understanding of the past: A basic asymmetry. *American Journal of Psychology* 106(1):1–24.

De Groot, M. H. 1970. *Optimal statistical decisions.* New York: McGraw-Hill (reprinted, 2004, Wiley Classics Library).

Diehl, M., and W. Stroebe. 1987. Productivity loss in brainstorming groups: Toward a solution of a riddle. *Journal of Personality and Social Psychology* 53(3):497–509.

Eisenhardt, K. M., J. L. Kahwajy, and L. J. Bourgeois, III. 1997. How management teams can have a good fight. *Harvard Business Review* 75(4):77–85.

Erikson, R. S., and C. Wlezien. 2008. Are political markets really superior to polls as election predictors? *Public Opinion Quarterly* 72(2):190–215.

Fiore, S. M., E. Salas, H. M. Cuevas, and C. A. Bowers. 2003. Distributed coordination space: Toward a theory of distributed team process and performance. *Theoretical Issues in Ergonomic Science* 4(3):340–364.

Fischhoff, B. 1975. Hindsight is not equal to foresight: The effect of outcome knowledge on judgment under uncertainty. *Journal of Experimental Psychology: Human Perception and Performance* 1(3):288–299.

Gigone, D. M., and R. Hastie. 1993. The common knowledge effect: Information sharing and group judgment. *Journal of Personality and Social Psychology* 65:959–974.

Gigone, D., and R. Hastie. 1997. The proper analysis of the accuracy of group judgments. *Psychological Bulletin* 121:149–167.

Gladwell, M. 2003. Connecting the dots: The paradoxes of intelligence reform. *The New Yorker* (March 10):83–89.

Gold, T., and B. Hermann. 2003. *The role and status of DoD Red Teaming activities.* Technical Report, September, No. A139714. Washington, DC: Storming Media USA.

Goodwin, D. K. 2005. *Team of rivals: The political genius of Abraham Lincoln.* New York: Simon and Schuster.

Graefe, A., and C. Weinhardt. 2008. Long-term forecasting with prediction markets—A field experiment on applicability and expert confidence. *Journal of Prediction Markets* 2(2):71–91.

Green, K. C., J. S. Armstrong, and A. Graefe. 2008. Methods to elicit forecasts from groups: Delphi and prediction markets compared. *Foresight: The International Journal of Applied Forecasting* 8:17–20.

Greitemeyer, R., S. Schulz-Hardt, F. C. Brodbeck, and D. Frey. 2006. Information sampling and group decision making: The effects of an advocacy decision procedure and task experience. *Journal of Experimental Psychology: Applied* 12(1):31–42.

Hackman, J. R. 2002. *Leading teams: Setting the stage for great performances.* Boston, MA: Harvard Business School Press.

Hackman, J. R., and N. Vidmar. 1970. Effects of size and task type on group performance and member reactions. *Sociometry* 33(1):37–54.

Hackman, J. R., S. M. Kosslyn, and A. W. Woolley. 2008. *The design and leadership of intelligence analysis teams.* Unpublished Technical Report No. 11. Available: http://groupbrain.wjh.harvard.edu [accessed February 2010].

Hammond, K. R., J. Rohrbaugh, J. Mumpower, and L. Adelman. 1977. Social judgment theory: Applications in policy formation. In M. F. Kaplan and S. Schwartz, eds., *Human judgment and decision processes in applied settings* (pp. 1–30). New York: Academic Press.

Hanson, R., R. Oprea, and D. Porter. 2006. Information aggregation and manipulation in an experimental market. *Journal of Economic Behavior and Organization* 60(4):449–459.

Hastie, R. 1986. Experimental evidence on group accuracy. In B. Grofman and G. Owen, eds., *Information pooling and group decision making* (pp. 129–157). Greenwich, CT: JAI Press.

Heuer, R. J., Jr. 2007. *Small group processes for intelligence analysis.* Unpublished manuscript, Sherman Kent School of Intelligence Analysis, Central Intelligence Agency. Available: http://www.pherson.org/Library/H11.pdf [accessed February 2010].

Heuer, R. J., Jr. 2008. Computer-aided analysis of competing hypotheses. In R. Z. George and J. B. Bruce, eds., *Analyzing intelligence: Origins, obstacles, and innovations* (pp. 251–265). Washington, DC: Georgetown University Press.

Hinsz, V. B., R. S. Tindale, and D. A. Vollrath. 1997. The emerging conception of groups as information processors. *Psychological Bulletin* 121(1):43–64.

Hollingshead, A. B. 1998. Group and individual training: The impact of practice on performance. *Small Group Research* 29(2):254–280.

Hulse, C. 2003. Pentagon abandons plans for futures market on terror. *New York Times.* July 2.

Janis, I. L. 1972. *Victims of Groupthink: A psychological study of foreign-policy decisions and fiascos.* Boston, MA: Houghton Mifflin.

Janis, I. L. 1982. *Groupthink: Psychological studies of policy decisions and fiascos,* 2nd ed. Boston, MA: Houghton Mifflin.

Jervis, R. 2006. Reports, politics, and intelligence failures: The case of Iraq. *Journal of Strategic Studies* 29(1):3–52.

Kelley, T., and J. Littman. 2001. *The art of innovation: Lessons in creativity from IDEO, America's leading design firm.* New York: Random House.

Kerr, N. L., and R. S. Tindale. 2004. Group performance and decision making. *Annual Review of Psychology* 55:623–655.

Klein, G., and T. E. Miller. 1999. Distributed planning teams. *International Journal of Cognitive Ergonomics* 3(3):203–222.

Klein, G., K. G. Ross, B. M. Moon, D. E. Klein, and E. Hollnagel. 2003. Macrocognition. *IEEE Intelligent Systems* May–June:81–85.

Kozlowski, S. W. J., and D. R. Ilgen. 2006. Enhancing the effectiveness of work groups and teams. *Psychological Science in the Public Interest* 7(3):77–124.

Kramer, T. J., G. P. Fleming, and S. M. Mannis. 2001. Improving face-to-face brainstorming through modeling and facilitation. *Small Group Research* 32(5):533–557.

Larson, J. R., Jr., P. G. Foster-Fishman, and C. B. Keys. 1994. Discussion of shared and unshared information in decision-making groups. *Journal of Personality and Social Psychology* 67(3):446–461.

Larson, J. R., Jr., C. Christensen, A. S. Abbot, and T. M. Franz. 1996. Diagnosing groups: Charting the flow of information in medical decision-making teams. *Journal of Personality and Social Psychology* 71(2):533–557.

Laughlin, P. R. 1999. Collective induction: Twelve postulates. *Organizational Behavior and Human Decision Processes* 80(1):50–69.

Lavery, T. A., T. M. Franz, J. R. Winquist, and J. R. Larson, Jr. 1999. The role of information exchange in predicting group accuracy on a multiple judgment task. *Basic and Applied Social Psychology* 21(4):281–289.

Lee, M. D., and T. D. R. Cummins. 2004. Evidence accumulation in decision making: Unifying the "take the best" and the "rational" models. *Psychonomic Bulletin and Review* 11(2):343–352.

Linstone, H. A., and M. Turoff, eds. 1975. *The Delphi Method: Techniques and applications.* Reading, MA: Addison-Wesley Educational. Available: http://www.is.njit.edu/pubs/delphibook/ [accessed February 2010].

Mannix, E., and M. A. Neale. 2005. What differences make a difference? The promise and reality of diverse teams in organizations. *Psychological Science in the Public Interest* 6(2):31–55.

Manski, C. F. 2006. Interpreting the predictions of prediction markets. *Economics Letters* 91(4):425–429.

Mathieu, J. E., T. S. Heffner, G. F. Goodwin, E. Salas, and J. A. Cannon-Bowers. 2000. The influence of shared mental models on team process and performance. *Journal of Applied Psychology* 85:273–283.

Moreland, R. L., and J. M. Levine. 1982. Socialization in small groups: Temporal changes in individual-group relations. *Advances in Experimental Social Psychology* 15:137–192.

Moreland, R. L., and L. Myaskovsky. 2000. Exploring the performance benefits of group training: Transactive memory or improved communication. *Organizational Behavior and Human Decision Processes* 82(1):117–133.

Moreland, R. L., L. Argote, and R. Krishnan. 1996. Socially shared cognition at work: Transactive memory and group performance. In J. L. Nye and A. M. Browker, eds., *What's social about social cognition* (pp. 128–141). Thousand Oaks, CA: Sage.

Nemeth, C. J. 1986. Differential contributions of majority and minority influence. *Psychological Review* 93(1):23–32.

Nemeth, C. J., K. Brown, and J. Rogers. 2001. Devil's advocate versus authentic dissent: Stimulating quantity and quality. *European Journal of Social Psychology* 31(6):707–720.

Nijstad, B. A., W. Stroebe, and H. F. M. Lodewijkx. 2003. Production blocking and idea generation: Does blocking interfere with cognitive processes? *Journal of Experimental Social Psychology* 39(4):531–548.

Okhuysen, G. A., and K. M. Eisenhardt. 2002. Integrating knowledge in groups: How formal interventions enable flexibility. *Organization Science* 13(4):370–386.

Oxley, N. L., M. T. Dzindolet, and P. B. Paulus. 1996. The effects of facilitators on the performance of brainstorming groups. *Journal of Social Behavior and Personality* 11(4): 633–646.

Page, S. E. 2007. *The difference: How the power of diversity creates better groups, firms, schools, and societies.* Princeton, NJ: Princeton University Press.

Paris, C. R., E. Salas, and J. A. Cannon-Bowers. 2000. Teamwork in multi-person systems: A review and analysis. *Ergonomics* 43(8):1,052–1,075.

Pashler, H., M. McDaniel, D. Rohrer, and R. Bjork. 2008. Learning styles: Concepts and evidence. *Psychological Science in the Public Interest* 9(3):105–119.

Paulus, P. B. 1998. Developing consensus about Groupthink after all these years. *Organizational Behavior and Human Decision Processes* 73(2/3):362–374.

Paulus, P. B., and H.-C. Yang. 2000. Idea generation in groups: A basis for creativity in organizations. *Organizational Behavior and Human Decision Processes* 82(1):76–87.

Plous, S. 1995. A comparison of strategies for reducing interval overconfidence in group judgments. *Journal of Applied Psychology* 80(4):443–454.

Puncochar, J. M., and P. W. Fox. 2004. Confidence in individual and group decision making: When "two heads" are worse than one. *Journal of Educational Psychology* 96(3):582–591.

Rescher, N. 1998. *Predicting the future*. Albany: State University of New York Press.

Rohrbaugh, J. 1979. Improving the quality of group judgment: Social judgment analysis and the Delphi technique. *Organizational Behavior and Human Performance* 24(1):73–92.

Rohrbaugh, J. 1981. Improving the quality of group judgment: Social judgment analysis and the nominal group technique. *Organizational Behavior and Human Performance* 28(2): 272–288.

Rouse, W. B., and N. M. Morris. 1986. On looking into the black box: Prospects and limits in the search for mental models. *Psychological Bulletin* 100(3):349–363.

Rowe, G., and G. Wright. 1999. The Delphi technique as a forecasting tool: Issues and analysis. *International Journal of Forecasting* 15(3):353–375.

Safire, W. 2004. *On language: Groupthink*. Available: http://www.nytimes.com/2004/08/08/magazine/the-way-we-live-now-8-8-04-on-language-groupthink.html?sec=&spon=&pagewanted=1 [accessed February 2010].

Schkade, D., C. R. Sunstein, and R. Hastie. 2007. What happened on deliberation day? *California Law Review* 95(3):915–940.

Schulz-Hardt, S., F. C. Brodbeck, A. Mojzisch, R. Kerschreiter, and D. Frey. 2006. Group decision making in hidden profile situations: Dissent as a facilitator for decision quality. *Journal of Personality and Social Psychology* 91(6):1,080–1,093.

Schum, D. A. 1987. *Evidence and inference for the intelligence analyst* (2 vols.). Lanham, MD: University Press of America.

Schweiger, D. M., W. R. Sandberg, and J. W. Ragan. 1986. Group approaches to improving strategic decision making: A comparative analysis of dialectical inquiry, devil's advocacy, and consensus. *Academy of Management Journal* 29(1):51–71.

Schwenk, C. R. 1988. *The essence of strategic decision making*. Lexington, MA: Lexington Press.

Schwenk, C. R. 1990. Effects of devil's advocacy and dialectical inquiry on decision making: A meta-analysis. *Organizational Behavior and Human Decision Processes* 47(1):161–176.

Senate Select Committee on Intelligence. 2004. *Report of the Select Committee on Intelligence on the U.S. intelligence community's prewar intelligence assessments on Iraq*. Available: http://www.gpoaccess.gov/serialset/creports/iraq.html [accessed June 2010].

Sniezek, J. A. 1992. Groups under uncertainty: An examination of confidence in group decision making. *Organizational Behavior and Human Decision Processes* 52(2):124–155.

Sorkin, R., C. Hays, and R. West. 2001. Signal-detection analysis of group decision making. *Psychological Review* 108(1):183–203.

Sorkin, R., S. Luan, and J. Itzkowitz. 2004. Group decision and deliberation: A distributed detection process. In D. J. Koehler and N. Harvey, eds., *Blackwell handbook of judgment and decision making* (pp. 464–484). Malden, MA: Blackwell.

Stasser, G., and M. Augustinova. 2007. Social engineering in distributed decision-making teams: Some implications for leadership at a distance. In S. P. Weisband, ed., *Leadership at a distance: Research in technologically supported work* (pp. 151–168). Mahwah, NJ: Erlbaum Associates.

Stasser, G., and W. Titus. 1985. Pooling of unshared information in group decision making: Biased information sampling during discussion. *Journal of Personality and Social Psychology* 48(6):1,467–1,478.

Stasser, G., and W. Titus. 2003. Hidden profiles: A brief history. *Psychological Inquiry* 14(3/4):304–313.

Stasser, G., D. D. Stewart, and G. M. Wittenbaum. 1995. Expert roles and information exchange during discussion: The importance of knowing who knows what. *Journal of Experimental Social Psychology* 31:244–265.

Steiner, I. D. 1972. *Group process and productivity*. San Diego, CA: Academic Press.

Straus, S. G., A. M. Parker, J. B. Bruce, and J. W. Dembosky. 2008. *The group matters: A review of the effects of group interaction processes and outcomes in analytic teams.* Working Paper WR-580-USG. Santa Monica, CA: RAND Corporation. Available: http://www.rand.org/pubs/working_papers/2009/RAND_WR580.pdf [accessed February 2010].

Sunstein, C. R. 2006. *Infotopia: How many minds produce knowledge.* New York: Doubleday.

Sunstein, C. R. 2009. *Going to extremes: How like minds unite and divide.* New York: Oxford University Press.

Surowiecki, J. 2004. *The wisdom of crowds.* New York: Doubleday.

Tapscott, D., and A. D. Williams. 2006. *Wikinomics: How mass collaboration changes everything.* New York: Penguin.

Tetlock, P. E. 2006. *Expert political judgment: How good is it? How can we know?* Princeton, NJ: Princeton University Press.

Turner, M. E., and A. R. Pratkanis. 1998. Twenty-five years of Groupthink theory and research: Lessons from the evaluation of a theory. *Organizational Behavior and Human Decision Processes* 73(2–3):105–115.

U.S. Government. (2009) *Tradecraft primer: Structured analytic techniques for improving intelligence analysis.* Available: https://www.cia.gov/library/center-for-the-study-of-intelligence/csi-publications/books-and-monographs/Tradecraft%20Primer-apr09.pdf [accessed February 2010].

Wageman, R. 2001. How leaders foster self-managing team effectiveness: Design choice versus hands-on coaching. *Organization Science* 12(5):559–577.

Whyte, G. 1998. Recasting Janis's Groupthink model: The key role of collective efficacy in decision fiascoes. *Organizational Behavior and Human Decision Processes* 73(2–3): 185–209.

Whyte, W. H., Jr. 1952. Groupthink. *Fortune Magazine* 45(March):6–7.

Wilson, J. R., and A. Rutherford. 1989. Mental models: Theory and application in human factors. *Human Factors* 31(5):617–634.

Winquist, J. R., and J. R. Larson, Jr. 1998. Information pooling: When it impacts group decision making. *Journal of Personality and Social Psychology* 74(2):371–377.

Wolfers, J., and E. Zitzewitz. 2004. Prediction markets. *Journal of Economic Perspectives* 18(2):107–126.

Yasin, R. 2009. National security and social networking are compatible. *Government Computer News*, July 23. Available: http://www.gcn.com/Articles/2009/07/23/Social-networking-media-national-security.aspx?Page=1 [accessed February 2010].

Zarnoth, P., and J. A. Sniezek. 1997. The social influence of confidence in group decision making. *Journal of Experimental Social Psychology* 33(4):345–366.

9

Social Categorization and Intergroup Dynamics

Catherine H. Tinsley

Imagine that the Central Intelligence Agency (CIA) suspects a Pakistani national living in Canada is planning a terrorist attack against the United States. The CIA has been working with Canadian authorities to track the man's movements and analyze his future intentions. Border patrol has been alerted because the suspect appears to be part of a Canadian-based terrorist cell that may soon try to enter the United States. The National Security Agency (NSA) has been contacted to monitor the suspect's telecommunications. Last week, the suspect phoned a U.S. citizen and resident, which triggered the involvement of the Federal Bureau of Investigation (FBI).

As this scenario illustrates, current threats to U.S. security can be global, can come from varied nonstate actors (including isolated individuals), and can require extensive coordination across intelligence community (IC) agencies. Indeed, the IC has recognized a need to integrate information and analysis, as captured in various agencies' strategic plans. The Director of National Intelligence writes that "information sharing is a top priority" and that we must move from a mentality of "need to know" to a mentality of "responsibility to provide" (Office of the Director of National Intelligence, 2008). The Defense Intelligence Agency (DIA) Strategic Plan lists "support[ing] unification of effort across the IC to promote horizontal integration fostering access to data and sharing information" as one of its five major strategic actions (Defense Intelligence Agency, 2007). This coordination goes beyond simply the need to share information with each other. Instead, it requires analysts to understand and appreciate the experience and knowledge that each different agency brings to the table. This deeper understanding will help attenuate communication problems (Fischhoff, this volume, Chapter 10), such as agents talking past each other or dismissing each other's analysis.

Unfortunately, cross-agency collaboration can be thwarted by the familiar pathologies found in all intergroup endeavors. These include misaligned organizational incentives, ossified bureaucratic policies, and conflicting political pressures. For example, agencies within the IC are "mission specific" (Sims, 2005), meaning they serve different customers who may be asking different analytic questions about the same target or event. Each agency in the IC naturally has "its own terminology, routines, and expectations about what people can ask for" (Simon, 2005, p. 150). Moreover, interagency "turf wars," which appear to arise from historical inertia and budgetary conflicts (Sims and Gerber, 2005), provide inherent challenges to interagency collaboration.

Discussing any particular bureaucratic, political, and budgetary conflicts is beyond the scope of this chapter, which instead focuses on how the pluralistic structure of the IC can engender cognitive and motivational biases that hinder effective cross-agency collaboration. Special attention is paid to the agency grouping and how social categorization processes can influence individual behavior. Social categorization is the process by which we make judgments about individuals (and who they are in relation to ourselves) based on their group membership. When we encounter other people, we tend to encode not only individual information about that person, but also social information—in particular, whether he or she is a member of one of our "in-groups"—the groups to which we belong—or is an "out-group" member, or outsider. In the context of the IC, where a salient group boundary is agency (or subagency) affiliation, social categorization suggests that analysts register whether other analysts are members of the same or different IC agency.[1] This encoding can produce mental roadblocks to coordination by eliciting well-documented intergroup dynamics, including differentiation, ethnocentrism, and integration neglect (explained below). These roadblocks are not unique to the IC, but rather are fundamental

---

[1]This agency grouping does not mean that other social groups are irrelevant. Indeed, within some agencies there are large distinctions between analysts and collectors (e.g., the CIA). Groups are people's subjective representations of others vis-à-vis the self. These groups may exist because people interact regularly and share a common fate (Campbell, 1958), such as with workgroups, or groups may be large collectives where individuals are connected by virtue of common symbolic attachments (Geertz, 1973). The motivational and cognitive biases discussed in this chapter would pertain to any social group distinction that is relevant for the actors involved. For simplicity of presentation, however, I choose the agency level as the focal social group because this follows both the formal organizational structure and other work describing agency affiliation as a dominant social category in the IC (see Sims and Gerber, 2005, or Fingar, this volume, Chapter 1).

aspects of organizational life, unless deliberate efforts are made to overcome them. More relevant to the IC is how these dynamics play out and how they might be managed.

Before describing the usual pathologies that can arise from an intergroup environment, I briefly detail research in organizational behavior to explain why these pluralistic structures evolve. In most organizations, and particularly for the mission-diverse IC, social groups function to simplify tasks and create high-quality (i.e., well-grounded and solidly analytic) products. The idea is not to restructure the IC to rid it of multiple social groups (which is likely to be impossible anyway), but rather to attenuate negative externalities that this intergroup environment can produce.

INTERGROUP DYNAMICS AS A FACT
OF ORGANIZATIONAL LIFE

Social groups exist in all organizations and often create cognitive and motivational roadblocks to cooperation and collaboration. Despite their pernicious consequences, organizations cannot eradicate groups. For organizations, groups are necessary for efficient coordinated action. For individual employees, groups are necessary for constructing identity and making sense of their workplace.

The Organization's Need to Form Groups

All organizations differentiate—meaning they split their employees into different groups (Lawrence and Lorsch, 1967). Differentiation allows for specialization, production efficiency, and accountability. Imagine if every employee was responsible for the same job tasks—no one would master any special skills, and failure to accomplish job tasks would rest with everyone and hence with no one. The IC can be modeled as a decentralized conglomerate organization (Chandler, 1962). In one organizational chart[2] the Office of the Director of National Intelligence is at the top. One level below it are the program agencies (CIA, DIA, FBI, NSA, etc.). On the next level are the "departmental agencies" or those that primarily report directly to a Cabinet member (Drug Enforcement Administration, Department of Homeland Security, Department of State's Bureau of Intelligence and Research (INR), Department of the Treasury, etc.). On the final level are the "service agencies" (Army, Air Force, Navy, Marine Corps, and Coast Guard Intelligence). Of course, the IC can be grouped in other ways (e.g., on the basis of whether the agencies' primary function is collection

---

[2]Chart published in *National Intelligence: A Consumer's Guide to National Intelligence* (Office of the Director of National Intelligence, 2009, p. 9).

or analysis, or whether their primary concern is foreign intelligence or law enforcement). Yet, alternative ways of grouping personnel does not threaten the central thesis that the multiorganizational character of the IC creates groups that differentiate themselves from one another and engender cultural barriers to collaboration.

The important point is that the IC *is* structured, and the basic structural unit is the agency. In the IC, the first order differentiation of analysts is based on agency affiliation. The structure allows each agency to produce intelligence products tailored to the needs of its primary customer base. For example, in April 2001, when a U.S. EP-3 surveillance aircraft collided in mid-air with a Chinese fighter plane and the EP-3 landed on the Chinese island of Hainan, different IC agencies produced intelligence assessments that answered very different types of questions reflecting the interests and responsibilities of their different customers. Thus, the INR, whose primary customer is the Department of State, produced intelligence to answer questions such as: What are the diplomatic implications of the collision? What signals has the Chinese government sent that might help to resolve the crisis? What is the government telling its own people about the incident? The DIA, whose primary customers are in the Department of Defense, addressed different questions: Are the Chinese moving any military assets? Are there any signs that units have increased readiness levels? What are Japanese and South Korean media saying about the incident and U.S. forces based in those countries?

The NSA and National Geospatial Agency (NGA) addressed more technical questions about the types of equipment on board and what the implications would be of some or all of it falling into the hands of the Chinese government. The CIA, reflecting its broad customer base and responsibilities, provided a second take on many of the questions posed and answered by other agencies. These illustrations make clear that specialization is necessary, appropriate, and essential to address specific customer concerns. Only by being close to customers can analysts know what they require and produce truly useful intelligence products.

Throughout the differentiation process, organizations make trade-offs about where and how much to differentiate, with the aim of maximizing goals such as: (1) resource efficiency, (2) time efficiency, (3) employee accountability, (4) responsiveness to the environment, and (5) adaptability over time (Nohria, 1991). For the IC, resource efficiency would be the ability to produce quality intelligence with economy of labor and capital; time efficiency would be the ability to do so rapidly. Employee accountability describes the ability to hold employees responsible for required activities. Responsiveness to the environment means satisfying the requirements of U.S. policy makers as well as the need to protect sources and methods. Finally, adaptability refers to the ability to innovate to meet changing security threats and policy decisions. To maximize this portfolio of issues, the organization decides how much to differentiate and where to draw the distinctions.

Naturally, this differentiation process creates groups (e.g., agencies) that have their own unique intelligence priorities and routines. Although agencies may share common rules for evaluating source reliability or explicating underlying assumptions, the agencies develop different decision rules on what topics to cover and different standard operating procedures on which streams of data are the most reliable to use. For example, the INR may rely more heavily on diplomatic and open-source information; the DIA may rely more heavily on military channels; the CIA may focus primarily on clandestine human intelligence collection; and the FBI may use other human informants with information relevant to law enforcement. These decision rules and procedures are likely to align with the agency's mission, but they will in some sense dictate how data are collected, fused, used or discarded, interpreted, and presented. Thus it is not surprising that differentiated agencies can produce intelligence that is not completely uniform, even if each is a well-researched product reflecting solid evidence and analysis. Some systemic tension is natural; the idea is to understand and manage it rather than try to eliminate it.

Individuals' Need to Group

Differentiation benefits organizations through efficiency gains and specialization. This specialization can also benefit individuals because it encourages employees' skill development. Yet skill specialization can also make the employee more dependent on the organization because high-asset specificity cuts both ways (Williamson, 2002). Do individuals benefit from the presence of multiple social groups in their environment?

Some have argued that social categorization processes (constructing social groups) is a natural human process. As social creatures, we tend to carve up our social landscape into groups (see social categorization theory, Deschamps and Doise, 1978; Vanbeselaere, 1991), in part to construct our own identities (Tajfel, 1969; Tajfel and Turner, 1979). Generally, we come to understand who we are by virtue of the groups to which we do and do not belong (Smith and Berg, 1987). In fact, we tend to view other people, first and foremost, as members of a particular social category (in-group or out-group) (Brewer and Feinstein, 1999; Fiske et al., 1999). This social categorization happens relatively effortlessly (Fiske, 1998) and is often based on visually prominent and culturally relevant features, such as age, race, and (here) agency affiliation (Brewer and Feinstein, 1999; Fiske, 1998). Of course, people have multiple in-group identities (Stryker and Statham, 1985; Tajfel, 1978), but when these categories compete for attention, one usually dominates, depending on contextual cues (Brewer and Pierce, 2005). For example, a female professional may think of herself as an analyst at work and as a mother at home. Moreover, an analyst might think of herself as an analyst when talking to collectors and as a CIA employee when talking to a DIA analyst.

This type of automatic characterization not only helps us self-identify, but also allows us to form a basic understanding of a socially different "other" (Bodenhausen et al., 1999). Social groups can be thought of as social categories, and people tend to form prototypic representations of these categories in the form of exemplary members (actual members who best embody group features) or ideal members (an amalgamated abstraction of group characteristics) (Kahneman and Miller, 1986). As individuals self-categorize, they represent themselves less as unique individuals and more as embodiments of the relevant prototypic features (Hogg and Terry, 2000). That is, self-categorization cognitively assimilates the self with the in-group prototype. Therefore, this social grouping process gives an individual direction or guidance because group prototypes "describe and prescribe perceptions, attitudes, feelings, and behavior" (Hogg and Terry, 2000, p. 124). People tend to conform to their groups (Asch, 1955) for both cognitive and motivational reasons. Cognitively, conformity reduces uncertainty—when confronted with a situation, individuals know how to react based on prototypical group norms. Social norms carry both a descriptive and injunctive/ prescriptive function (Cialdini and Trost, 1998). Motivationally, conformity increases that member's attractiveness in the eyes of other in-group members (Mowday and Sutton, 1993).

Thus social categorization processes give people a sense of identity at work (who they are) and provide them with guidance on how to behave. Yet, these processes function like any other heuristic in constraining people's thoughts (e.g., expectations and attitudes about people and situations, and attributions for events) (Salancik and Pfeffer, 1978) and behavioral repertoire. Social categorization may be natural, effortless, and in some ways beneficial, but is not without the ethnocentric consequences discussed next.

HOW SOCIAL CATEGORIZATION INFLUENCES INDIVIDUALS

As noted above, individual thought and behavior is influenced by the social environment, such as how employees are split into groups, what behavior is rewarded, and what institutional routines develop. Interestingly, people are often unaware of the extent to which their thought and behavior have been shaped by their social context. We often believe that we think and act as unconstrained free agents, when in fact, our "rational" thoughts and behavior, including our awareness and imagination, are bounded by our own frames of reference. In particular, we underestimate the extent to which our thoughts and behaviors are shaped by subjective construal rather than direct perceptions of an objective reality (Griffin and Ross, 1991).

"Culture" is one term that is often used to label a shared frame of reference or a shared social context. Culture can be defined as a constellation of values, assumptions, beliefs, behavioral norms, and routines that define a group of people united by ethnic or organizational membership (Benedict, 1934). It is what makes a collection of people a "group" (or as Tylor, 1871, first described it—culture is a "superorganic" entity). Culture offers members a social blueprint that interprets stimuli and guides group members (Boas, 1940). Groups can differ according to how tight or how loose their culture is, meaning how much "deviance" group members are allowed before being sanctioned (Triandis, 2002).[3] Most groups have complex cultures, meaning one type of behavior (e.g., competition) is rewarded in some contexts and a different behavior (e.g., cooperation) is rewarded in another context.[4] Yet, all cultures outline expected beliefs and behaviors (although they may be context dependent) and reward conformity to these ideals. In this way, cultures shape individual thought and behavior.

Decades of research supports the idea that culture influences group members' thought and behavior by showing that people of different cultures respond to the same stimuli with different attitudes, beliefs, and activities (Berry, 1980; De Vos, 1975; Erez, 1986; Leung and Bond, 1984; Triandis, 1989; Wagner, 1995). Dearborn and Simon (1958), for example, showed that socialization through organizational training systems produces "managerial mindsets" that limit how people conceptualize problems and solutions. In their study, they asked groups of executives from a manufacturing firm to study a particular company, and asked the executives to identify the company's most pressing problem. The study had three groups from three functional cultures—sales executives, production executives, and human and public relations executives. Each cultural group viewed the same company data through a different lens, and thus offered three entirely different proposals about the company's most pressing problem (sales, operations, and human relations, respectively).

---

[3]Furthermore, depending on the size of the cultural group boundary, cultures can include "subcultures." Echoing footnote 1, for example, the CIA can have a dominant culture (certain values, norms, and routines), then different subcultures for analysts versus collectors. This level of analysis issue should not detract from the basic sociocognitive dynamics outlined in the chapter. Social categorization processes can occur at any organizational level. The purpose here is simply to document the intergroup dynamics that emanate once these categorization processes occur.

[4]For more on cultural complexity and its relation to context-dependent behavior, see Brett et al. (2007).

Similarly, Tinsley and Pillutla (1998) found that socialization into different national cultures led people to interpret the same negotiation task in different ways. One cultural group assumed the goal of the negotiation was to maximize joint gain, whereas the other cultural group assumed the goal was to minimize the difference between each party's outcomes. This goal discrepancy corresponded with the groups' actual outcomes and with parties' satisfaction with those outcomes.

In sum, cultural profiles offer members a roadmap for interpreting stimuli and guiding behavioral reactions. At the same time, by focusing attention and behavior, these roadmaps also constrain thought and action. By institutionalizing an optimal way to think and behave, these roadmaps can suggest that other thoughts and behaviors are suboptimal or even wrong. Accordingly, interactions among members of different cultural groups that have different missions, approaches, and routines can be strained.

INTERGROUP DYNAMICS FROM
SOCIAL CATEGORIZATION PROCESSES

One of the most robust findings from cultural research is that of ethnocentrism, which literally means putting one's own group at the center of the universe. Anthropologists (Boas, 1940; Mead, 1964; Kroeber and Kluckhohn, 1952; Lowie, 1966; Malinowski, 1944) find that people learn to be ethnocentric through socialization in a particular social system, which rewards appropriate thought and behavior while sanctioning inappropriate thought and behavior. Hence, members come to believe that their group's values, beliefs, behaviors, and organizing principles are superior to those of any other group. In the IC, this might be reflected in the CIA believing its practices to be "the gold standard" (Goss, 2005) or in the INR being promoted as "the biggest little intelligence shop in town" (Aspin quoted in Ignatius, 2004). Evolutionary psychology considers ethnocentrism to be an innate outgrowth of nepotism (van de Berghe, 1981), meaning ethnocentrism has a natural survival value for the group.

In-Group Bias

Psychologists tend to focus on the costs of ethnocentrism, including "ingroup bias" or the tendency to see members of one's own group in a more positive light relative to members of other groups (Tajfel, 1970). For example, in the IC, this might be reflected in a predisposition to favor types of information (e.g., clandestine human intelligence) produced by the agency in which the analyst is embedded. Across a variety of studies outside the IC, people have judged members of their in-groups to be smarter, more attractive, more cooperative, fairer, more trustworthy, and more hard working than members of out-groups (cf., Brewer, 1979; Tajfel, 1970, 1982). This prejudice generally seems to entail withholding positive traits from the out-group rather than actively assigning negative traits to them (Fiske et al., 1999), and it is found to enhance the status of the in-group rather than degrade the out-group (Tajfel, 1982). Strikingly, this in-group bias occurs not only across real-life groups, but also can be activated with groups created in the laboratory based on minimal or random criteria, such as having the same birthday or similar final digits in Social Security numbers (Brewer, 1979; Brewer and Kramer, 1982). Moreover, in-group bias can occur with or without direct interaction (e.g., attitudinal biases that arise simply through observation or awareness of an out-group member), and without any prior personal history between the parties involved (Kahn and Zald, 1990).

From a practical standpoint, in-group favoritism is problematic in social landscapes with more than one group. First, it leads to discrimination, with in-group members being treated better than out-group members. People award higher monetary payouts and emotional payouts, such as helping behavior, to in-group members than to out-group members. Second, the bias leads to perhaps the most common problem in intergroup relations, "reciprocal antipathy," or the difficulty of getting groups to cooperate with each other. As Kramer notes (2005, p. 407):

> The problem of securing cooperation between interdependent groups has been a central and recurring theme in the study of intergroup relations from its inception (Sherif, 1966a; Sumner, 1906). Whether they are minimal groups created in laboratory settings (Tajfel, 1970), groups of boys at summer camp (Sherif et al., 1961), groups within organizations (Mouton and Blake, 1986), or even nation-states (Kahn and Zald, 1990), reciprocal antipathy between groups seems to develop with surprising frequency and alacrity.

In the IC, for example, this might create problems with respect to information sharing and create various "security regulations" that make it difficult for analysts to access information not collected or disseminated to their agency, or rules that limit access to certain databases (see Fingar, this volume, Chapter 1).

In-group bias impairs actors from different groups from cooperating with each other, even to achieve a mutually desired end state. Often simply associating oneself with an in-group leads to biases favoring one's group over others (Cadinu and Rothbart, 1996; Smith and Henry, 1996; Turner, 1987). Homophily, or the tendency to be attracted to those who are similar to oneself (Blau, 1977; Berscheid and Reis, 1998), suggests that the simple categorization of others into a different group can produce bias and decrease cooperation.

Therefore, in-group favoritism does not necessarily stem from faulty incentive structures. Actors from two different groups can be given incentives to solve a particular problem or to share mutually needed information, yet still suffer coordination difficulties. Rather, in-group favoritism is rooted in the sociocognitive categorization mechanism, which primes a sense of difference that eschews cognitive and motivational roadblocks to cooperation. Recall that self-categorization is a process where someone cognitively assimilates his or her self-concept to the in-group prototype. A critical feature of group prototypes is that of meta-contrast, meaning prototypes maximize similarities within each group and differences across social groups (Hogg and Terry, 2000). For example, Ledgerwood and Chaiken (2007) find that people tend to radicalize their attitudes to assimilate to those of the in-group and contrast from those of the out-group. This might play out in the IC, for example, in predispositions to dismiss alternative judgments and hypotheses that originate outside of one's agency (the "not invented here" problem).

Out-Group Homogeneity

A second outgrowth of ethnocentrism is the "out-group homogeneity effect," or the tendency to see members of one's own group as differentiated, but to perceive out-group members as similar and unvaried (Quattrone and Jones, 1980). Seeing in-group members as more varied cannot be attributed to knowledge and exposure, as this effect is found between groups, such as "men" and "women," who interact frequently (Mullen and Hu, 1989).

The problem that arises from out-group homogeneity is stereotyping. A stereotype is a mental model that an actor has of another person based on the target's social category membership (Lippman, 1922; Fiske and Taylor, 1991), so that the actor ascribes personality traits to the whole social category and subsequently confers these personality traits onto any member of that social group (Spencer-Rogers et al., 2007). Holding stereotypes about another social group is useful to the extent that members of the group behave in stereotype-consistent ways. Unfortunately, research shows that actors tend to discount stereotype-inconsistent behavior from targets. For example, actors tend to follow stereotypic information about an interdependent work partner, even when this information is fictitious and assigned on a random basis (Tinsley et al., 2002; O'Connor and Tinsley, 2009).

Although stereotypes are technically a cognitive phenomenon, they elicit an emotional concomitant that can be negative.[5] The IC, like other

---

[5]Although most stereotypes are thought to elicit negative emotions toward others, not all stereotypes do so. Fiske and colleagues (1999, 2002) detail four general types of stereotypes

organizations, has many stereotypes that affect the way analysts in one agency think of and deal with their counterparts in other agencies. Common stereotypes include the perception that INR analysts are predisposed to believe what foreign officials claim to be the case and attach greater weight to diplomatic reporting than other forms of intelligence; that CIA analysts give greater credence to clandestinely acquired human intelligence; and that DIA analysts are prone to exaggerate military threats and to favor worst case possibilities.

Whether these stereotypes are true or not (or are based on truth but exaggerated, or were true but no longer are so) is irrelevant. Any stereotypes that analysts hold of each other will influence their expectations of each other and their decisions about whether or not to reach out and ask one another for help. Stereotypes can cause collaboration problems because the actor is conferring group-level information on an individual, who may or may not "fit the profile." Thus, analysts can misunderstand each other's needs and abilities. Moreover, because we tend to discount situational explanations for others' behavior (Ross, 1977; Jones and Harris, 1967), and these attribution errors are more pernicious for out-group members (Allison and Messick, 1985), an actor could easily misperceive a target's intent and ascribe a more sinister motive, making any interaction more emotionally trying than it needs to be.

Do these intergroup problems pervade every organizational interaction? Of course not, but social categorization and intergroup dynamics represent the backdrop against which everyday organizational activities occur. Like background music that sometimes fades out of awareness and at other times becomes an annoying distraction, intergroup issues can remain quiet or create a disconcerting amount of static. The next sections describe research on when intergroup dynamics are relatively dormant versus when they come forward as a powerful force shaping the interaction.

WHEN MIGHT INTERGROUP DYNAMICS BE MORE ACUTE?

In certain circumstances intergroup biases have an especially acute influence on members' cognitions and behaviors. Generally, the degree of

---

along two dimensions, the warmth of the target and the presumed competence of the target. Thus, an actor's social categorization of a target can elicit feelings of: (1) low warmth/low competence, (2) low warmth/high competence, (3) high warmth/low competence, or (4) high warmth/high competence. Presumably, actors who think the target belongs to this last social group should have a relatively easier time working with this target than with a target categorized in one of the other three groups. Indeed, in a collaboration task, O'Connor and Tinsley (2009) found that people's positive stereotypes of each other lead to high collaboration and high output, even when the information was false and even when only one party made such a positive inference about the other. Unfortunately, however, Fiske et al. (1999) find that people tend to reserve this high-warmth/high-competence stereotype for fellow in-group members.

entitativity of the social landscape, meaning the salience and perceived permanence of the group boundaries (because of simple, distinct, and consensual group prototypes), correlates to the amount of intergroup static. One context that tends to elicit intergroup categorizations and bias is a threatening situation. Realistic group conflict theory (Campbell, 1965; Sherif, 1966a) argues that resource threat leads to intergroup salience, and thus to ethnocentrism and intergroup conflict. This theory has received strong empirical support (Sherif, 1966b; Tajfel, 1970; Alexander et al., 1999). Similarly, Derks et al. (2008) delineate several types of social identity threat, such as the threat that one's group might be devalued or lacks distinctiveness, and show that social identity threat also leads to "compensatory in-group bias." In other words, not only can resource threat trigger differentiation and ethnocentrism, but also identity threat can trigger differentiation and prejudice against the out-group. In general, threats tend to activate a competitive mindset, which triggers ethnocentrism (Mussweiler and Bodenhausen, 2002; Stapel and Koomen, 2005).

A second context that evokes intergroup categories is when decision making requires speed or unusual cognitive effort. Recall that social categorizations can be automatic processes that offer a heuristic for how to approach and manage interactions with a target "other." Such automatic processes tend to be activated when the mind is focused elsewhere. Time constraints, deadlines, or "high cognitive load" (complex tasks that require much thoughtful effort) tend to increase the use of cognitive short-cuts such as social categorization processes. For IC analysts this might mean that analyses that are particularly complex and/or time sensitive (that put stress on the analyst) will activate their intergroup categories. In these situations of tight deadlines and problem complexity, analysts are more likely to look to those within their own agency for help, rather than solicit the assistance of those in other agencies.

A final context in which group categorization and intergroup bias may be particularly acute is when individuals have a strong attachment to their own cultural group. Individuals generally become attached to strong cultures (Triandis, 2002), which create a high cohesion among group members, increasing group entitativity (Hogg, 1992, 1993). Cultures are strong when member consensus and intensity exists (O'Reilly, 1989). Specifically, members agree on the attitudes and beliefs they value and on normative behaviors; they also feel strongly about the importance of these values, beliefs, and norms. In this way, an individual's in-group category is particularly accessible because it is valued or important (Hogg and Terry, 2000).

In industry, a strong culture is positively regarded. Management scholars point to successful companies (as measured by long-term stock performance) and argue that the organization's strong culture contributed to its success (e.g., Walmart, Southwest Airlines, Nordstrom) (O'Reilly and Pfeffer, 1995). The belief is that a strong culture represents a unique competitive advantage because it is an enduring and inimitable resource (unlike capital, which is easy to raise, or technology, which is often either shared or stolen).

A strong culture can improve employees' commitment by giving them identity and meaning (Schein, 1988), and it can boost performance by serving as an informal control system. Formal control systems exist through appraisal and reward systems, yet such metrics can be imperfect, and at times, neither behavior nor outcomes can be adequately monitored (Dornbusch and Scott, 1975). Thus, culture can serve as a social control system that regulates behavior, particularly in the face of unusual or unpredictable situations that require initiative, flexibility, and innovation. In fact, many culture researchers argue that the less formal direction employees receive, the more ownership they take over their actions and performance. For example, at Nordstrom, associates are simply told to "use their good judgment in all situations" (Goodall, 1992). At Southwest Airlines, employees are instructed to do what it takes to make the customer happy.[6] At the Ritz Carlton, associates learn to think of themselves as "ladies and gentlemen assisting other ladies and gentlemen" and are given large discretionary budgets to address customer complaints (Fisher, 2009).

Although many industry corporations strive for strong cultures, an important difference to note is that these organizations are building (or trying to build) one uniform culture throughout the organization rather than several different strong cultures unique to any division. Within the IC, building and maintaining a strong agency culture may be beneficial. However, the costs of these strong agency cultures can be salient intergroup boundaries.

HOW HAVE NEGATIVE INTERGROUP EFFECTS BEEN ATTENUATED?

Contexts in which groups show less bias against each other are mirror images of those above—that is, when there is little situational threat, low stress, few time constraints for problem solving, or weak group boundaries. Imagining the IC having many problems that are not complex, time sensitive, and potentially threatening is difficult, so the most useful approach may be to focus on situations that weaken the salience of the group borders. Two types of interventions seem to weaken the salience of the group category. The first is when attention is directed "up a level" to focus on a

---

[6]See the Southwest Airlines customer service commitment at http://www.southwest.com/about_swa/customer_service_commitment/csc.pdf [accessed October 2010].

broader, more inclusive in-group with which all important actors can be members. The second is when attention is directed "down a level" to highlight that each analyst is his or her own unique, individual actor (a process called "individuation").

Focusing Upward: Creating Larger In-Groups

Allport's (1954) contact hypothesis argues that intergroup prejudice will decrease when the intergroup contact is structured so that: (1) groups have equal status, (2) groups share a common goal, (3) groups experience some initial cooperation with each other, and (4) group integration is supported by authority figures. A recent meta-analysis of this hypothesis (analyzing 515 independent studies over seven decades) finds good empirical support that intergroup contact eases intergroup prejudice, particularly when Allport's conditions are followed (Pettigrew and Tropp, 2006).

To increase the chance that Allport's conditions are met, many organizations try to construct a strong, companywide culture, whereby groups share a common status and goals and are encouraged to cooperate by organizational leaders. In the context of the IC, this might mean focusing on the IC as a whole or on the analytic slice of the IC, and creating a strong group identification for all IC analysts. Some evidence shows that when different groups are given a common, superordinate goal, their group identities merge and their collaboration increases. The common goal decreases the tendency to "free-ride" or simply abdicate any responsibility (Olson, 1965), and increases identification-based trust (Lewicki and Bunker, 1996).

Yet building a strong culture goes beyond sharing a common, superordinate goal. Generally senior managers (those with status and legitimacy) focus on three levers for building and maintaining a strong culture. The first is selection, or how new members are chosen. Organizations are advised to select new members based on "values fit" rather than on specific skills (Schneider, 1987). For example, General Electric looks for candidates who "stimulate and relish change and are not frightened or paralyzed by it" and "have a passion for excellence, hating bureaucracy and all the nonsense that comes with it" (Chatman and Cha, 2003). Cisco Systems recruits candidates who are frugal, enthusiastic about the Internet, and not obsessed with status (O'Reilly, 1989). The second lever is the socialization process, or how members learn the ropes. Two key aspects of socialization are the acquisition of knowledge (of formal and informal processes) and bonding with other members of one's group. Socialization includes learning stories about the organization's history, myths about heroic acts by past employees, behavioral rituals, and sacred symbols (Blumer, 1962). Socialization also includes participation in the organization (O'Reilly, 1989) because people's attitudes often adjust to their behaviors rather than vice versa (Festinger,

1957). The final lever for managing culture is a system of punishment-and-reward mechanisms that cause members to experience the consequences of their actions. These mechanisms are often not financial. For example, at computer retailer CompUSA, regional sales meetings occur around a U-shaped table; those whose quarterly sales are lowest are assigned to sit "front and center" because they are presumed to need to pay closest attention. Similarly, CompUSA name badges also include their store's "shrink number"—the amount of inventory lost to theft (Puffer, 1999, p. 29).

According to Heath and Staudenmayer (2000), most organizations suffer from "partition focus" and "integration neglect." That is, organizations focus the majority of their resources on how to differentiate (divide their employees into groups) and neglect the question of how to bring them back together to coordinate action. This emphasis on partitioning may stem from how we are taught to solve complex problems—by breaking a seemingly intractable issue into its component parts and trying to isolate and solve each part individually. Yet, integration neglect is an unfortunate byproduct.[7]

Aside from strong organizational cultures, how do companies integrate and shift employee focus to the larger organization level? The most common choice is through managerial hierarchy. Differentiated units all report to a centralized "superior" unit that is responsible for synthesizing information from subordinate units. This type of integration is called "pooled integration" (Thompson, 1967) because the subordinate units pool information in the common superior unit. This process requires no interaction among subordinate units for routine tasks that can be parsed and delegated. By contrast, "linked interdependence" occurs when work flows from one unit to another, as in an assembly line, and "reciprocal interdependence" describes the flow of work back and forth between two or more units, as might be the case with intelligence analysis (Thompson, 1967).

These latter types of integration can also be managed through a superior unit, though this may not be the most efficient way of coordinating. More typically, the superior unit uses its authority to instruct the subordinate units to coordinate with each other. Some evidence shows that this "instruction to cooperate" works in laboratory settings. In controlled research experiments, "units" were more likely to cooperate with each other on a

---

[7]This integration neglect is particularly unfortunate given that many bureaucratic partitions of personnel into groups (i.e., most differentiation mechanisms) reflect past, rather than future, environments. For example, the 9/11 Commission's report argues that the (then) partitioning of the IC into agencies that focused on domestic threats versus those that focused on foreign threats was a differentiation that reflected dated cold war logic (National Commission on Terrorist Attacks, 2004). Because organizations cannot continuously reinvent their partitioning to match the current environment, with much less partition to match the unknown future environment, integration becomes critical.

mixed-motive task when they were told by an authority figure to cooperate with each other, as compared to when they were given no such instruction and were left to make their own choices (Sally, 1995). Moreover, Gaertner and various sets of colleagues (1994, 1996, 1999) found that when groups were instructed to cooperate with each other and experienced nonhostile interaction with each other, group members started to see themselves as two groups *within* a larger group. This happened both in the laboratory and in naturally occurring workgroups. Yet such cooperation may be short lived; once the authority figure is no longer monitoring behavior, cooperation may decrease. Moreover, cooperation under these circumstances may be nominal because it is externally rather than internally motivated.

Aside from simple instructions to collaborate, authority figures can reconfigure the inter-group landscape, forming new groups that cut across old group boundaries. In the IC, these cross-cutting groups might be special task forces formed to investigate a particular topic (human trafficking in Asia, drug smuggling across the Mexican–U.S. border). The salience of the new group may degrade the perceived strength of the old group boundary. Recall that individuals are members of multiple in-groups and that context cues which identity is elicited. When investigating this special topic, then, the new salient group might be the task force, increasing interagency collaboration.

One unanswered question from the literature is the extent to which individuals can hold loyalties to multiple, competing, and complementary in-groups. For example, can an analyst simultaneously have a strong identity with her agency, her particular topical task force, and the IC as a whole?

Marilyn Brewer's work (Brewer and Pierce, 2005; Roccas and Brewer, 2002) suggests that some people may be able to multiple identify better than others. She and her colleagues note that people differ as to their "social identity complexity," whereby people who are high on social identity complexity can see that they have divergent in-groups with different types of members, which tends to make them more open and tolerant of others. On the other hand, people who are low on social identity complexity perceive that their in-groups are highly convergent, making them less open and tolerant of others. That is, it does not matter how many different groups to which one is a member, per se, but rather how they are subjectively represented and combined that determines one's level of inclusiveness for the in-group. Those individuals with high social identity complexity tend to construct an in-group as the union of all the various groups to which they belong, whereas those individuals with low social identity complexity tend to construct an in-group as the intersection of all the various groups to which they belong. Thus, IC analysts who are high on social identity complexity might respond much better to being regrouped into special task forces than those low on social identity complexity. Being a member of a special task force might induce the former to construct a more inclusive and broader in-group, expanding the community of other analysts with whom they cooperate. Yet, this type of intervention might prompt the latter type of analysts to construct an even more exclusive and smaller "in-group," further restricting the unit for which they might naturally cooperate.

Integration Through Individuation and Social Networks

Aside from focusing "up a level" on how all agents are members of the larger IC or on forming broader and more expansive "in-groups," intergroup dynamics diminish when attention is focused down a level—when others are seen as individual agents more than as members of a social group. There are two processes: individuation and connecting these individual agents together through agent-to-agent networks.

Individuation

Individuation is the opposite of self-categorization. Individuation is the process of coming to see oneself and others as individuals rather than merely as members of a social group (Jung, 1971). The more personalized an actor's contact with someone, the less the actor stereotypes that individual (Brewer, 1996). Unfortunately, this individuation process requires mental energy (Neuberg and Fiske, 1987; Wegner and Wenzlaff, 1996). Thus, ironically, some research shows that intentional suppression of stereotypic thought can produce the very thoughts one is trying to suppress (Macrae et al., 1994; Wegner, 1994). Moreover, suppression can function as a repetitive prime that actually increases a stereotype's accessibility (Macrae et al., 1994; Higgins, 1989). Thus, intentionally trying to ignore someone's different group membership is not likely to produce favorable results.

By contrast, perspective taking, a process in which one attempts to merge the self with the other (Davis et al., 1996), may be one mechanism that can be used to induce individuation. Perspective taking means to imagine one's self in another person's position. When a person engages in perspective taking, his or her self-concept is activated, and because only one mental category seems to dominate at a certain time (Macrae et al., 1995), the self-concept is then applied to the target. Perspective taking is a conscious mental process that appears to elicit a subconscious recategorization of the target. Thus, perspective taking increases an actor's empathy for and assistance to a target (Bateson, 1991) and tendency to attribute target behaviors to the situation rather than to target dispositions (Regan and Totten, 1975). Galinsky and Moskowitz (2000) found that asking people to imagine a day in the life of an out-group target decreased stereotype activation and in-group favoritism.

Similarly, decreasing group distinctiveness by having out-group members disclose personal information or by removing cues of social dissimilarity likewise decreases intergroup bias (Bettencourt et al., 1992; Brewer and Miller, 1984; Gollwitzer et al., 1999). All these interventions are likely to reduce in-group favoritism because they function subconsciously on the actor. The actor is not aware of the social categorization processes or, more specifically, that the target's categorical distinction from the self has evaporated.

Social Networks

Once actors are individuated, integration still requires a way for them to connect. Network scholars insist that every organization has a complex web of informal ties among individual employees (Krackhardt, 1990; Granovetter, 1985). Many kinds of social networks exist, such as advice networks, trust networks, and communication networks. These networks can literally be mapped by asking employees whom they go to for advice, whom they trust, whom they talk to every day, whose job they could assume with only 1 day of training, or whom they would recruit to support a proposal that might be unpopular. Generally a tie is said to exist between two people only if both individuals claim it does (Wellman and Berkowitz, 1988).

Network scholars also advance the idea that these social ties grow organically during the natural course of task accomplishment and that they can either be functional or dysfunctional to the organization (Krackhardt, 1990). Because managerial perceptions of social networks are usually inaccurate, upper managers are exhorted to uncover these networks through objective mapping. One configuration that is particularly problematic is an "imploded relationship," in which a group of actors tightly linked within a group have no (or few) links outside the group. Also problematic is the "bow tie," in which two imploded groups are linked to each other by only one (or a few) connections (Krackhardt, 1990).

Most prescriptive research in this area focuses on how individuals can build more personally useful social networks. Granovetter (1985) discusses the "strength of weak ties," or the notion that the most useful people in your network may be those who are one tie removed from you, as they are likely to have access to novel information and opportunities; by contrast, people to whom you are immediately linked tend to have the same information you have. Thus, Uzzi and Dunlap (2005) caution us to beware of networking only with people we like or with those who are geographically convenient because they are not likely to offer new information or perspectives.

Because most scholars look at networks within firms, where they appear to flourish without encouragement, only scant research is available on how to promote the organic growth of networks. Gulati's work (1995; Gulati and Nickerson, 2008) that looks at network ties across firms discusses the importance of trust in alliance formation. Generally, alliances grow from the motivation and instigation of individual actors. Actors must feel they need something the target has (e.g., another type of intelligence) and must trust that if they ask for it, the target will be responsive. When someone allows himself or herself to be vulnerable and the other person does not violate that vulnerability, trust grows.

In the context of the IC, collaboration across agencies both requires trust and can engender trust. Collaboration requires trust because the initiating analyst will identify and admit to a need (making the initiating analyst vulnerable) and responding analysts will share sensitive information to meet these needs (making responding analysts vulnerable). Trust helps bridge this chasm of risk. When initial acts of faith result in fulfilled promises, reciprocal disclosures, and non-opportunistic behavior, then trust builds.

Unfortunately, the process of building trust can take some time. Building trust among analysts of different agencies can be difficult to engineer from above. "Bonding" experiences, such as Outward Bound trips that are not task relevant, risk becoming trite. However, creating a work-related task in which analysts from different agencies must cooperate with each other should build trust, assuming the agents perform well together. Allowing these agents space to cooperate in a task-focused manner, and giving them a little extra time to get to know each other, might foster mutual trust.

One intriguing idea is that analysts may be able to develop "swift trust" (Myerson et al., 1996), which is the collective perception that vulnerability that may exist in temporary systems will not be exploited. Swift trust seems to occur for people whose personalities predispose them to trusting others. Highly trusting people look for confirmation in other's behavior, in particular whether those others have been helpful and enthusiastic (Popa, 2007). Therefore, some (e.g., high trusting) analysts who might be able to achieve a high rate of production collaborate rather quickly, despite the temporary nature of this interaction.

Online tools such as A-Space, Intellipedia, and the Analysts Resource Catalogue offer resources for analysts wishing to network with each other in real-time to solve discrete tasks and find answers to less well-defined research questions. In these new communication spaces, people may feel less vulnerable, and this "swift trust" might develop more readily. The burgeoning research on social networking sites, such as Facebook and LinkedIn, might be useful to investigate because many of these social networking sites are now being used for transactional purposes (e.g., online marketing and product promotion). Traditional communication literature makes a great distinction between the types of messages that can be effectively communicated online versus face to face. For example, Media Richness Theory (Daft and Lengel, 1984; Daft et al., 1987) contends that the more ambiguous and uncertain a task is or the more equivocal the communication needs, the richer[8] the communication medium should be. However, whether this is still true for the generation bred on virtual communications and connections is unclear.

Casciaro and Lobo (2005) instruct upper managers to leverage the power of likable people to initiate connections among various unconnected individuals. They find that most people would rather interact with a "lovable fool" than a "competent jerk" in an interdependent work task. Thus, they argue that likable people (those who are empathetic, generous, and socially skilled) can reach out to others and even serve as brokers among different groups. Although the idea that people will respond to likable others makes sense (even if they are relative strangers asking for resources), whether any of these connections would flourish once the "likables" are no longer involved is uncertain.

The emphasis on likability calls to mind Cialdini's extensive work on persuasion—how to get people to do something for you that they otherwise might not do. His six "weapons of influence" (Cialdini, 2008) include (1) likability—we are more likely to say yes to someone we like than to someone we do not like; (2) authority—we are more likely to say yes if we've been instructed by an authority figure to do so (see above section on integration through managerial hierarchy); (3) commitment and consistency—we are more likely to commit to larger favors after having already done a smaller favor (the "foot-in-the-door" technique); (4) social proof—we are more likely to do something if we see others doing it (see above section on culture and conformity); (5) reciprocity—we are more likely to do something for someone who has done something for us; and (6) scarcity—we are more likely to do something if we will get something scarce in return. Future research might look at whether these principles can be applied by analysts to encourage others to collaborate with them. Moreover, do analytic networks grow organically, emanating from pockets of likability, commitment, and scarcity?

---

[8]A communication medium richness is a function of (1) the medium's capacity for immediate feedback; (2) the number of cues and channels available; (3) language variety; and (4) the degree to which intent is focused on the recipient. Richer media are said to create a greater "social presence," immediacy, and warmth.

CONCLUSION: WHY INTERAGENCY COLLABORATION IS VITAL

Hazards flourish in areas where no one is directly responsible. In the IC's current environment of complex interconnected systems, risks are difficult to monitor, and uncertainty is inescapable. Unfortunately, because of this complex interconnectivity, even minor hazards can escalate to have large consequences (Perrow, 1984). This uncertainty is not all bad. New situations can bring new opportunities for process of innovation. At the same time, meeting new challenges can eschew unintended negative results that can be disastrous. Thus, integration processes should be undertaken mindfully. Intelligence needs to be as interconnected as the system of potential hazards might be. This interconnectivity means integrating intelligence analysis across agencies to help IC members "work the spaces between the cases" (Hayden, 2009).

REFERENCES

Alexander, M. G., M. B. Brewer, and R. K. Herman. 1999. Images and affect: A functional analysis of out-group stereotypes. *Journal of Personality and Social Psychology* 77:78–93.

Allison, S. T., and D. M. Messick. 1985. The group attribution error. *Journal of Experimental Social Psychology* 21:563–579.

Allport, G. W. 1954. *The nature of prejudice*. Reading, MA: Addison Wesley.

Asch, S. E. 1955. Opinions and social pressure. *Scientific American* 193:31–35.

Bateson, G. 1991. *Sacred unity: Further steps to an ecology of mind*. Chicago, IL: University of Chicago Press.

Benedict, R. F. 1934. *Patterns of culture*. Boston, MA: Houghton Mifflin Co.

Berry, J. W. 1980. Introduction to methodology. In H. C. Triandis and J. W. Berry, eds., *Handbook of cross-cultural psychology*, vol. 2. Boston, MA: Allyn and Bacon.

Berscheid, E., and H. T. Reis. 1998. Attraction and close relationships. In D. T. Gilbert, S. T. Fiske, and G. Lindzey, eds., *The handbook of social psychology*, 4th ed. (pp. 193–281). New York: McGraw-Hill.

Bettencourt, B. A., M. B. Brewer, M. Croak, and N. Miller. 1992. Cooperation and the reduction of intergroup bias: The role of reward structure and social orientation. *Journal of Experimental Social Psychology* 28(4):301–319.

Blau, P. M. 1977. *Inequality and heterogeneity: A primitive theory of social structure*. New York: Free Press.

Blumer, H. 1962. Society as symbolic interaction. In A. M. Rose, ed., *Human behavior and social process: An interactionist approach*. New York: Houghton-Mifflin.

Boas, F. 1940. *Race, language, and culture*. New York: MacMillan.

Bodenhausen, G. V., C. N. Macrae, and J. W. Sherman 1999. On the dialectics of discrimination: Dual processes in social stereotyping. In S. C. Trope, ed., *Dual process theories in social psychology* (pp. 271–290). New York: Guilford.

Brett, J. M., C. H. Tinsley, D. L. Shapiro, and T. Okumura. 2007. Intervening in employee disputes: How and when will managers from Japan, China, and the U.S. act differently? *Management and Organization Review* 3(2):183–204.

Brewer, M., and A. Feinstein. 1999. Dual processes in the cognitive representation of persons and social categories. In S. Chaiken and Y. Trope, eds., *Dual processes in social pyschology* (pp. 255–270). New York: Guilford Press.

Brewer, M. B. 1979. Ingroup bias in the minimal intergroup situation: A cognitive–motivational analysis. *Psychological Bulletin* 86:307–324.

Brewer, M. B. 1996. When stereotypes lead to stereotyping: The use of stereotype in person perception. In C. N. Macrae, C. Stangor, M. Hewstone, eds., *Stereotypes and stereotyping* (pp. 254–275). New York: Guilford Press.

Brewer, M. B., and R. M. Kramer. 1982. Choice behavior in social dilemmas: Effects of social identity, group size, and decision framing. *Journal of Personality and Social Psychology* 50:543–549.

Brewer, M. B., and N. Miller. 1984. Beyond the contact hypothesis: Theoretical perspectives on desegregation. In N. M. Brewer, ed., *Groups in contact: The psychology of desegregation*. New York: Academic Press.

Brewer, M. B., and K. P. Pierce. 2005. Social identity complexity and outgroup tolerance. *Personality and Social Psychology Bulletin* 31(5):428–437.

Cadinu, M. R., and M. Rothbart. 1996. Self-anchoring and differentiation process in the minimal group setting. *Journal of Personality and Social Psychology* 70(4):661–677.

Campbell, D. 1958. Common fate, similarity, and other indices of the status of aggregates of persons as social entities. *Behavioral Science* 3:14–25.

Campbell, D. T. 1965. Ethnocentric and other altruistic motives. In D. Levine, ed., *Nebraska symposium on motivation*. Vol. 1 (pp. 283–311). Lincoln: University of Nebraska Press.

Casciaro, T., and M. S. Lobo. 2005. Competent jerks, lovable fools and the formation of social networks. *Harvard Business Review* 83(6):92–99.

Chandler, A. D. 1962. *Strategy and structure: Chapters in the history of the American industrial enterprise.* Cambridge, MA: MIT Press.

Chatman, J. A., and S. E. Cha. 2003. Leading by leveraging culture. *California Management Review* 45(4):20–34.

Cialdini, R. 2008. *Influence, science and practice*, 4th ed. Needham Heights, MA: Allyn and Bacon.

Cialdini, R. B., and M. R. Trost. 1998. Social influence: Social norms, conformity, and compliance. In D. T. Gilbert, S. T. Fiske, and G. Lindzey, eds., *The handbook of social psychology*, 4th ed. vol. 2 (pp. 151–192). Boston, MA: McGraw-Hill.

Daft, R. L., and R. H. Lengel. 1984. Information richness: A new approach to managerial behavior and organizational design. In L. L. Cummings and B. M. Staw, eds., *Research in organizational behavior, vol. 6* (pp. 191–233). Homewood, IL: JAI Press.

Daft, R. L., R. H. Lengel, and L. K. Trevino. 1987. Message equivocality, media selection, and manager performance: Implications for information systems. *MIS Quarterly* (Sept.):355–366.

Davis, M. H., L. Conklin, A. Smith, and C. Luce. 1996. Effect of perspective taking on the cognitive representation of person: A merging of self and other. *Journal of Personality and Social Psychology* 70:713–726.

De Vos, G. 1975. Apprenticeship and paternalism. In E. G. Vogel, ed., *Modern Japanese organization and decision-making* (pp. 228–248). Tokyo, Japan: Charles E. Tuttle.

Dearborn, D. C. and H. A. Simon. 1958. Selective perception: A note on the departmental identification of executives. *Sociometry* 21:140–144.

Defense Intelligence Agency. 2007. *Strategic plan 2007–2012.* Available: http://www.dia.mil/thisisdia/2007-2012_DIA_Strategic_Plan.pdf [accessed May 2010].

Derks, B. I., M. Inzlicht, and S. Kang. 2008. The neuroscience of stigma and stereotype threat. *Group Processes and Intergroup Relations* 11(2):163–181.

Deschamps, J. C., and W. Doise. 1978. Crossed category memberships in intergroup relations. In H. Tajfel, ed., *Differentiation between social groups* (pp. 141–158). Cambridge, UK: Cambridge University Press.

Dornbusch, S. M., and W. R. Scott. 1975. *Evaluation and the exercise of authority.* San Francisco, CA: Jossey-Bass.

Erez, M. 1986. The congruence of goal-setting strategies with sociocultural values, and its effect on performance. *Journal of Management* 12:585–592.

Festinger, L. 1957. *A theory of cognitive dissonance.* Evanston, IL: Row, Peterson.

Fisher, B. 2009. *Connect with customers on a whole-new level.* Available: http://www.successmagazine.com/article/print?articleId=785 [accessed October 2010].

Fiske, S. T. 1998. Stereotyping, prejudice, and discrimination. In D. T. Gilbert, S. T. Fiske, and G. Lindzey, eds., *Handbook of social psychology*, vol. 2 (pp. 357–411). Boston, MA: McGraw-Hill.

Fiske, S. T., and S. E. Taylor. 1991. *Social cognition*, 2nd ed. New York: McGraw-Hill.

Fiske, S., M. Lin, and S. Neuberg. 1999. The continuum model: Ten years later. In S. Chaiken and Y. Trope, eds., *Dual process theories in social psychology* (pp. 231–254). New York: Guilford Press.

Fiske, S. T., A. J. C. Cuddy, P. Glick, and J. Xu. 2002. A model of (often mixed) stereotype content: Competence and warmth respectively follow from perceived status and competition. *Journal of Personality and Social Psychology* 86(6):878–902.

Gaertner, S. L., M. C. Rust, J. F. Dovidio, B. A. Bachman, and P. A. Anastasio. 1994. The contact hypothesis: The role of a common ingroup identity on reducing intergroup bias. *Small Groups Research* 25:224–249.

Gaertner, S. L., J. F. Dovidio, and B.A. Bachman. 1996. Revisiting the contact hypothesis: The introduction of a common intergroup identity. *Journal of Intercultural Relationships* 20:271–290.

Gaertner, S. L., J. F. Dovidio, M. C. Rust, B. S. Banker, C. M. Ward, G. R. Mottola, M. Houlette, and J. A. Nier. 1999. Reducing intergroup bias: Elements of intergroup cooperation. *Journal of Personality and Social Psychology* 76(3):388–402.

Galinsky, A., and G. B. Moskowitz. 2000. Perspective taking: Decreasing stereotype expression, stereotype accessibility and ingroup favoritism. *Journal of Personality and Social Psychology* 78(4):708–724.

Geertz, C. J. 1973. *The interpretation of cultures.* New York: Basic Books.

Gollwitzer, P. M. 1999. *Implementation effects on stereotype and prejudice activation.* Unpublished manuscript. Psychology Department, New York University.

Goodall, H. L., Jr. 1992. Empowerment, culture, and postmodern organizing: Deconstructing the Nordstrom Employee Handbook. *Journal of Organizational Change Management* 5(2):25–30.

Goss, P. 2005. Goss: CIA is "gold standard" for intel ops. *Associated Press.* November 29. Available: http://www.foxnews.com/story/0,2933,176996,00.html [accessed October 2010].

Granovetter, M. 1985. Economic action and social structure: The problem of embeddedness. *American Journal of Sociology* 91(3):481–510.

Griffin, D. W., and L. Ross. 1991. Subjective construal, social inference, and human misunderstanding. In M. P. Zanna, ed., *Advances in experimental social psychology*, vol. 24 (pp. 319–359). San Diego, CA: Academic Press.

Gulati, R. 1995. Does familiarity breed trust? The implications of repeated ties on contractual choice in alliance. *Academy of Management Journal* 38:85–112.

Gulati, R., and J. Nickerson. 2008. Interorganizational trust, governance choice, and exchange performance. *Organization Science* 19(5):688–708.

Hayden, M. V. 2009. Defenders at risk: How blame games are costing spy agencies. *Washington Post*. June 19. Available: http://www.washingtonpost.com/wp-dyn/content/article/2009/06/18/AR2009061803494.html [accessed October 2010].

Heath, C., and N. Staudenmeyer. 2000. Coordination neglect: How lay theories of organizing complicate coordination in organizations. *Research in Organizational Behaviour* 22:155–193.

Higgins, E. T. 1989. Continuities and discontinuities in self-regulatory and self-evaluative processes: A developmental theory relating self and affect. *Journal of Personality* 57(2):407–444.

Hogg, M. A. 1992. *The social psychology of group cohesivenesss: From attraction to social identity theory*. London, UK: Harvester Wheatsheaf.

Hogg, M. A. 1993. Group cohesiveness: A critical review and some new directions. *European Review of Social Psychology* 4:85–111.

Hogg, M. A., and D. J. Terry. 2000. Social identity and self-categorization processes in organizational contexts. *Academy of Management Review* 25(1):121–140.

Ignatius, D. 2004. Some good intelligence gatherers. *Washington Post*. April 30.

Jones, E. E., and V. A. Harris. 1967. Attribution of attitudes. *Journal of Experimental Social Psychology* 3(1):1–24.

Jung, C. G. 1971. *Psychological types*. Vol. 6. Princeton, NJ: Princeton University Press.

Kahn, R., and M. Zald. 1990. *Organizations and nation-states: New perspectives on conflict and cooperation*. San Francisco, CA: Jossey-Bass.

Kahneman, D., and D. T. Miller. 1986. Norm theory: Comparing reality to its alternatives. *Journal of Personality and Social Psychology* 93(2):136–153.

Krackhardt, D. 1990. Assessing the political landscape: Structure, cognition, and power in organizations. *Administrative Science Quarterly* 35(2):342–369.

Kramer, R. 2005. A failure to communicate: 9/11 and the tragedy of the informational commons. *International Public Management Journal* 8(3):397–416.

Kroeber, A. L., and F. R. Kluckhohn. 1952. *Culture: A critical review of concepts and definitions*. Peabody Museum papers, 47(1). Cambridge, MA: Harvard University.

Lawrence, P. A., and J. Lorsch. 1967. Differentiation and integration in complex organizations. *Administrative Science Quarterly* 12:1–30.

Ledgerwood, A., and S. Chaiken. 2007. Priming us and them: Automatic assimilation and contrast in group attitudes. *Journal of Personality and Social Psychology* 93(6):940–956.

Leung, K., and M. H. Bond. 1984. Some determinants of conflict avoidance. *Journal of Cross-Cultural Psychology* 19:125–136.

Lewicki, R. J., and B. B. Bunker. 1996. Developing and maintaining trust in work relationships. In R. M. Kramer and T. R. Tyler, eds., *Trust in organizations: Frontiers of theory and research* (pp. 114–139). Thousand Oaks, CA: Sage.

Lippman, W. 1922. *Public opinion*. New York: Harcourt Brace.

Lowie, R. H. 1966. *Culture and ethnography*. New York: Basic Books.

Macrae, C. N., G. V. Bodenhausen, A. B. Milne, and J. Jetten. 1994. Out of mind but back in sight: Stereotypes on the rebound. *Journal of Personality and Social Psychology* 67:808–817.

Macrae, C. N., G. V. Bodenhausen, and A. B. Milne. 1995. The dissection of selection in person perception: Inhibitory processes in social stereotyping. *Journal of Personality and Social Psychology* 69:397–407.

Malinowski, B. 1944. *A scientific theory of culture and other essays*. Chapel Hill, NC: University of North Carolina Press.

Mead, M. 1964. *Continuities in cultural evolution*. New Haven, CT: Yale University Press.

Mouton, J., and R. Blake. 1986. *Executive achievement*. New York: McGraw Hill Higher Education.

Mowday, R. T., and R. I. Sutton. 1993. Organizational behavior: Linking individuals and groups to organizational contexts. *Annual Review of Psychology* 44:195–229.

Mullen, B., and L. Hu. 1989. Perceptions of ingroup and outgroup variability: A meta-analytic integration. *Basic and Applied Social Psychology* 10:233–252.

Mussweiler, T., and G. V. Bodenhausen. 2002. I know you are but what am I? Self-evaluative consequences of judging ingroup and outgroup members. *Journal of Personality and Social Psychology* 82:19–32.

Myerson, D., K. E. Weick, and R. M. Kramer. 1996. Swift trust and temporary groups. In R. M. Kramer and T. R. Tyler, eds., *Trust in organizations: Frontiers of theory and research* (pp. 166–195). Thousand Oaks, CA: Sage.

National Commission on Terrorist Attacks Upon the United States. 2004. *The 9/11 Commission report*. New York: W. W. Norton. Available: http://www.9-11commission.gov/report/911Report.pdf [accessed April 2010].

Neuberg, S. L., and S. T. Fiske. 1987. Motivational influences on impression formation: Outcome dependency, accuracy driven attention, and individuating processes. *Journal of Personality and Social Psychology* 53:431–444.

Nohria, N. 1991. *Note on organization structure*. Boston, MA: Harvard Business School.

O'Connor, K. E., and C. H. Tinsley. 2009. Looking for a strategic advantage at the negotiating table? Cultivate a reputation for mutually-beneficial dealmaking. Under review, *Organizational Behavior and Human Decision Processes*.

Office of the Director of National Intelligence. 2008. *United States intelligence community information sharing strategy*. February 22. Available: http://www.dni.gov/reports/IC_Information_Sharing_Strategy.pdf [accessed May 2010].

Office of the Director of National Intelligence. 2009. *National intelligence: A consumer's guide*. Available: http://www.dni.gov/IC_Consumers_Guide_2009.pdf [accessed March 2010].

Olson, M. 1965. *The logic of collective action*. Boston, MA: Harvard University Press.

O'Reilly, C. 1989. Corporations, culture and commitment: Motivation and social control in organizations. *California Management Review* 31:9–25.

O'Reilly, C., and J. Pfeffer. 1995. *Southwest Airlines: Using human resources for competitive advantage (A)*. HR-1 A. Case Study from Graduate School of Business, Stanford University. Available from Harvard Business Publishing.

Perrow, C. 1984. *Normal accidents: Living with high-risk technologies*. Princeton, NJ: Princeton University Press.

Pettigrew, T. F., and L. R. Tropp. 2006. A meta-analytic test of intergroup contact theory. *Journal of Personality and Social Psychology* 90(5):751–783.

Popa, C. L. 2007. *Testing a model of swift trust in temporary groups*. Paper presented at the annual meeting of the International Communication Association, San Francisco, CA. Available: http://www.allacademic.com//meta/p_mla_apa_research_citation/1/7/3/0/1/pages173019/p173019-1.php [accessed May 2010].

Puffer, S. 1999. CompUSA's CEO James Halpin on technology, rewards, and commitment. *Academy of Management Executive* 13:29–36.

Quattrone, G. A., and E. E. Jones. 1980. The perception of variability within in-groups and out-groups: Implications for the law of small numbers. *Journal of Personality and Social Psychology* 38(1):141–152.

Regan, D. T., and J. Totten. 1975. Empathy and attribution: Turning observers into actors. *Journal of Personality and Social Psychology* 32:850–856.

Roccas, S., and M. B. Brewer. 2002. Social identity complexity. *Personality and Social Psychology Review* 6(2):88–106.

Ross, L. 1977. The intuitive psychologist and his shortcomings: Distortions in the attribution process. In L. Berkowitz, ed., *Advances in experimental social psychology,* vol. 10 (pp. 173–220). New York: Academic Press.

Salancik, G., and J. Pfeffer. 1978. A social information processing approach to job attitudes and task design. *Administrative Sciences Quarterly* 23:224–253.

Sally, D. 1995. Conversation and cooperation in social dilemmas: A meta-analysis of experiments from 1958 to 1992. *Rationality and Society* 7(1):58–92.

Schein, E. H. 1988. *Process consultation.* Reading, MA: Addison-Wesley.

Schneider, B. 1987. The people make the place. *Personnel Psychology* 40:437–453.

Sherif, M. 1966a. *In common predicament.* Boston, MA: Houghton Mifflin.

Sherif, M. 1966b. *Intergroup conflict and cooperation: The Robber's Cave experiment.* Norman, OK: University Book Exchange.

Sherif, M., L. J. Harvey, B. J. White, W. R. Hood, and C. W. Sherif. 1961. *Intergroup cooperation and competition: The Robber's Cave experiment.* Norman, OK: University Book Exchange.

Simon, J. M., Jr. 2005. Managing domestic, military, and foreign policy requirements. In J. E. Sims and B. Gerber, eds., *Transforming U.S. intelligence* (pp. 149–161). Washington, DC: Georgetown University Press.

Sims, E. R. 2005. Understanding ourselves. In J. E. Sims and B. Gerber, eds., *Transforming U.S. intelligence* (pp. 32–59). Washington, DC: Georgetown University Press.

Sims, J. E., and Gerber, B., eds. 2005. *Transforming U.S. intelligence.* Washington, DC: Georgetown University Press.

Smith, E. R., and S. Henry. 1996. An in-group becomes part of the self: Response time evidence. *Personality and Social Psychology Bulletin* 22:635–642.

Smith, K. K., and D. N. Berg. 1987. *Paradoxes of group life: Understanding conflict, paralysis and movement in group dynamics.* San Francisco, CA: Jossey-Bass.

Spencer-Rodgers, J., M. J. Williams, D. L. Hamilton, K. Peng, and L. Wang. 2007. Culture and group perception: Dispositional and stereotypic inferences about novel and national groups. *Journal of Personality and Social Psychology* 93(4):525–543.

Stapel, D., and W. Koomen. 2005. When less is more: The consequences of affective primacy for subliminal priming effects. *Personality and Social Psychology Bulletin* 31:1286–1295.

Stryker, A., and A. Statham. 1985. Symbolic interaction and role theory. In G. Lindsey and E. Aronson, eds., *Handbook of social psychology,* 3rd ed. (pp. 311–378). New York: McGraw-Hill.

Sumner, W. 1906. *Folkways.* Boston, MA: Gin and Company.

Tajfel, H. 1969. Cognitive aspects of prejudice. *Journal of Social Issues* 25:79–97.

Tajfel, H. 1970. Experiments in intergroup discrimination. *Scientific American* 223(5):96–102.

Tajfel, H. 1978. *Differentiation between social groups: Studies in the social psychology of intergroup relations.* London, UK: Academic Press.

Tajfel, H., and J. C. Turner. 1979. An integrative theory of intergroup conflict. In W. G. Worchel, ed., *The social psychology of intergroup relations.* Monterey, CA: Brooks-Cole.

Tajfel, J. 1982. Instrumentality, identity and social comparisons. In J. Tajfel, ed., *Social identity and intergroup relations.* New York: Cambridge University Press.

Thompson, J. 1967. *Organizations in action: Social science bases of administrative theory.* Piscataway, NJ: Transaction.

Tinsley, C. H., and M. Pillutla. 1998. The influence of culture on business negotiations in the U.S. and Hong Kong. *Journal of International Business Studies* 12(4):711–728.

Tinsley, C. H., K. O'Connor, and B. Sullivan. 2002. "Tough" guys finish last: The perils of a distributive reputation. *Organization Behavior and Human Decision Processes* 88:621–642.

Triandis, H. C. 1989. Cross-cultural studies of individualism-collectivism. In J. J. Berman, ed., *Nebraska Symposium on Motivation: Cross-cultural perspectives*, vol. 37 (pp. 41–133). Lincoln, NE: University of Nebraska Press.

Triandis, H. C. 2002. Subjective culture. In W. J. Lonner, D. L. Dinnerl, S. A. Hayes, and D. N. Sattler, eds., *Online readings in psychology and culture*. Bellingham, WA: Center for Cross-Cultural Research, Western Washington University. Available: http://www.ac.wwu.edu/~culture/ [accessed May 2010].

Turner, J. C. 1987. *Rediscovering the social group: A self-categorization theory.* Oxford, UK: Basical Blackwell.

Tylor, E. B. 1871. *Primitive culture.* London, UK: J. Murray.

Uzzi, B., and S. Dunlop. 2005. How to build your network. *Harvard Business Review* 83(12):53–60.

van de Berghe, P. L. 1981. *The ethnic phenomenon.* Westpoint, CT: Praegar.

Vanbeselaere, N. 1991. The impact of in-group and out-group homogeneity/heterogeneity upon intergroup relations. *Basic and Applied Social Psychology* 12:291–301.

Wagner, J. A., III. 1995. Studies of individualism–collectivism: Effects on cooperation in groups. *Academy of Management Journal* 38(1):152–172.

Wegner, D. M. 1994. Ironic processes of mental control. *Psychological Review* 101:34–52.

Wegner, D. M., and R. M. Wenzlaff. 1996. Mental control. In E. T. Higgins and A. W. Kruglanski, eds., *Social psychology: Handbook of basic principles.* (pp. 466–492). New York: Guilford Press.

Wellman, B., and S. D. Berkowitz, eds. 1988. *Social structures: A network approach.* Cambridge, UK: Cambridge University Press.

Williamson, O. E. 2002. The theory of the firm as governance structure: From choice to contract. *Journal of Economic Perspectives* 16(3):171–195. Available: http://groups.haas.berkeley.edu/bpp/oew/choicetocontract.pdf [accessed May 2010].

Part IV

Organizations

Part IV focuses on research into organizational factors that affect the effectiveness of the intelligence community (IC) in its missions. All organizations face challenges, but the application of well-researched theories and practices can be of great benefit. The four chapters comprising this final section of the volume discuss some of the most significant organizational challenges to IC agencies: communications, accountability, workforce, and adaptation.

In Chapter 10, Baruch Fischhoff draws on decision science and communication research to characterize communications within the IC and between it and the clients for its analyses. He describes natural barriers to analysts' understanding of clients' analytical needs when formulating analyses, and to their assessments of how well clients have understood the conclusions and limitations of the resulting analyses. He shows the scientific foundations and methods for improved internal and external communication. For example, value-of-information analysis allows identification of information most important for clients' decisions, and sensitivity analysis allows identification of the facts most valuable for understanding ongoing situations.

In Chapter 11, Philip E. Tetlock and Barbara A. Mellers note that the IC has faced recurrent demands for greater accountability, typically focused on high-profile errors, that can produce short-term shifts in error-avoidance priorities ("don't make the last mistake"—be it a false positive or a false negative) without improving long-term forecasting accuracy. They also note that working analysts are often more accountable for following procedures than for accuracy (which is assumed to follow from adherence to the procedures). Tetlock and Mellers show how, in other domains, research has documented the benefits and limitations to such practices, while focusing the feedback that is needed for improved accuracy. They show how the IC might close this critical knowledge gap.

In Chapter 12, Steve W. J. Kozlowski summarizes research relevant to how organizations acquire, build, and sustain effective workforces. He distinguishes their needs in acquiring human resources and building human capital, then identifies practices relevant to each. For the former, he stresses the demonstrated importance of having people with the right combinations of cognitive ability, personality, and values. For the latter, he stresses the training needed to provide people with mission-specific knowledge and skills (e.g., languages and country-specific knowledge). He also reports on research into creating effective performance incentives.

In Chapter 13, Amy Zegart addresses research on organizational change. She describes obstacles to adopting new practices in private sector firms and the special challenges that make adaptation even more difficult for intelligence agencies. She then considers research showing the crucial and often hidden importance of organizational structure for aggregating information and organizational learning. Next, she turns to political science, examining the limits of personal leadership and the power of harnessing individual incentives to foster change. Finally, she cautions against using much of the popular management literature as a guide for intelligence reform.

10

Communicating About Analysis

Baruch Fischhoff

Useful analysis requires effective communication among diverse individuals. Members of an analytical community must communicate with each other and with their clients. Both kinds of communication can bring into contact individuals with very different missions, backgrounds, and perspectives. Within an analytical community, a single analysis might require communication among individuals with expertise in economics, anthropology, psychology, engineering, and logistics. Each contributing discipline might have subfields and competing theories, each needing to be heard. Setting the terms of an analysis and reporting its results might require communication with clients who differ from the analysts in their objectives, careers, and education. These professional differences overlay the cultural, socioeconomic, and other differences that can complicate any communication in a diverse society.

Other chapters in this volume document the threats to mutual understanding that arise in the absence of clear communication. One such threat arises when members of a group interact intensely with one another, but lose touch with how differently the world looks to members of other groups (see Tinsley, this volume, Chapter 9). A second threat arises when individuals misread one another's objectives (see Arkes and Kajdasz, this volume, Chapter 7). A third arises when different experiences and objectives lead individuals to evaluate the quality of analyses differently (see this volume's McClelland, Chapter 4; Spellman, Chapter 6; and Kozlowski, Chapter 12).

This chapter considers social, behavioral, and decision science research about overcoming such threats in order to improve communications about analysis. It considers communication both between analysts and their clients and among analysts themselves. It considers the communication issues raised by analytical methods, psychological processes, and management practices. (For analytical methods, see this volume's Kaplan, Chapter 2; Bueno de Mesquita, Chapter 3; McClelland, Chapter 4; and Skinner, Chapter 5. For psychological processes, see this volume's Kaplan, Chapter 2; Spellman, Chapter 6; Arkes and Kajdasz, Chapter 7; and Hastie, Chapter 8, For management practices, see this volume's Fingar, Chapter 1; Tetlock and Mellers, Chapter 11; and Kozlowski, Chapter 12). Like the other chapters, this chapter recognizes the need for additional research dedicated to the specific needs of analysts and their clients. Where it refers to general principles of decision science, additional sources include Clemen and Reilly (2002), Hastie and Dawes (2001), Raiffa (1968), and vonWinterfeldt and Edwards (1986). Where it refers to general principles of communicating decision-relevant information, additional sources include Fischhoff (2009), Morgan et al. (2001), Slovic (2001), Schwarz (1999), and Woloshin et al. (2008).

In a well-known essay, philosopher Paul Grice (1975) described the obligations of communication as saying things that are (1) relevant, (2) concise, (3) clear, and (4) truthful. Fulfilling the last of these conditions is at the core of the analytical enterprise. Taking full advantage of that commitment requires effective two-way communication, allowing analysts to understand their clients' information needs and present their answers comprehensibly. After presenting the science available to meet those goals, the chapter outlines the organizational challenges to mobilizing it.

ANALYST–CLIENT COMMUNICATIONS

At times, analysts' clients face specific decisions, such as whether to enter an international coalition, deploy military forces, suspend diplomatic relations, or reduce foreign aid. Serving such clients means efficiently communicating the information most critical to their choices. At other times, analysts' clients face no specific decisions, but want the situational awareness needed for future decisions (e.g., what conditions affect the stability of international coalitions, the effectiveness of military deployments, the impacts of diplomatic sanctions, or the usefulness of foreign aid?). Serving such clients means communicating information that might be useful one day. The former might be called *need-to-know communication* and the latter *nice-to-know communication*.

In both cases, the communication task is the same as that of everyday life: Listening well enough to identify relevant facts and to convey them comprehensibly. Unlike most everyday life, for analysts, the set of things that might be said can be very large and the communication window very small. The behavioral, social, and decision sciences offer methods for overcoming these barriers to communication.

Need-to-Know Communication

For need-to-know communication, *value-of-information analysis* (Clemen and Reilly, 2002; Raiffa, 1968) is the formal name (in decision analysis) for evaluating facts by their ability to increase the expected utility of recipients' choices. Consider, for example, a client considering whether to strengthen sanctions on a target country. The most valuable information, for that decision, might pertain to the cohesiveness of the international coalition enforcing the sanctions, the strength of the target country's economy, the vulnerability of its industries, the strength of its political opposition, or the probability of sanctions rallying nationalist feelings. Identifying the most valuable information requires knowing how clients see their choices, including their *goals*, the action *options* that they contemplate, and the *probabilities* of achieving each goal with each option. For example, when deciding about sanctions, some clients may be especially concerned about effects on civilian populations. They will need more information on those effects, on alternatives to sanctions, and on the probability of sustaining sanctions. If analysts fail to see these concerns, then they will not produce the relevant analyses. Conversely, if they see concerns where none exist, then they may produce analyses without an audience.

Value-of-information analysis provides a structured way to characterize decision-relevant information needs. It begins by sketching a client's *decision tree*, then examines the impact of possible analytical results on identifying the best choice. Its product is a *supply curve* (to use the economic term), which orders information in terms of decreasing marginal contribution to improved decision making. The communication window is used best by providing the most valuable analytical results first. At some point, it may pay to close that window, when additional results cannot improve the decision or the cost is too high (in terms of the time spent conveying analyses or the opportunities lost while waiting for analytic results to be produced).

Decision theory offers formal procedures for computing the expected utility of choices and the value of information in aiding them. Used slavishly, these procedures can undermine analysts' work, especially if the calculations are done outside the analytical team or by computer programs whose results must be taken on faith. However, understanding the principles underlying these procedures, which show how to think about making various kinds of decisions, can help to structure communications and the analyses that precede them.

These formal procedures assume that decision makers are *rational* when integrating new information with their existing beliefs and values. Such rationality is unattainable when inevitably fallible individuals face complex choices (see this volume's Spellman, Chapter 6; Arkes and Kajdasz, Chapter 7; Hastie, Chapter 8; and Tinsley, Chapter 9). However, the assumption of rationality allows analysts to evaluate information needs in an orderly way. It also fits their organizational role. Whatever they think about their clients in private, analysts are expected to treat them as rational individuals, able to make good use of analytical results. Fortuitously, decision research has found that many choices tolerate modest imprecision in how well decision makers understand and integrate their facts (Dawes, 1979; Dawes et al., 1989; vonWinterfeldt and Edwards, 1986). With such decisions, analysts who create and convey relevant facts may have done all that is needed to allow imperfect clients to make good choices.

Nice-to-Know Communication

As mentioned, sometimes clients are not making choices, but looking for signs that decisions might need to be made—or remade. In order to "follow the action," they need to understand the factors that shape the outcomes that matter most to them. *Influence diagrams* (Clemen and Reilly, 2002; Horvitz, 2005; Howard, 1989) provide a general way to represent such understanding, consistent with most of the models described in chapters in this volume by Kaplan (Chapter 2), Bueno de Mesquita (Chapter 3), McClelland (Chapter 4), and Skinner (Chapter 5). Figure 10-1 provides a highly simplified example of an influence diagram. In it, the nodes represent variables describing a situation, whereas the arrows represent the relationships between them. The nodes require observation, whereas the arrows require theory. Between them, they provide a standard, transparent representation of what analysts (and their clients) believe.

With such models, *sensitivity analysis* (Clemen and Reilly, 2002; Raiffa, 1968) plays the role that value-of-information analysis plays with specific decisions. It asks how "sensitive" predictions are to variations in each variable (node) or relationship (arrow). For example, if clients want to predict a country's political stability, then analysts might examine how sensitive that stability is to variables such as the health of the country's major industries, news media, police force, and public health system. Further analyses can then focus on the most important of these factors. For example, if the country's leadership is vulnerable to its public's perception that it cannot handle emergencies, then analysts might study the adequacy of the country's disease surveillance, risk communication, and disaster response systems.

The most useful communications contain information with high predictive value that is not already known. Telling people what they already know wastes their time and trust. Thus, if clients already know how public perceptions of their leaders' competence affect public morale, then they just

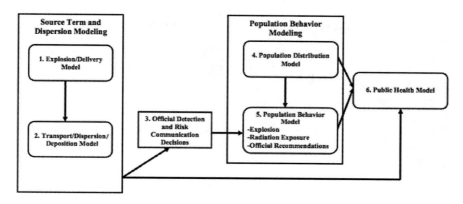

FIGURE 10-1 An influence diagram.
NOTE: Simplified version of an influence diagram for predicting the public health consequences of a radioactive dispersion device (RDD). Each of the six nodes summarizes one subset of the analysis in a form that can be used to predict the variables in the next nodes to which it is connected. Any RDD scenario can be represented as an instantiation of each element of the model (e.g., one *source term* for the amount of material dispersed, one official communication, one degree of public compliance).
SOURCE: Dombroski and Fischbeck (2006). Reprinted with permission from John Wiley and Sons. Original publication available: http://onlinelibrary.wiley.com/journal/10.1111/(ISSN)1539-6924.

need to be told the state of those perceptions. If they do not understand those processes, then they first need background information on the roles played by public opinion. In psychological jargon, they need help creating a *mental model* of the processes being described; that is, an intuitive representation, in which they can accommodate new information and from which they can derive predictions (Bartlett, 1932; Gentner and Stevens, 1983; Rouse and Morris, 1986).

Assessing Clients' Knowledge and Needs

Setting communication priorities requires knowing how clients currently view their choices. What are their goals? What options will they consider? What do they believe about the expected outcomes of choosing different options? How accurate and certain are those beliefs? Given the well-established limits to interpersonal understanding (see this volume's Arkes and Kajdasz, Chapter 7; Hastie, Chapter 8; and Tinsley, Chapter 9), it would be perilous to assume that clients' views are accessible to analysts by observation alone.

Scientific approaches to assessing others' views can be categorized as *open-ended, structured, inferred,* and *indexed* methods—in order of roughly decreasing sensitivity to individual differences in those views (e.g., Converse and Presser, 1986; Fischhoff, 2009; Schwarz, 1996; Sudman and Bradburn, 1982). Applying these methods before an analysis allows assessment of clients' information needs. Applying them after communicating analytical results allows assessment of how well those needs have been met; that is, to what extent clients have learned what they most need to know. The opportunities to apply these methods will depend on the clients, the analysts' relationship with them, and the resources devoted to communication. Knowing what scientifically sound assessment entails can help analysts to make the best of whatever opportunities they have—and to recognize the barriers to understanding their clients.

Open-Ended Methods

The best way to understand clients (or anyone else) is to work closely and continuously with them, learning their views and receiving feedback on how well one is communicating (and saying things that seem worth knowing). If analysts lack access to the ultimate client, they may still be able to talk with surrogates, such as current staff members or previous holders of the client's position—recognizing that these surrogates may not understand the client's view and may not faithfully represent it even if they do (when they have agendas of their own).

Effective consultation must have both enough structure to identify clients' specific needs and enough freedom to allow clients to express themselves in their own words on topics of their own choosing. A common research procedure for addressing these somewhat conflicting goals is the *semi-structured, open-ended interview*. It entails asking increasingly specific questions, based on preliminary analysis of the client's decision (Morgan et al., 2001). The opening section of an interview allows the client to raise any issue on the general topic. The middle section asks the client to elaborate on all those issues. The final section asks about issues that arose in the preliminary decision analysis, but not in the interview. Thus, an interview might gravitate from "What do you see as the main factors in South Asia?" to "How do you characterize the Taliban in Afghanistan?" to "What about [X]?" (where X is a seemingly important local leader who has not been mentioned). Such interviews allow analysts to follow their clients' lead, without inadvertently missing topics because the discussion drifts in other directions.

Structured Methods

Open-ended interviews demand quality time from busy clients, while allowing them to speak their minds in their own terms. When such interviews are impossible, structured methods might be an alternative. Indeed, there are often standard ways for clients to communicate their perceived needs to the intelligence community (e.g., Requests for Information, Collection Directives). For analysts to produce and communicate useful results, these structured communications must capture the decisions that their clients are facing. Unfortunately, such communications have well-known limits. Their contents are limited to issues that those who use them see as relevant and to terms that users expect to be understood. They offer little opportunity for analysts to request clarifications or to reveal the need for them. Thus, structured methods can leave an illusion of understanding in situations where analysts and clients are talking past one another.

Some misunderstandings have been extensively documented. For example, verbal quantifiers (e.g., "most," "likely," "rare") can mean different things to different people and to the same person in different contexts (Kent, 1964; O'Hagan et al., 2006; Wallsten et al., 1993). People prefer receiving numeric estimates (which are more informative), but prefer giving verbal ones (which are easier to produce) (Erev and Cohen, 1990). From a cognitive perspective, this problem is easily addressed. Probabilities are everyday terms, readily applied to any well-specified event (e.g., "What is the probability that at least 10 percent of voters will support far-right parties?"). Studies find that people typically provide probabilities having good *construct validity*, in the sense of being systematically related to their other beliefs. Such probabilities still may not have *external validity*, in the sense of predicting what will happen. However, those errors reflect misinformation, rather than an inability to translate beliefs into numbers (Fischhoff, 2008, 2009).

There is less consensus on how to express the uncertainty surrounding analyst's knowledge (e.g., how much confidence can be placed in predictions, see Funtowicz and Ravetz, 1990; Politi et al., 2007). Researchers focused on specific domains have found how differently people can use everyday terms such as "inflation" (Ranyard et al., 2008) and "safe sex" (McIntyre and West, 1992) or how they express race and ethnicity (McKenney and Bennett, 1994). If analysts and their clients unwittingly use terms differently, then analyses may not be understood as intended (Fischhoff, 1994).

When limited to structured communications with their clients, analysts might use two procedures familiar to survey researchers (Converse and Presser, 1986). One is the *cognitive interview*, which asks people like the intended users of a structured instrument to think aloud as they attempt to use it (Ericsson and Simon, 1994). Allowing these test readers to say whatever comes to mind when they use a communication instrument allows them to surprise its designer with interpretations that they never imagined.

The second procedure is the *manipulation check*, which asks users to report how they interpreted selected items. Without such empirical checks, it is hard to assess a communication channel's noisiness.

Inferred Methods

Without direct or indirect communication, analysts are left watching their clients, wondering what decisions they are facing now or might be considering in the future. Applied economics has formalized the process of inferring intentions from actions in *revealed preference analysis*. For example, many studies attempt to discern the importance of various housing features (e.g., size, style, age, school district) from purchase prices (e.g., Earnhart, 2002). A controversial application involves inferring the value of a human life from the wage premium paid for riskier jobs (Viscusi, 1983).

Revealed preference analyses have the attraction of examining actual behavior, rather than verbal expressions, as with open-ended interviews or structured surveys. However, economic research has also demonstrated how difficult it is to isolate the role that each goal and belief plays in a decision. Economists typically simplify their task by assuming that decision makers accurately perceive the expected outcomes of their choices. That allows them to focus on deducing decision-makers' goals.

Analysts cannot make that simplifying assumption. Rather, they must face the full complexity of inferring what their clients believed and wanted when they make a decision. As a further complication, their clients may make choices that are designed to hide their beliefs and values (unlike home buyers and workers in hazardous industries). Those beliefs and values may change over time, as circumstances change. Decisions that they never made cannot be observed. "Reading the boss's mind" is a perennial workplace activity. However, it provides weak guidance for communicating with clients.

Indexed Methods

If analysts can neither communicate with nor observe their clients adequately, they may be left thinking about how people like those clients view their decisions. That means asking questions such as "How much do they know about human rights (smuggling, corruption . . .)?" "How much do they care?" "What are their blind spots?" "Which options are unthinkable for them?" Analysts placed in this position need, in effect, a theory of how people like their clients think.

Some of the science relevant to that understanding appears elsewhere in this volume. For example, organizational research (see this volume's Hastie, Chapter 8; Tinsley, Chapter 9; Tetlock and Mellers, Chapter 11; and Kozlowski, Chapter 12) can describe clients in terms such as:

- What kinds of people end up in those positions (e.g., by ethnicity, politics, socioeconomic background)?
- What cross-cultural experiences have they had?
- What disciplines have they studied?
- What do they read?
- Whom do they consult?
- Are they rewarded for bold or for conservative decisions?
- Do they find statistical or case-study evidence more persuasive?
- Do they find particular words offensive?

To use such general information, analysts must overcome judgmental challenges such as those presented in chapters in this volume by Spellman (Chapter 6), Arkes and Kajdasz (Chapter 7), and Tinsley (Chapter 9). For example, weak anecdotal evidence about a specific client might overwhelm strong *base-rate* knowledge about what such people generally do. Decisions dominated by situational constraints might be misattributed to individual preferences. Undue confidence may be placed in small samples. However, reading about the limits to intuitive judgment (e.g., Ariely, 2009; Poulton, 1994; Thaler and Sunstein, 2008) provides no guarantee of being able to overcome them (Milkman et al., 2009).

Communication Strategies

Knowing their clients' views allows analysts to focus their work, thereby producing the most useful analyses. This knowledge also positions them to report that work effectively, by choosing the best language, examples, and background information. As with assessing clients' needs, the weaker the connection is between analyst and client, the greater the need is to rely on general behavioral principles when designing communications. Some examples follow, building on the principles of chapters in this volume by Spellman (Chapter 6), Arkes and Kajdasz (Chapter 7), Hastie (Chapter 8), and Tinsley (Chapter 9). (See also National Research Council, 1996, 1989.)

Need-to-Know Communication

Decision makers often need to know the probability of an event happening. Communicating such predictions requires unambiguous events and numeric probabilities. Figure 10-2 shows one apparent consequence of communicating analytical results imprecisely. It summarizes judgments of "the probability of efficient human-to-human transmission of the H5N1 [avian flu] virus within 3 years." These judgments were elicited in October 2005 from a group of leading public health experts and a group of similarly accomplished non-medical experts (associated with technologies that might ameliorate a pandemic). At the time, the news media were saturated with flu-related reporting. However, those reports had few quantitative estimates. In the absence of such estimates, these nonmedical "experts" saw much higher risks than did the medical experts, a miscommunication that was revealed once their beliefs were made explicit. In retrospect, the 15 percent chance seen by the medical experts seems like a reasonable value, whereas the 60 percent chance imputed to them seems alarmist. Thus, poor communication encouraged unduly harsh judgment of these analysts' work (see McClelland, this volume, Chapter 4).

An event is unambiguous if one could, eventually, tell whether it has occurred. When events are ambiguous, predictions are confusing, even for people comfortable with probabilities. In the late 1970s, the National Weather Service experienced resistance to the probability-of-precipitation forecasts that it had introduced a decade earlier. Studies found that the problem was not with the probabilities, but with the events. Did a "70 percent chance of rain" mean "rain over 70 percent of the period," "rain

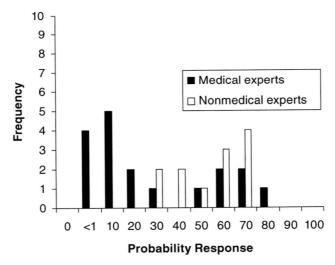

FIGURE 10-2 Probability judgments for efficient human-to-human transmission of avian flu.
NOTE: Responses to "What is the probability that H5N1 will become an efficient human-to-human transmitter (capable of being propagated through at least two epidemiological generations of humans) sometime during the next 3 years?" Answers were from 19 public health experts (median = 15 percent) and 18 experts in other fields, primarily technology (median = 60 percent).
SOURCE: Bruine de Bruin et al. (2006). Reprinted by permission of the publisher (Taylor and Francis Group, http://www.informaworld.com).

over 70 percent of the area," or "70 percent chance of measurable rain?" The answer is the last one (Joslyn and Nichols, 2009; Murphy et al., 1980).

Research has found that some details are particularly hard to communicate (Fischhoff, 2009; Schwarz, 1996). For example, people often overlook quantitative details of an event's *scope* (e.g., how broad an area is involved; how often the event will be repeated). One possible solution is highlighting quantitative details (e.g., how long a medical procedure lasts) that might be overshadowed by more tangible qualitative ones (e.g., how much it hurts). A second possible solution is using the most natural scope. The formulation in Figure 10-2 reflected public health experts' belief that 3 years is the normal planning horizon for pandemic preparations. Box 10-1 shows four other design problems, along with solutions suggested by the research literature (Fischhoff, 2009; Slovic, 2001).

Nice-to-Know Communication

Even when individuals understand the intended meaning of an analytical result, they may lack an intuitive feeling for why it was made and how much to trust it. Without that understanding, they may lack the feeling of self-efficacy needed to rely on it. They would, in effect, be forced to make and defend decisions based on "what my staff [or contractors] tell me,

---

BOX 10-1
Four Communication Design Problems and Solutions

1. Risks are seen differently when reported in relative terms (e.g., "twice as great") and in absolute terms (e.g., "2 in a million vs. 1 in a million"). Because the relative-risk perspective is incomplete, it should be avoided.

2. People may not see the equivalence of numerically identical rates (e.g., 20 die per 10,000 afflicted) and ratios (e.g., for each person who died, 500 survive). If one perspective is more natural, communications should use it; if not, then presenting both perspectives allows recipients to triangulate.

3. Risks can look different when expressed in different units (e.g., probability of premature death vs. expected life-years lost from premature deaths). Because different units express different values (e.g., whether to consider the age of the deceased), communications should use those that the recipient prefers.

4. People can neglect the cumulative risk of repeating a decision. When they consider cumulative risk, they often underestimate it. For example, it seems unintuitive that while only one car ride in 5 million ends in a fatal crash, one life in 200 does. Communications should do the math for them.

SOURCE: Drawn from Fischhoff (2009) and Slovic (2001).

although I can't really explain why." They would also lack the substantive knowledge needed to identify new options or tell when circumstances have changed enough to require new analyses.

Psychology has a long tradition of studying the *mental models* that individuals use when thinking about how their world works (Johnson-Laird, 1983; Rouse and Morris, 1986). Studies have examined thinking in domains as diverse as reading maps, reasoning syllogistically, following instructions, interpreting personal health signs, predicting physical mechanics, making sense of physiological processes (e.g., the circulatory system), and grasping the interplay of physical, biological, and social forces associated with climate change. These studies all begin with a *normative analysis*, summarizing the relevant science in something like influence-diagram form. They proceed to *descriptive* studies capable of revealing intuitive beliefs, including ones very different from the normative standard. The studies then seek *prescriptive* interventions for bridging the gap between the normative ideal and descriptive reality.

The descriptive studies often reveal *heuristics*, or rules of thumb, that allow people to approximate solutions to problems for which they lack needed information or skills. Some heuristics apply to broad classes of inferences. A classic source is Pólya's (1957) *How to Solve It*, with heuristics such as, "Can you find an analogous problem and solve that?" "Can you draw a picture of the problem?" "Have you used everything that you know about it?" Communications that evoke these ways of thinking might help clients to think like analysts. Thus, it may help to draw analogies, use pictures (e.g., influence diagrams), or invoke otherwise forgotten facts (Larkin and Simon, 1987).

The judgment heuristics described by Spellman (this volume, Chapter 6) and Arkes and Kajdasz (this volume, Chapter 7) might be used similarly, while taking care to avoid the biases they can produce. For example, using the availability heuristic means evaluating the probability of an event by how easily instances come to mind. It can be a useful guide, unless some examples are disproportionately available (e.g., Munich, shark attacks). Analysts might reduce this threat by presenting balanced sets of examples and explicitly noting ones that might be neglected.

Other heuristics are domain specific, like those used to predict how explosives work, gases disperse, traffic moves, or inflation behaves. Communications may fail unless they make sense to people, given these normal ways of thinking (or mental models). For example, when analyses predict human behavior (see this volume's Kaplan, Chapter 2; Bueno de Mesquita, Chapter 3; McClelland, Chapter 4; and Skinner, Chapter 5), their work will be interpreted in terms of clients' "folk wisdom" heuristics about human behavior (see this volume's Spellman, Chapter 6; Arkes and Kajdasz, Chapter 7; and Tinsley, Chapter 9). When those heuristics are accurate, that part of the analytical story need not be explained. For example, if clients share the heuristic that "Everyone has sacred values that they will not compromise," communications can focus on what is sacred to the specific people being analyzed. If clients lack that heuristic, then it needs to be explained in intuitively plausible terms (e.g., by reference to values that they themselves hold sacred). If clients hold contradictory heuristics, then evoking both may help, so that clients can think about their relative strength. For example, "If we make that gesture, it will be interpreted as a drop in the bucket, rather than as a foot in the door, toward deeper engagement."

If clients' common sense is wrong, then better intuitions are needed. For example, typically seeing people in similar circumstances leads to the *fundamental attribution error* (Arkes and Kajdasz, this volume, Chapter 7), whereby observers exaggerate the power of personality factors, relative to situational pressures, in shaping behavior. One possible antidote is suggesting missing behaviors (e.g., "We've never seen him without his advisors. Would he be so brave alone?"). Similarly, analyses that predict orderly public reaction to emergencies may confront the widespread *myth of mass panic*. It might be undermined by noting (1) that memory can conflate movie scenes with reality, (2) that people running from problems may be acting rationally and cooperatively (as in the 9/11 evacuations), (3) that feeling panicky rarely leads to panic behavior, and (4) that, in emergencies, most people are rescued by "ordinary citizens," who happen to be there, before professional rescuers arrive to do their brave work trying to save the last few lives (Wessely, 2005). Such explanations replace faulty elements of mental models with sound ones, while building on client's existing knowledge.

Extrapolation

The relevancy of these results (and others like them) to communicating analytical results in any specific setting depends on how different the real situation is from the conditions that behavioral scientists have studied. Three general aspects of the research that merit attention are:

1. *The people involved in the research.* To a first approximation, basic decision-making skills are acquired by the mid-teen years and retained through life (Fischhoff, 2008; Reyna and Farley, 2006). Thus, *how* people think in behavioral studies should not be that different from how people think in other settings. However, most behavioral research involves individuals without subject matter expertise. As a result, conclusions based on *what* people think must be generalized cautiously.

2. *The prevalence of the effects.* Like other sciences, the behavioral sciences often create conditions that exaggerate effects, so as to

observe their operation more closely. As a result, effects can be larger in the lab than in life. Like other sciences, the behavioral sciences often focus on problems. As a result, people can look worse in the lab than in life. The scientific reason for focusing on problems is that there are often many explanations for good performance (e.g., instruction, inference, trial and error), but few explanations that fit a pattern of errors.

3. *The soundness of the normative analyses.* The rhetoric of behavioral research tends to emphasize problems. However, claims of bias are not always supported by normative analyses of what constitutes sound decision making (see this volume's Kaplan, Chapter 2; Bueno do Mesquita, Chapter 3; McClelland, Chapter 4; and Skinner, Chapter 5). For example, people respond differently to reports of absolute and relative risk (see Box 10-1). Although this difference is sometimes identified as a bias, there is no necessary connection between the two judgments: People who only hear relative risk estimates must guess at the associated absolute risks. If they guess wrong, then they should see the risks differently than do people who know the correct values.

Extrapolating results from research settings to other ones requires understanding both. The chapters of this volume seek to make behavioral and social research accessible to those knowledgeable about the world of analysis. Fully examining these connections requires collaborations between people with expertise in both domains.

Measuring Communication Success

The success of communications is an empirical question. Without evidence, one must guess whether clients have absorbed what they need. When direct assessment is possible, measures include (1) clients' *memory* of what has been reported; (2) *manipulation checks* of whether information was interpreted as intended; (3) *active mastery* of the content, allowing clients to make valid inferences from it; (4) *predictive ability*, enhanced by the analysis; (5) *calibration of confidence judgments* in the analysis, expressing recognition of its limits; and (6) *coherence*, showing internal consistency of beliefs (see Fischhoff, 2009, for details and references). When direct assessment is impossible, analysts are left guessing how well they have achieved these goals.

ANALYST–ANALYST COMMUNICATIONS

To meet client needs, analysts must predict the outcomes that those clients value. Typically they must assemble knowledge distributed among diverse individuals, some with established working relations, some without. These analyst–analyst communications face challenges analogous to those of analyst–client communications, with analogous opportunities to bridge the gaps. These are covered in the next two sections, which draw on Fischhoff et al. (2006), Morgan et al. (2001), Morgan and Henrion (1990), and O'Hagan et al. (2006). The chapters in this volume by Tetlock and Mellers (Chapter 11), Kozlowski (Chapter 12), and Zegart (Chapter 13) discuss institutional arrangements needed to allow such collaboration.

Task Analysis of Challenges in Analytical Collaboration

Analyses take varied forms, ranging from fully computational to purely narrative (see this volume's Kaplan, Chapter 2; Bueno de Mesquita, Chapter 3; McClelland, Chapter 4; and Skinner, Chapter 5). Whatever methods an analytical team uses, it faces common communication challenges. In influence diagram terms, a fully computational model is represented by the *variables* and *relationships* in a diagram, while a fully specified narrative analysis describes a path through a diagram, instantiating its variables and relationships.

Assessing the variables in an analysis requires eliciting experts' beliefs with the precision required of probability judgments (see Figure 10-2). Without that precision, other analysts cannot know what they believe about, say, a regime's stability, an army's readiness, or a leader's health. When experts disagree, other analysts need to know the distribution of their answers (and not just a verbal summary of their degree of consensus). Experts in one domain also need to know the assumptions made by experts in other ones. For example, in Figure 10-1, experts in official responses (node 3) need some assumptions about the kinds of attack (node 1) and dispersion (node 2) scenarios they must consider. Dispersion modelers need some assumptions about the kinds of input that officials need. Without good communication, their work may not connect.

Specifying the relationships in an analysis requires similar clarity. Analysts need to know the functional form of each dependency. For example, do experts believe that deterrence increases monotonically with armament levels or does it only "kick in" after they pass some threshold? Do experts believe that a single act of humiliation can radicalize a young person or that radicalization reflects a cumulative effect? Here, too, analysts need to know the degree of consensus in the fields on which they depend.

Clear communication about uncertainties and disagreements is essential to determining how much they matter. Even fields that are full of disputes and uncertainties may still have all the precision that clients need. For example, Morgan and Keith (1995) conducted extensive interviews with climate scientists, representing the range of expert opinions—and found that nearly all their experts saw a significant chance of major warming, seemingly enough to convince any policy maker that a large gamble is being taken with the environment. Seemingly different theories can make similar predictions when they add up related factors (Dawes et al., 1989).

Communication between analysts may have special value when it allows triangulating the perspectives produced by using narrative and computational methods. Computational models create scenarios from individually plausible links, then assess their overall probability. However, in the life of a person (or political movement), individual links can be plausible, yet add up to an implausible story. For example, someone who perceives deep personal humiliation may be more likely to accept radical ideologies, while someone who accepts radical ideologies may be more likely to be recruited to commit violent acts. However, deep personal humiliation may leave psychological scars that forestall such action (Ginges and Atran, 2008).

Examining the coherence of a sequence of links is at the heart of narrative analysis. Conversely, ensuring the completeness and precision of an account is at the heart of quantitative analysis. At times, practitioners of the two approaches mistrust one another's work. Narrative analysts fear undue pressure for quantification, which can happen when easily quantified factors (e.g., estimates of materiel) are privileged over more qualitative ones (e.g., political sentiment). Quantitative analysts fear undue opacity in narratives, which can happen when good writing takes precedence over clear thinking. A possible compromise is requiring narratives to be clear enough to allow creating models that could be computed, were the data available. Conversely, quantitative models should not be constrained by data concerns when identifying potentially relevant predictors. Fischhoff and colleagues (2006) use *computable* to describe models that are designed to facilitate such communication between qualitative and quantitative analysts.

Communication Methods

Methods for analyst–analyst communication parallel those for analyst–client communication, with similar strengths, weaknesses, and supporting science.

Open-ended methods involve direct interactions among analysts, designed to allow disagreements about variables, relationships, and terms to emerge. Jointly creating influence diagrams is one such method. Electronic media offer new possibilities for understanding (e.g., collaborative workspaces) and misunderstanding (e.g., flaming, Wiki wars).

Structured methods elicit experts' judgments (as in Figure 10-2), allowing other analysts to consult the summaries. Omitting direct communication among analysts increases the importance of asking precise questions and eliciting precise answers.

Inferred methods involve reading other experts' analyses, hoping to grasp their reasoning. Narrative analyses can be misread, when the ability to read their lines suggests the ability to read between their lines. Quantitative analyses can be misread, when their lack of transparency leads them to be taken on faith or rejected outright.

Indexed methods summarize a field's typical results, in stylized form, for others' use. In order to represent a field responsibly, they must also reveal its controversies and uncertainties. The Cochrane Collaboration offers valuable procedures for that process on its website.[1]

Chapters in this volume by Spellman (Chapter 6), Arkes and Kajdasz (Chapter 7), Hastie (Chapter 8), and Tinsley (Chapter 9) describe some of the perils to understanding, even among individuals with shared goals. Sound analyst–analyst communication increases the chances of analysts having something valuable to communicate to clients.

MANAGING FOR COMMUNICATION SUCCESS

As with other vital organizational functions, effective communications require proper people and processes (see this volume's Tetlock and Mellers, Chapter 11, and Kozlowski, Chapter 12). Figure 10-3 shows a model for integrating communication with analysis and action (National Research Council, 1996, described a process that is similar in spirit). The central column in the picture depicts a fairly conventional analytical process, beginning with problem formulation and proceeding to action. (It has noteworthy reality checks between stages, asking whether the work bears continuing.)

The left-hand bar requires ongoing two-way communication between clients and analysts. In the early stages, analysts are in the center column, learning what their clients need to know, while preparing them with nice-to-know background information. In the later stages, analysts are in the left column, communicating their analyses and listening for future analytical needs, as they observe their clients taking action.

Management must create these channels to make communication possible. It must also staff them properly. To implement the methods described here, analytical teams need *subject matter* expertise (regarding potentially

---

[1]See http://www.cochrane.org [accessed October 2010].

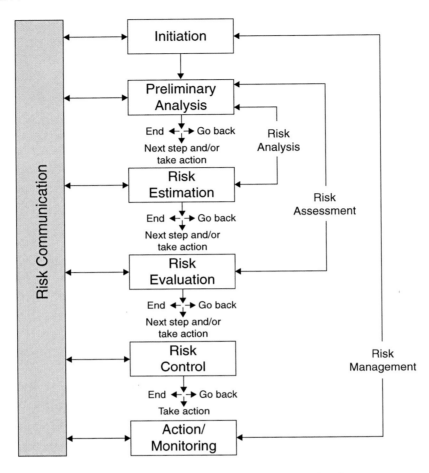

Note: *Risk communication with stakeholders is an important part of each step in the decision process.*

FIGURE 10-3 A model for integrating analysis and communication.
NOTE: The center column shows the stages in a conventional, analytically driven decision-making process (here, expressed in terms of risks). The right shows the needed strategic commitment to two-way communication at all stages of the process. SOURCE: Canadian Standards Association (1997). Reproduced with the permission of Canadian Standards Association from CAN/CSA-0850-97 (R2009)—*Risk Management: Guideline for Decision Makers*, which is copyrighted by CSA, 5060 Spectrum Way, Mississauga, ON, L4W 5N6 Canada. While use of this material has been authorized, CSA shall not be responsible for the manner in which the information is presented, nor for any interpretations thereof. For more information on CSA or to purchase standards, please visit our website at http://www.shopcsa. ca or call 1-800-463-6727.

relevant facts), *methodological* expertise (for identifying and synthesizing those facts), and *communication* expertise (for designing and evaluating communications).

Although having subject matter expertise is natural for analytical organizations, having the other two kinds may not be. Without them, it is not possible to take full advantage of the behavioral, social, and decision science research available to the intelligence community. Given the diversity of that research, such expertise might be provided through a central unit available to all analytical teams, with matrix management to ensure that the unit's members are integrated with analytical teams. An alternative management approach is to secure the needed behavioral expertise through external contracts. For such outsourcing to succeed, an analytical organization needs the internal expertise to evaluate service providers. Choosing between internal and external expertise requires balancing the short-term benefits of improving specific analyses against the long-term benefits of enhancing an organization's own human capital.

CONCLUSION

Effective communication is essential to effective analysis. It is needed to identify the questions that clients need to have answered, to coordinate the expertise relevant to providing those answers, and to ensure that analytical results are understood as intended. A scientific approach to communication entails both analytical and empirical research. The former involves decision analysis of information needs and task analysis of information flows. The latter involves assessment of beliefs before and after receiving analytical results.

The execution of that research can draw on behavioral and decision science theory and method. Decision science provides methods for identifying the information that needs to be known, by clients with well-formulated decisions, and the information that would be nice to know, for clients hoping to create decision options, monitor changes in their environment, or understand what information they need to know. Behavioral science provides guidance on obstacles to understanding analytical results and on ways to overcome them, along with organizational guidance on securing and deploying the needed human resources.

Communication is sometimes seen as a tactical step, transmitting results to clients. However, unless communication also plays a strategic role, those analyses may be off target and incompletely used. If an analytical organization makes a strategic commitment to communication, behavioral science can help with its execution, overcoming some of the flawed intuitions that can lead people to exaggerate how well they understand one another.

REFERENCES

Ariely, D. 2009. *Predictably irrational.* New York: Harper.

Bartlett, F. C. 1932. *Remembering.* Cambridge, UK: Cambridge University Press.

Bruine de Bruin, W., B. Fischhoff, L. Brilliant, and D. Caruso. 2006. Expert judgments of pandemic influenza. *Global Public Health* 1(2):178–193.

Canadian Standards Association. 1997. *Risk management: Guideline for decision makers* (reaffirmed 2002). Etobicoke, Ontario, Canada: Canadian Standards Association.

Clemen, R. T., and R. Reilly. 2002. *Making hard decisions: An introduction to decision analysis.* Belmont, CA: Duxbury.

Converse, J. M., and S. Presser. 1986. *Survey questions. Handcrafting the standardized questionnaire.* Thousand Oaks, CA: Sage Publications.

Dawes, R. M. 1979. The robust beauty of improper linear models in decision making. *American Psychologist* 34:571–582.

Dawes, R. M., D. Faust, and P. E. Meehl. 1989. Clinical vs. actuarial judgment. *Science* 243:1668–1674.

Dombroski, M. J., and P. S. Fischbeck. 2006. An integrated physical dispersion and behavioral response model for risk assessment of radiological dispersion device (RDD) events. *Risk Analysis* 26:501–514.

Earnhart, D. 2002. Combining revealed and stated data to examine housing decisions using discrete choice analysis. *Journal of Urban Economics* 51:143–169.

Erev, I., and B. L. Cohen. 1990. Verbal versus numerical probabilities: Efficiency, biases, and the preference paradox. *Organizational Behavior and Human Decision Processes* 45:1–18.

Ericsson, A., and H. A. Simon. 1994. *Verbal reports as data.* Cambridge, MA: MIT Press.

Fischhoff, B. 1994. What forecasts (seem to) mean. *International Journal of Forecasting* 10:387–403.

Fischhoff, B. 2008. Assessing adolescent decision-making competence. *Developmental Review* 28:12–28.

Fischhoff, B. 2009. Risk perception and communication. In R. Detels, R. Beaglehole, M. A. Lansang, and M. Gulliford, eds., *Oxford textbook of public health,* 5th ed. (pp. 940–952). Oxford, UK: Oxford University Press.

Fischhoff, B., W. Bruine de Bruin, U. Guvenc, D. Caruso, and L. Brilliant. 2006. Analyzing disaster risks and plans: An avian flu example. *Journal of Risk and Uncertainty* 33:133–151.

Funtowicz, S., and J. Ravetz. 1990. *Uncertainty and quality in science for policy.* Dordrecht, The Netherlands: Kluwer.

Gentner, D., and A. L. Stevens, eds. 1983. *Mental models.* Hillsdale, NJ: Erlbaum.

Ginges, J., and S. Atran 2008. Humiliation and the inertia effect. *Journal of Cognition and Culture* 8:281–294.

Grice, P. 1975. Logic and conversation. In P. Cole and J. L. Morgan, eds., *Syntax and semantics: Speech acts.* Vol. 3 (pp. 133–168). New York: Guilford Press.

Hastie, R., and R. M. Dawes. 2001. *Rational choice in an uncertain world,* 2nd ed. Thousand Oaks, CA: Sage.

Horvitz, E., ed. 2005. Special issue on graph-based representation. *Decision Analysis* 2(4): 183–244.

Howard, R. A. 1989. Knowledge maps. *Management Science* 35:903–922.

Johnson-Laird, P. N. 1983. *Mental models.* New York: Cambridge University Press.

Joslyn, S. L., and R. M. Nichols. 2009. Probability or frequency? Expressing forecast uncertainty in public weather forecasts. *Meteorological Applications* 90:185–219.

Kent, S. 1964. *Words of estimative probability.* Available: https://www.cia.gov/library/center-for-the-study-of-intelligence/csi-publications/books-and-monographs/sherman-kent-and-the-board-of-national-estimates-collected-essays/6words.html [accessed May 2010].

Larkin, J., and H. A. Simon. 1987. Why a diagram is (sometimes) worth ten thousand words. *Cognitive Science* 11(1):65–99.

McIntyre, S., and P. West. 1992. What does the phrase "safer sex" mean to you? Understanding among Glaswegian 18 year olds in 1990. *AIDS* 7:121–126.

McKenney, N. R., and C. E. Bennett. 1994. Issues regarding data on race and ethnicity: The Census Bureau experience. *Public Health Reports* 109:16–25.

Milkman, K. L., D. Chugh, and M. H. Bazerman. 2009. How can decision making be improved? *Perspectives on Psychological Science* 4:379–383.

Morgan, M. G., and M. Henrion. 1990. *Uncertainty.* New York: Cambridge University Press.

Morgan, M. G., and D. W. Keith. 1995. Subjective judgments by climate experts. *Environmental Science and Technology* 29:468A–476A.

Morgan, M. G., B. Fischhoff, A. Bostrom, and C. Atman. 2001. *Risk communication: The mental models approach.* New York: Cambridge University Press.

Murphy, A. H., S. Lichtenstein, B. Fischhoff, and R. L. Winkler. 1980. Misinterpretations of precipitation probability forecasts. *Bulletin of the American Meteorological Society* 61:695–701.

National Research Council. 1989. *Improving risk communication.* Committee on Risk Perception and Communication, Commission on Physical Sciences. Commission on Behavioral and Social Sciences and Education. Washington, DC: National Academy Press.

National Research Council. 1996. *Understanding risk: Informing decisions in a democratic society.* P. C. Stern and H. V. Fineberg, eds. Committee on Risk Characterization. Commission on Behavioral and Social Sciences and Education. Washington, DC: National Academy Press.

O'Hagan, A., C. E. Buck, A. Daneshkhah, J. R. Eiser, P. H. Garthwaite, D. J. Jenkinson, J. E. Oakley, and T. Rankow. 2006. *Uncertain judgments: Eliciting expert probabilities.* Chichester, UK: Wiley.

Politi, M. C., P. K. J. Han, and N. Col. 2007. Communicating the uncertainty of harms and benefits of medical procedures. *Medical Decision Making* 27:681–695.

Pólya, G. 1957. *How to solve it,* 2nd ed. Princeton, NJ: Princeton University Press.

Poulton, E. C. 1994. *Behavioral decision making.* Hillsdale, NJ: Erlbaum.

Raiffa, H. 1968. *Decision analysis.* Reading, MA: Addison-Wesley.

Ranyard, R., F. Del Missier, N. Bonini, D. Duxbury, and B. Summers. 2008. Perceptions and expectations of price changes and inflation: A review and conceptual framework. *Journal of Economic Psychology* 29:378–400.

Reyna, V., and F. Farley. 2006. Risk and rationality in adolescent decision making: Implications for theory, practice, and public policy. *Psychology in the Public Interest* 7(1):1–44.

Rouse, W. B., and N. M. Morris. 1986. On looking into the black box: Prospects and limits in the search for mental models. *Psychological Bulletin* 110:349–363.

Schwarz, N. 1996. *Cognition and communication: Judgmental biases, research methods, and the logic of conversation.* Hillsdale, NJ: Erlbaum.

Schwarz, N. 1999. Self reports. *American Psychologist* 54:93–105.

Slovic, P., ed. 2001. *The perception of risk.* London, U.K.: Earthscan.

Sudman, S., and N. Bradburn. 1982. *Asking questions: A practical guide to questionnaire design.* San Francisco, CA: Jossey-Bass.

Thaler, R. H., and C. R. Sunstein. 2008. *Nudge: Improving decisions about health, wealth, and happiness.* New Haven, CT: Yale University Press.

Viscusi, W. K. 1983. *Risk by choice: Regulating health and safety in the workplace.* Cambridge, MA: Harvard University Press.
vonWinterfeldt, D., and W. Edwards. 1986. *Decision analysis and behavioral research.* New York: Cambridge University Press.
Wallsten, T. S., D. V. Budescu, and R. Zwick. 1993. Comparing the calibration and coherence of numerical and verbal probability judgments. *Management Science* 39:176–190.
Wessely, S. 2005. Don't panic! *Journal of Mental Health* 14(1):1–6.
Woloshin, S., L. M. Schwartz, and H. G. Welch. 2008. *Know your chances: Understanding health statistics.* Berkeley: University of California Press.

11

Structuring Accountability Systems in Organizations: Key Trade-Offs and Critical Unknowns[1]

Philip E. Tetlock and Barbara A. Mellers

When things go wrong, one rarely needs to wait long to hear angry cries to "hold the rascals accountable." Intelligence agencies are no exception to this blame game, as we can see by surveying the past decade of recriminations over the failures to predict the 9/11 attacks and the lack of weapons of mass destruction in Iraq (Posner, 2005a). But "accountability" is no panacea, as we can see by surveying the sprawling experimental and field research literatures on the impact of various types of accountability on various forms of human judgment (Lerner and Tetlock, 1999). If "accountability cures" exist for what ails intelligence analysis, those cures will need to be far more complex and carefully calibrated than cries for "greater accountability" imply—and will need to be implemented in carefully controlled and phased field research trials to ensure that the desired effects outweigh the undesired.

The research literature on accountability spans work in social psychology, organization theory, political science, accounting, finance, and microeconomics (agency theory)—and offers us an initially confusing patchwork quilt of findings guaranteed to frustrate those looking for quick fixes. Sometimes "accountability" helps. Researchers have documented conditions under which accountability improves the calibration of probability estimates (Siegel-Jacobs and Yates, 1996; Tetlock and Kim, 1987), checks

---

[1]We are grateful to Cherie Chauvin, Jeffrey Cooper, Tom Fingar, Daniel Kahneman, Robert Jervis, John Morgan, Paul Tetlock, and Amy Zegart for helpful comments on earlier versions of this chapter. We especially thank Baruch Fischhoff for his assistance in sharpening our argument.

self-enhancement biases (Sedikides et al., 2002), makes people attend more seriously to hypothesis-disconfirming evidence (Kruglanski and Freund, 1983), and makes people more self-aware and accurate judges of covariation in their environment (Hagafors and Brehmer, 1983; Murphy, 1994). Other times, "accountability" has perverse effects, increasing defensiveness and escalating commitment to sunk costs (Simonson and Staw, 1992), increasing susceptibility to being distracted by low-diagnosticity cues (Tetlock and Boettger, 1989) and superficially plausible but specious reasoning (Barber et al., 2003), and inducing rather indiscriminant ambiguity aversion (Curley et al., 1986) and risk aversion (Tetlock and Boettger, 1994).

At other times, achieving consensus on whether "accountability" is helping, hurting, or having no effect is impossible because so much hinges on observers' sympathies and perceptions of whose ox is about to be gored. Examples of such accountability controversies include debates over how to structure relations between auditors and their corporate clients (Moore et al., 2006) or between legislators and citizens (Kono, 2006), how to make teachers accountable for improving student performance (Chubb and Moe, 1990), and how to hold managers accountable for making decisions on race-and-gender neutral grounds (Kalev et al., 2006; Tetlock and Mitchell, 2009). Setting up rules and incentives to encourage desired—and discourage undesired—behavior is a much-discussed problem that is far from fully solved (Kerr, 1975).

Understanding the effects of accountability requires clear definitions for both the independent and dependent variables, as well as a conceptual scheme for characterizing the myriad organizational processes for implementing accountability. On the independent-variable side, accountability is an omnibus term for a complex bundle of variables captured by the multipronged question: Who must answer to whom for what—under what normative ground rules and with what consequences for passing or failing performance standards (Schlenker, 1985; Scott and Lyman, 1968; Tetlock, 1985, 1992)? This definition could apply to virtually any level of analysis, from the societal to the interpersonal. One could hold governments accountable for policy miscalculations; governments could hold intelligence agencies accountable for flawed guidance; agency heads could hold their managers accountable for failure to check errors; and managers could hold individual analysts accountable for making the initial errors. To make this chapter manageable, we focus on the accountability pressures operating on individual analysts in their immediate working environment.

Even within this restricted focus, our definition still allows for enormous parametric complexity. One could hold analysts accountable to colleagues of the same or higher status whose own views are either well known or unknown before analysts submit their work, whose interpersonal style is more collaborative or adversarial, who are focused more on the process by which analysts reach conclusions or on the bottom-line accuracy of those conclusions, who are known to be tolerant or intolerant of dissent, or who are known to be moderate or extreme in their reactions to success or failure. Each of these variations has the potential to influence either what analysts say they think (e.g., public attitude shifting) or how they actually think (e.g., private thought processes shift toward self-criticism or self-justification) (Tetlock, 1992). For these reasons, accountability is often viewed as a crucial construct for bridging more micro, behavioral science approaches (that focus on inside-the-head processes of decision makers) and social science approaches (that focus on the organizational and political structures within which individuals are embedded). Any reasonably complete characterization of the environment within which analysts work cannot ignore the accountability relationships that bind them to key constituencies and that can influence both what and how they think (March and Olsen, 1989).

On the dependent-variable side, policy debates over accountability systems invariably pivot on implicit or explicit conceptions of what would constitute enhanced performance. The official answer for intelligence agencies in the early 21st century—providing timely and accurate information that enables policy makers to advance our national interest—is too open-ended to be of much practical value. We need specific guidance on the types of "criterion variables" that proposed accountability systems are supposed to be maximizing or minimizing. Do we want analysts to focus on "policy-maker (customer) satisfaction," even if that means subtly signaling them to engage in sycophantic attitude shifting to support politicians' flawed world views (Prendergast, 1993; Tetlock, 1992)? Do we want to insulate analysts from political pressures, even if that means they become less responsive to policy makers' legitimate and often urgent needs? Do we want to incentivize only accuracy, with no regard for the inherent unpredictability of the environment, and risk rewarding analysts who play fast and loose with evidence, but just happen to be lucky on some recent big calls? Do we want to put the spotlight on measures of how analysts think—and reward the rigorous, punish the sloppy, and attach virtually no weight to "who gets what right?" How should we balance timeliness and accuracy as analysts move from cases that require rapid action to those that allow for more leisurely contemplation of ambiguities and trade-offs?

This chapter wrestles with the foundational questions: What insights can we glean from the vast interdisciplinary literature on accountability on how to balance the relevant trade-offs—and how the organizations dedicated to analyzing national security information should structure the work lives of those charged with offering useful guidance to decision makers? Furthermore, if one were to design—from scratch—the accountability ground rules for monitoring the "performance" of intelligence analysts and incentivizing "improvement," what should one do?

Initially, the complexity of the choice set looks overwhelming. Accountability systems can be classified in so many ways—indeed, in principle, there are as many forms of accountability as there are distinct relationships among human beings. That said, two key issues loom especially large in political debates over how to structure responsibility for intelligence analysis processes and products (Posner, 2005a, b). The first is beyond the control of intelligence agencies—the degree of autonomy they should possess vis-à-vis their political overseers—and we touch on this briefly. The second is very much under the control of intelligence agencies—how they should structure their internal accountability systems for defining and facilitating excellence—and we devote most attention to this topic.

#1 Balancing Clashing Needs for Professional Autonomy and Political Responsiveness

How dependent should those who preside over intelligence analysis be on the approval or disapproval of their democratically elected political masters in Congress and the Executive Branch of government? Should they enjoy as much autonomy as, say, the Federal Reserve or should they—like most other political appointees—serve strictly at the pleasure of the President?

At one end of the continuum are those who insist on complete subordination of intelligence analysis to the political priorities of policy makers. Some might even argue that democratic political theory requires nothing else: analysts' overriding concern should be satisfying their "customers" in congressional committees and Executive Branch offices. But this argument may be too extreme in light of the substantial independence enjoyed by the Federal Reserve in analyzing economic trends and setting monetary policy, and in light of the evidence that the more independent central banks are, the better they manage complex trade-offs between unemployment and inflation (Alesina and Summers, 1993; Fischer, 1995). Complete subordination of intelligence analysis to political masters raises the risk of incentivizing analysts to be sycophants who fear telling their political bosses anything that could incur their wrath, thereby facilitating groupthink-like insulation from dissonant insights.

At the other end of the continuum are those who argue for the independence that the Federal Reserve exercises in analyzing monetary policy or that the National Science Foundation exercises in choosing which grants to fund. Some might insist that the power to punish intelligence agencies for offering ideologically unwelcome reports is incompatible with the goal of getting ruthlessly objective analysis. But this argument also may go too far. In an open and pluralistic society, politicians may often pay a steep penalty for politicizing intelligence assessments—and consumers of intelligence need some leverage over the suppliers to ensure responsiveness to legitimate needs. Few would want analysts to be as free to ignore policy demands as they would be if they enjoyed the job security of tenured professors. Analysts who feel accountable only to each other in this scenario might start writing like academics: only for each other.

Whether the current system has found a sound compromise between these clashing values is beyond the purview of this chapter. But there should be little doubt about the need to factor these trade-offs into organizational design. Furthermore, there should be little doubt that where one comes down on this continuum of accountability design options will be influenced by one's assumptions about relative risks of excessively pushy politicians and of an excessively insulated analytical community that exploits lax oversight to pursue its own agenda.

#2 Balancing Clashing Needs for Rigor in Processes and for Creativity in Coping with Rapidly Changing Events

Whatever degree of institutional independence one prefers for intelligence agencies, how should we gauge the performance of analysts working in these agencies? Should we embrace pure process accountability and focus solely on the rigor of the underlying analytic process? Or should we embrace outcome accountability and focus solely on who gets what right across issue domains and time frames (pure outcome accountability)? Or should we embrace some form of hybrid process-outcome system that assigns adjustable weights to rigor and accuracy and that, depending on the task requirements of the moment, allows for the possibility of letting process trump outcome in some settings, of letting outcome trump process in other settings, and of assigning equal weights in yet other settings?

Advocates of process accountability maintain that the best way to reach the optimal forecasting frontier—and stay there—is to hold analysts responsible for respecting certain logical and empirical guidelines. As we can see from the list of standards for analytic tradecraft contained in Intelligence Community Directive No. 203, June 21, 2007 (Director of National Intelligence, 2007, pp. 3-4), the current emphasis appears to be on process accountability within the Office of the Director of National Intelligence:

- Properly describes quality and reliability of underlying sources (how do you know what you claim to know?);
- Properly caveats and expresses uncertainties or confidence in analytic judgments;
- Properly distinguishes between underlying intelligence and analysts' assumptions and judgments;

- Incorporates alternative analysis where appropriate;
- Demonstrates relevance to U.S. national security;
- Uses logical argumentation;
- Exhibits consistency of analysis over time, or highlights changes and explains rationale; and
- Makes accurate judgments and assessments—although this comes with the understandable caveat: make the most accurate judgments and assessments possible given the information available . . . and known information gaps. . . . Accuracy is sometimes difficult to establish and can only be evaluated retrospectively if necessary information is collected and available.

Indeed, strong arguments can be made for stressing process over outcome accountability. Proponents of process accountability warn that it is unfair and demoralizing to hold analysts responsible for outcomes palpably outside their control—and doing so may stimulate either risk-averse consensus forecasts (herding of the sort documented among managers of mutual funds—whereby individuals believe, they can't fire all of us—Bikhchandani et al., 1998; Scharfstein and Stein, 1990) or, when retreat is impossible, escalating commitment to initially off-base forecasts (defending those positions as fundamentally right but just off on timing—Simonson and Staw, 1992; Tetlock, 2005).

A large body of work shows how easily outcome-accountability systems can be corrupted—even in competitive private-sector firms (Bertrand and Mullainathan, 2001; Sappington, 1991). For example, when H. J. Heinz division managers received bonuses only if earnings increased from the prior year, managers found ways to deliver consistent earnings growth by manipulating the timing of shipments to customers and by prepaying for services not yet received, both at a cost to the firm as a whole (Baker et al., 1994). One can easily imagine analogs in which managers of analysts find ways of inflating their "accuracy scores" by increasing the number of "easy things" they are responsible for predicting or by introducing more generous scoring rules that permit reclassifying errors as "almost right" or "just off on timing" or derailed by inherently unpredictable exogenous shocks. Furthermore, one also can easily imagine how outcome-accountability pressures operating on individual analysts could lead to information hoarding and even sabotage of each other's efforts (although this classic problem can be mitigated by emphasizing outcome accountability for team performance—and by designing disincentives for hoarding).

Process-accountability proponents also warn of how impractical—as well as unfair—outcome-accountability systems can be. They are certainly right that assessing the accuracy of real-world political forecasts is a nontrivial undertaking. Below we list seven often-offered objections to the feasibility of factoring accuracy metrics into the standards to which analysts are held accountable:

1. Self-negating prophecies in which initially sound predictions (that would have been right if policy makers had not acted on them) now appear incorrect because policy makers did act on them (one still much-debated example: Y2K).
2. Self-fulfilling prophecies in which initially unsound predictions (that would have been wrong if policy makers had not acted on them) become correct because policy makers did act on them (one possible example: aggressive counterinsurgency measures against a subpopulation that was not pro-Taliban beforehand, but becomes pro-Taliban as a result of the measures).
3. Exogenous shocks or missing information on key variables that cause lower probability outcomes to occur—and cast into false doubt fundamentally sound analyses of causal dynamics.
4. Exogenous shocks that cause credit to be assigned to far-fetched theories.
5. Arbitrary time frames for assessing the accuracy of many predictions (should we call a Sovietologist wrong if he or she thought in 1988 that the Union of Soviet Socialist Republics would disintegrate within a 10-year frame, but not the 5-year frame—or should we praise him for being so much closer to right than the expert consensus in 1988?).
6. When forecasts are premised on conditional adoption of policy x, how can we know whether the forecasts were right when non-x was adopted.
7. The "I-made-the-right-mistake" defense (the consequences of making a Type 2 error of underestimating the enemy are vastly greater than those of making a Type 1 error of overestimating the enemy). Inflating the probabilities of the more serious error is reasonable if that it is the only way to achieve the desired policy outcome.

Proponents of outcome accountability reply that, although accuracy is indeed an elusive construct, there are ways to address these objections—and that rough measures with known limitations are vastly better than no measures (Tetlock, 2005). Properly implemented, outcome accountability empowers people to seek ingenious analytic strategies not formally embodied in process guidelines (Wilson, 1989). Proponents of outcome accountability also worry that: (1) process accountability can readily ossify into bureaucratic rituals and mutual backscratching—Potemkin-village facades of process accountability and rigor designed to deflect annoying questions from external critics (Edelman, 1992; Meyer and Rowan, 1977); and (2) process accountability can distract analysts from the central task of understanding the external world by squandering cognitive resources on impression management aimed at convincing superiors of how rigorous their analytical processes are (Lazear, 1989). A healthy dose of outcome accountability alerts us to the possibility that even the best on-paper, process-accountability mechanisms can be corrupted in a multitude of ways—whether they are opinionated managers who suppress information or peer reviewers who fail to catch errors in draft reports because the reviewers are too homogeneous in outlook or because they have been intimidated by dogmatists higher up in the bureaucratic food chain. Outcome accountability sends a much-needed signal to beleaguered dissenters that, although they may suffer the slings and arrows of short-term career damage by taking unpopular positions (e.g., being labeled as "process deficient" by groupthink mindguards [Janis, 1972]), formal mechanisms will be in place to compensate them for the losses—and then some. The logic here is akin to that in whistleblower protection legislation—namely, to encourage the sort of dissent that is often suppressed even in relatively well-functioning organizational systems. Inasmuch as process-accountability systems can fail in a host of unintended ways—many of which can be offset by carefully calibrated doses of outcome accountability—it becomes harder to defend a categorical rejection of all efforts to explore the potential value-added of outcome accountability.

Again, whether the current system has found a sound compromise between competing accountability design templates is beyond the purview of this chapter. But again there should be little doubt about the need to factor these trade-offs into organizational design, and little doubt that where one comes down on this continuum of accountability design options will be influenced by one's implicit or explicit assumptions about the relative risks of process accountability being corrupted and degenerating into a bureaucratic formality versus the relative risks of holding people unfairly accountable for the inherently unforeseeable, and prompting them to engage in ever more elaborate forms of trickery designed to inflate their accuracy scores.

Of course, the choice between process and outcome accountability is not dichotomous. One can easily imagine an enormous range of blends of process and outcome accountability, many of which can be found in the private sector. One well-known process-outcome hybrid in the world of finance is RAROC (risk-adjusted return on capital) guidelines, which place constraints on the risks that decision makers are allowed to take with firm money, but still incentivize decision makers to maximize returns within those guidelines.[2] Within a RAROC world, one can profit handsomely

---

[2]RAROC was developed and first implemented by Charles Sanford at Banker's Trust Company in the mid-1970s.

from being right if one works within the firm's process guidelines on acceptable risk taking—but one can also lose one's job if one makes "too much money" by violating those guidelines and exposing the firm to unacceptable potential risk.

In judging the wisdom of infusing more outcome accountability into intelligence analysis, much hinges on one's answers to the following question: Are current systems already functioning so close to the optimal forecasting frontier that additional outcome accountability is unlikely to improve aggregate performance—and likely instead simply to shift error-tolerance thresholds?

THE INFORMATION ENVIRONMENT

The performance of any analytical system, and the contribution of any attempt to improve it, depends on the difficulty of the task. That depends, in turn, on the difficulty of extracting a signal from the world being analyzed and the error tolerances of those who depend on the system for useful insights.

Figure 11-1 formalizes these demands, drawing on signal detection theory, a mainstay of behavioral science (Green and Swets, 1966; as well as this volume's McClelland, Chapter 4, and Arkes and Kajdasz,

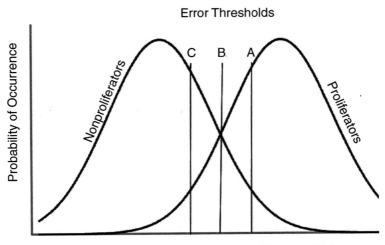

FIGURE 11-1 A world that permits modest predictability.
SOURCE: Generalized from Green and Swets (1966).

Chapter 7). In Figure 11-1, the analytical task is to assess the risk of nuclear proliferation, in a world where the two distributions represent the behavior of nations that truly are and are not proliferators. Imagine that each observation is drawn at random from the appropriate distribution. In most cases, analysts can tell whether an observation comes from a proliferator or a nonproliferator. However, in some cases in the middle range, the evidence is either hard to assign to one kind of country or even misleading (such that proliferators look like nonproliferators and vice versa). Analysts cannot avoid making errors when the evidence falls in the overlapping zone, no matter how strong or what types of accountability pressures are on them.

Which errors analysts make will, however, depend on how they interpret those accountability pressures. Imagine three political forecasters who are equally skilled at discriminating proliferation signals from noise, but differ in the error thresholds they believe their task requires. These thresholds are indicated by vertical lines A, B, and C. They represent the balance of evidence that each forecaster uses to distinguish "nonproliferators" and "proliferators." Forecaster C will tolerate many false alarms to avoid one miss, and so is more likely to overconnect the dots. An extreme example of this value orientation was the position allegedly taken by Vice President Dick Cheney with respect to the invasion of Iraq in 2003: Even a 1 percent probability of a nuclear weapon falling into the hands of terrorists was "too much" (Suskind, 2006). Forecaster B assigns equal weight to the two types of errors. Forecaster A will tolerate many misses to avoid a single false alarm, so will not make the proliferation "call" on a nation that sends only weak indicators, either because intelligence gathering is weak or the target nation is skilled at deception.

Figure 11-2 displays the same dilemma in a different way, plotting hit rates against false alarm rates. Perfect forecasters achieved a 100 percent hit rate at 0 percent cost in false alarms, falling at the point in the top left corner. Forecasters with no ability, who simply guessed, would fall along the main diagonal, at a point reflecting their understanding of the system's tolerance for hits versus false alarms. For example, forecasters with a strong aversion to misses would consider nearly every observation to be evidence of proliferation and end up near the upper right corner (in Figure 11-2). The three forecasters from Figure 11-1 appear on the same curve, representing their (identical) ability to extract signals about proliferation, but their differing understanding of the appropriate error thresholds. Note that A and C, who see strong aversion to false alarms or misses respectively, produce forecasts not that different from forecasters who just guess. Of course, that divergence could be vitally important.

The area between the curve and the diagonal in Figure 11-2 represents the value that forecasters add, above chance. To move to a higher

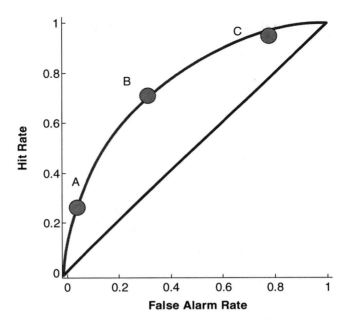

FIGURE 11-2 Possible hit-versus-false-alarm trade-offs in a world of modest predictability (see Figure 11-1).
SOURCE: Generalized from Green and Swets (1966).

ability curve, forecasters need to be better analysts or to have better information—or live in a world where the two kinds of nations behave more distinctly. Unless an accountability system changes forecasters' analytical ability—how they process information or the types of information they process—all it can do is change the relative mix of errors. Getting analysts' thresholds attuned to those that the organization desires can have value. However, that is a different enterprise from attempting to improve their aggregate forecasting performance. Indeed, if the threshold shifts are seen as serving political fashions, they may even discourage thoughtful analysis (why bother thinking when the best way to get ahead is simple conformity?).

Figure 11-3 depicts a more highly predictable world, with less overlap between distributions, in which analysts can more readily distinguish proliferators from non-proliferators. However, because the thresholds remain the same, in absolute terms, they reflect much different (and much higher) levels of knowledge. The solid curve in Figure 11-4 shows that the corresponding forecasting frontier has been pushed toward the top left corner. As a result, analysts can now achieve the same hit rate with a much lower

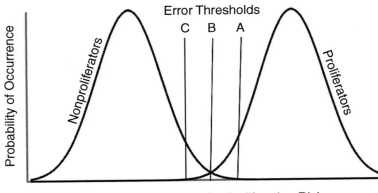

FIGURE 11-3 A world that permits a very high degree of predictability.
SOURCE: Generalized from Green and Swets (1966).

false alarm rate, or the same false alarm rate with a much higher hit rate. However, exploiting this new forecasting ability requires understanding the quality of the judgments that it allows. Unfortunately, although people are more confident when they are more knowledgeable, the correlation is weaker than it should be.

Observers tend to be overconfident in domains where they know little—and underconfident in domains where they know a lot (Erev et al., 1994; Lichtenstein and Fischhoff, 1977; Moore and Healy, 2008). As a result, analysts and their clients might not take full advantage of improved ability unless they knew how good it was. This is likely to happen only if the analytical organization is committed to evaluating its accuracy systematically. That requires comparing analyses with actual events, while maintaining a consistent threshold for calling events (in this case, whether nations are proliferators or not). Maintaining that threshold requires a clear and effectively communicated organizational philosophy, implemented with appropriate incentives, the topic of the next section.

Does anyone, however, know how close we are to the optimal forecasting frontier? How can we determine whether we are living in a Figure 11-1 or 11-3 world? Here awareness of and candor about ignorance are essential: No one has a strong scientific claim to know. Assessing where the prediction ceiling might be in political–military–economic domains of highest priority to the intelligence community is an inherently open-ended assignment (short of the absolute and extremely improbable ceiling defined by R-squared values of 1.0)—and the peer-reviewed literature, notwithstanding some heroic efforts (Armstrong, 2005; Bueno de Mesquita, 2009),

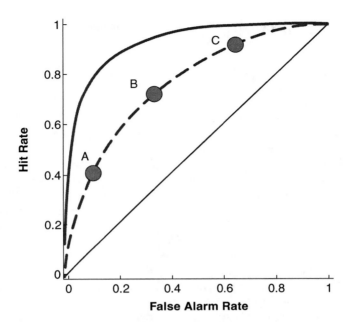

FIGURE 11-4 Possible hit-versus-false-alarm trade-offs in a world with a very high degree of predictability (see Figure 11-3).
SOURCE: Generalized from Green and Swets (1966).

has barely scratched the surface of this massive undertaking. This means that, although many may have opinions about the wisdom of exploring the feasibility and desirability of closer scrutiny of the accuracy of analytical judgment, no one knows how much—or little—we stand to learn from such studies. This sort of ignorance can be extraordinarily expensive even if we assume the possibility of only modest increments in performance—a reasonable assumption in light of evidence that just a single round of feedback can substantially improve calibration (in the long run, modest increments could save lives and money on a massive scale for military and economic decisions that hinge on accurate subjective-probability estimates [Lichtenstein and Fischhoff, 1980]).

This mix of deep ignorance with high stakes makes a strong case for conducting low-cost studies designed to explore the likely yield from developing sophisticated accuracy metrics and then institutionalizing level playing-field competitions that pit different analytical mindsets/methods against each other repeatedly across domains and time. Setting the scope for such competitions is beyond that of this chapter, but to ensure reasonably comprehensive coverage, these competitions should vary along at least five dimensions, each with the potential to change the rank ordering in predictive power of mindsets/methods:

1. **Skewed versus evenly balanced base rates.** Events can range from the extremely rare (genuine black swans) to the quite routine (things that happen between 30 and 70 percent of the time). Being right is easy when predicting events with extremely skewed base rates, such as whether Phoenix, Arizona, will have rain on a summer day: Just predict no rain all of the time.

2. **Stable versus unstable environments.** Incrementalist analytical approaches, which update their predictions in light of experience, should perform best in environments with well-defined, slowly changing base rates. Such approaches fail dramatically, however, in unstable environments when "base rates," whether defined in cross-sectional or longitudinal terms, lose meaning: In 1991, what was the base-rate probability of a multiethnic empire, such as the Union of Soviet Socialist Republics, disintegrating? In 2001, what was the probability of a fundamentalist Islamic terrorist group pulling off an unprecedented mass-casualty attack on American soil? Available evidence suggests that expert judgment and statistical models alike do a poor job at identifying punctuated-equilibrium points, at transitions between stable and unstable environments—and then back again (Armstrong, 2005; Taleb, 2007; Tetlock, 2005).

3. **Relative severity of asymmetry of Type 1 versus Type 2 errors.** Rare events—such as the 9/11 strikes or a terrorism-sponsoring state acquiring nuclear capabilities—are often those for which we have great (although not infinite) tolerance for false alarms—and little patience for misses, even if accompanied by the excuse—"well, 99 percent of our reports were right." If proficiency can be acquired in predicting such rare events, such proficiency quite possibly has been purchased at the expense of accuracy in analyzing more mundane events. To check this possibility—and the acceptability of the price—researchers need to conduct comparisons of forecasting accuracy for both low and high base-rate outcomes, and managers need to communicate to analysts the value-weighted accuracy functions that they want analysts to maximize (e.g., I am willing to tolerate dozens of false alarms to avoid a single miss for these rare events, but I attach equal importance to avoiding false alarms and misses for these more common events).

4. **Temporal distance.** Although imagining exceptions is possible— such as processes with lots of short-term volatility that settle down over time—analyses should be more accurate for events closer in

time. Indeed, as Kahneman and Klein (2009) suggest, beyond a certain point, long-range political forecasting may become impossible because of the potential for trivially small causes to have enormous and inherently unforeseeable effects. (They pose the following counterfactual thought experiment: How much different would 20th century history be if the three fertilized eggs—Stalin, Hitler, and Mao—had been female rather than male?).

5. **Different levels of analysis.** Performance may differ for micro and macro levels of analysis. Analysts are unlikely to be equally proficient in assessing the chances, say, of "the leadership of country X will make decision Y," "the European Commission passing resolution Z," "the voters of country Y electing candidate A," "financial markets dropping by XX percent," and "the alliance between countries C and D holding firm."

Such distinctions matter. Each of these factors may affect analysts' performance—as well as the power of accountability norms and incentives to improve performance. There is no guarantee that those methods or mindsets that have an edge in predicting lower base-rate, longer run shifts in macro processes, such as nation-state disintegration and the rise or fall of religious fundamentalism, will be the same as those that have an edge in predicting short-term tactical shifts in the behavior of individual leaders, such as shifts in trade negotiation stances. Indeed, considerable evidence shows there will be no all-round winner (Armstrong, 2005)—and it is prudent to think of prediction competitions as complex, Olympics-like tournaments, with numerous qualitative and quantitative subdivisions of events.

THE EVALUATIVE STANDARD

The signal detection theory framework, embodied in Figures 11-1 through 11-4, assumes that what matters, when holding analysts accountable, is their ability to reduce the risks of false negatives and false positives, weighted by the costs of each type of error. Such a long-term, large-sample perspective protects analysts who have had bad luck on an issue—and protects policy makers from analysts who get lucky. However, analysts' working conditions can impose other incentives, such as "pleasing one's immediate boss" or "policy maker (customer) satisfaction," which can translate into sycophantic attitudes shifting toward managers' and/or politicians' flawed world views (Prendergast, 1993). Conversely, efforts to insulate analysts from political pressures may make them less responsive to policy makers' legitimate and often urgent needs—in which case the value of their knowledge may be lost. Moreover, accuracy alone may have relatively little value unless the information arrived in a timely, comprehensible fashion, so that its full meaning can be extracted.

Agency theory (Baker et al., 1994; Gibbons, 1998; Sappington, 1991) provides an account of how to align the goals of principals and agents linked by contracts and organizational ties. Here, the principals are the policy maker clients and the agents are the analysts, respectively. We start with the following four simplifying assumptions that treat principals and agents as rational egoists:

1. Assume a linear production function: $y = a + e$, where y is all intelligence products that the principal (the U.S. government) values; a is the effort that agents (analysts) must expend to produce y (and which is under their control); and e is noise that causes production to rise or fall, in unpredictable ways, outside analysts' control. Assume that outcome accuracy is the analytical product that policy makers value most.

2. Assume a linear wage contract: $w = s + by$, where w is wages, s is a fixed salary, agreed upon before knowing how productive an agent will be, and b is the bonus rate (at which the bonus rises per unit increase in y). The slope, b, is zero for process-accountability systems in which analysts' wages are all salary, with no bonus for predictive accuracy.

3. Assume a linear pay-off function for agents: $w - c(a)$, the realized wage minus the disutility of doing the work. Analysts' intrinsic motivation makes the utility term, $-c(a)$, less negative.

4. Assume a linear pay-off function for the principal, $y - w$, or the realized output net of wages.

According to agency theory, the more random the environment, the more workers will prefer the security of wage compensation, which imposes no risk on the agent $(b = 0)$. Given the randomness that intelligence analysts see in their world, they should adopt a risk-averse position and prefer a guaranteed salary that comes with process compliance over the uncertain bonuses that come with big prediction successes. One might generalize the empirical claim by positing that the larger the value of e, the more employees will be willing to trade increments in b for higher salary guarantees. The preferred compensation scheme from the government's perspective, as e increases, however, is less clear. On the one hand, the government wants to reward its workforce for skill, not luck. On the other hand, as e rises, it might become increasingly attractive to transfer responsibility for mistakes to intelligence agencies, then down the chain of command to analysts.

Applying agency theory runs into the same problem as applying accountability schemes. There is no unbiased measure of y, the output of good analysis. The same problem arises in other domains, where employers struggle with finding performance goals and aligning accountability norms and incentives with them, even when the goals are well defined (Kerr, 1975). In principal–agent theory, this is called the "hidden action problem" of how to induce the agent to take a "correct" action that the principal wants, but cannot directly observe (Holmström and Milgrom, 1991). The technical solution is easy to prescribe, but hard to follow: Evaluate agents with metrics that most closely correlate with the observed but desired action. In the intelligence context, achieving this solution requires identifying process or outcome metrics that correlate with rigorous, open-minded analyst behavior that maximizes the chances of political assessments that are useful to analysts' clients.

Unfortunately, agency theory does not offer off-the-shelf solutions. Process metrics are closer to the behavior that employers hope to shape, but their application can rely on potentially faulty supervisor judgments (see this volume's Hastie, Chapter 8, and Kozlowski, Chapter 12), including cases where supervisors' preconceived theories of the outcome affect their judgments of the process. Process metrics can also lead to mechanical adherence to process over substance. Outcome-accountability metrics allow analysts the freedom to find the best ways to work through their problems, keeping them focused on the ultimate goal of their labors. They allow, even require, formal recognition of past difficulty and reporting thresholds, as conceptualized in signal detection theory. Of course, as the fine print in promotions for financial products reminds us, past performance is no guarantee of future performance. Moreover, cross-context consistency in the accuracy of political forecasts has been found to be low, although significantly above zero (e.g., Tetlock, 2005).

In brief, agency theory cannot conclusively answer the process–outcome question. But it does suggest the value of experimenting with process–outcome hybrids, and it does identify the institutional incentives that must be considered when conducting assessments of analysts' performance. Those incentives are expressed in organizations' formal rules, as in incentive schemes and in supervisors' rating procedures. If properly set, they express the signal-detection-theory formalisms in practical terms, recognizing both the limits to analysis and its goals. Agency theory provides guidance on how this can be done, as well as cautionary tales on how it can be corrupted, by those hoping to dodge accountability or to skew analyses.

CLOSING THOUGHTS

Accountability norms and incentives are essential to coping with the core challenges that all organizations confront: overcoming the constraints of bounded rationality (Kahneman, 2003; March and Simon, 1993) and parochial interests (Pfeffer and Sutton, 2006), and enabling more effective use of information and expertise than would have been possible if we had relied on randomly selected individual or small-group components of the organization. We can easily see why so many reach reflexively for accountability solutions when things go wrong. The "woulda-coulda-shoulda" counterfactuals are too tempting: "surely we could have avoided that stupid error if we had just tweaked these accountability guidelines in this direction and those other guidelines in this other direction."

But such reflexive fixes are as likely to make things worse as they are to make things better. As should now be obvious, we cannot deduce from first principles an optimal accountability system for monitoring intelligence analysts and incentivizing them to add "more value"—even if we possessed clear-cut consensus metrics of "value." But we can take the following three constructive steps, as described in the paragraphs below.

Step #1: Be More Explicit About Strengths and Weaknesses of Competing Models

First, we can be more explicit about the strengths and weaknesses of competing models for how to organize accountability systems, such as process versus outcome versus process-outcome hybrid forms of accountability. Here it is also worth keeping in mind the larger context of this debate, which recurs across diverse policy domains. Observers' preferences for process versus outcome accountability tend to be correlated with how much or how little observers trust the organization and the human beings staffing it. The greater the distrust, the greater the likelihood that observers will worry about how readily process-accountability systems can be corrupted or diluted and thus favor "more loophole-resistant" outcome-accountability systems (Tetlock, 2000). For instance, critics of corporate America tend not to trust corporate personnel managers to implement affirmative action programs rigorously and tend to suspect that companies' process-accountability systems for ensuring equal employment opportunity are mere Potemkin village facades of compliance. They demand numerical goals and statistical-outcome monitoring of treatment of minority groups (Tetlock and Vieider, 2011). Conversely, critics of public schools tend not to trust public school administrators and teachers to run a rigorous curriculum, and suspect that process-accountability systems for monitoring school performance are mere Potemkin village facades. They demand objective outcome testing data (Tetlock and Vieider, 2011). Organizations can sense when they are not trusted—and it is crucial to avoid the emergence of perceived correlations between recommendations of process accountability and "we trust you" and recommendations of outcome accountability and "we do not trust you." The intended message is: We just want to find out what works best.

Step #2: Be More Open About Our Knowledge of Optimal Forecasting

Second, we can be more open about our limited knowledge of where the optimal forecasting frontier lies for various categories of intelligence problems—and of what value we believe could be added by commitment to developing better accuracy measures and to conducting experiments on the power of various interventions to move analytic performance closer to the forecasting frontier. Here again, the context to the debate is larger. Some observers explicitly argue that much talk about intelligence reform is ill conceived and rests on occasionally ridiculous and unrealistic expectations about what reform can deliver. In this view, the major political challenge is not improving analyst performance; it is reducing expectations for that performance (Betts, 2009). Organizations do, of course, often welcome lowering of performance expectations—and harm can be done by demanding the impossible—but one would not be doing intelligence agencies a long-term favor by incorrectly concluding there is no room for improvement if subsequent events reveal improvement to have been possible. Imagine that 10 years from now, various private-sector and prediction-market initiatives start reliably outperforming intelligence agencies in certain domains—and, during his or her daily intelligence briefing, the President turns to the Director of National Intelligence and says: "I can get a clearer sense of the odds of this policy working by averaging public sources of probability estimates."

Step #3: Preempt Politicization and Clarify Arguments

Third, we can do a better job of preempting politicization and clarifying where the factual-scientific arguments over enhancing intelligence analysis should end and the value-driven political ones should begin. Once the scientific community has enumerated the organizational design tradeoffs and key uncertainties, and has compared the opportunity costs of inaction with the tangible costs of the needed research, policy makers must set value priorities, asking: Do the net potential benefits of undertaking the embedded-organizational experiments and validity research sketched here outweigh the net observed benefits of not rocking the bureaucratic boat and continuing to insulate current policies and procedures from scientific scrutiny and challenge?

REFERENCES

Alesina, A., and L. H. Summers. 1993. Central bank independence and macroeconomic performance: Some comparative evidence. *Journal of Money, Credit, and Banking* 25(2):151–162.

Armstrong, J. S. 2005. *Principles of forecasting.* Boston, MA: Kluwer Academic.

Baker, G., R. Gibbons, and K. J. Murphy. 1994. Subjective performance measures in optimal incentives contracts. *Quarterly Journal of Economics* 109(4):1,125–1,156.

Barber, B. M., C. Heath, and T. Odean. 2003. Good reasons sell: Reason-based choice among group and individual investors in the stock market. *Management Science* 49(12):1,636–1,652.

Bertrand, M., and S. Mullainathan. 2001. Are CEOs rewarded for luck? The ones without principals are. *Quarterly Journal of Economics* 116(3):901–932.

Betts, R. 2009. *Enemies of intelligence: Knowledge and power in American national security.* New York: Columbia University Press.

Bikhchandani, S., D. Hirshleifer, and I. Welch. 1998. Learning from the behavior of others: Conformity, fads, and informational cascades. *Journal of Economic Perspectives* 12(3):151–170.

Bueno de Mesquita, B. 2009. *The predictioneer's game: Using the logic of brazen self-interest to see and shape the future.* New York: Random House.

Chubb, J., and T. Moe. 1990. *Politics, markets and schools.* Washington, DC: Brookings Institution Press.

Curley, S. P., J. F. Yates, and R. A. Abrams. 1986. Psychological sources of ambiguity avoidance. *Organizational Behavior and Human Decision Processes* 38:230–256.

Director of National Intelligence. 2007. Intelligence Community Directive (ICD) 203: Analytic standards. June 21. Available: http://www.dni.gov/electronic_reading_room/ICD_203.pdf [accessed May 2010].

Edelman, L. B. 1992. Legal ambiguity and symbolic structures: Organizational mediation of civil rights law. *American Journal of Sociology* 97:1531–1576.

Erev, I., T. Wallsten, and D. Budescu. 1994. Simultaneous over-and-under confidence: The role of error in judgment processes. *Psychological Review* 10:519–527.

Fischer, S. 1995. Central-Bank independence revisited. *American Economic Review* 85(2):201–206.

Gibbons, R. 1998. Incentives in organizations. *Journal of Economic Perspectives* 12(4):115–132.

Green, D. M., and J. Swets. 1966. *Signal detection theory and psychophysics.* New York: Wiley.

Hagafors, R., and B. Bremer. 1983. Does having to justify one's judgments change the nature of the judgment process? *Organizational Behavior and Human Performance* 31(2):223–232.

Holmström, B., and P. Milgrom. 1991. Multitask principal–agent analyses: Incentive contracts, asset ownership, and job design. *Journal of Law, Economics, and Organization* 7:24–52.

Janis, I. L. 1972. *Victims of groupthink: A psychological study of foreign-policy decisions and fiascos.* Boston, MA: Houghton Mifflin.

Kahneman, D. 2003. A perspective on judgment and choice: Mapping bounded rationality. *American Psychologist* 58:697–720.

Kahneman, D., and G. Klein. 2009. Conditions for intuitive expertise: A failure to disagree. *American Psychologist* 64(6):515–526.

Kalev, A., F. Dobbin, and E. Kelly. 2006. Best practices or best guesses? Assessing the efficacy of corporate affirmative action and diversity practices. *American Sociological Review* 71:589–617.

Kerr, S. 1975. On the folly of rewarding A, while hoping for B. *Academy of Management Journal* 18(4):769–783. Republished in 1995 in *Academy of Management Executive* 9(1):7–14.

Kono, D. Y. 2006. Optimal obfuscation: Democracy and trade policy transparency. *American Political Science Review* 100(3):369–384.

Kruglanski, A. W., and T. Freund. 1983. The freezing and unfreezing of lay-inferences: Effects on impressional primacy, ethnic stereotyping, and numerical anchoring. *Journal of Experimental Social Psychology* 19(5):448–468.

Lazear, E. P. 1989. Pay equality and industrial politics. *Journal of Political Economy* 97(3):561–580.

Lerner, J., and P. E. Tetlock. 1999. Accounting for the effects of accountability. *Psychological Bulletin* 125:255–275.

Lichtenstein, S., and B. Fischhoff. 1977. Do those who know more also know more about how much they know? The calibration of probability judgments. *Organizational Behavior and Human Performance* 20:159–183.

Lichtenstein, S., and B. Fischhoff. 1980. Training for calibration. *Organizational Behavior and Human Performance* 26:149–171.

March, J. G., and J. P. Olsen. 1989. *Rediscovering institutions: The organizational basis of politics*. Stanford, CA: Stanford University Press.

March, J. G., and H. A. Simon. 1993. *Organizations*. Cambridge, MA: Blackwell.

Meyer, J. W., and B. Rowan. 1977. Institutionalized organizations: Formal structure as myth and ceremony. *American Journal of Sociology* 83:340–363.

Moore, D. A., and P. Healy. 2008. The trouble with overconfidence. *Psychological Review* 11:502–517.

Moore, D., P. E. Tetlock, L. Tanlu, and M. Bazerman. 2006. Conflicts of interest and the case of auditor independence: Moral seduction and strategic issue cycling. *Academy of Management Review* 31:10–29.

Murphy, R. 1994. The effects of task characteristics on covariation assessment: The impact of accountability and judgment frame. *Organizational Behavior and Human Decision Processes* 60(1):139–155.

Pfeffer, J., and R. Sutton. 2006. *Hard facts, dangerous half-truths and total nonsense*. Cambridge, MA: Harvard Business School Press.

Posner, R. A. 2005a. *Preventing surprise attacks: Intelligence reform in the wake of 9/11*. Lanham, MD: Rowman and Littlefield.

Posner, R. A. 2005b. *Remaking domestic intelligence*. Stanford, CA: Hoover Institution Press.

Prendergast, C. 1993. A theory of "yes men." *American Economic Review* 83(4):757–770.

Sappington, D. E. M. 1991. Incentives in principal–agent relationships. *Journal of Economic Perspectives* 5(2):45–66.

Scharfstein, D. S., and J. C. Stein. 1990. Herd behavior and investment. *American Economic Review* 80(3):465–479.

Schlenker, B. R. 1982. Translating actions into attitude: An identity-analytic approach to the explanation of social conduct. In L. Berkowitz, ed., *Advances in Experimental Social Psychology*, vol. 15 (pp. 194–208). New York: Academic Press.

Scott, M., and S. Lyman. 1968. Accounts. *American Sociological Review* 33:46–62.

Sedikides, C., K. C. Herbst, D. P. Hardin, and G. J. Dardis. 2002. Accountability as a deterrent to self-enhancement: The search for mechanisms. *Journal of Personality and Social Psychology* 83(3):592–605.

Siegel-Jacobs, K., and J. F. Yates. 1996. Effect of procedural accountability and outcome accountability on judgment quality. *Organizational Behavior and Human Decision Processes* 65(1):1–17.

Simonson, I., and B. M. Staw. 1992. Deescalation strategies: A comparison of techniques for reducing commitment to losing courses of action. *Journal of Applied Psychology* 77(4):419–426.

Suskind, R. 2006. *The one-percent doctrine: Deep inside America's pursuit of its enemies since 9/11.* New York: Simon and Schuster.

Taleb, N. N. 2007. *The black swan: The impact of the highly improbable.* New York: Random House.

Tetlock, P. E. 1985. Accountability: The neglected social context of judgment and choice. In B. Staw and L. Cummings, eds., *Research in organizational behavior,* vol. 7 (pp. 297–332). Greenwich, CT: JAI Press. Reprinted in L. Cummings and B. Staw, eds., *Research in organizational behavior: Judgment processes.* Greenwich, CT: JAI Press.

Tetlock, P. E. 1992. The impact of accountability on judgment and choice: Toward a social contingency model. In M. Zanna, ed., *Advances in experimental social psychology,* vol. 25 (pp. 331-376). New York: Academic Press.

Tetlock, P. E. 2000. Cognitive biases and organizational correctives: Do both disease and cure depend on the ideological beholder? *Administrative Science Quarterly* 45:293–326.

Tetlock, P. E. 2005. *Expert political judgment: How good is it? How can we know?* Princeton, NJ: Princeton University Press.

Tetlock, P. E., and R. Boettger. 1989. Accountability: A social magnifier of the dilution effect. *Journal of Personality and Social Psychology* 57(3):388–398.

Tetlock, P. E., and R. Boettger. 1994. Accountability amplifies the status quo effect when change creates victims. *Journal of Behavioral Decision Making* 7:1–23.

Tetlock, P. E., and L. I. Kim. 1987. Accountability and judgment processes in a personality prediction task. *Journal of Personality and Social Psychology* 52(4):700–709.

Tetlock, P. E., and G. Mitchell. 2009. Implicit bias and accountability systems: What must organizations do to prevent discrimination? In B. M. Staw and A. Brief, eds., *Research in organizational behavior,* vol. 29 (pp. 3–38). New York: Elsevier.

Tetlock, P. E., and F. Vieider, 2011. *Accountability, agency, and ideology: Exploring managerial preferences for process versus outcome accountability.* Unpublished manuscript, Wharton School of Business, University of Pennsylvania.

Wilson, J. Q. 1989. *Bureaucracy: What government agencies do and why.* New York: Basic Books.

12

Workforce Effectiveness:
Acquiring Human Resources and
Developing Human Capital

Steve W. J. Kozlowski

Among the many important ingredients in the complex alchemy of organizational effectiveness is a capable, highly motivated, and adaptive workforce. To accomplish mission objectives, organizations must navigate the complexities, uncertainties, and dynamics of their external environments, outperforming and counteracting competitors and adversaries, by being better, faster, or more innovative. They must build a uniquely capable workforce, then leverage its special talents. This is accomplished by developing a strategy to meet mission objectives, and aligning the internal organization with respect to leadership, administrative structure, work processes (i.e., technology), and human resource management (HRM) practices to support strategy execution. In that sense, acquiring and building an effective workforce is predicated on providing the organization with unique capabilities, enabling it to meet strategic objectives, and simultaneously making it difficult for adversaries to be successful.

The purpose of this chapter is to describe behavioral science theory and research findings from organizational psychology and human resource management that underpin the *acquisition of human resources* and *development of human capital*, both of which are essential for creating a capable, innovative, and adaptive workforce. I will begin by providing a brief overview of the shifting strategic landscape faced by the intelligence community (IC) and implications of this shift for IC strategy and internal alignment. I will then discuss strategic HRM, which describes how the workforce can be aligned to help accomplish IC strategic objectives, and I will present a strategic HRM architecture for acquiring human resources and developing human capital. I will then describe in detail specific clusters of HRM practices that implement strategic HRM: recruitment and selection, training and development, performance management and incentives, and work design and teamwork. Finally, I will close with research issues relevant to sustaining employee development, collaboration, and organizational learning for the long haul.

STRATEGIC ALIGNMENT

The IC as an Organization

Some readers are likely to assert that the IC is not like other organizations and that behavioral science knowledge about the effective functioning of business organizations is not relevant to the IC because it is so uniquely different. I will not make the claim that the IC is exactly like other organizations in all ways, but I will claim that it is quite similar to nearly any other organization in many important ways. With respect to differences, Zegart (this volume, Chapter 13) identifies some key factors that make public institutions and the IC less sensitive to the adaptive pressures that commercial firms face. That is, the benefits of competition for adaptation are limited because survival within the IC is less of an issue; IC agencies do not compete directly. Rather, they are aligned to serve unique customer needs (Fingar, this volume, Chapter 1) and, thus, the IC is arrayed more as a loosely coupled divisional structure than a set of centralized units competing in the same environmental niche (Galbraith, 1972). In that sense, the basic mechanisms of organizational alignment—external and internal—apply equally well or well enough to the IC so that theory and research findings from organizational science are relevant. This chapter is intended to summarize lessons from research on organizational effectiveness that can be applied to improving workforce development and organizational learning in the IC.

The Strategic Environment and IC Strategy

As described by Fingar (this volume, Chapter 1), the strategic environment of the IC has shifted dramatically in the post-Soviet Union era. Following the end of World War II, the IC had been arrayed to assess and counteract a large, militarily capable, state actor and its many coaligned proxy states. Although many uncertainties were inherent in the strategic balance between the United States and the Union of Soviet Socialist Republics, there was also a high degree of stability in the nature of the relationship, the intentions of key actors, and their likely means of action.

Stability calls for an organizational strategy that exploits what is known, with internal alignments relying on tight structural control.

The previous strategic environment of the IC has shifted dramatically. As described by the National Intelligence Strategy (NIS):

> The United States faces a complex and rapidly changing national security environment in which nation-states, highly capable non-state actors, and other transnational forces will continue to compete with and challenge U.S. national interests. Adversaries are likely to use asymmetric means and technology (either new or applied in a novel way) to counter U.S. interests at home and abroad. (Office of the Director of National Intelligence, 2009a, p. 3)

Environmental turbulence calls for an organizational strategy based on exploration and innovation. This strategic shift requires an internal alignment that enables unique capabilities to be acquired, developed, and leveraged to promote flexibility, agility, and adaptability. Indeed, the NIS specifies two overarching "Enterprise Goals" focused on internal alignment that are designed to help it accomplish its "Mission Goals" (i.e., external alignment) (Office of the Director of National Intelligence, 2009a, p. 9):

- Deliver balanced and improving capabilities that leverage the diversity of the community's unique competencies and evolve to support new missions and operating concepts.
- Operate as a single integrated team, employing collaborative teams that leverage the full range of IC capabilities to meet the requirements of our users, from the President to deployed military units.

With the NIS as a point of departure, I now turn to how the behavioral science literature on strategic HRM and HRM practices can be instrumental in achieving these IC strategic goals.

Implications for Strategic Alignment

The dominant conceptualization of organizations is that they are systems of interacting elements at multiple levels of analysis (i.e., individuals, teams, subsystems, and the organization); open to environmental inputs (e.g., resources and stakeholders; competitors and adversaries); and purposeful as they seek to accomplish goals, maintain balance between external environmental demands and internal structure, and adapt to their environmental niche (Katz and Kahn, 1966).

Macro-Level: The Environment–Organization Interface

Organizations seek alignment with their external *environment*. They pursue a *mission* that exploits an environmental niche—to accomplish goals by providing products or services that are supported by customers and stakeholders. Competitors seek to exploit the same niche and to gain advantage. For the IC, "competitors" are adversaries to U.S. national interests in the form of nations, nonstate actors, and their intelligence operations. Thus, senior leaders craft a *strategy* to accomplish mission goals, with the intent of being superior relative to competitors. In general, strategy is designed to exploit environmental stability through control and efficiency (defender), create environmental turbulence through flexibility and innovation (prospector), or achieve a balance of both strategic orientations (analyzer) (Miles et al., 1978).

From a contingency perspective, different strategic orientations need different internal alignments. A defender strategy requires routine, well-known core technologies (i.e., product or service delivery systems) and tight bureaucratic structures to achieve control and efficiency. A prospector strategy needs reconfigurable technologies and a discretionary, organic structure to achieve flexibility and innovation. An analyzer strategy needs to manage and balance both forms of technology-structure fit. Looking at the IC with limited insight from the outside, the IC strategy appears to conform roughly to the analyzer archetype, although the exact balance of exploitation and exploration is difficult to characterize.

The reason this macro perspective is important is because strategic alignment has implications for HRM, meaning the types of human resources the firm seeks—the knowledge, skills, abilities, and other characteristics, or KSAOs (e.g., personality, interests, and values), of its people—and the management approach used to lead, develop, and motivate the workforce (Miles et al., 1978). In general, a defender strategy uses an authoritative management approach (i.e., directive), an analyzer strategy is more participative (i.e., seeks employee input, but maintains control), and a prospector strategy encourages employee empowerment (i.e., shifts discretion to employees and teams to fuel innovation). This is an early conceptualization and, as I will discuss later, it is evolving. However, it illustrates the important connections among organizational strategy, internal alignment, and the link to HRM.

Meso-Level: Workgroups and Teams

The macro-level is important for shaping the internal organization—that is, the way the workforce experiences the implications of technology systems, administrative structures, and leadership approaches. However, employees do not experience such factors directly. Rather, it is the direct experience with their job, their connection to coworkers in a workflow (which may be tightly or only loosely coupled) and in social groups, and the relationship enacted with their leader that characterizes their primary experience of the organization. Thus, although the macro context is important for constraining and shaping the nature of the proximal context, the meso-level is what employees experience directly (Indik, 1968). The work unit, the workgroup, or the team is where people "live" in the organization. The meso-level sits at the juncture between the organization as a broad entity and the individual in isolation. It is "where the rubber meets the road" in organizational behavior (Kozlowski and Bell, 2003; Kozlowski and Ilgen, 2006).

In addition, over the past two decades, organizations worldwide have shifted the structure of work from individual jobs in a functional structure to team-based structures (Devine et al., 1999). This shift has many drivers, including increased problem complexity, demands for rapid decision making, and the need for adaptability in turbulent environments. The advantages of work teams is that they can bring diverse and specific expertise to bear on problems; team members can back each other up, catch errors, and correct them; and they can flexibly adapt to the emergent needs of the problem situation (Kozlowski et al., 1999; Marks et al., 2001; LePine et al., 2008). Teams enable collective, "macro cognition" to be applied to high-stakes, challenging, and critical problems (Fiore et al., 2010).

Micro-Level: Individuals and Their Capabilities

At the micro-level, we focus on the capabilities that individuals bring to the organization, including their knowledge, skills, abilities, and other characteristics (Ployhart, 2011). A simplistic but useful heuristic is to view human performance as resulting from a combination of ability and motivation (Campbell et al., 1993). KSAOs encompass both ability ("can do") and motivational ("will do") factors (Cronbach, 1970). Motivation is also shaped by meso-level factors (e.g., effective leadership, supportive peers, engaging work). Thus, at a fundamental level, the organizational design target is one of achieving external and internal alignment. Workforce effectiveness is a product of selecting the right mix of individuals, based on their KSAOs, to create a pool of human resources consistent with the organization's strategic alignment, then to invest in human capital by developing and motivating the workforce so the organization can accomplish its mission more effectively than its competitors.

STRATEGIC HUMAN RESOURCE MANAGEMENT

Systemic Fit Perspective

Until the early 1980s, HRM was regarded as an important functional area in organizations, but not as a critical aspect of organizational strategy. The "strategic alignment and adaptation" perspective advanced by Miles et al. (1978), which I highlighted previously, began to bring HRM practices more directly into the strategic equation, with HRM as an integral support for organizational strategy. Snow and Snell (2011) characterize this early view as a *systemic fit perspective* that focused on aligning HRM policies and practices with strategy. Strategy was a deliberate effort to maintain organizational fit with a dynamic external environment and to align internal systems, including HRM, to execute the strategy well. In a systemic fit perspective, HRM is strategy driven. This orientation is a basic foundation for effective HRM design.

Strategic Capabilities Perspective

More recent work has begun to explore how HRM can create sustained competitive advantage by building organizational capabilities. The *strategic capabilities perspective* is future oriented and focused on fostering learning, motivation, and innovation. This shifts the view from one of just having the right pool of *human resources* to one of also being able to build *human capital* by investing in the development of the workforce to create unique capabilities. Key talent pools are identified and targeted for specific human capital investments (Boudreau and Ramstad, 2005, 2007). Human capital propels strategy formulation (Snow and Snell, 2011); it allows novel strategies to be developed based on the unique capabilities of organizational members. If such capabilities are difficult to imitate and hard for adversaries to replicate, and if they cannot be substituted by other resources, they provide a foundation for long-term competitive advantage (Barney and Wright, 1998; Ployhart, 2006, 2011). With respect to the IC, the lesson is to recruit and select the right people to acquire a pool of high-quality human resources and then to develop, motivate, and integrate that talent to create unique capabilities for the IC.

IC Workforce Strategy

Previously I described the strategic environment of the IC and highlighted its two internally oriented enterprise goals documented in the NIS (Office of the Director of National Intelligence, 2009a, Sec 1:16). Those two enterprise goals are intended to be implemented by six more specific "enterprise objectives (EOs)." *EO 6: Develop the Workforce* is directly relevant to the current discussion. Actions specified to meet EO 6 include (1) build a diverse and balanced workforce, (2) enhance professional development, (3) cultivate relevant expertise, (4) support an entrepreneurial ethos, (5) deploy integrated agile teams, and (6) build a culture of leadership excellence. The material that follows describes research-based applications that can enable this HRM strategy for the IC workforce to be accomplished.

AN ARCHITECTURE FOR STRATEGIC HUMAN RESOURCE MANAGEMENT

Individual Differences

People differ from one another on a wide range of characteristics. Individuals differ on demographic features (e.g., age, sex, race), abilities (e.g., cognitive, physical), and preferences (e.g., personality, values). The focus from a human resources perspective is on differences in KSAOs (e.g., personality, interests, and values) that are linked to differences in, for example, educational attainment, vocational preferences, job performance, and career success. At the most basic level, KSAOs are individual differences that contribute to job performance. At the aggregate level, the collection of KSAOs across the workforce comprises an organization's human resource pool.

Stable and Malleable Individual Differences

KSAOs can be divided into those that are stable and those that are malleable. Stable KSAOs include factors such as cognitive ability, personality, and values that are relatively enduring across the span of adult development. Malleable KSAOs include factors such as domain knowledge, job-specific skills, and motivational characteristics. For example, cognitive ability, which is a generalized predictor of learning and performance effectiveness and has a high genetic component, is very stable across a person's career (Lyons et al., 2009), whereas domain knowledge and job-specific skills accrue over time through experience and training. Over lengthy periods of experience, very high levels of domain-specific expertise develop (Charness and Tuffiash, 2008). Importantly, stable KSAOs influence malleable KSAOs. In particular, individuals with higher cognitive ability gain more from experience than those with less cognitive ability. For example, researchers have shown that individuals with higher cognitive ability have steeper trajectories of career success, as indexed by salary growth, relative to those with lower cognitive ability. Factors that accounted for their increasingly greater success over time include: they sought more training, gravitated to more complex jobs, and pursued higher status occupations (Judge et al., 2010). They invested in their human resource endowment, gained human capital, and were able to leverage it at an *increasing rate* over time.

Human Resources and Human Capital

This distinction between stable and malleable KSAOs is important because it underpins a way of conceptualizing the distinction and relationship between human resources and human capital. This conceptual distinction links back to the systemic fit and strategic capabilities perspectives and, thus, sketches a basic architecture for the mechanisms of achieving strategic HRM. This architecture is illustrated in Figure 12-1.

Stable KSAOs cannot be changed; they are human resource endowments. They are generic in that they are applicable to a wide range of jobs, situations, and organizations. In general, we know that individuals who have high cognitive ability (Schmidt and Hunter, 2004) and a conscientious personality profile (Barrick and Mount, 1991) perform at a higher level across a wide range of jobs. In that sense, those endowments are valuable in the broad labor market and allow individuals who possess them to seek the highest pay-off in organizational fit. Thus, organizations have to invest to recruit and select the best candidates with high-valued KSAOs. Those investments yield an aggregate pool of human resources. From a systemic fit perspective, strategic HRM should target selection of individuals with KSAO profiles that are consistent with the existing organizational strategy. The value of the resource pool for the organization is that positive effects manifest quickly in the form of performance effectiveness. Moreover, from a strategic capabilities perspective, efforts to maximize the quality of the resource pool have the potential, with additional investments, to develop human capital.

Malleable KSAOs are targets for human capital investments. Although they are influenced by stable individual differences, their value to the organization can be enhanced by targeted development. From an organizational perspective, the more job specific, unique, difficult to replicate, and nonsubstitutable the knowledge and skills are that are developed, the better the organization fares (Barney and Wright, 1998; Ployhart, 2006, 2011). Why? Because investments in general knowledge or skills are valuable in the broader labor market, whereas specific skills are not as easily marketed by the individual, poached by other organizations, or imitated. Thus, for example, investing in job-specific training makes more sense for an organization because it can be applied immediately and is difficult for an individual to market elsewhere, whereas an investment in, say, an advanced

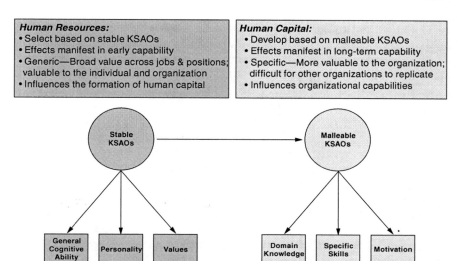

FIGURE 12-1 Knowledge, skills, abilities, and other characteristics (KSAOs): Human resources and human capital.

degree is valuable in many different jobs and organizations.[1] More importantly, from a strategic capabilities perspective, the goal is to create human capital that is valuable, unique, and difficult for other organizations to replicate and that can be leveraged to create competitive advantage. With respect to the IC, application of this approach would create unique analytic capabilities, and mechanisms to link analysts collaboratively, to gain advantage over adversaries.

HUMAN RESOURCE MANAGEMENT PRACTICES

Translating Strategic HRM into Action

Human resources and human capital provide a basis for understanding the differences in resource endowments and capabilities that in aggregate distinguish organizations competing in a particular environmental niche. At the firm level, one can liken them to aggregate individual abilities or "can do" characteristics. They are necessary, but not sufficient. What is also needed is motivation among employees to engage in human capital

---

[1]This is not to say that encouraging advanced education is always poor HRM policy. I merely illustrate that human capital investment implications must be carefully considered with respect to strategic HRM goals. Under the right set of assumptions and constraints, a policy supporting advanced degrees may yield strategic advantage.

development and to collectively apply their KSAOs for the benefit of the organization. HRM practices are designed to enhance an organizational workforce's ability to perform and/or their motivation to do so (Becker and Huselid, 1998; Delery and Shaw, 2001). Many of these practices—such as recruitment, selection, training, performance management, compensation, and work design—have been used for quite some time, but only within the past few decades have researchers engaged in concerted efforts to empirically link HRM practices to indicators of organizational effectiveness. This link provides the means to implement the strategic HRM architecture.

Early research in this area examined individual practices. For example, Holzer (1987) showed that investments in more extensive recruiting efforts were associated with organizational productivity. Terpstra and Rozell (1993) reported positive relations between specific selection practices and organizational performance. McEvoy and Cascio (1985) showed that job enrichment reduced employee turnover (which is associated with organizational productivity) (Brown and Medoff, 1978), and Gerhart and Milkovich (1992) reported that incentive compensation plans were positively related to productivity. An early meta-analysis reported that training, goal setting, and sociotechnical systems were positively associated with productivity (Guzzo et al., 1985). This early research provided recognition that HRM practices were linked to firm effectiveness. These HRM practices were labeled high-performance work practices by the U.S. Department of Labor (1993), and they use a variety of other names, including high-involvement, high-commitment, and high-performance work systems.

The next generation of research advances has been aimed at resolving two primary limitations. First, the early research efforts tended to examine single practices, whereas strategic HRM theory suggests that "bundles" of aligned practices (MacDuffie, 1995) or particular combinations of practices (Youndt et al., 1996) work in synergistic fashion. Second, the methodology of the early research was less than ideal because the designs were typically cross-sectional (i.e., all data collected simultaneously), thereby yielding causal ambiguity, and the data were often self-reported (i.e., a manager was the sole data source), yielding concerns about response biases that could artificially inflate the observed relations (Huselid, 1995). Subsequent research has sought to address these limitations, solidify the linkage between HRM practices and organizational effectiveness (Delery and Doty, 1996; Hatch and Dyer, 2004; Huselid, 1995; Koch and McGrath, 1996; MacDuffie, 1995), and resolve causal ambiguity (Ployhart et al., 2009; Wright et al., 2005; Van Iddekinge et al., 2009). For example, Delery and Doty (1996) showed that HRM practices were associated with profits for a sample of banks, and MacDuffie (1995) found positive associations between HRM practice bundles with productivity and quality in a sample of automobile assembly plants. Although research by Wright et al. (2005) concluded that a causal linkage between HRM practices and organizational effectiveness is ambiguous, Van Iddekinge et al. (2009) showed that the implementation of selection and training at the unit level was positively predictive of *future* unit performance (see also Ployhart et al., 2009).

In the ensuing years, research has developed and several qualitative reviews have concluded that HRM practices positively influence organizational performance (Becker and Huselid, 1998; Lepak et al., 2006; Wright and Boswell, 2002). More recently, the empirical foundation became sufficient to enable a meta-analytic review of the relationship between HRM practices and organizational effectiveness.[2] Combs et al. (2006) cumulated findings from 92 studies that examined HRM practice relationships across 19,319 organizations. They reported a corrected overall correlation between HRM practices and indicators of organizational effectiveness of .20, which was significantly stronger for bundles ($r_c = .28$) than for individual practices ($r_c = .14$). Although a relationship of .20 might not appear to be very large, it is statistically and practically significant; increasing HRM practices by one standard deviation increases firm performance by 20 percent of a standard deviation. As the authors note, "In this sample, a one standard deviation increase in the use of HRM practices translates, on average, to a 4.6 percentage-point increase in gross return on assets from 5.1 to 9.7 and a 4.4 percentage-point decrease in turnover from 18.4 to 14 percent. Thus, HRM practices' impact on organizational performance is not only statistically significant, but managerially relevant" (Combs et al., 2006, p. 518). Moreover, a recent meta-analysis of 66 primary studies (68 samples with 12,163 observations) found that the positive relationship between human capital and firm performance was significantly stronger ($r_c = .14$) when the measures of human capital were form specific rather than general (Crook et al., in press), a key point made in this chapter. Although there is a need to improve methodological rigor and to refine understanding of the mechanisms that account for these relations (Becker and Huselid, 2006; Ostroff and Bowen, 2000), there is a sufficient basis to conclude that HRM practices are a viable means to implement strategic HRM, develop the workforce, and enhance organizational effectiveness.

---

[2]A meta-analysis quantitatively cumulates indicators of relationship or effect size, correcting for statistical artifacts (e.g., measurement error), and reporting an estimate of the "true" magnitude of the relationship in question.

TABLE 12-1 Core Human Resource Management Practices for
Developing an Effective Workforce

Human Resources		Human Capital Investments	
Acquire stable KSAOs	Build malleable KSAOs	Motivate the workforce	Foster organizational learning
↓	↓	↓	↓
Recruitment and selection	Training and development	Performance management and compensation	Work design and teamwork

Developing an Effective Workforce

Although many different HRM practices are used, I will provide a discussion focused on four clusters of core practices (Table 12-1): (1) *recruitment and selection*, (2) *training and development*, (3) *performance management and incentives*, and (4) *work design and teamwork*. I focus on these four core activities because they are consistent with the strategic HRM architecture illustrated in Figure 12-1 and because they are based on well-developed methodologies and practices and/or they have an extensive literature and research foundation. Each separate practice is represented by a relatively independent literature and area of practice. However, there are conceptual *and* operational overlaps, so I have categorized the practices into coherent clusters of related activities. I have also ordered them in logical progression. The purpose is to provide a concise overview of key issues and the approach for each cluster.

Recruitment and Selection

Recruitment and selection practices are critical to the quality of an organization's human resource pool. Recruitment is directed toward identifying, reaching, and attracting job applicants (Barber, 1998). Selection is the use of psychometric assessment techniques to measure applicant KSAOs and then to select those applicants with the highest predicted job performance.[3] Recruitment and selection must work in concert. Extensive recruiting enhances the degree to which an organization can exercise selec-

---

[3]Comprehensive reviews of the recruitment literature can be found in Rynes and Cable (2003) and Yu and Cable (2011); a comprehensive review of the selection literature can be found in Ployhart (2011). For selection, an analysis of jobs and their task requirements is used to identify KSAOs necessary to perform those jobs to a given performance criterion. Measures (i.e., tests and other assessments) of the relevant KSAOs are then used to select individuals with desired KSAO profiles, with the intent of improving aggregate work performance. At the aggregate level, the collection of KSAOs across the workforce is an organization's resource pool.

tivity during hiring. The larger and more diverse the applicant pool is on KSAOs, the more that can be gained via scientific selection (Cascio, 2000). For example, IC-wide recruitment events (job fairs) with multiple agencies represented likely allow each agency access to a wider pool of candidates than they could attract on their own; however, the selection process also becomes more critical because more general candidates may attend who do not possess the specific qualities needed by a particular agency. Recruitment and selection are costly activities, but the costs have to be viewed in perspective. If the organization fails to recruit a sufficiently large and diverse pool of applicants, then even the best selection practices cannot be optimally effective. Similarly, if recruitment yields a large and diverse applicant pool, but the organization fails to use appropriate selection practices, it cannot gain maximum utility from its hiring decisions. Both aspects have to work in concert.

A considerable amount of recruitment research has focused on recruiter characteristics, recruitment sources, and recruitment policies and practices (Rynes, 1991). Research on recruiter characteristics suggests that recruiters who are job incumbents (relative to personnel recruiters), personable, and knowledgeable about the job have more positive effects on job choice, although the effects are quite small (Rynes, 1991). Thus, although involving current analysts in the recruitment and hiring process may have some benefit, this research suggests it is unnecessary for successful hiring as long as recruitment officers have a full understanding of the relevant KSAOs necessary for the position. With respect to sources, research suggests that recruitment via employee referral has more positive effects on job outcomes (e.g., low turnover, low absenteeism, positive job attitudes) relative to those recruited directly or through advertisements or employment agencies (Yu and Cable, 2011). Research on recruitment practices has focused largely on the provision of realistic information through actual job previews intended to sensitize applicants at risk for turnover to self-select out of the hiring process. Although there is some support for realistic job previews in the literature, meta-analytic evidence indicates that the effects are weak (Phillips, 1998). Thus, the IC should not be overly concerned about the challenges of providing unclassified realistic job previews for a classified job because they have a limited effect on turnover. However, more recent research on recruiting has shifted toward the "signaling" that the recruitment process conveys to applicants about the organization, its culture, and the "fit" for the applicant. This work indicates that organizational image and reputation are more important factors than job characteristics such as pay and location and thus are key factors for attracting high-quality applicants (Cable and Turban, 2001; Cable and Yu, 2006; Yu and Cable, 2011). Therefore, the IC should be concerned with the image it presents to potential applicants through signals such as inefficient security clearance processing.

Scientific selection is a well-developed and proven methodology and set of practices that have been in general, though by no means universal, use for a century. The essence of selection is to assess applicant KSAOs that are predictive of future job performance and then to hire the best applicants. The development of a selection system has several key steps. Job analysis is the bedrock of selection system development. It is a systematic process to identify the important and critical task behaviors that comprise a job and the underlying KSAOs required for effective job performance. Many techniques can be used to generate job analysis data, which typically involves observing, interviewing, or surveying subject matter experts or job incumbents. Task-oriented job analyses focus on compiling task behaviors and then inferring underlying KSAOs. Worker-oriented job analyses assess KSAOs directly. Other approaches target job competencies—clusters of capabilities—that are at a higher level of specificity. Although competencies are easier to communicate to lay audiences, their link to underlying KSAOs is often imprecise, making them more difficult to assess with rigor. For example, the IC has developed a set of qualification and performance standards (i.e., competencies) for four hierarchical levels of analyst position (Homeyer and Madsen, 2009), although the precise KSAOs linked to these competencies that would guide selection design are not specified.

Job analysis provides the data needed to define the criterion—job performance that is to be predicted—and to identify potential predictor constructs and measures of the KSAOs underlying job performance. A validation study is then conducted whereby job applicants (predictive validity design) or job incumbents (concurrent validity design) are assessed on the predictor measures, and then job performance data are correlated with the predictors. Significant correlations provide evidence for validity, and the validation process provides data that can be used to develop a selection decision system to be applied to future applicants.

Predictor domains include general cognitive ability (GCA), psychomotor and physical abilities, job- or domain-relevant knowledge, personality, and interests and values. GCA is a robust predictor. Meta-analytic evidence indicates that it is an effective predictor of performance for virtually all jobs (Schmidt and Hunter, 1998) and that it is also an effective predictor of training success (Ree and Earles, 1991). Research also suggests that GCA is a good predictor of performance adaptability (Kozlowski and Rench, 2009). In addition, to the extent that cognitive ability is a more important aspect of job performance, its validity increases (Hunter and Hunter, 1984). Thus, GCA should be a particularly effective predictor of intelligence analyst effectiveness. A disadvantage of GCA is large racial–ethnic score differences. As a result, an effort is often made to supplement GCA assessment with other predictors in selection system design (Drasgow, 2003; Ployhart, 2011). Psychomotor and physical abilities are important for some jobs (e.g., firefighters, analysts deployed to combat zones), but they are generally not useful for knowledge work. The use of personality for selection was out of favor for decades, primarily because the mass proliferation of personality facets made validation difficult. However, simplification of normal personality assessment around the Five Factor Model—conscientiousness, openness to experience, being agreeable, extroversion, and low neuroticism—allowed personality to emerge as a viable predictor over the past two decades. In general, meta-analytic evidence indicates that high conscientiousness and low neuroticism are predictive of strong job performance, whereas the usefulness of other factors is job dependent (e.g., extroversion for sales jobs) (Barrick and Mount, 1991). Moreover, aggregate, firm-level personality is associated with firm performance (Ployhart et al., 2006). Finally, values and interests represent general preferences. Although they are not very effective predictors of job performance, they are useful predictors of person–job fit and are used to aid career choice.

In summary, recruitment and selection work in tandem. By recruiting a large and diverse pool of applicants, assessing them with validated predictors, and then selecting the most qualified applicants, an organization can ensure that it is acquiring a high-quality pool of human resources. This HRM strategy has immediate and long-term pay-offs in terms of performance effectiveness. Moreover, the output of this strategy—the quality of the aggregate resource pool—is a direct input to the next strategy, which is designed to further enhance capabilities.

Training and Development

These HRM strategies target malleable KSAOs, which can be tailored to enhance individual competencies and organizational capabilities. Training is the systematic acquisition (i.e., learning) of KSAOs that are designed to improve performance on the job (i.e., transfer). In that sense, training is a formal activity directed by the organization and backed by a well-developed methodology and tool set. Development is more informal and encompasses a mix of activities (Salas et al., 2011) including socialization and informal learning (Chao, 1997) during organizational entry (Chao, 2011), mentoring during early career development (Eby, 2011), and a variety of activities associated with development across the career span (London, 2011). Unlike recruitment and selection, which are in essence one-shot strategies, training and development can be viewed as a series of organization-directed interventions and self-directed activities to meet just-in-time job demands, plans for career progression, and capabilities configuration for sustained competitive advantage. They are flexible strategies.

Training effectiveness presents two critical issues. First, employees have to *learn* the knowledge and skills conveyed during training. Second, the trained KSAOs have to *transfer* to yield improved performance on the job, which means they have to be job relevant, acquired, and exhibited. The instructional systems design model is a systematic methodology for the design, delivery, evaluation, and improvement of training programs that consists of three critical phases: (1) needs assessment, (2) training design and delivery, and (3) evaluation and feedback (Goldstein and Ford, 2002).

Needs assessment is the means by which targeted KSAOs, the objectives of training, are identified and specified. An organizational analysis addresses whether training is the solution to the problem (i.e., the problem may have other root causes), whether organizational resources are sufficient to support training and transfer (i.e., training takes time, money, and managerial commitment), and whether system support is adequate so trainees will be receptive (i.e., the organization has policies, practices, and climate that are supportive of training). Task analysis identifies and operationally defines the desired KSAOs—the training objectives—that need to be delivered by the training experience. For knowledge workers, a traditional task analysis may be supplemented or replaced by a cognitive task analysis that traces cognitive operations, decision skills, and capabilities needed to perform the task effectively (Schraagen et al., 2000). Given that the tasks of intelligence analysis are largely "in the head," cognitive task analysis should be an important tool for mapping knowledge and skills needed for IC analyst jobs. Finally, person analysis identifies who needs what kind of training. The same training may be delivered to everyone; training may be targeted to those with specific skill needs (e.g., predeployment training or specialist training for analysts working with a single intelligence collection discipline or "INT"); or training may be tailored to the patterns of individual needs. Uniform delivery is most common, as is the case in the IC, which requires that all new employees below a certain pay grade (or pay band) or military rank attend IC and agency-specific 101 courses. The needs assessment process yields a set of training objectives that specify training goals and desired competencies.

The *training design and delivery* phase is concerned with determining the training setting and delivery medium (e.g., classroom, on the job, web based), developing training content, and creating experiences that provide a vehicle for learning and engaging trainee motivation. Training design has a well-documented tendency to be faddish (Goldstein and Ford, 2002), often driven by the newest technology. Technology is not training. Training design has to be aligned with instructional goals (Kozlowski and Bell, 2007). Instructional goals vary in complexity from basic facts (i.e., declarative knowledge) to procedures (i.e., procedural knowledge or concept application) to strategies (i.e., underlying principles) and adaptability (i.e., performance modifications to meet contingencies), with higher levels encompassing lower order ones. As targeted competencies become more advanced, more complex learning processes are implicated. These, in turn, drive necessary features of the instructional design. If you need people to acquire declarative knowledge, reading (rereading and memorizing) a book or manual may be sufficient. But if you need deeper comprehension of decision-making strategies and the capability to adapt those strategies, then you need to engage active, mindful, effortful learning. These higher level competencies may require systematic, guided hands-on experience in the work context or a "synthetic world" simulation (Bell and Kozlowski, 2007; Cannon-Bowers and Bowers, 2009). Indeed, one of the key challenges for improving analytic skills in the IC is that timely feedback and evaluation of the accuracy of a forecast is typically lacking (e.g., the time frame is too long, the forecast influenced events, etc.). Because simulation incorporates "ground truth" or an objective solution, it could be used effectively to provide analysts with wide-ranging synthetic experience, exposure to low-frequency events, and opportunities to calibrate forecasts with the provision of timely, accurate, and constructive feedback and evaluation. For example, the Defense Intelligence Agency has recently begun using analytic simulation to enhance analysis and decision skills (Peck, 2008). These initial efforts could be augmented substantially by incorporating explicit instructional models in simulation design (Bell et al., 2008).

Evaluation and feedback are critical to training effectiveness. Kirkpatrick (1976) proposed a classic typology for training evaluation. Each additional evaluative criterion as one proceeds from reactions to results adds rigor to the evaluative process. Reactions refer to an assessment of trainees' affective response to the training: Did they like it and think it was useful? This question should be familiar to anyone who has taken a professional development course because it is often asked in end-of-course surveys. Although satisfaction with training is not in and of itself an indication of training effectiveness, a lack of satisfaction is a sign of motivational problems. If trainees did not like the training or did not see it as relevant, they are unlikely to have been motivated to learn the material and are unlikely to transfer it to the job. Learning refers to knowledge and skill acquisition relevant to the training objectives. If the material is not learned effectively, it cannot enhance job performance. Reactions and learning criteria are internal to training. Behavior addresses whether the training yielded performance improvement in the job setting; did training transfer to performance? Results link to more macro organizational outcomes that were the original driver of training. It is possible for training to yield transfer but fail to solve the original problem. Behavior and results are external criteria. Finally, evaluation loops feedback to the needs assessment phase in a continuing process of improvement. If training yields learning and transfer, roll it out. If not, it means the objectives need to be reconsidered (back to needs assessment) or delivery needs redesign.

The design of effective training is a science, not an art (Kozlowski and

Salas, 2009). Transfer, however, tends to be more challenging (Salas et al., 2011). Training does not occur in a vacuum; it is embedded in the broader organizational context that can influence pretraining expectations, motivation during training, and motivation to transfer. Trainees have expectations about training before it occurs, which can have a substantial impact on whether they are motivated to gain from the experience. Expectations are influenced by how training is framed and used in the organization. If it is used as a Band-Aid—slapped onto a problem to signal concern, but not supported by policies, practices, and rewards—then it is likely that employees will view required training with skepticism.

Motivation and learning during training are a matter of training design and delivery. If they are based on the latest fad, they are less likely to yield learning, whereas when training design is scientifically based, it will yield learning of targeted knowledge and skills. A key challenge for training design is to create experiences that impart targeted KSAOs. Stimulating trainees' motivation so they learn is an integral aspect of effective training design. However, an organizational context that supports development and skill application is important for prompting trainee motivation during the training phase. In other words, this is where pretraining expectations, positive or negative, impact motivation to learn (Colquitt et al., 2000).

Although training will typically yield learning, it is of little direct value to the organization unless it also yields improvements in job performance or other relevant behavior changes (i.e., desirable behavior changes aligned with the targeted KSAOs). This highlights the importance of the issue of training transfer (Baldwin and Ford, 1988). Motivation again plays a central role in trainee willingness to try things in a different way and apply their newly acquired knowledge and skills. In that sense, transfer is largely a matter of support in the job setting, which can either directly prompt transfer or interfere with the link between learning and transfer. If the organization is indifferent to the use of trained skills or if supervisors and peers disparage training concepts ("we don't do things that way here"), transfer is unlikely. Thus, a supporting organizational climate for transfer, peers who encourage change, and leadership that facilitates application of the new knowledge and skills are critical for transfer to occur (Kozlowski and Salas, 1997); training must be aligned with the organizational system (Kozlowski et al., 2000). When organizational leadership, culture, and practices are aligned with training, transfer is supported and enhanced. Thus, for example, specific questions included in the annual IC Employee Climate Survey could be designed to assess leadership, climate, and peer supports for training and to determine the longer term benefits of job-related training provided to analysts. Moreover, employees also need an opportunity to practice or apply the skills. Research shows that without such opportunities, trained skills decay (Ford et al., 1992).

The topic of development is quite broad, so here I focus on those informal development activities that are important (1) during initial entry into the organization as the newcomer is socialized, assimilated, and enculturated; (2) during the early career stage where the individual may have the opportunity to be mentored; and (3) over the long-term career trajectory in terms of lifelong learning. Each topic represents substantial empirical literatures, so this section is designed to summarize some of the more pertinent highlights.[4]

Socialization is the informal process by which newcomers learn about, adjust to, and assimilate the norms, values, and perspectives of other organizational members (Bauer et al., 1998). Early research on socialization tended to view it as a one-way process with the organization exerting forces to assimilate the newcomer. Recent research more often views the process as bidirectional, with the organization exerting forces for assimilation and the newcomer, as a proactive agent, also seeking to tailor the role to best fit them. Indeed, March (1991) suggests it is not desirable for organizations to assimilate newcomers too quickly. Rapid socialization prevents newcomers from bringing in new ideas that can enrich the existing knowledge base; there is a fine balance between socialization and organizational learning. Learning during socialization has positive effects on long-term career success (Chao et al., 1994). Socialization is an informal process whereby newcomers learn about their job, role, workgroup, and the organization by communicating with coworkers and supervisors, from observation and experimentation, and from manuals and other objective sources of information (Ostroff and Kozlowski, 1992; Morrison, 1993). In general, research shows that the development of a good relationship with the newcomer's immediate supervisor is important for learning and adjustment (Liden et al., 1993; Ostroff and Kozlowski, 1992; Major et al., 1995).

Research indicates that newcomers are especially open to influence during entry. Some researchers have suggested that this is an opportune time for an organization to exert leverage to influence this informal process (Ostroff and Kozlowski, 1992) because it has long-term implications for performance effectiveness (Chao et al., 1994). Interestingly, organizations do little, if anything, to shape this process deliberately; it is a major lost opportunity.

"Mentoring refers to a developmentally oriented interpersonal relationship between two individuals: a more senior or experienced organizational insider (the mentor) and a more junior or less experienced organizational member (the protégé). . . . " (Eby, 2011, p. 3). Kram (1985) conceptualized the relationship as providing two types of developmental support: (1) career support (e.g., coaching, sponsorship, etc.), and

---

[4]For comprehensive reviews on socialization, mentoring, and lifelong learning, see Chao (2011), Eby (2011), and London (2011), respectively.

(2) psychosocial support (e.g., enhancing the protégé's identity and sense of competence). Protégés have the potential to gain many benefits from mentoring (Eby et al., 2008). Indeed, meta-analytic evidence indicates that protégés have more positive work and career attitudes and better career outcomes, including higher salary, salary growth, and promotion rates (Allen et al., 2004). Mentors also benefit (Allen, 2007). Although mentoring relationships are generally viewed as positive, some evidence shows that like any other close interpersonal connection, there can also be negative outcomes, ranging from minor hassles to major drama, for the protégé and the mentor (Eby, 2007). Much of the research in this area focuses on protégé and mentor characteristics that lead to the formation of this informal relationship and to the outcomes received by both the protégé and mentor.

Because mentoring is valued for its many benefits, organizations including IC agencies have fostered formal mentoring programs by providing structure, guidance, and assistance to initiate and maintain such relationships. Evidence on the effectiveness of formal mentoring programs relative to naturally occurring informal mentoring is mixed (Finkelstein and Poteet, 2007), although many studies find that formal programs are not as effective as informal mentoring (Chao et al., 1992; Noe, 1988; Wanberg et al., 2003). Some authors suggest that the informal–formal distinction is too imprecise and that inspection of the specific aspects of formal mentoring programs may help to identify features needed for success. Finkelstein and Poteet (2007) identify "best practices" for formal mentoring programs, which could benefit existing agency mentoring programs and provide insight for potential designs of an IC-wide mentoring program.

Development over the long term is characterized as lifelong learning; combinations of informal and formal learning activities; activities that are job and career focused; and experiences that relate to off-work interests. Lifelong learning involves development and continuity (London, 2011). To keep this discussion manageable, I will focus on learning that is directly relevant to the workplace. "Workplace learning is task focused, collaborative, often stems from problem-solving experiences, and occurs in a political and economic environment of behavior expectations and consequences," London wrote (2011, p. 5). A wide range of activities are relevant, such as taking job-specific courses to aid current or future performance, seeking challenging assignments to stretch skills, rotating jobs or cross-training on different positions to broaden skills, taking continuing education courses to maintain professional accreditation, attending work conferences, and writing or presenting a professional paper, among many other examples (Kozlowski and Farr, 1988; Maurer et al., 2003; Noe and Wilk, 1993).

A primary focus of research in this area has been identifying the factors that facilitate employee participation in continuous development activities. Job challenge is one important factor because it forces the individual to stretch skills and to seek expanded capabilities. Jobs with well-established routine procedures are less likely to prompt development activities (Kozlowski and Farr, 1988). Another key factor is a general individual tendency to have the motivation to learn (Birdi et al., 1997; Hurtz and Williams, 2009; Maurer and Turulli, 1994; Maurer et al., 2003; Noe and Wilk, 1993). Finally, management and peer support are important facilitators for participation in developmental activities (Birdi et al., 1997; Hurtz and Williams, 2009; Kozlowski and Farr, 1988; Kozlowski and Hults, 1987; Noe and Wilk, 1993). For example, research has shown that an organizational climate supportive of development predicted higher participation rates in development activities and better supervisor ratings of job performance, with performance increasing over time (Kozlowski and Farr, 1988; Kozlowski and Hults, 1987).

In summary, training and development are important practices for building human capital; that is, improving and shaping KSAOs to build unique capabilities for the organization. Training has a strong empirical foundation, a well-developed methodology and tool set, and robust theories to guide instructional design. Development includes a more diverse set of primarily informal activities, but the general conclusion is that developmental activities have important positive outcomes for employees and organizations. The key is for organizations to craft cultures that prompt and facilitate development by supporting managerial policies and leveraging appropriate informal processes. Aligning informal development with formal training processes can leverage and shape organizational learning (Kozlowski et al., 2009). In other words, the value of development activities is in their contribution to current and future organizational capabilities; that is, to their fit with strategic HRM. In this regard, one can view informal developmental activities as part of an organizational learning process in which formal training and informal developmental activities are aligned across levels of the system and with organizational strategy. I will return to this point in the discussion.

Performance Management and Incentives

These high-performance work practices target the process of continual improvement of employee job performance and the linkage of incentives to motivate the achievement of work outcomes that contribute to organizational objectives. Aguinis defines performance management as " . . . a continuous process of identifying, measuring, and developing the performance of individuals and teams and aligning performance with the strategic goals of the organization" (Aguinis, 2007, p. 2). Incentives are rewards, generally

monetary, that are used to make targeted work outcomes salient and motivating to employees (Bartol and Locke, 2000). Incentives, of course, are
one aspect of a broader organizational compensation policy that is also
important for recruiting and retaining talent; that broader discussion is
beyond the scope of my treatment here.[5]

Performance management has emerged from decades of prior research
on performance evaluation that was primarily measurement oriented (i.e.,
the challenges of measuring performance via rater judgment) and represents a paradigm shift (Smither, 2011). Performance evaluation is generally
an annual review of employee performance conducted by the immediate
supervisor. Sometimes it is developmental (i.e., feedback for areas of needed
improvement), sometimes motivationally oriented (i.e., there is a process of
setting goals; management by objectives), and sometimes linked to rewards
(i.e., it is used to determine pay raises, bonuses, and promotions). These
multiple purposes create a clash of competing motives for raters who have
been known to distort evaluations to achieve specific outcomes for employees (Kozlowski et al., 1998). By contrast, performance management is an
integrated approach designed to influence employee attention, motivate
action, reward success, and develop capabilities.

Core elements of performance management include goal setting, feedback, coaching and development, performance evaluation, and rewards
(Smither, 2011). I will briefly highlight each element, but I must note that
each has an extensive underlying literature. Goal setting is a work motivation approach that has amassed considerable support and has a high efficacy, as shown by meta-analytic evidence at the individual (Mento et al.,
1987) and team levels (O'Leary-Kelly et al., 1994). The central tenant of
goal setting is that goals should be specific and difficult to achieve. Goals
have an orienting property, and specificity is important for setting a standard so that progress toward goal accomplishment can be monitored. Individuals accepting or committing to accomplishing goals is often important;
operationally this is often implemented by having supervisors and employees mutually negotiate the goals to be accomplished (Smither, 2011). This
is the case in at least some IC agencies, where supervisors and employees
agree to annual job expectations and supervisors conduct mid-term reviews.

Aguinis (2007) asserts that performance standards should be position
specific, concrete, practical to measure, meaningful, achievable, and reviewed
regularly. An employee needs feedback to monitor progress toward goal
accomplishment. Some tasks provide direct feedback. For example, sales positions often have monthly, quarterly, and yearly revenue goals that are easy

---

[5]See Smither (2011) for a comprehensive review of performance management (PM), Aguinis
(2007) for detailed performance management applications, and Rynes and Gerhart (2000) for
a review of broader compensation topics.

to monitor. However, managerial and technical positions rarely provide such clearly tangible outputs and must be augmented by regular supervisory review. An evaluation of goal progress gives one a sense of confidence in one's capability (i.e., self-efficacy). The nature of feedback and how it is provided can either help to build or to undermine self-confidence and motivation (Kluger and DeNisi, 1996). Feedback is specific and process oriented so that performance information is given. Coaching is provided to support self-confidence and develop capabilities. Finally, incentives are linked to goal accomplishment.

Performance management systems can also be devised that link to team goals and beyond.[6] In particular, Pritchard and his colleagues (1988) developed an approach described as The Productivity Measurement and Enhancement System (ProMES) that is targeted at the group or team level. ProMES implements a system of goals, feedback, and incentives defined in terms meaningful to group members. The initial validation effort reported substantial productivity improvements, relative to baseline, as each element was implemented. Feedback was first (50 percent improvement), followed by goal setting (75 percent improvement) and incentives (76 percent improvement). A recent meta-analysis summarizing 83 implementations of ProMES (Pritchard et al., 2008) concluded that the overall effects on productivity improvement across a variety of organizations and team tasks were substantial (i.e., a large effect size) and the improvements were robust, persisting over years.

The use of incentives is more of a set of practices than a well-developed research domain. Aguinis (2007), for example, highlights incentives typically used in organizations, including base pay (which is most useful for recruitment and retention) and contingent pay increases for merit. Merit increases can go into the base or they can be one-time bonuses; many IC agencies already offer both kinds of merit incentives. Firms may also provide short- (e.g., bonus pay or a merit day off) or long-term (e.g., pay step increase or promotion) incentives to motivate employee effort. Bartol and Locke (2000) provide guidelines for the use of monetary incentives, recommending that pay policy should be (1) clearly specified and communicated, (2) fair and objective, (3) aligned with challenging goals and building confidence, (4) contingent on high performance, (5) substantial enough to be highly valued, (6) focused on upside potential, and (7) aligned with team, unit, and organizational objectives. Promised incentives must be consistently delivered. Not unusually, incentives may be limited by economic factors or policy shifts, which undermine subsequent trust and, thus, the motivating potential of incentives in the future.

Incentives are most useful when integrated into a well-developed performance management system. The implementation problems of moving the

---

[6]See Kozlowski and Ilgen (2006) for a comprehensive review of the research on team effectiveness.

Department of Defense and IC into new civilian compensation programs, "designed to reward superior performance and boost the recruitment and retention of civilian employees" (Office of the Director of National Intelligence, 2009b, p. 2), may have effects on employee trust and motivation that will not be fully realized for several years (see National Academy of Public Administration, 2010, for a detailed discussion of the Defense Civilian Intelligence Personnel System).

Highlighting some concerns about the use of incentives is also important. A close, clear coupling is needed between the measures of performance used to provide incentives and desired employee behaviors; financial incentives *will* increase the behaviors measured and rewarded. For example, Lawler and Rhode (1976) described the dysfunctional effects of measurement in terms of rigid bureaucratic behavior (i.e., behave in ways that influence the measures, but are misaligned with organizational goals), strategic behavior (i.e., more time-focused efforts to influence measurement), and invalid data reporting (i.e., deliberately distorting information). This is a classic conundrum (Kerr, 1975) because performance measures are often deficient (i.e., they do not fully capture performance) and contaminated (i.e., they may assess other factors that do not represent performance). The 2008 IC Employee Climate Survey indicates that 88 percent of employees believe their work is important. However, only 29 percent believe pay raises depend on how well an employee performs, and only 30 percent believe steps are taken to deal with poor performers who either cannot or will not improve (Office of the Director of National Intelligence, 2008). The adage is: Be careful what you reward, because you will get it!

In summary, performance management and incentives are potent practices designed to motivate employee performance by directing attention to important objectives, enhancing the commitment of effort, promoting persistence in the face of difficulties and obstacles, and rewarding effectiveness. The foundation elements of performance management, including goal setting, feedback, and developmental coaching, have good support in the literature. Specific implementations, such as ProMES, have solid evidence of effectiveness. Incentives can be useful adjuncts to a well-developed performance management system, although the linkage between measurement and incentives must be carefully considered and monitored.

Work Design and Teamwork

Work design and teamwork are HRM practices intended to enhance employee involvement, stimulate motivation, and leverage distributed expertise. Work design comprises " . . . the content, structure and organization of tasks and activities that are performed by an individual on a day-to-day basis in order to generate work products" (Cordery and Parker, 2011, p.

6). It focuses on the structural properties of jobs that engage employee interest and motivation, which then influence employee commitment, job satisfaction, and performance. Although much of the research on work design has focused on individual jobs, a focus is emerging on work teams emanating from early work on sociotechnical systems (Trist and Bamforth, 1951). The ongoing evolution of work, which is shifting from a focus on individual jobs to team work systems (Devine et al., 1999), is also energizing this expanded interest. Researchers have studied small-group and team effectiveness for well over half a century, creating a substantial body of knowledge on team effectiveness independent of the work design literature. I will briefly highlight key findings from this research foundation.[7]

Work design has a long history. Early efforts at the turn of the 20th century applied an industrial engineering approach with the intent of simplifying, standardizing, and routinizing work processes to simplify selection and training, create predictable work outputs, and enable easy replacement of personnel. Although the approach yields efficient work systems, it also yields boredom, alienation, and counterproductive behavior (e.g., sabotage) that are well documented. Since the mid-20th century, research on work design has shifted to the enrichment of job content to make the work more meaningful, challenging, and motivating. For example, Herzberg (1968) proposed that work needed to entail challenge and meaning to motivate employees. Early research on sociotechnical systems focused on designs that provided work groups with sufficient autonomy to control (e.g., control over who and how) task accomplishment. A theory of job design developed by Hackman and Oldham (1976) had a strong influence on the field for the rest of the century. They postulated a set of structural characteristics that can be designed into jobs—skill variety, task identity, task significance, autonomy, and feedback—that stimulated psychological states of meaningfulness, responsibility, and knowledge of results. These characteristics, in turn, enhanced internal motivation, job satisfaction, and high-quality performance and lessened withdrawal (i.e., absenteeism, turnover). Although the theory has more precise details, these core aspects are generally supported by meta-analytic evidence (Fried, 1991; Humphrey et al., 2007; Johns et al., 1992). More recent developments have elaborated on the framework, in particular expanding job characteristics to include cognitive and emotional demands, social contact, and opportunities to develop skills (Parker et al., 2001).

Moreover, the scope of work design research has expanded to encompass work teams (Cordery and Parker, 2011). In the past two decades, organizations worldwide have engaged in a major shift in the structure of work moving from functional clusters of individual jobs to team-based work systems. The reasons for this restructuring are many, but primary advantages

---

[7]For comprehensive reviews of the literature on work design, see Cordery and Parker (2011).

are to push decisions closer to the origins of problems, capitalize on diverse expertise, encourage innovation, and enhance adaptability. Psychologists have researched small groups, work team processes, and team effectiveness for more than 50 years, and recent reviews have summarized that substantial research foundation (Ilgen et al., 2005; Kozlowski and Bell, 2003; Kozlowski and Ilgen, 2006; Mathieu et al., 2008). In particular, research has identified several key cognitive, motivational, and behavioral team processes associated with team effectiveness. For example, meta-analytic support and solid research results highlight the importance of team cognitive processes—a shared team climate (i.e., common understanding of strategic imperatives), team mental models (i.e., shared model of the task, team, equipment, and system), and team learning (i.e., seeking feedback, backing up, correcting errors); motivational team processes—collective efficacy (i.e., shared sense of competence and capability), and team cohesion (i.e., member attraction and task commitment); and behavioral team processes—team regulation (i.e., goal selection, effort, feedback, and adaptation), coordination, and back-up/error correction—for team effectiveness (Kozlowski and Ilgen, 2006).

Acknowledging the rise of virtual and ad hoc networked teams is also important, particularly for "knowledge work" that entails information processing, problem solving, and flexible responses (Kirkman et al., 2011). Technology increasingly enables "communities of practice" to emerge around important topics so that knowledge workers can share information, collaborate on problem solving, and generate innovative solutions (e.g., A-Space and Intellipedia). These emergent and self-organizing processes at the intersection of work design and teamwork are motivating and empowering, and contribute to the development of a learning organization.

In summary, work design and teamwork provide a set of techniques for enriching the structure of jobs; creating a sense of capability, energy, and engagement; and linking employees in meaningful ways to others to leverage their knowledge and diverse capabilities. The practices arise from distinct literatures, but have complementary effects in terms of designing jobs that motivate and engage, and providing a means for distributed expertise to be applied flexibly to solve challenging problems. They are useful for workforce development and for developing effective ways for the organization to leverage its human resources and human capital.

CONCLUSION

Review Approach and Objectives

The purpose of this chapter is to provide a concise summary of the scientific literature on developing an effective workforce. Workforce development is not an art; it is a science. I structured the review to place workforce development in the broader context of organizational mission and strategy, and their alignment with strategic human resource management focused on acquiring valuable human resource endowments, building targeted human capital capabilities, and sustaining human capability development and performance over the long haul.

The specific HRM practices examined are those considered core activities—recruitment and selection, training and development, performance management and incentives, and work design and teamwork—with respect to acquiring, building, and sustaining an effective workforce. Many other topics relevant to organizational effectiveness—including leadership (Day, 2011) and organizational climate and culture (Zohar and Hofmann, 2011)—could, and perhaps should, be considered, but are beyond my charge for this chapter. I have tried to keep the discussion focused on those HRM practices with well-supported evidentiary foundations focused on workforce development.

Strengths, Weaknesses, and Focal Research Targets

This chapter focused on HRM practices that are well developed and supported in the literature. On balance I would say that the literature evidences several strengths, which I have highlighted, and relatively few weaknesses. However, I wish to emphasize a few areas worthy of special attention and areas where the literature needs more development.

First, although the HRM practices each represent specific literatures, I have presented them in a conceptual framework that treats them as an integrated set of activities. This is consistent with contemporary theory, but not much direct empirical evidence exists to support the integration argument. Obviously, this is a target for future research. However, even without direct evidence, integration just plain makes sense.

Second, the presumption is that HRM practices are causally linked to organizational performance; however, rigorous empirical data supporting this causality are sparse (see Ployhart et al., 2009; Van Iddekinge et al., 2009), and some studies suggest caution (Wright et al., 2005). The causal link makes sense, but the jury is still out; more definitive research is needed. On the other hand, many of these techniques have been used successfully for decades and supporting evidence is considerable. We knew that smoking and cancer were highly connected long before we could prove the causal link. In the meantime, it makes sense to go with what you know.

Third, with respect to the specific HRM practices, there are some important points of intersection. Selection is a well-developed methodology, and we know it improves the quality of the human resources pool. It cannot work to optimal effectiveness without a large and diverse applicant pool. Recruitment is not a methodology, but a set of practices. Sometimes the practices are "traditional" (e.g., there are pathways for new hires from prior institutions—such as the military or candidates who already possess a security clearance—that yield good candidates for the IC). Although the use of current employees to target potential recruits can help identify specialized talent, it can also yield restrictions on the diversity of the applicant pool. Such practices merit scrutiny and should be supplemented by more pathways to improve diversity in the pool of applicant KSAOs.

Training is a well-developed methodology. The primary challenges are at the intersection with the work context: Will the skills transfer? Will they be supported? Will they influence organizational performance? Ensuring that the context is aligned to support training is critical. Moreover, alignment will also prompt development. Kozlowski et al. (2009) describe this alignment between formal and informal learning, across levels of the organizational system, and consistent with organizational strategy as an "infrastructure" to promote a learning organization.

Performance management comprises a set of well-supported techniques for developing skills and improving performance. Its effectiveness is in the implementation, and a critical element is how well performance is measured. If performance measurement does not capture desired behaviors, the system will be seriously flawed. This is the linchpin. The importance of the measurement issue is compounded by the use of financial incentives. For example, if rewards place an emphasis on the quantity of analytic products produced (because it is easy to count), quality may suffer. You will get what you pay for, so make sure it is exactly what you want.

Finally, work design is well supported, and tools are available to analyze and implement work design changes. We know a lot about team effectiveness. Teams are not a panacea, and the general advice is not to form teams to perform jobs that an individual can perform alone (Steiner, 1972). On the other hand, for problem-solving tasks in which performance is enhanced by diverse expertise, multiple perspectives, and collaboration, teams are a viable HRM practice. On the horizon, virtual teams, network-centric problem solving, and self-organizing communities of practice represent a peek at exciting, technology-fueled, and team-enabled learning organizations of the future. These forms of work and organizational design are emergent, with little systematic research, and this is an obvious and important research target. The key is to make all these elements work in concert.

A Broader Research Question: The IC as a Learning Organization

The systems character of organizations, their multilevel structures, and their need to adapt to dynamic, often unpredictable, environmental shifts has placed the concept of organizational learning central to understanding organizational behavior and effectiveness (Cyert and March, 1963; Fiol and Lyles, 1985; March and Simon, 1958). The problem is that in organizational behavior—a domain with more than its fair share of fuzzy concepts—organizational learning is among the fuzziest because it encompasses nearly everything, including formal and informal mechanisms; processes and outcomes; and a wide range of phenomena at multiple levels, including learning, development, leadership, and culture (Fiol and Lyles, 1985).

Recent theoretical work intended to make the concept more tractable for research and application developed an infrastructure for organizational learning based on three primary features: (1) alignment of informal and formal learning mechanisms, (2) specification of different developmental targets and outcomes at different levels of the system, and (3) alignment of the multilevel system around strategic imperatives (Kozlowski et al., 2009). One key assumption in this approach is that learning is inherently a psychological phenomenon at the individual level. Thus, the theory is built around the construction of an aligned system that fosters learning at the individual level and promotes its emergence as a collective phenomenon. It conceptualizes organizational learning as a bottom-up process. Organizational change, a challenging endeavor fraught with failure (Zegart, this volume, Chapter 13), is a management initiated, top-down process. From a complexity theory perspective, long-term, lasting change in multilevel systems occurs via bottom-up emergent processes (Kozlowski and Klein, 2000).

What I sketch above is theoretical. Simulated data support some basic mechanisms of emergence, but no empirical foundation has been well developed. There are case-based exemplars as organizations implement tools designed to promote learning as an emergent process of change. Interestingly, the IC has already embarked on analyses and initial interventions consistent with a bottom-up approach to foster organizational learning. The IC is a set of units with divisions under the umbrella of the U.S. government. The units are "analytic boutiques" (Fingar, this volume, Chapter 1) attached to the unique sensibilities and needs of different customers. This arrangement provides much more flexibility than a centralized structure (Galbraith, 1972), but it also promotes information silos (Zegart, this volume, Chapter 13).

The big challenge is to retain the flexibility of this distributed architecture, while breaking down barriers that impede collaboration. That means capitalizing on the HRM practices reviewed previously and building an infrastructure to promote organizational learning. So, for example, the IC has developed performance standards (i.e., competencies) and qualification standards for positions across agencies. It has systematically identified the content of expertise across IC units, providing a map of the distribution and location of key knowledge (Fingar, this volume, Chapter 1). It has inventoried intelligence analyst skills in the Analytic Resources Catalog, which represents the KSAO capability pool (Fingar, this volume, Chapter 1). These acts provide some basic actions needed to target desired human resources, locate key talent, and identify human capital to be developed. This is a good start. Moreover, it has implemented Intellipedia, a secure wiki site to share information and catalog intelligence (Andrus, 2005), and A-Space, a web-enabled networking tool to promote collaborative problem solving (Dixon, 2009). These tools enable bottom-up, self-organizing forms of learning, dynamic team networks, adaptation, and system evolution. Good tools will survive and thrive.[8] Poor ones will die from disuse.

The IC has shown a willingness to try new approaches, experiment, and see what works. Improving intelligence analysis will require more than the use of mathematically based decision-making tools and techniques. Such tools will help improve and reduce variance in some aspects of individual decision effectiveness. That is a good start, but it is not enough. Improving intelligence analysis requires harnessing the workforce as a collective. It requires integration and networking mechanisms to link disparate expertise spread across the IC architecture, foster collaborative learning and information amplification, and provide process feedback and peer input to advance critical thinking. It requires crafting the IC into a learning organization. This is an extraordinary opportunity to research the emergence of collaborative networks, to map them, and to develop a living model of organizational learning in the IC.

REFERENCES

Aguinis, H. 2007. *Performance management.* Upper Saddle River, NJ: Pearson Prentice Hall.
Allen, T. D. 2007. Mentoring relationships from the perspective of the mentor. In B. R. Ragins and K. E. Kram, eds., *The handbook of mentoring: Theory, research and practice* (pp. 123–147). Thousand Oaks, CA: Sage.
Allen, T. D., L. T. Eby, M. L. Poteet, E. Lentz, and L. Lima. 2004. Career benefits associated with mentoring protégés: A meta-analysis. *Journal of Applied Psychology* 89(1):127–136.
Andrus, D. C. 2005. The wiki and the blog: Toward a complex adaptive intelligence community. *Studies in Intelligence* 49(3). Available: http://papers.ssrn.com/sol3/papers.cfm?abstract_id=755904 [accessed June 2010].
Baldwin, T. T., and J. K. Ford. 1988. Transfer of training: A review and directions for future research. *Personnel Psychology* 41(1):63–105.
Barber, A. E. 1998. *Recruitment employees.* Thousand Oaks, CA: Sage.

---

[8]A briefing by the Office of the Director of National Intelligence to the National Research Council, August 18, 2009, indicated that in approximately one year of operation, of 12,800 analysts, A-Space had acquired about 11,000 voluntarily registered users, with 30 percent of those users contributing to A-Space. That indicates a high implementation rate relative to typical implementations of new technology in organizations.

Barney, J. B., and P. W. Wright. 1998. On becoming a strategic partner: The role of human resources in gaining competitive advantage. *Human Resource Management* 37(1):31–46.

Barrick, M. R., and M. K. Mount. 1991. The big five personality dimensions and job performance: A meta-analysis. *Personnel Psychology* 44:1–26.

Bartol, K. M., and E. A. Locke. 2000. Incentives and motivation. In S. L. Rynes and B. Gerhart, eds., *Compensation in organizations: Current research and practice.* (pp. 104–147). San Francisco, CA: Jossey-Bass.

Bauer, T. N., E. W. Morrison, and R. R. Callister. 1998. Organizational socialization: A review and directions for future research. In G. R. Ferris, ed., *Research in personnel and human resources management,* vol. 16 (pp. 149–214). Stamford, CT: JAI Press.

Becker, B. E., and M. A. Huselid. 1998. High performance work systems and firm performance: A synthesis of research and managerial implications. In G. R. Ferris, ed., *Research in personnel and human resources management,* vol. 16 (pp. 53-101). Stamford, CT: JAI Press.

Becker, B. E., and M. A. Huselid. 2006. Strategic human resource management: Where do we go from here? *Journal of Management* 32(6):898–925.

Bell, B. S., and S. W. J. Kozlowski. 2007. Advances in technology-based training. In S. Werner, ed., *Managing human resources in North America* (pp. 27–42). Oxon, UK: Routledge.

Bell, B. S., A. M. Kanar, and S. W. J. Kozlowski. 2008. Current issues and future directions in simulation-based training in North America. *International Journal of Human Resource Management* 19(8):1,416–1,434.

Birdi, K., C. Allan, and P. Warr. 1997. Correlates and perceived outcomes of four types of employee development activity. *Journal of Applied Psychology* 82(6):845–857.

Boudreau, J. W., and P. M. Ramstad. 2005. Talentship and the evolution of human resource management: From "professional practices" to "strategic talent decision science." *Human Resource Planning Journal* 28:17–26.

Boudreau, J. W., and P. M. Ramstad. 2007. *Beyond HR: The new science of human capital.* Boston, MA: Harvard Business School.

Brown, C., and J. Medoff. 1978. Trade unions in the production process. *Journal of Political Economy* 86(3):355–378.

Cable, D. M., and D. Turban. 2001. Recruitment image equity: Establishing the dimensions, sources and value of job seekers' employer knowledge during recruitment. In G .R. Ferris, ed., *Research in personnel and human resources management,* vol. 20 (pp. 115–163). Stamford, CT: JAI Press.

Cable, D. M., and K. Y. T. Yu. 2006. Managing job seekers' organizational image beliefs: The role of media richness and media credibility. *Journal of Applied Psychology* 91(4):828–840.

Campbell, J. P., R. A. McCloy, S. H. Oppler, and C. E. Sager. 1993. A theory of performance. In N. Schmitt and W. C. Borman, eds., *Personnel selection in organizations* (pp. 35–70). San Francisco, CA: Jossey-Bass.

Cannon-Bowers, J., and C. Bowers. 2009. Synthetic learning environments: On developing a science of simulation, games, and virtual worlds for training. In S. W. J. Kozlowski and E. Salas, eds., *Learning, training, and development in organizations* (pp. 229–260). New York: Routledge.

Cascio, W. F. 2000. *Costing human resources: The financial impact of behavior in organizations.* Cincinnati, OH: Southwestern.

Chao, G. T. 1997. Unstructured training and development: The role of organizational socialization. In J. K. Ford, S. W. J. Kozlowski, K. Kraiger, E. Salas, and M. Teachout, eds., *Improving training effectiveness in work organizations* (pp. 129–151). Mahwah, NJ: Erlbaum.

Chao, G. T. 2011. Socialization in organizations. In S. W. J. Kozlowski, ed., *Oxford handbook of industrial-organizational psychology*. New York: Oxford University Press.

Chao, G. T., P. M. Walz, and P. D. Gardner. 1992. Formal and informal mentorships: A comparison on mentoring functions and contract with nonmentored counterparts. *Personnel Psychology* 45(3):619–636.

Chao, G. T., A. M. O'Leary-Kelly, S. Wolf, H. J. Klein, and P. D. Gardner. 1994. Organizational socialization: Its content and consequences. *Journal of Applied Psychology* 79(5):730–743.

Charness, N., and M. Tuffiash. 2008. The role of expertise research and human factors in capturing, explaining, and producing superior performance. *Human Factors* 50(3):427–432.

Colquitt, J. A., J. A. LePine, and R. A. Noe. 2000. Toward an integrative theory of training motivation: A meta-analytic path analysis of 20 years of research. *Journal of Applied Psychology* 85(5):678–707.

Combs, J., Y. Liu, A. Hall, and D. Ketchen. 2006. How much do high-performance work practices matter? A meta-analysis of their effects on organizational performance. *Personnel Psychology* 59(3):501–528.

Cordery, J., and S. Parker. 2011. Work design: Creating jobs and roles that promote individual effectiveness. In S. W. J. Kozlowski, ed., *Oxford handbook of industrial-organizational psychology*. New York: Oxford University Press.

Cronbach, L. J. 1970. *Essentials of psychological testing*, 3rd ed. New York: Harper and Row.

Crook, R. T., S. Y. Todd, J. G. Combs, D. J. Woehr, and D. J. Ketchen. in press. Does human capital matter? A meta-analysis of the relationship between human capital and firm performance. Submitted to *Journal of Applied Psychology*.

Cyert, R. M., and J. G. March. 1963. *A behavioral theory of the firm*. Oxford, UK: Blackwell.

Day, D. V. 2011. Leadership. In S. W. J. Kozlowski, ed., *Oxford handbook of industrial-organizational psychology*. New York: Oxford University Press.

Delery, J. E., and D. H. Doty. 1996. Modes of theorizing in strategic human resource management: Tests of universalistic, contingency and configurational performance predictions. *Academy of Management Journal* 39(4):802–835.

Delery, J. E., and J. Shaw. 2001. The strategic management of people in work organizations: Review, synthesis, and extension. In G. R. Ferris, ed., *Research in personnel and human resources management*, vol. 20 (pp. 167–197). Stamford, CT: JAI Press.

Devine, D. J., L. D. Clayton, J. L. Phillips, B. B. Dunford, and S. B. Melner. 1999. Teams in organizations: Prevalence, characteristics, and effectiveness. *Small Group Research* 30(6):678–711.

Dixon, N. M. 2009. *How A-Space is shaping analysts' work*. Washington, DC: Defense Intelligence Agency.

Drasgow, F. 2003. Intelligence in the workplace. In W. C. Borman, D. R. Ilgen, and R. J. Klimoski, eds., *Handbook of psychology: Industrial and organizational psychology*, vol. 12 (pp. 107–130). Hoboken, NJ: Wiley.

Eby, L. T. 2007. Understanding problems in mentoring: A review and proposed investment model. In B. R. Ragins and K. E. Kram, eds., *Handbook of mentoring* (pp. 323–344). Thousand Oaks, CA: Sage.

Eby, L. T. 2011. Workplace mentoring: Past, present and future perspectives. In S. W. J. Kozlowski, ed., *Oxford handbook of industrial-organizational psychology*. New York: Oxford University Press.

Eby, L. T., T. D. Allen, S. C. Evans, T. Ng, and D. L. DuBois. 2008. Does mentoring matter? A multidisciplinary meta-analysis comparing mentored and non-mentored individuals. *Journal of Vocational Behavior* 72(2):254–267.

Finkelstein, L. M., and M. L. Poteet. 2007. Best practices in workplace formal mentoring programs. In T. D. Allen and L. T. Eby, eds., *The Blackwell handbook of mentoring* (pp. 345–367). Malden, MA: Blackwell.

Fiol, C. M., and M. A. Lyles. 1985. Organizational learning. *Academy of Management Review* 10(4):803–813.

Fiore, S. M., M. A. Rosen, K. A. Smith-Jentsch, E. Salas, M. Letsky, and N. Warner. 2010. Toward an understanding of macrocognition in teams: Predicting processes in complex collaborative contexts. *Human Factors* 52(2):203–224.

Ford, J. K., M. A. Quiñones, D. J. Sego, and J. S. Sorra. 1992. Factors affecting the opportunity to perform trained tasks on the job. *Personnel Psychology* 45(3):511–527.

Fried, Y. 1991. Meta-analytic comparison of the job diagnostic survey and job characteristics inventory as correlates of work satisfaction and performance. *Journal of Applied Psychology* 76(5):690–697.

Galbraith, J. 1972. Organization design: An information processing view. In J. Lorsch and P. Lawrence, eds., *Organizational planning: Cases and concepts* (pp.530–548). Homewood, IL: Irwin-Dorsey.

Gerhart, B., and G. T. Milkovich. 1992. Employee compensation: Research and practice. In M. D. Dunnette and L. M. Hough, eds., *Handbook of industrial and organizational psychology*, vol. 3 (pp. 481–569). Palo Alto, CA: Consulting Psychologists Press.

Goldstein, I. L., and J. K. Ford. 2002. *Training in organizations: Needs assessment, development, and evaluation*, 4th ed. Belmont, CA: Wadsworth.

Guzzo, R. A., R. D. Jette, and R. A. Katzell. 1985. The effect of psychologically based intervention programs in worker productivity: A meta-analysis. *Personnel Psychology* 38(2):275–291.

Hackman, J. R., and G. R. Oldham. 1976. Motivation through design of work: Test of a theory. *Organisational Behaviour and Human Performance* 16(2):250–279.

Hatch, N. W., and J. H. Dyer. 2004. Human capital and learning as a source of sustainable competitive advantage. *Strategic Management Journal* 25(12):1,155–1,178.

Herzberg, F. 1968. One more time: How do you motivate employees? *Harvard Business Review* 46(1):53–62.

Holzer, H. J. 1987. *Hiring procedures in the firm: Their economic determinants and outcomes.* NBER Working Paper Series (No. 2185). Cambridge, MA: National Bureau of Economic Research.

Homeyer, J., and A. R. Madsen. 2009. *IC analyst qualification standards.* PowerPoint slides presented at National Research Council meeting of the Committee on Behavioral and Social Science Research to Improve Intelligence Analysis for National Security, Washington, DC, May 14.

Humphrey, S. E., J. D. Nahrgang, and F. P. Morgeson. 2007. Integrating motivational, social, and contextual work design features: A meta-analytic summary and theoretical extension of the work design literature. *Journal of Applied Psychology* 92(5):1,332–1,356.

Hunter, J. E., and R. F. Hunter. 1984. Validity and utility of alternative predictors of job performance. *Psychological Bulletin* 96(1):72–98.

Hurtz, G. M., and K. J. Williams. 2009. Attitudinal and motivational antecedents of participation in voluntary employment development activities. *Journal of Applied Psychology* 94(3):635–653.

Huselid, M. A. 1995. The impact of human resource management practices on turnover, productivity, and corporate financial performance. *Academy of Management Journal* 38(3):635–672.

Ilgen, D. R., J. R. Hollenbeck, M. Johnson, and D. Jundt. 2005. Teams in organizations: From input-process-output models to IMOI models. *Annual Review of Psychology* 56:517–543.

Indik, B. P. 1968. The scope of the problem and some suggestions toward a solution. In B. P. Indik and F. K. Berren, eds., *People, groups, and organizations* (pp. 3–30). New York: Teachers College Press.

Johns, G., J. L. Xie, and Y. Fang. 1992. Mediating and moderating effects in job design. *Journal of Management* 18(4):657–676.

Judge, T. A., R. Klinger, and L. Simon. 2010. Time is on my side: Time, general mental ability, human capital, and extrinsic career success. *Journal of Applied Psychology* 95(1):92–107.

Katz, D., and R. L. Kahn. 1966. *The social psychology of organizations*. New York: Wiley.

Kerr, S. 1975. On the folly of rewarding A, while hoping for B. *Academy of Management Journal* 18(4):769–783. Republished in 1995 in *Academy of Management Executive* 9(1):7–14.

Kirkman, B. L., C. B. Gibson, and K. Kim. 2011. Across borders and technologies: Advancements in virtual teams research. In S. W. J. Kozlowski, ed., *Oxford handbook of industrial-organizational psychology*. New York: Oxford University Press.

Kirkpatrick, D. L. 1976. Evaluation of training. In R. L. Craig, ed., *Training and development handbook*. New York: McGraw-Hill.

Kluger, A. N., and A. DeNisis. 1996. The effects of feedback interventions on performance: A historical review, a meta-analysis, and a preliminary feedback intervention theory. *Psychological Bulletin* 119(2):254–284.

Koch, M. J., and R. G. McGrath. 1996. Improving labor productivity: Human resource management policies do matter. *Strategic Management Journal* 17(5):335–354.

Kozlowski, S. W. J., and B. S. Bell. 2003. Work groups and teams in organizations. In C. Borman, D. R. Ilgen, and R. J. Klimoski, eds., *Handbook of psychology: Industrial and organizational psychology*, vol. 12 (pp. 333–375). London, UK: Wiley.

Kozlowski, S. W. J., and B. S. Bell. 2007. A theory-based approach for designing distributed learning systems. In S. M. Fiore and E. Salas, eds., *Where is the learning in distance learning? Toward a science of distributed learning and training* (pp. 15–39). Washington, DC: APA Books.

Kozlowski, S. W. J., and J. L. Farr. 1988. An integrative model of updating and performance. *Human Performance* 1:5–29.

Kozlowski, S. W. J., and B. M. Hults. 1987. An exploration of climates for technical updating and performance. *Personnel Psychology* 40(3):539–563.

Kozlowski, S. W. J., and D. R. Ilgen. 2006. Enhancing the effectiveness of work groups and teams. *Psychological Science* Supplemental:77–124.

Kozlowski, S. W. J., and K. J. Klein. 2000. A multilevel approach to theory and research in organizations: Contextual, temporal, and emergent processes. In K. J. Klein and S. W. J. Kozlowski, eds., *Multilevel theory, research and methods in organizations: Foundations, extensions, and new directions* (pp. 3–90). San Francisco, CA: Jossey-Bass.

Kozlowski, S. W. J., and T. Rench. 2009. *Individual differences, adaptability, and adaptive performance: A conceptual analysis and research summary*. Final Report; Contract No. W911NF-07-D-0001, TCN: 08146. Research Triangle Park, NC: Battelle Scientific Services.

Kozlowski, S. W. J., and E. Salas. 1997. An organizational systems approach for the implementation and transfer of training. In J. K. Ford, S. W. J. Kozlowski, K. Kraiger, E. Salas, and M. Teachout, eds., *Improving training effectiveness in work organizations* (pp. 247–287). Mahwah, NJ: Erlbaum.

Kozlowski, S. W. J., and E. Salas, eds. 2009. *Learning, training, and development in organizations*. New York: Routledge Academic.

Kozlowski, S. W. J., G. T. Chao, and R. F. Morrison. 1998. Games raters play: Politics, strategies, and impression management in performance appraisal. In J. W. Smither, ed., *Performance appraisal: State of the art methods for performance appraisal* (pp. 163–205). San Francisco, CA: Jossey-Bass.

Kozlowski, S. W. J., S. M. Gully, E. R. Nason, and E. M. Smith. 1999. Developing adaptive teams: A theory of compilation and performance across levels and time. In D. R. Ilgen and E. D. Pulakos, eds., *The changing nature of work performance: Implications for staffing, personnel actions, and development* (pp. 240–292). San Francisco, CA: Jossey-Bass.

Kozlowski, S. W. J., K. G. Brown, D. Weissbein, J. A. Cannon-Bowers, and E. Salas. 2000. A multilevel approach to training effectiveness: Enhancing horizontal and vertical transfer. In K. J. Klein and S. W. J. Kozlowski, eds., *Multilevel theory, research and methods in organizations: Foundations, extensions, and new directions* (pp. 157–210). San Francisco, CA: Jossey-Bass.

Kozlowski, S. W. J., G. T. Chao, and J. M. Jensen. 2009. Building an infrastructure for organizational learning: A multilevel approach. In S. W. J. Kozlowski and E. Salas, eds., *Learning, training, and development in organizations* (pp. 361–400). New York: Routledge Academic.

Kram, K. E. 1985. *Mentoring at work.* Glenview, IL: Scott, Foresman and Company.

Lawler, E. E., and J. G. Rhode. 1976. *Information and control in organizations.* Pacific Palisades, CA: Goodyear.

Lepak, D. P., H. Liao, Y. Chung, and E. E. Harden. 2006. A conceptual review of human resource management systems in strategic human resource management research. In J. J. Martocchio, ed., *Research in personnel and human resources management*, vol. 25 (pp. 217–271). Stamford, CT: JAI Press.

LePine, J. A., R. F. Piccolo, C. L. Jackson, J. E. Mathieu, and J. R. Saul. 2008. A meta-analysis of teamwork processes: Tests of a multidimensional model and relationships with team effectiveness criteria. *Personnel Psychology* 61(2):273–307.

Liden, R. C., S. J. Wayne, and D. Stilwell. 1993. A longitudinal study on the early development of leader–member exchanges. *Journal of Applied Psychology* 78(4):662–674.

London, M. 2011. Lifelong learning. In S. W. J. Kozlowski, ed., *Oxford handbook of industrial-organizational psychology.* New York: Oxford University Press.

Lyons, M. J., T. P. York, C. E. Franz, M. D. Grant, L. J. Eaves, K. C. Jacobson, K. W. Schaie, M. S. Panizzon, C. Boake, H. Xian, R. Toomey, S. A. Eisen, and W. S. Kremen. 2009. Genes determine stability and the environment determines change in cognitive ability during 35 years of adulthood. *Psychological Science* 20(9):1,146–1,152.

MacDuffie, J. P. 1995. Human-resource bundles and manufacturing performance: Organizational logic and flexible production systems in the world auto industry. *Industrial and Labor Relations Review* 48(2):197–221.

Major, D. A., S. W. J. Kozlowski, G. T. Chao, and P. D. Gardner. 1995. A longitudinal investigation of newcomer expectations, early socialization outcomes, and the moderating effects of role development factors. *Journal of Applied Psychology* 80(3):418–431.

March, J. G. 1991. Exploration and exploitation in organizational learning. *Organization Science* 2(1):71–87.

March, J. G., and H. A. Simon. 1958. *Organizations.* New York: John Wiley.

Marks, M. A., J. E. Mathieu, and S. J. Zaccaro. 2001. A temporally based framework and taxonomy of team processes. *Academy of Management Review* 26(3):356–376.

Mathieu, J., M. T. Maynard, T. Rapp, and L. Gilson. 2008. Team effectiveness 1997–2007: A review of recent advancements and a glimpse into the future. *Journal of Management* 34(3):410–476.

Maurer, T. J., and B. A. Tarulli. 1994. Investigation of perceived environment, perceived outcome and person variables in relationship to voluntary development activity by employees. *Journal of Applied Psychology* 79(1):3–14.

Maurer, T. J., E. M. Weiss, and F. G. Barbeite. 2003. A model of involvement in work-related learning and development activity: The effects of individual, situational, motivational, and age variables. *Journal of Applied Psychology* 88(4):707–724.

McEvoy, G. M., and W. F. Cascio. 1985. Strategies for reducing employee turnover: A meta-analysis. *Journal of Applied Psychology* 70(2):342–353.

Mento, A. J., R. P. Steel, and R. J. Karren. 1987. A meta-analytic study of the effects of goal-setting on task performance—1966–1984. *Organizational Behavior and Human Decision Processes* 39(1):52–83.

Miles, R. E., C. C. Snow, A. D. Meyer, and H. J. Coleman. 1978. Organizational strategy, structure and process. *Academy of Management Review* 3(3):546–562.

Morrison, E. W. 1993. Longitudinal study of the effects of information seeking on newcomer socialization. *Journal of Applied Psychology* 78(2):173–183.

National Academy of Public Administration. 2010. *The Defense Civilian Intelligence Personnel System: An independent assessment of design, implementation, and impact*. Washington, DC: National Academy of Public Administration. Available: http://www.napawash.org/dcips/DCIP_2158/FINAL%20DCIPS%20REPORT%20June%202010.pdf [accessed June 2010].

Noe, R. A. 1988. An investigation of the determinants of successful assigned mentoring relationships. *Personnel Psychology* 41(3):457–479.

Noe, R. A., and S. L. Wilk. 1993. Investigation of the factors that influence employee participation in development activities. *Journal of Applied Psychology* 78(2):291–302.

Office of the Director of National Intelligence. 2008. *IC 2008 Employee Climate Survey: Summary of results*. Available: http://www.dni.gov/reports/IC-Survey_2008.pdf [accessed June 2010].

Office of the Director of National Intelligence. 2009a. *National intelligence strategy of the United States of America*. Available: http://www.dni.gov/reports/2009_NIS.pdf [accessed June 2010].

Office of the Director of National Intelligence. 2009b. *Intelligence community workers give their employers high marks for job satisfaction and identify remaining challenges, 2008 survey shows*. ODNI News Release No. 13-09. Available: http://www.dni.gov/press_releases/20090409_release.pdf [accessed June 2010].

O'Leary-Kelly, A. M., J. J. Martocchio, and D. D. Frink. 1994. A review of the influence of group goals on group-performance. *Academy of Management Journal* 37(5):1,285–1,301.

Ostroff, C., and D. E. Bowen. 2000. Moving HR to a higher level: HR practices and organizational effectiveness. In K. J. Klein and S. W. J. Kozlowski, eds., *Multilevel theory, research and methods in organizations: Foundations, extensions, and new directions* (pp. 211–266). San Francisco, CA: Jossey-Bass.

Ostroff, C., and S. W. J. Kozlowski. 1992. Organizational socialization as a learning process: The role of information acquisition. *Personnel Psychology* 45(4):849–874.

Parker, S. K., T. D. Wall, and J. L. Cordery. 2001. Future work design and practice: Towards an elaborated model of work design. *Journal of Occupational and Organizational Psychology* 74:413–440.

Peck, M. 2008. U.S. spies use custom videogames to learn how to think. *Wired*. April 24. Available: http://www.wired.com/politics/security/news/2008/04/spy_games?currentPage=all# [accessed June 2010].

Phillips, J. M. 1998. Effects of realistic job previews on multiple organizational outcomes: A meta-analysis. *Academy of Management Journal* 41(6):673–690.

Ployhart, R. E. 2006. Staffing in the 21st century: New challenges and strategic opportunities. *Journal of Management* 32(6):868–897.

Ployhart, R. E. 2011. Personnel selection: Ensuring sustainable organizational effectiveness through the acquisition of human capital. In S. W. J. Kozlowski, ed., *Oxford handbook of industrial-organizational psychology*. New York: Oxford University Press.

Ployhart, R. E., J. A. Weekley, and K. Baughman. 2006. The structure and function of human capital emergence: A multilevel examination of the ASA model. *Academy of Management Journal* 49(4):661–677.

Ployhart, R. E., J. A. Weekley, and J. Ramsey. 2009. The consequences of human resource stocks and flows: A longitudinal examination of unit service orientation and unit effectiveness. *Academy of Management Journal* 52(5):996–1,015.

Pritchard, R. D., S. D. Jones, P. L. Roth, K. K. Stuebing, and S. E. Ekeberg. 1988. The effects of feedback, goal setting, and incentives on organizational productivity. *Journal of Applied Psychology Monograph Series* 73(2):337–358.

Pritchard, R. D., M. M. Harrell, D. DiazGranados, and M. J. Guzman. 2008. The productivity measurement and enhancement system: A meta-analysis. *Journal of Applied Psychology* 93(3):540–567.

Ree, M. J., and J. A. Earles. 1991. Predicting training success: Not much more than *g*. *Personnel Psychology* 44(2):321–332.

Rynes, S. L. 1991. Recruitment, job choice, and post-hire consequences: A call for new research directions. In M. D. Dunnette and L. M. Hough, eds., *Handbook of industrial and organizational psychology*, 2nd ed. vol. 2 (pp. 399–444). Palo Alto, CA: Consulting Psychologists Press.

Rynes, S. L., and D. M. Cable. 2003. Recruitment research in the twenty-first century. In W. C. Borman and D. R. Ilgen, eds., *Handbook of psychology: industrial and organizational psychology*, vol. 12 (pp. 55–76). New York: John Wiley and Sons.

Rynes, S. L., and B. Gerhart, eds. 2000. *Compensation in organizations: Current research and practice*, vol. 1. San Francisco, CA: Jossey-Bass.

Salas, E., S. J. Weaver, and M. S. Porter. 2011. Learning, training, and development in organizations. In S. W. J. Kozlowski, ed., *Oxford handbook of industrial-organizational psychology*. New York: Oxford University Press.

Schmidt, F. L., and J. E. Hunter. 1998. The validity and utility of selection methods in personnel psychology: Practical and theoretical implications of 85 years of research findings. *Psychological Bulletin* 124(2):262–274.

Schmidt, F. L., and J. Hunter. 2004. General mental ability in the world of work: Occupational attainment and job performance: General intelligence, objectively defined and measured. *Journal of Personality and Social Psychology* 86(1):162–173.

Schraagen, J. M., S. F. Chipman, and V. L. Shalin, eds. 2000. *Cognitive task analysis*. Mahwah, NJ: Erlbaum.

Smither, J. W. 2011. Performance management. In S. W. J. Kozlowski, ed., *Oxford handbook of industrial-organizational psychology*. New York: Oxford University Press.

Snow, C. C., and S. A. Snell. 2011. Strategic human resource management. In S. W. J. Kozlowski, ed., *Oxford handbook of industrial-organizational psychology*. New York: Oxford University Press.

Steiner, I. D. 1972. *Group process and productivity*. New York: Academic Press.

Terpstra, D. E., and E. J. Rozell. 1993. The relationship of staffing practices to organizational level measures of performance. *Personnel Psychology* 46(1):27–48.

Trist, E. L., and K. M. Bamforth. 1951. Some social and psychological consequences of the longwall method of coal-getting. *Human Relations* 4:3–38.

U.S. Department of Labor. 1993. *High performance work practices and firm performance*. Washington, DC: U.S. Government Printing Office.

Van Iddekinge, C., G. R. Ferris, P. L. Perrewe, A. Z. Perryman, F. R. Blass, and T. D. Heetderks. 2009. Effects of selection and training on unit-level performance over time: A latent growth modeling approach. *Journal of Applied Psychology* 94(4):829–843.

Wanberg, C. R., E. T. Welsh, and S. A. Hezlett. 2003. Mentoring research: A review and dynamic process model. In J. J. Martocchio and G. R. Ferris, eds., *Research in personnel and human resources management,* vol. 22 (pp. 39–124). Stamford, CT: JAI Press.

Wright, P. M., and W. Boswell. 2002. Desegregating HRM: A review and synthesis of micro and macro human resource management research. *Journal of Management* 28(3):247–276.

Wright, P. M., B. D. Dunford, and S. A. Snell. 2001. Human resources and the resource based view of the firm. *Journal of Management* 27(6):701–721.

Wright, P. M., T. M. Gardner, L. M. Moynihan, and M. R. Allen. 2005. The relationship between HR practices and firm performance: Examining causal order. *Personnel Psychology* 58(2):409–446.

Youndt, M. A., S. A. Snell, J. W. Dean, and D. P. Lepak. 1996. Human resource management, manufacturing strategy, and firm performance. *Academy of Management Journal* 39(4):836–866.

Yu, T. K. Y., and D. M. Cable. 2011. Recruitment and competitive advantage: A brand equity perspective. In S. W. J. Kozlowski, ed., *Oxford handbook of industrial-organizational psychology.* New York: Oxford University Press.

Zohar, D., and D. A. Hofmann. 2011. Organizational culture and climate. In S. W. J. Kozlowski, ed., *Oxford handbook of industrial-organizational psychology.* New York: Oxford University Press.

13

Implementing Change: Organizational Challenges

Amy Zegart

Improving organizational performance is never easy. As sociologist Jim March has noted, success requires that organizations balance exploration—the search for new ways of doing things—with exploitation, the ability to harness new practices and jettison older, less effective ones (March, 1991). These challenges confront all organizations, but two factors make them more acute for intelligence agencies. The first is bounded rationality (Simon, 1976). In the theoretical world, individuals have the luxury of perfect rationality, seeing all of the relevant options, assessing trade-offs with clarity, and making the best decisions. The real world is not as nice. There, rationality is inherently limited or bounded by uncertainty, imperfect information, and cognitive constraints that lead individuals to make decisions that appear to be "good enough"—but may turn out to be nowhere close (Simon, 1976). Intelligence officials have the toughest time of all, confronting bounded rationality problems in spades. Their job is to give policy-making customers decision advantage amidst swirling uncertainty, missing information, enemy deception and denial, and fast-changing events that are often unforeseeable, even to the participants themselves.

The second acute intelligence challenge is secrecy. As I discuss below, the more specialized any organization becomes, the harder it is for any one part of the organization to understand or improve what another part is doing, a phenomenon that sociologists call "structural secrecy" (Vaughan, 1996). In the classified universe, of course, this structural secrecy is compounded by actual secrecy, which protects vital information from adversaries, but also compartmentalizes information, ideas, organizations, and practices to a much greater extent.

Despite the intelligence community's (IC's) unique challenges, the fields of organization theory and political science offer useful insights and cautionary warnings about the organizational side of improving intelligence analysis. The chapters in Part II (Analytic Methods) of this volume mine an array of relevant literature for the best *analytic tools* to improve intelligence analysis. Here, we turn to a different task: Examining a broad sweep of relevant social science research with an eye to identifying which *organizational factors* impede or facilitate effective analysis. Worth underscoring, though, is the fact that social science does not offer ready-made instructions about how to make intelligence analytic improvements stick. However, it does offer some useful generalizations that can illuminate the trade-offs and challenges involved to guide more effective implementation.

INSIGHTS AND LIMITATIONS OF ORGANIZATION THEORY

Organization theory is a wide-ranging, multidisciplinary field that includes sociology, psychology, political science, economics, and professional school fields such as urban planning and management. Although organization theorists tackle vastly different questions using a multitude of methodologies, they all share an interest in understanding how organizations behave, and why. In general, the field's research is animated by three central issues: (1) how internal organizational structures and features affect organizational outcomes (particularly efficiency and survival); (2) how external factors influence what goes on inside an organization; and (3) how the interaction between internal and external forces shapes an organization's prospects for survival.

For our purposes, the field offers three insights for improving intelligence analysis, described in the following pages.

Insight #1: Adopting New Practices Is Difficult Even for Firms

This idea is more important than it sounds. Critics frequently bemoan that government is not run more like a business, and recommend exporting private-sector practices into public-sector bureaucracies (Osborne and Gaebler, 1993; Osborne and Plastrik, 1998). The data show, however, that most businesses are not run like businesses. Consider survival, which is the most rudimentary indicator of firm adaptation (Aldrich, 1999).[1] According to the U.S. Census Bureau, nearly a third of the 5.5 million American businesses that existed in 1990 failed within four years (Aldrich, 1999).

---

[1] As Aldrich points out, such findings most likely understate adaptation failure because they focus only on surviving populations, excluding all of the organizations that never made it past the start-up phase, when survival rates are considerably lower.

Every year, more than half a million American businesses go bust. That's about 1,500 per day or 1 business every minute (U.S. Census Bureau, 2009, Table 739).[2] What's more, social science research suggests that corporate fads often flop. Pfeffer and Sutton (2006), for example, note that studies repeatedly find that the majority of corporate mergers (some estimates are 70 percent or more) fail to deliver promised benefits and actually end up destroying value. Analysis of 93 studies covering more than 200,000 mergers published in peer-reviewed journals found that on average, the negative effects of a merger on shareholder value appeared within days after the merger was announced (Pfeffer and Sutton, 2006).

Even top-performing firms struggle to sustain their performance. Between 1955 and 2005, for example, nearly 2,000 companies made *Fortune* magazine's list of the largest 500 U.S. corporations. Of these, only three held the number one spot for more than a single year; 27 made the list once without ever appearing again; and just 71, or 3.8 percent, managed to stay on the list for the entire 50-year span (Schlosser and Florian, 2004).[3] Between 2000 and 2003, more than 400 public companies went bankrupt, including Enron, which rose to seventh on the *Fortune* 500 list, and Bethlehem Steel, one of the great industrial giants of the 20th century (Loomis, 2004; Serwer, 2002). Their combined liabilities reached more than $500 billion, a figure 10 times greater than the annual budget for all U.S. intelligence agencies combined (Office of the Director of National Intelligence, 2007).[4] As Lewin and colleagues (2004) conclude, the empirical data clearly support the observation that "most firms are selected out" (p. 108).

These findings describe organizational adaptation prospects in the best of circumstances; adaptation challenges are likely to be far greater in public-sector agencies. As Allison (1980), Moe (1989), Wilson (2000), Zegart (2007), and others have noted, private-sector firms enjoy key adaptation advantages that government agencies lack. Four are paramount. First, market competition incentivizes firms to adapt or die. Indeed, population ecology theorists argue that private-sector innovation arises *between* organizations, not within them: Newer, fitter firms are constantly replacing older, outdated ones through a Darwinian process of natural selection (Hannan and Freeman, 1977, 1984). But this degree of organizational churn does not exist in government. As many have observed, government agencies are notoriously hard to kill because some interest groups and

---

[2]Note that these figures cover firm deaths each year from 1990 to 2005. Because they predate the current economic recession, they are likely to underestimate current firm death rates.

[3]The three firms that remained at number one for more than a single year are General Motors, Exxon Mobil, and Walmart. Rankings are based on previous year's revenues.

[4]Intelligence budget calculations based on an Office of the Director of National Intelligence press release, which reported the first post-9/11 declassified National Intelligence Program budget: $43.7 billion for FY 2007 (Office of the Director of National Intelligence, 2007).

elected officials out there will always resist (Downs, 1967; Stinchecombe, 1965; Lowi, 1979; Kaufman, 1976; Lewis, 2003).[5] Public-sector agencies—especially intelligence agencies—rarely fear they will go out of business.[6] Instead, history has shown that policy makers usually respond to perceived government failures by creating new agencies, not eliminating existing ones. Although intelligence agencies may have other incentives to adapt, the market's powerful imperative to change or close up shop is not one of them.

These realities suggest that the benefits of competition are naturally more limited in the IC than in the private sector. On the one hand, competition can stimulate ideas, sharpen analysis, guard against groupthink and other pitfalls, and generate new ways of doing things. Yet because intelligence agencies compete without the shadow of organizational death, weak practices in one agency are likely to linger alongside better ones elsewhere.

The second advantage that firms enjoy in the adaptation struggle is that their creators and employees want them to succeed (Moe, 1990; Zegart, 1999, 2007). In the business world, no one foists a new company on reluctant owners and no employee cheers silently for the day when company profits plummet. Instead, businesses are filled with organizational well-wishers who have vested interests in the organization's continued success. Government agencies, by contrast, are created by many who want them to fail. In politics, new agencies are forced into existence by winning political coalitions who impose their will on the losers. This means that losers have a say in the new organization's design and operation. The fragmented structure of the American political system ensures that political opponents have many opportunities to sabotage the creation of a new agency at the outset, hobbling it with all sorts of structures, rules, and requirements that hinder its performance over time (Moe, 1989; Zegart, 1999, 2007). As Terry Moe writes, "American public bureaucracy is not designed to be effective" (Moe, 1989, p. 267). Whether it's the Environmental Protection Agency or the Office of the Director of National Intelligence (ODNI), government agencies are constrained from the start by the politics of their own creation.

The third advantage businesses have when it comes to driving organizational change is managerial discretion. Subject only to minimal legal requirements, managers in private firms can determine or change their

---

[5]David Lewis has questioned the immortality thesis, finding that 438 new agencies were created between 1946 and 1997. But to put those numbers into perspective, more businesses are born in a single day before lunch.

[6]Indeed, congressional scholars have made much of Congress's oversight powers. See McCubbins (1985); Weingast and Moran (1983); and Epstein et al. (1999). But Congress's oversight weapons are much weaker than they appear and at times create perverse incentives, rewarding failures by granting bigger budgets, more personnel, and other corrective measures that bureaucracies value (see Moe, 1987).

organization's mission; hire and fire whomever they choose; institute whatever procedures, policies, and customs they believe are necessary; and attract capital from a multitude of sources. As James Q. Wilson shows in detailed case studies that range from prisons to schools to the Central Intelligence Agency (CIA), public-sector managers are far more constrained. They can only dream of exercising this kind of discretion to shape the organization's mission and match resources against priorities (Wilson, 2000).

Fourth and finally, businesses typically have an easier time instituting major change because chief executive officers (CEOs) usually stay on the job longer than their public-sector counterparts. Although CEO tenure has declined in recent years, it still averages 7 years (Kaplan and Minton, 2006; Kelman and Myers, 2009). That's more than twice as long as the 3.3-year median tenure of Senate-confirmed Cabinet secretaries and three times longer than the median service of deputy-secretary–level appointees in the first Bush and Clinton Administrations (Dull and Roberts, 2008). Average tenure of top intelligence officials is even shorter: Since 9/11, CIA director tenure has averaged 2 years, and directors of national intelligence (a position created in April 2005) have averaged 1.47 years. Although the Federal Bureau of Investigation (FBI) director holds a 10-year fixed term, the Bureau's top counterterrorism position has been held by eight people since 9/11, averaging just 1 year each (Stein, 2006).[7] These figures are particularly noteworthy given the fact that organization theorists consistently have found that frequent leadership turnover hurts firm performance.[8]

In sum, organization theory tells us that adaptation is difficult under the best of circumstances. Businesses are fortunate. They are fueled by market competition and its shadow of death, focused by a unified mission, filled with stakeholders seeking success, armed with broad managerial discretion to match resources against organizational needs, and led by senior executives who stay long enough to see major changes implemented. But even these blessings lead to failure more frequently than one might expect.

---

[7]Since the article was printed, Arthur Cummings became executive assistant director of the National Security Branch, making him the eighth top counterterrorism official.

[8]Classic early work in the 1960s and 1970s examined sports teams and found that frequent coaching turnover was correlated with poor team performance. Since the 1990s, a robust literature has found the relationship between executive tenure and firm performance to be curvilinear. Organizational performance typically rises with CEO tenure to a point, then falls as executives and organizations get stuck in outmoded thinking and practices. Importantly, Kelman and Myers (2009) note that the CEO tenure inflection point (when performance starts to diminish) is 5 years or more. This is substantially longer than the tenure of most intelligence agency heads. For turnover literature, see Kesner and Sebora (1994); Dull and Roberts (2008); Rainey and Steinbauer (1999); and Kelman and Myers (2009). For related work on institutional change and the survival of political leaders, see Bueno de Mesquita et al. (2003).

Insight #2: Organizational Structure Matters More Than We Think

The second insight focuses on the relationship between an organization's structure and its ability to learn. Cyert and March's 1963 classic, *A Behavioral Theory of the Firm*, first introduced the idea that organizations were not fixed and rigid, but adaptive learning systems. Subsequent research was quite diffuse, but generally agreed on four important points: (1) organizational learning involves acquiring, processing, and integrating information important to the functioning of the organization; (2) organizational learning positively affects future performance (Fiol and Lyles, 1985; Levitt and March, 1988); (3) organizations learn in a host of directed and spontaneous ways; and (4) organizational structure can influence learning in profound and often hidden ways.

This last point is particularly important for intelligence agencies because they are in the information learning business, confront extreme levels of uncertainty, and have faced persistent calls for structural overhaul since World War II. The list of reorganization efforts is long, including the CIA's creation in 1947; the National Security Agency's establishment in 1952; the consolidation of imagery into the National Imagery and Mapping Agency in 1996; the creation of the Terrorist Threat Integration Center in 2003 and its successor, the National Counterterrorism Center, in 2004; the creation of the ODNI in 2005; and repeated counterterrorism, intelligence, and national security reorganizations inside the FBI from the 1990s to the present. In each case, reformers sought to improve the IC's performance by restructuring the organizations within it. As Hammond (2009) writes, "while many prescriptions for intelligence community 'reform' have proved difficult to implement, structure seems to have been subjected to reforms and reorganizations fairly often, perhaps because structural problems are seen, whether correctly or not, as more easily solved" (p. 4).

Organization theorists have not settled the question of which structural arrangements are best, even in private industry. However, they have illuminated more clearly *why* no one best structure exists.

Briefly put, organization theorists have found neutral design to be impossible; the structure of the organization itself—its hierarchy, its arrangement of subunits—affects how information is organized and what decisions result (Simon, 1976; Hammond and Thomas, 1989; Seidman, 1998). A hypothetical example illustrates the point. Imagine for a moment that you are the head of an agency, and you possess magical powers to eliminate all conceivable sources of bias so that your decisions are based solely on the information provided by your subordinates. Waving your wand, you eliminate the personal and cognitive biases of everyone in the organizational chain of command, including yourself. You neutralize the pressures of political interests and external stakeholders seeking a particular outcome. You eliminate the pathologies of small-group decision making. You ensure that information does not get filtered or altered in the communications process, so each subordinate unit passes along all the information it has. You align incentives so that everyone has every reason in the world to provide "just the facts," information that is unvarnished, untainted, and unconnected to personal or career objectives. Furthermore, let's assume that all the information you receive is highly credible. Even in these ideal circumstances, your decision will be biased, and it may turn out to be wholly inconsistent with the data. Why? Because how you organize units in the bureaucracy determines whether the same pieces of information get concentrated as signals or dispersed as noise (Wohlstetter, 1962).

Bendor and Hammond (2010) provide two simple examples that show these structural forces at work. In the first, an intelligence agency director has three bureaus monitoring terrorist groups. The director will alert the President about a possible impending attack only if at least two of the three bureau chiefs report that they are concerned about terrorist activity patterns in their domains. Bureau chiefs, in turn, operate with the same decision rule: A bureau chief will send a report expressing concern to the director only if at least two of his three subordinates raise a red flag. Reporting is determined by answering the following question: "Do you believe that the groups in your jurisdiction are intensifying their terrorist activity?" A "0" means "no," and a "1" means "yes." Table 13-1 shows the same data aggregated in two different structures.

The first structure organizes bureaus by geography: Regions A, B, and C. Inside each regional bureau, subordinates are responsible for tracking the activities of al Qaeda-affiliated, Iran-affiliated, and unaffiliated terrorist groups. The bureau chief from region A gets signals of concern from all three subordinates (1,1,1), so he sends a report to the agency director. Region B's bureau chief gets only one signal of concern (1,0,0), so he does not send a report to the director. Region C also has only one signal (0,1,0), so does not report a concern. In this structure, because only one of the three regional bureaus raises a red flag, the director does not alert the President.

Now consider the second structure, which organizes bureaus by the

TABLE 13-1 The CIA Reporting Problem

	Region A	Region B	Region C
AQ-affiliated groups	1	1	0
Iran-affiliated groups	1	0	1
Unaffiliated groups	1	0	0

NOTE: AQ = al Qaeda.
SOURCE: Bendor and Hammond (2010, p. 651:Table 27.2). Reprinted by permission of Oxford University Press, see http://www.oup.com.

type of terrorist groups they monitor. Within each bureau, subordinates track activities in different geographic regions. The bureau that monitors al Qaeda-affiliated groups receives two reports from regional subordinates (1,1,0), so it reports concern to the director. The Iran-affiliated group bureau also receives two signals from different regions (1,0,1), so it reports concern. Because two of three bureaus have reported concern, the director alerts the President. *The data and decision rules are exactly the same in both structures. But because these two structures aggregate the information differently, the director warns in one case, but not the other.*

In the second example, Bendor and Hammond (2010) also show how hierarchies can produce counterintuitive judgments. Now an agency director wants to know whether al Qaeda-affiliated groups are more or less likely than Iran-affiliated terrorist groups to commit attacks in the near future (see Table 13-2). There are two bureaus. Bureau A's information suggests that 20 percent of al Qaeda-affiliated groups (10 of 50) are planning terrorist attacks, while no Iran-affiliated groups are planning attacks. Bureau A therefore concludes that al Qaeda-affiliated groups are more likely to commit terrorist activities in the near future. Bureau B has different data showing that 100 percent of al Qaeda-affiliated groups (10 of 10) are planning terrorist attacks, while 80 percent (40 of 50) of Iran-affiliated groups are planning attacks. Based on these data, Bureau B also reports to the director that al Qaeda-affiliated groups are more likely to commit near-term attacks.

However, when the director aggregates the data from both bureaus, she finds a very different picture: One-third of al Qaeda-affiliated groups (20 of 60) are planning near-term attacks, while two-thirds of Iran-affiliated groups (40 of 60) are planning attacks. Using the same metrics (percentage

TABLE 13-2 Terrorist Activities Reports

Bureau A			Bureau B		
	Terrorist Activities Planned	No Terrorist Activities Planned		Terrorist Activities Planned	No Terrorist Activities Planned
AQ-affiliated groups	10	40	AQ-affiliated groups	10	0
Iran-affiliated groups	0	10	Iran-affiliated groups	40	10

NOTE: AQ = al Qaeda.
SOURCE: Bendor and Hammond (2010). Original publication included two tables: Original table: 27.3 Terrorist Activities Reports—Bureau A (p. 652) and 27.4 Terrorist Activities Reports—Bureau B (p. 652). Reprinted by permission of Oxford University Press, see http://www.oup.com.

TABLE 13-3 Director's Aggregated Data from Bureaus A and B

	Terrorist Activities Planned	No Terrorist Activities Planned
AQ-affiliated groups	20	40
Iran-affiliated groups	40	20

NOTE: AQ = al Qaeda.
SOURCE: Table derived from Bendor and Hammond (2010).

of affiliated groups planning attacks) and the same decision rule (select the group type with the higher percentage of member organizations planning attacks), the director reaches the opposite conclusion of Bureaus A and B. She judges that Iran-affiliated groups are more likely to commit near-term attacks (see Table 13-3).

As this example illustrates, data collected in subunits can lead every subunit to the same evidence-based hypothesis, *even when the aggregation of data across subunits suggests the exact opposite belief.* Called Simpson's paradox, this problem is well known among statisticians and occurs when associations between variables in smaller datasets become inverted once the data are combined (Simpson, 1951). One of the more popular examples of Simpson's paradox involves the batting averages of baseball stars Dave Justice and Derek Jeter. Although Justice had a higher batting average than Jeter in 1995 and 1996, Jeter had a higher batting average when data from both years were totaled. The reason: large differences in the number of at-bats each year (Ross, 2004).

Intelligence experts, of course, have long been aware of structural dilemmas. In 1949, Sherman Kent explicitly contemplated the trade-offs between a centralized versus decentralized intelligence system as well as the relative costs and benefits of organizing units by geography or function (Kent, 1949). No arrangement, he concluded, was ideal.[9] But more recent organization theory suggests that these structural problems may be even more pernicious than many realize. The Bendor and Hammond examples provide a cautionary warning: Robust analytic techniques are not enough. Organizational structures can exert enormous, unseen, and unexpected influence over how information is aggregated and what hypotheses emerge (Bendor and Hammond, 2010).

Organizational structure also affects an organization's ability to learn

---

[9]Kent (1949) came down in favor of "the regional breakdown as far as possible," but acknowledged that such a structure posed two problems: "how to handle matters which defy regionalization" and "how to handle those problems of a multinational nature for which the organization provides no full-time functional supervisor or coordinator" (pp. 122–123). See also Hammond (2009).

and improve its own performance. As Vaughan (1996) and Zegart (2007) have noted, the structure of an organization can impede its ability to adapt, even when the need to adapt is clear. The key here is specialization. In their quest for efficiency, organizations create subunits to break down large tasks into smaller ones. Each subunit becomes specialized, using particular skills, employing particular people, and developing particular knowledge so each part of the organization does what it does best. But these pockets of specialization make it difficult for one part of the organization to understand the work of another, complicate coordination by creating distance between managers and operators, and foster standardized ways of communicating and operating across organizational divisions. Although March and Simon's (1958) classic work finds many benefits to standard operating procedures,[10] more recent research finds that standard operating procedures are a double-edged sword, increasing organizational reliability but hampering innovation.[11] Standard forms, automated computer systems, and reporting procedures help managers across an organization to perform the same tasks in the same ways each time. These measures, however, also weed out new ideas and stifle improvements that do not fit easily into existing forms, channels, or procedures—a phenomenon Vaughan calls "structural secrecy" (1996).

Two examples show the powerful effects of structural secrecy at work. First, Vaughan's case study of the Space Shuttle *Challenger* disaster finds that Morton Thiokol engineers were gravely concerned about the resilience of the shuttle's O-ring joints in cold weather. They turned out to be right: In 1986, *Challenger* exploded shortly after launch because abnormally cold weather had caused the O-rings on the solid rocket boosters to fail. The night before the disaster, Thiokol's engineers desperately tried to abort the launch. But their warnings were muted and ultimately disregarded in large part because of the National Aeronautics and Space Administration's (NASA's) own standard operating processes, structures, and norms. No minimum temperature launch criterion had been established, so NASA managers did not see the urgency of creating one the night before a launch. Thiokol's crucial presentation relied on qualitative judgments from previous flights (the putty damage between the O-rings *looked* different in colder weather flights than others) rather than NASA's standard "engineering-supported" technical positions that were based on quantitative analysis. Because the Shuttle program's division of labor physically separated key

---

[10]March and Simon argued that standard operating procedures help organizations cope with two problems: too much information and too little information. Standard procedures, they noted, simplify the task of management and provide useful feedback loops that enable managers to identify trends early enough to take corrective action before problems turn into crises.

[11]For problems with standard operating procedures, see Allison (1971); Vaughan (1996); and Sagan (1993).

participants in different locations, the pivotal communication occurred in a three-way teleconference, with no video transmission. As Vaughan notes, "many visual cues that normally aid interpretation—such as gestures, facial expressions, body posture, activity—were unavailable." Instead, "communication depended on individual willingness to speak to an unseen audience" (Vaughan, 1996, p. 357). Paradoxically, the very structures, rules, and technologies designed to improve organizational efficiency sabotaged NASA's ability to learn.

Zegart finds that structural secrecy also hindered the FBI's ability to penetrate the 9/11 plot. In a 7-week period during the summer of 2001, three FBI field offices uncovered what turned out to be key clues. In Phoenix, Special Agent Kenneth Williams identified a disturbing trend, wrote a memo warning that Osama bin Laden might be sending terrorists to train in U.S. flight schools, and recommended several specific steps, including notifying other intelligence agencies. As FBI Director Robert Mueller later reflected, "You are not going to have a better intelligence product than the Phoenix memo."[12] During the same period, FBI agents in Minneapolis detained a suspicious foreign flight school student named Zacarias Moussaoui, a self-proclaimed Jihadist who wanted to fly 747s and later became the only person convicted in the United States in connection with the attacks. Third and finally, the FBI's New York office began searching for Khalid al-Mihdhar and Nawaf al-Hazmi, two suspected al Qaeda operatives who later hijacked American Airlines Flight 77 and flew it into the Pentagon. But because the FBI was divided into 56 largely independent and autonomous field offices (one longstanding joke at the Bureau was that the FBI consisted of 56 field offices with a headquarters attached), none of the agents working these cases knew about the others. On three separate occasions in that 7-week period, the threat of a domestic terrorist attack caught the attention of someone in the FBI, but failed to trigger a broader effort to collect information, share information, or take stock of what the FBI already knew. The Bureau's field office structure enhanced specialization—enabling individual field offices to address local law enforcement priorities—but prevented officials in one part of the organization from learning what others in the organization already knew (Zegart, 2007).

In sum, organizational learning research suggests that structure matters much more than most people believe, that organizational reliability and innovation are often mutually exclusive, that managers must work outside standard operating procedures to identify obsolete practices and foster innovation, and that officials must be vigilant about monitoring how structural arrangements aggregate, or fail to aggregate, information to guard against misleading analytic judgments.

---

[12]Personal communication, Robert Mueller, FBI, January 2007.

Insight #3: Internal Barriers to Organizational Change Are Powerful

Social science research finds what intelligence insiders already know to be true: employees become wedded to organizational routines, thinking, norms, ideas, and identities and these attachments make change difficult (see Tinsley, this volume, Chapter 9, for discussion of these issues in greater depth). Here, a point worth underscoring is that resistance to innovation stems more from the everyday aspects of organizational life than from a few old-timers or old-thinkers. Levitt and March argue that organizational performance often falls victim to "competency traps," which are routines that were once beneficial, but have become obsolete over time (Levitt and March, 1988; March, 1981). Avoiding competency traps requires systemic and careful work to identify and exploit "old knowledge" that still works (March, 1991; Crossan et al., 1999), "unlearn" routines that do not (Hedberg, 1981), and explore new approaches that might work better (March, 1991; Levinthal and March, 1993). For intelligence, this research suggests that improving analysis requires more than hiring talent or generating good ideas and new tools. It requires an explicit management program to identify and shed maladaptive practices, encourage the search for new and better ones, foster supportive cultures and habits, and erode counterproductive ones.

Limitations

The most serious limitation of organization theory is its focus on firms. As Steve Kelman (2007, p. 226) writes, "Improving government performance is a topic worthy of significant research attention, yet dramatically insufficient scholarly firepower is directed at it." The result is that organization theory pays relatively little attention to political incentives, institutions, and power, forces that are crucial for understanding adaptation challenges in government agencies (Zegart, 2007).

INSIGHTS AND LIMITATIONS OF POLITICAL SCIENCE

The political science literature offers different insights and limitations for improving intelligence analysis, as described in the paragraphs below.

Insight #1: Institutional Incentives Drive Behavior

Although the political science literature is vast, the discipline's dominant approach for the past 20 or 30 years has been rational choice. See Chapter 3, this volume, by Bruce Bueno de Mesquita for discussion of rational choice analysis in much greater depth and for an examination of how game theoretic models offer useful analytic tools. But rational choice also illuminates the "how to make good analytic practices stick" side of the equation.

Put simply, theories of rational choice focus on what makes individuals alike, not what makes them different. Rational choice theorists argue that all individuals, whatever their personalities, wants, and needs, act in predictable and systematic ways for predictable and systematic reasons: Namely, they select alternatives and conduct activities that maximize net benefits to themselves. In politics, individuals are driven by the incentives of office to maximize their *political* advantages. No normative judgment is implied; rational choice describes the way the political world works, not the way reformers wish it to be.[13]

Legislators, for example, select committee assignments that deliver benefits to folks back home because they prefer winning reelection to losing (Mayhew, 1974). Similar dynamics explain Presidential behavior. Although no two Presidents are alike, all of them wield the same powers, confront the same institutional players, seek to secure their place in history, and make decisions based on which policies produce the greatest advantages for their administration at the lowest political cost. For political scientists, outcomes stem less from the idiosyncratic personalities or beliefs of individuals, and more from the forces that transcend them (Moe, 1985, 2009).

For intelligence analysis, rational choice theories remind us that leadership is not a panacea; institutional incentives frequently explain why people and organizations behave in the ways they do—for example, why constituent elements of the IC historically resisted centralization under the CIA, and why they are likely to continue resisting centralization under the new ODNI, including efforts to improve analytic practices, even now.[14]

At the ground level, rational choice theory suggests that bad incentives often prevent good people from improving organizational performance. A new analytic technique, for example, may produce better judgments. But getting analysts to use it requires convincing them, and their managers, that the costs of learning and using something new are worth it. Although charismatic leadership can help foster change, institutionalizing these kinds of improvements requires structuring incentives and communicating them clearly. Net career benefits—for each person involved—matter a great deal.

In short, the literature suggests that making improvements stick means relying less on the force of individual personalities and more on harnessing the incentives that motivate us all.

---

[13]Three seminal works in rational choice are Arrow (1951); Downs (1957); and Olson (1965). For an important critique, see Green and Shapiro (1996).

[14]I do not mean to suggest that rational self-interest is the *only* reason intelligence elements might resist centralization. But it is an important and often underappreciated one.

Insight #2: Individual Rational Decisions, Collective Suboptimal Results

Political science research also cautions that individually rational decisions can produce collectively suboptimal results. The classic example is the tragedy of the commons, where individual farmers seek to gain advantage by allowing their sheep to graze as much as possible on public lands. Yet, because every farmer has the same cost–benefit calculation, they all make the same choice. Overgrazing ensues, the fields become fallow, and everyone suffers. Current examples of tragedy of the commons problems abound. Nobody likes wasteful government spending, but every member of Congress has strong incentives to draft legislative earmarks to fund his or her district's pet projects, leading to wasteful earmark proliferation. When the stock market starts falling dramatically, the natural reaction among nonprofessional investors (and some professional ones) is often to avoid bigger losses by selling fast. But when many respond to these incentives in the same way, the market plummets even more and losses grow. Rational behavior for one becomes detrimental for all. This same basic logic explains in part why intelligence agencies in the Pentagon and other parts of the IC historically have fought against centralized control by the Director of Central Intelligence (DCI) and its ODNI successor, even though doing so hinders the coordination and collaboration essential to intelligence success. One reason agency employees circumvent or resist central directives is that they see personal or organizational benefits to protecting their own agency's turf and costs to ceding it. The result, however, is that the entire intelligence system suffers.[15]

Limitations

Political science has been hampered by two key weaknesses. The first is that the field rarely treats agencies as dependent variables. Organizations are inputs to policy outcomes, not phenomena to be studied in their own right. Most political scientists are uninterested in internal organizational forces such as norms, routines, and cultures, precisely the forces that fuel bureaucratic resistance to change. Indeed, "culture" is something of a dirty word in the discipline, denoting a residual, "squishy" variable that cannot be measured clearly and that is usually employed only when all other explanations fall short.

The second limitation stems from the first: Political science pays little attention to the nuts and bolts of how agencies actually work. Although public administration and political science used to be closely aligned fields,

---

[15]Of course, there are also pathological and psychological reasons for resisting centralization, including rigid adherence to outdated agency cultures, traditions, and identities, and more general aversion to change.

they split decades ago. For years now, political science has considered public administration to be too practically oriented, too atheoretical, and too methodologically weak. The claims are not entirely without merit (Kelman, 2007). But the effect has been to create a yawning gap between theory and practice, and a dearth of policy-relevant political science work to inform public management. It is no coincidence that the "reinventing government" movement, which gave rise to the Clinton–Gore National Performance Review, came from practitioners instead of scholars (Kettl, 1998, 2005; Aberbach and Rockman, 2000).

A WORD ABOUT THE BUSINESS MANAGEMENT LITERATURE

A separate and growing body of research concerns the practical interests of managers. In the early days, the debate focused mostly on how to improve firm efficiency. Taylor's seminal work in 1911 argued that managers' core challenge was to institute practices that increased managerial control, reduced worker discretion, and broke down tasks into smaller and smaller pieces. Rejecting the aphorism that "Captains of industry are born, not made," Taylor sought, as he put it, "to try to convince the reader that the remedy for . . . inefficiency lies in systematic management, rather than in searching for some unusual or extraordinary man" (Taylor, 1911, p. 7). Starting in the 1930s and 1940s, Harvard Business School produced an alternative "human relations" approach that found workers also needed to be motivated to be productive.[16]

After World War II, business programs skyrocketed, producing major changes and a growing popular orientation. In 1956, fewer than 4,000 students received a Master's in Business Administration (MBA). By 2003, that number had topped 100,000 (U.S. Department of Education, 2005).[17] In a 20-year period alone—from 1974 to 1994—the number of American universities offering MBA degrees doubled, from 389 to nearly 800 (Deutsch, 1993). Because business schools are in the business of training managers, they have an incentive to produce research that highlights the importance of leadership and the role of managers inside organizations (Kelman, 2007). Although important social science research has continued to be developed inside business schools, a cottage industry of best-selling leadership and management books has also arisen, dispensing advice to business leaders

---

[16]In a series of famous experiments at the Hawthorne Western Electric Plant, Roethlisberger and Dickson (1949) found that worker productivity increased under *any* form of attention. One of the seminal theoretical works in the field is Barnard (1938). For an excellent overview of the literature, see Charles Perrow (1986).

[17]That's five times the number of students studying for Master's Degrees in Public Policy or Public Administration (Kelman, 2007).

and general audiences alike.[18] Despite its popularity, however, this literature has substantial limitations in improving intelligence analysis. Two reasons explain why.

First, the literature assumes away nearly all of the most important constraints on government agencies. Wallace Sayre's oft-quoted law that public and private management are fundamentally alike in all unimportant respects has fallen by the wayside (Allison, 1980). To be clear, this literature does not assert that its lessons apply well to government agencies; it neglects government agencies altogether (Kelman, 2007). General rules of thumb are drawn almost entirely from private-sector cases and are intended for private-sector audiences. Grafting these ideas from firms to intelligence agencies is difficult. For example, Jim Collins's (2001) book, *Good to Great*, examines the factors that distinguish high-performing firms from average ones in the same industry. One of his key findings is personnel, or as he puts it, "getting the right people on the bus and getting the wrong people off the bus." This advice makes good sense for companies, but overlooks important intelligence realities. In the intelligence world, anticipating who the "right people" are and how many of them you'll need is riddled with uncertainty. The right people at one point in time (say, Warsaw Pact experts) may turn out to be the wrong people later. Conversely, some employees (e.g., Pashtu speakers) may seem relatively insignificant one day and indispensable the next. Aligning the workforce will always lag substantially behind an intelligence agency's needs because hiring people entails undergoing a lengthy security clearance process and firing them requires dealing with onerous civil service procedures and regulations. Selecting the "right people" hinges as much on identifying intangible qualities—a willingness to embrace change and take intellectual risks, a drive to get things done, an aptitude for working well with intelligence customers and colleagues—as substantive knowledge or other measurable skills. Finally, for decades intelligence agency cultures have prized lifetime service to the mission and country, not "here today, gone tomorrow" labor markets where organizations and employees alike expect to move on as conditions warrant.[19] Getting on and off the intelligence bus is not so fast or easy.[20]

The second limitation of this work is methodological. With some important exceptions (Collins, 2001), the popular management literature

---

[18]Some of the best known examples are Collins (2001); Useem (1999); and Kotter (1996).

[19]The demographics of today's IC workforce raise new questions about career tenure—specifically, whether the post-9/11 generation of analysts expects more fluid career paths into and out of government and, if so, how the IC can harness top talent either through modifying retention practices or developing career paths that enable analysts to move in and out of government more easily.

[20]Collins defends the applicability business practices to nonprofits and government agencies in *Good to Great and the Social Sectors: A Monograph to Accompany Good to Great* (2005).

commits many of the selection bias errors discussed by Bueno de Mesquita (this volume, Chapter 3). In general, the literature presents sweeping conclusions, nostrums, and top-10 lists based on illustrative case studies and weak causal reasoning rather than more rigorous experimental testing, surveys, or systematic research methods. Peters and Waterman's *In Search of Excellence* (1981) is a classic example. The authors examine several top-performing companies, find a few things these companies have in common, and conclude that the commonalities must be the keys to success. Peters and Waterman might be right. Or they could be terribly wrong, identifying traits that are shared by *most* companies—successes and failures alike—and that have little or no bearing on performance.

These methodological weaknesses have created a great deal of conventional management wisdom with questionable results. In 1996, John Kotter published one of the best known change-management books ever written, *Leading Change*. Kotter's book contained no references, footnotes, or rigorous empirical research unless one counts occasional references to "that reminds me of a story" illustrative examples. Nevertheless, *Leading Change* spawned a huge change-management movement that produced thousands of articles and books. Yet in 2008, a McKinsey and Company survey of 3,199 executives around the world reported that only a third of all transformations succeeded, the same percentage that Kotter found 12 years earlier. The McKinsey study concluded, "It seems that, despite prolific output, the field of change management hasn't led to more successful change programs" (Aiken and Keller, 2009 p. 100).[21]

The point here is not to criticize for the sake of criticizing. It is to shine a light on which social science research paths offer dead ends and which offer promising avenues to improve the implementation of analytic practices. In the final analysis, organization theory and political science offer some important, relevant insights. The popular management literature, however, appears far less promising for improving intelligence analysis.

REFERENCES

Aberbach, J. D., and B. A. Rockman. 2000. *In the web of politics: Three decades of the U.S. federal executive.* Washington, DC: Brookings Institution Press.

Aiken, C., and S. Keller. 2009. The irrational side of change management. *McKinsey Quarterly* 2:100–109.

Aldrich, H. 1999. *Organizations evolving.* Englewood Cliffs, NJ: Prentice-Hall.

Allison, G. 1971. *Essence of decision: Explaining the Cuban missile crisis*, 1st ed. Boston, MA: Little Brown.

---

[21] These authors go on to commit the same methodological mistakes, proffering advice about how to handle "the irrational side of change management" based largely on their own professional experiences working with companies attempting transformations.

Allison, G. 1980. *Public and private management: Are they fundamentally alike in all unimportant respects?* Proceedings of the Public Management Research Conference, November 19–20, 1979 (pp. 27–38). OPM Document 127-53-1. Washington, DC: Office of Personnel Management.

Arrow, K. J. 1951. *Social choice and individual values.* New Haven, CT: Yale University Press.

Barnard, C. 1938. *The functions of the executive.* Cambridge, MA: Harvard University Press.

Bendor, J., and T. Hammond. (2010). Choice-theoretic approaches to bureaucratic structure. In F. R. Durant, ed., *The Oxford handbook of American bureaucracy* (pp. 638–665). London, UK: Oxford University Press.

Bueno de Mesquita, B., A. Smith, R. Siverson, and J. Morrow. 2003. *The logic of political survival.* Cambridge, MA: MIT Press.

Collins, J. 2001. *Good to great: Why some companies make the leap . . . and others don't.* New York: Harper Business.

Collins, J. 2005. *Good to great and the social sectors: A monograph to accompany good to great.* New York: HarperCollins.

Crossan, M. M., H. W. Lane, and R. E. White. 1999. An organizational learning framework: From intuition to institution. *Academy of Management Review* 24(3):522–537.

Cyert, R. M., and J. G. March. 1963. *A behavioral theory of the firm.* Oxford, UK: Blackwell.

Deutsch, C. H. 1993. MBA programs fight for shrinking pool of students interested in business. *New York Times*, November 14.

Downs, A. 1957. *An economic theory of democracy.* New York: Harper and Row.

Downs, A. 1967. *Inside bureaucracy.* Upper Saddle River, NJ: Scott Foresman and Company.

Dull, M., and P. S. Roberts. 2008. Continuity, competence, and the succession of Senate-confirmed agency appointees, 1989–2009. *Presidential Studies Quarterly* 39(3):432–453.

Epstein, D., S. O'Halloran, R. Calvert, and T. Eggertsson. 1999. *Delegating powers.* New York: Cambridge University Press.

Fiol, C. M., and M. A. Lyles. 1985. Organizational learning. *Academy of Management Review* 10(4):803–813.

Green, D. P., and I. Shapiro. 1996. *Pathologies of rational choice theory.* New Haven, CT: Yale University Press.

Hammond, T. H. 2009. *Intelligence organizations and the organization of intelligence: On the problem of drawing inferences from data scattered around the bureaucracy.* Unpublished manuscript. Department of Political Science, Michigan State University.

Hammond, T. H., and P. Thomas. 1989. The impossibility of a neutral hierarchy. *Journal of Law, Economics, and Organization* 5(1):155–184.

Hannan, M. T., and J. H. Freeman. 1977. Population ecology of organizations. *American Journal of Sociology* 82(5):929–964.

Hannan, M. T., and J. H. Freeman. 1984. Structural inertia and organizational change. *American Sociological Review* 49(2):149–164.

Hedberg, B. 1981. How organizations learn and unlearn. In P. Nystrom and W. H. Starbuck, eds., *Handbook of organizational design* (pp. 3–27). London, UK: Oxford University Press.

Kaplan, S. N., and B. A. Minton. 2006. *How has CEO turnover changed? Increasingly performance sensitive boards and increasingly uneasy CEOs.* NBER Working Papers 12465. Cambridge, MA: National Bureau of Economic Research.

Kaufman, H. 1976. *Are government organizations immortal?* Washington, DC: Brookings Institution Press.

Kelman, S. 2007. Public administration and organization studies. In A. Brief and J. P. Walsh, eds., *Academy of Management Annals* (pp. 225–267). New York: Erlbaum.

Kelman, S., and J. Myers. 2009. *Successfully executing ambitious strategies in government: An empirical analysis.* Faculty Research Working Paper Series (#RWP09-009). Boston, MA: Harvard University, Kennedy School of Government.

Kent, S. 1949. *Strategic intelligence for American world policy.* Princeton, NJ: Princeton University Press.

Kesner, I. F., and T. C. Sabora. 1994. Executive succession: Past, present and future. *Journal of Management* 20(2):327–372.

Kettl, D. 1998. *Reinventing government: A fifth-year report card.* Washington, DC: Brookings Institution Press.

Kettl, D. 2005. *The global public management revolution,* 2nd ed. Washington, DC: Brookings Institution Press.

Kotter, J. P. 1996. *Leading change.* Cambridge, MA: Harvard Business School Press.

Levinthal, D., and J. G. March. 1993. The myopia of learning. *Strategic Management Journal* 14(SI):95–112.

Levitt, B., and J. G. March. 1988. Organizational learning. *Annual Review of Sociology* 14:319–340.

Lewin, A. Y., C. B. Weigelt, and J. D. Emery. 2004. Adaptation and selection in strategy and change: Perspectives on strategic change in organizations. In M. S. Poole and A. H. Van de Ven, eds., *Handbook of organizational change and innovation.* New York: Oxford University Press.

Lewis, D. E. 2003. *Presidents and the politics of agency design: Political insulation in the United States government bureaucracy, 1946–1997.* Stanford, CA: Stanford University Press.

Loomis, C. J. 2004. The sinking of Bethlehem Steel. *Fortune* 5:174.

Lowi, T. J. 1979. *The end of liberalism: The second republic of the United States.* New York: W. W. Norton.

March, J. G. 1981. Footnotes to organizational change. *Administrative Science Quarterly* 26 (Dec.):563–577.

March, J. G. 1991. Exploration and exploitation in organizational learning. *Organization Science* 2(1):71–87.

March, J. G., and H. A. Simon. 1958. *Organizations.* New York: John Wiley.

Mayhew, D. 1974. *Congress: The electoral connection.* New Haven, CT: Yale University Press.

McCubbins, M. D. 1985. The legislative design of regulatory structure. *American Journal of Political Science* 29(4):721–748.

Moe, T. M. 1985. The politicized presidency. In J. E. Chubb and P. E. Peterson, eds., *The new direction in American politics.* Washington, DC: Brookings Institution Press.

Moe, T. M. 1987. An assessment of the positive theory of "Congressional Dominance." *Legislative Studies Quarterly* 12(4):475–520.

Moe, T. M. 1989. The politics of bureaucratic structure. In J. E. Chubb and P. E. Peterson, eds., *Can the government govern?* (pp. 267–330). Washington, DC: Brookings Institution Press.

Moe, T. M. 1990. The politics of structural choice: Toward a theory of public bureaucracy. In O. E. Williamson, ed., *Organization theory, from Chester Barnard to the present and beyond.* New York: Oxford University Press.

Moe, T. M. 2009. The revolution in Presidential studies. *Presidential Studies Quarterly* 39(4):701–724.

Office of the Director of National Intelligence. 2007. *DNI releases budget figure for National Intelligence Program.* News Release No. 22-07. Washington, DC: Office of the Director of National Intelligence. Available: http://www.dni.gov/press_releases/20071030_release.pdf [accessed June 2010].

Olson, M., Jr. 1965. *The logic of collective action.* Cambridge, MA: Harvard University Press.

Osborne, D., and T. Gaebler. 1993. *Reinventing government: How the entrepreneurial spirit is transforming the public sector.* New York: Penguin.

Osborne, D., and P. Plastrik. 1998. *Banishing bureaucracy: The five strategies for reinventing government.* New York: Penguin.

Perrow, C. 1986. *Complex organizations: A critical reader.* New York: McGraw-Hill.

Peters, T. J., and R. H. Waterman. 1981. *In search of excellence: Lessons from America's best-run companies.* New York: Warner.

Pfeffer, J., and R. I. Sutton. 2006. *Hard facts, dangerous half-truths, and total nonsense: Profiting from evidence-based management.* Cambridge, MA: Harvard Business School Press.

Rainey, H. G., and P. Steinbauer. 1999. Galloping elephants: Developing elements of a theory of effective government organizations. *Journal of Public Administration Research and Theory* 9(1):1–32.

Roethlisberger, F. J., and W. Dickson. 1949. *Management and the worker.* Cambridge, MA: Harvard University Press.

Ross, K. 2004. *A mathematician at the ballpark: Odds and probabilities for baseball fans.* New York: Pi Press.

Sagan, S. D. 1993. *The limits of safety: Organizations, accidents, and nuclear weapons.* Princeton, NJ: Princeton University Press.

Schlosser, J., and E. Florian. 2004. The biggest moneymakers! The best investments! The hall-of-famers and the one-hit-wonders! The triumphs, the failures, the milestones! Fifty years of . . . amazing facts! *Fortune* 5:152.

Seidman, H. 1998. *Politics, position, and power: The dynamics of federal organization*, 5th ed. New York: Oxford University Press.

Serwer, A. 2002. Breaking records—for bankruptcies: Chapter 11 is the hottest fad in business. But that's not even the half of it. *Fortune* 5:22.

Simon, H. A. 1976. *Administration behavior: A study of decision-making processes in administrative organizations*, 3rd ed. New York: Free Press.

Simpson, E. H. 1951. The interpretation of interaction in contingency tables. *Journal of the Royal Statistical Society* (Series B), 13:238–241.

Stein, J. 2006. FBI picks its seventh counterterrorism chief since September 11, 2001. *Congressional Quarterly.*

Stinchecombe, A. L. 1965. Social structures and organizations. In J. G. March, ed., *Handbook of organizations.* Chicago, IL: Rand McNally.

Taylor, F. 1911. *Principles of scientific management.* New York: Harper Bros.

U.S. Census Bureau. 2009. Firm births and deaths by employment size of enterprise: 1990 to 2005. Table 739. *Statistical abstract of the United States: 2009.* Washington, DC: U.S. Census Bureau. Available: http://www.census.gov/compendia/statab/cats/business_enterprise/establishments_employees_payroll.html [accessed June 2010].

U.S. Department of Education. 2005. *Earned degrees in business conferred by degree-granting institutions, by level of degree and sex of student: Selected years, 1955–56 to 2002–03.* Table 278. Washington, DC: U.S. Department of Education. Available: http://nces.ed.gov/programs/digest/d04/tables/dt04_278.asp [accessed June 2010].

Useem, M. 1999. *The leadership moment: Nine true stories of triumph and disaster and their lessons for us all.* New York: Three Rivers Press.

Vaughan, D. 1996. *The Challenger launch decision: Risk technology, culture, and deviance at NASA.* Chicago, IL: University of Chicago Press.

Weingast, B., and M. Moran. 1983. Bureaucratic discretion or congressional control? Regulatory policymaking by the Federal Trade Commission. *Journal of Political Economy* 91(5):765–800.

Wilson, J. Q. 2000. *Bureaucracy: What government agencies do and why they do it.* New York: Basic Books.

Wohlstetter, R. 1962. *Pearl Harbor: Warning and decision.* Stanford, CA: Stanford University Press.

Zegart, A. B. 1999. *Flawed by design: The evolution of the CIA, JCS, and NSC.* Stanford, CA: Stanford University Press.

Zegart, A. B. (2007) *Spying blind: The CIA, the FBI, and the origins of 9/11.* Princeton, NJ: Princeton University Press.

A

Contents List for
Intelligence Analysis for Tomorrow:
Advances from the
Behavioral and Social Sciences

B

Biographical Sketches of
Authors and Staff

Baruch Fischhoff (*Chair*) is Howard Heinz University Professor in the Departments of Social and Decision Sciences and of Engineering and Public Policy at Carnegie Mellon University. His research includes risk communication, analysis, and management; adolescent and medical decision making; national security; and environmental protection. He is a past president of the Society for Risk Analysis and a recipient of its Distinguished Achievement Award, and he is a past president of the Society for Judgment and Decision Making. He is a fellow of the American Psychological Society and of the American Psychological Association, and he is an elected member of the Institute of Medicine. He chairs the Food and Drug Administration's Risk Communication Advisory Committee. He is a current member of the Department of Homeland Security's Science and Advisory Committee and past member of the Environmental Protection Agency Scientific Advisory Board where he chaired the Homeland Security Advisory Committee. He holds a B.S. in mathematics and psychology from Wayne State University and an M.A. and Ph.D. in psychology from the Hebrew University of Jerusalem.

Hal R. Arkes is a professor in the Department of Psychology and a fellow at the Moritz College of Law at Ohio State University. His research focuses on judgment and decision making, medical decision making, and economic decision making. He serves on the editorial boards for the *Journal of Behavioral Decision Making*, the *Journal of Judgment and Decision Making*, the *Journal of Medical Decision Making*, and *Psychological Science*. He is an elected fellow of the American Psychological Society and has served as president for the Society for Judgment and Decision Making. He has received the Outstanding Teaching Award from Ohio University's College of Arts and Sciences and two Teaching Recognition Awards from Ohio University. He has a B.A from Carleton College, an M.S. in psychology from the University of Michigan, and a Ph.D. in psychology from the University of Michigan.

Bruce Bueno de Mesquita is a senior fellow at the Hoover Institution and the Silver professor of politics at New York University. In the broad context of international conflict, foreign policy formation, and nation building, his current research focuses on the links between political institutions, economic growth, and political change. He is also investigating the causes and consequences of international conflict, as well as national security policy forecasting and analysis. He is an elected member of the American Academy of Arts and Sciences and a member of the American Political Science Association, the International Studies Association, and the Peace Science Society. He is also a member of the board of advisers of the James A. Baker III Institute for Public Policy at Rice University. He has a B.A. from Queens College, an M.A. and a Ph.D. in political science from the University of Michigan, and an honorary doctorate from the University of Groningen in the Netherlands.

Cherie Chauvin, *Study Director,* is a program officer at the National Research Council, working on several studies and workshops relevant to defense and national security issues. Previously, she held several positions with the U.S. Department of Defense's Defense Intelligence Agency (DIA), where her work included support for military operations and liaison relationships in Japan, South Korea, and Mongolia, as well as conducting intelligence collection operations in Afghanistan to answer strategic and tactical military intelligence requirements. In recognition of her service, she was awarded the DIA Civilian Expeditionary Medal, the Department of the Army Commander's Award for Civilian Service, and the Office of the Director of National Intelligence National Meritorious Unit Citation. She holds a B.S. in cognitive science from the University of California at San Diego, an M.A. in international relations from The Maxwell School at Syracuse University, and an M.S. in strategic intelligence from the National Defense Intelligence College.

Thomas Fingar is a research scholar at Stanford University. Previously, he served as deputy director of national intelligence for analysis at the Office of the Director of National Intelligence and chairman of the National Intelligence Council, and as assistant secretary of the Bureau of Intelligence and Research at the U.S. Department of State. Prior to joining the State

Department, he held several research appointments at Stanford University, including senior research associate in the Center for International Security and Arms Control and director of the Stanford U.S.–China Relations Program. His many books and articles have focused mostly on national security and aspects of Chinese politics and policy making. He is a recipient of the Presidential Rank Award of Distinguished Executive. He has a B.A. in government and history from Cornell University and an M.A. and a Ph.D. in political science from Stanford University.

Reid Hastie is Robert S. Hamada Professor of Behavioral Science in the Graduate School of Business at the University of Chicago. Previously, he held positions at Harvard University, Northwestern University, and the University of Colorado. His primary research interests are in the areas of judgment and decision making (managerial, legal, medical, engineering, and personal), memory and cognition, and social psychology. Currently, he is studying the psychology of investment decisions; the role of explanations in category concept representations (including the effects on category classification, deductive, and inductive inferences); civil jury decision making (punitive damages and sexual harassment); the primitive sources of confidence and probability judgments; decision-making competencies across the adult life span; and neural substrates of risky decisions. He has a Ph.D. in psychology from Yale University.

James Kajdasz, Lieutenant Colonel in the U.S. Air Force, is an instructor at the National Defense Intelligence College, Joint Base Anacostia–Bolling, DC. He has held a variety of assignments in both military intelligence and academia, including at Hurlburt Field, Florida; Prince Sultan Air Base, Kingdom of Saudi Arabia; and Osan Air Base, Republic of Korea; as well as an assistant professor of behavioral sciences and leadership at the U.S. Air Force Academy. His mixed background in academia and operational intelligence has led to his major focus on applying academic theory to, and empirical study of, intelligence analysis methods that can improve the quality of intelligence training and analysis. He has a B.S. from the U.S. Air Force Academy, an M.A. from George Mason University, and a Ph.D. in quantitative psychology from Ohio State University.

Edward H. Kaplan is the William N. and Marie A. Beach Professor of Management Sciences at the School of Management, a professor of public health at the School of Public Health, and a professor of engineering in the School of Engineering and Applied Science, all at Yale University. He also codirects the Daniel Rose Technion–Yale Initiative in counterterror and homeland security operations research. His work is in operations research, mathematical modeling, and statistics, focusing on problems in public policy and management. His recent research has focused on issues in counterterrorism, including the tactical prevention of suicide bombings, bioterror preparedness, and response logistics in the event of a smallpox or anthrax attack. His work on smallpox received the 2003 Koopman Prize of the Institute for Operations Research and the Management Sciences, and his research evaluating suicide bomber detector schemes received the same award in 2005. He is an elected member of the National Academy of Engineering and of the Institute of Medicine. He has a B.A. from McGill University in economic and urban geography and master's degrees in operations research, city planning, and mathematics along with a Ph.D. in urban studies from the Massachusetts Institute of Technology.

Steve W. J. Kozlowski is professor of organizational psychology at Michigan State University. His research is focused on the design of active learning systems and the use of "synthetic experience" to train adaptive skills, systems for enhancing team learning and team effectiveness, and the critical role of team leaders in the development of adaptive teams. The goal of his programmatic research is to generate actionable theory, research-based principles, and deployable tools to facilitate the development of adaptive individuals, teams, and organizations. He is the editor of the *Journal of Applied Psychology*, and he has served on the editorial boards of the several other journals. He is a fellow of the American Psychological Association, the Association for Psychological Science, the International Association for Applied Psychology, and the Society for Industrial and Organizational Psychology. He holds a B.A. in psychology from the University of Rhode Island and an M.S. and a Ph.D. in organizational psychology from Pennsylvania State University.

Gary H. McClelland is professor of psychology at the University of Colorado and a faculty fellow of the Institute of Cognitive Science. His research interests include judgment and decision making, psychological models of economic behavior, experimental economics, statistics and data analysis, measurement and scaling, mathematical psychology, and graphical data displays on the web and on paper. His major books and articles focus on such topics as optimal design in psychological research, testing treatment by covariate interactions when treatment varies within subjects, continuing issues in the everyday analysis of psychological data, statistical difficulties of detecting interactions and moderator effects, insurance for low-probability hazards, and preference reversals and the measurement of environmental values. He received a Ph.D. from the University of Michigan.

Barbara Mellers is the Heyman University Professor in the Department of Psychology and the Wharton School of Business at the University of